Nineteenth-Century Major Lives and Letters

Series Editor: Marilyn Gaull

This series presents original biographical, critical, and scholarly studies of literary works and public figures in Great Britain, North America, and continental Europe during the nineteenth century. The volumes in *Nineteenth-Century Major Lives and Letters* evoke the energies, achievements, contributions, cultural traditions, and individuals who reflected and generated them during the Romantic and Victorian period. The topics: critical, textual, and historical scholarship, literary and book history, biography, cultural and comparative studies, critical theory, art, architecture, science, politics, religion, music, language, philosophy, aesthetics, law, publication, translation, domestic and public life, popular culture, and anything that influenced, impinges upon, expresses or contributes to an understanding of the authors, works, and events of the nineteenth century. The authors consist of political figures, artists, scientists, and cultural icons including William Blake, Thomas Hardy, Charles Darwin, William Wordsworth, William Butler Yeats, Samuel Taylor Coleridge, and their contemporaries.

The series editor is Marilyn Gaull, PhD (Indiana University), FEA. She has taught at William and Mary, Temple University, New York University, and is Research Professor at the Editorial Institute at Boston University. She is the founder and editor of *The Wordsworth Circle* and the author of *English Romanticism: The Human Context*, and editions, essays, and reviews in journals. She lectures internationally on British Romanticism, folklore, and narrative theory, intellectual history, publishing procedures, and history of science.

PUBLISHED BY PALGRAVE MACMILLAN:

Shelley's German Afterlives, by Susanne Schmid
Coleridge, the Bible, and Religion, by Jeffrey W. Barbeau
Romantic Literature, Race, and Colonial Encounter, by Peter J. Kitson
Byron, edited by Cheryl A. Wilson
Romantic Migrations, by Michael Wiley
The Long and Winding Road from Blake to the Beatles, by Matthew Schneider
British Periodicals and Romantic Identity, by Mark Schoenfield
Women Writers and Nineteenth-Century Medievalism, by Clare Broome Saunders
British Victorian Women's Periodicals, by Kathryn Ledbetter
Romantic Diasporas, by Toby R. Benis
Romantic Literary Families, by Scott Krawczyk
Victorian Christmas in Print, by Tara Moore
Culinary Aesthetics and Practices in Nineteenth-Century American Literature,
    edited by Monika Elbert and Marie Drews
Reading Popular Culture in Victorian Print, by Alberto Gabriele
Romanticism and the Object, edited by Larry H. Peer
Poetics en passant, by Anne Jamison
From Song to Print, by Terence Hoagwood
Gothic Romanticism, by Tom Duggett
Victorian Medicine and Social Reform, by Louise Penner
Populism, Gender, and Sympathy in the Romantic Novel, by James P. Carson
Byron and the Rhetoric of Italian Nationalism, by Arnold A. Schmidt
Poetry and Public Discourse in Nineteenth-Century America, by Shira Wolosky
The Discourses of Food in Nineteenth-Century British Fiction, by Annette Cozzi
Romanticism and Pleasure, edited by Thomas H. Schmid and Michelle Faubert

Royal Romances, by Kristin Flieger Samuelian
Trauma, Transcendence, and Trust, by Thomas J. Brennan, S.J.
The Business of Literary Circles in Nineteenth-Century America, by David Dowling
Popular Medievalism in Romantic-Era Britain, by Clare A. Simmons
Beyond Romantic Ecocriticism, by Ashton Nichols
The Poetry of Mary Robinson, by Daniel Robinson
Romanticism and the City, by Larry H. Peer
Coleridge and the Daemonic Imagination, by Gregory Leadbetter
Dante and Italy in British Romanticism, edited by Frederick Burwick and Paul Douglass
Jewish Representation in British Literature 1780–1840, by Michael Scrivener
Romantic Dharma, by Mark Lussier
Robert Southey, by Stuart Andrews
Playing to the Crowd, by Frederick Burwick
The Regions of Sara Coleridge's Thought, by Peter Swaab
John Thelwall and the Wordsworth Circle, by Judith Thompson
Wordsworth and Coleridge, by Peter Larkin
Turning Points in Natural Theology from Bacon to Darwin, by Stuart Peterfreund
Sublime Coleridge, by Murray Evans
Longing to Belong, by Sarah Juliette Sasson
British Literary Salons of the Late Eighteenth and Early Nineteenth Centuries,
    by Susanne Schmid
Emily Dickinson's Rich Conversation, by Richard E. Brantley

ALSO BY RICHARD E. BRANTLEY

Wordsworth's "Natural Methodism"
Locke, Wesley, and the Method of English Romanticism
Coordinates of Anglo-American Romanticism: Wesley, Edwards, Carlyle, and Emerson
Anglo-American Antiphony: The Late Romanticism of Tennyson and Emerson
Experience and Faith: The Late-Romantic Imagination of Emily Dickinson

EMILY DICKINSON'S RICH CONVERSATION
POETRY, PHILOSOPHY, SCIENCE

Richard E. Brantley

palgrave
macmillan

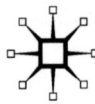

First published in 2013 by
PALGRAVE MACMILLAN®
in the United States—a division of St. Martin's Press LLC,
175 Fifth Avenue, New York, NY 10010.

Where this book is distributed in the UK, Europe and the rest of the world,
this is by Palgrave Macmillan, a division of Macmillan Publishers Limited,
registered in England, company number 785998, of Houndmills,
Basingstoke, Hampshire RG21 6XS.

Palgrave Macmillan is the global academic imprint of the above companies
and has companies and representatives throughout the world.

Palgrave® and Macmillan® are registered trademarks in the United States,
the United Kingdom, Europe and other countries.

ISBN: 978–0–230–34063–3

Reprinted by permission of the publishers and the Trustees of Amherst
College from THE POEMS OF EMILY DICKINSON, Ralph W. Franklin, ed.,
Cambridge, Mass.: The Belknap Press of Harvard University Press, Copyright
© 1998, 1999 by the President and Fellows of Harvard College. Copyright
© 1951, 1955, 1979, 1983 by the President and Fellows of Harvard College.

Reprinted by permission of the publishers from THE LETTERS OF EMILY
DICKINSON, Thomas H. Johnson, ed., Cambridge, Mass.: The Belknap Press
of Harvard University Press, Copyright © 1958, 1986, The President and
Fellows of Harvard College; 1914, 1924, 1932, 1942 by Martha Dickinson
Bianchi; 1952 by Alfred Leete Hampson; 1960 by Mary L. Hampson.

Copyright © 2007 by The Johns Hopkins University Press. Chapter Four first
appeared in *The Emily Dickinson Journal* 16.1 (2007), 27–52. Revised and
reprinted with permission by The Johns Hopkins University Press.

Library of Congress Cataloging-in-Publication Data

Brantley, Richard E.
    Emily Dickinson's rich conversation : poetry, philosophy, science / by
Richard E. Brantley.
        pages cm—(Nineteenth Century Major Lives and Letters)
    Includes bibliographical references and indexes.
    ISBN 978–0–230–34063–3 (alk. paper)
        1. Dickinson, Emily, 1830–1886—Criticism and interpretation.
    2. Philosophy in literature. I. Title.

PS1541.Z5B558 2013
811'.4—dc23   2012050197

A catalogue record of the book is available from the British Library.

Design by Newgen Imaging Systems (P) Ltd., Chennai, India.

First edition: June 2013

10 9 8 7 6 5 4 3 2 1

Transferred to Digital Printing in 2013

To Diana

CONTENTS

Acknowledgments   ix

List of Abbreviations   xi

Introduction   1

Part I   Gathering Experience

1   Proclaiming Empiricism   33

2   Guiding Experiment   71

Part II   Extending Experience

3   Gaining Loss   103

4   Despairing Hope   125

Conclusion   153

Appendix A   *Empiricism and Evangelicalism:*
                A Combination of Romanticism   175

Appendix B   *Locke and Wesley: An Essence of Influence*   179

Appendix C   *Wadsworth and Dickinson: A Marriage*
                of Minds   187

Notes   201

Works Cited   239

Index of Poems Cited   259

Index   263

ACKNOWLEDGMENTS

Audiences at Wake Forest University (2006), Brunel University (2007), Suffolk University (2009), Oxford University (2010), Glasgow University (2011), the Wordsworth Summer Conference (2011), Virginia Intermont College (2011), Haverford College (2012), Brunel University (2013), and the University of Maryland (2013) modeled lively give-and-take. Especially helpful on these occasions were formal suggestions and friendly amendments made by Wai Chee Dimock, Stephen Finley, Richard Gravil, Samantha Harvey, Cynthia MacKenzie, Amelia Osborne, James Osborne, Clo Phillips, Nicholas Roe, Elizabeth Scheer, Robert Scholnick, Edwin G. Wilson, and Eric G. Wilson. Readers of all or parts of the manuscript—Paul Crumbley, Jane Donahue Eberwein, Burton John Fishman, Chris Gair, Kenneth Godwin, Gillian Hillis, David Leverenz, Roger Lundin, Mikesch Meucke, Cristanne Miller, Melvyn New, Marianne Noble, Joel Pace, Georgiana Strickland, and Miriam Zach—showed how "opposition is true friendship." The editor of *Nineteenth-Century Major Lives and Letters*, Marilyn Gaull, accorded this project the pointed but generous and indispensable criticism for which this "Maxwell Perkins" of studies in Romanticism remains renowned; scholarly conversation is richer for her inimitable mix of rigorous reading, fair hearing, common sense, and academic wisdom. Finally, just as dialogue with all these others produced this book, so Diana Brantley's near influence took the primary form, this time, of daily exchanges about Dickinson's art; the dedication signifies gratitude for Diana's colloquy over the years—and for the spirited but unstrained copresence of her life-affirming love.

Scattered sections of chapter 1 appeared as "Emily Dickinson's Empirical Voice," *Symbiosis: A Journal of Anglo-American Literary Relations* 15.1 (April 2011): 105–32. Several consecutive pages of chapter 2 are forthcoming as "The Interrogative Mood of Emily Dickinson's Quarrel with God," *Religion & Literature*. A shorter version of chapter 3 appeared as "From Loss to Gain: Aftermath in the Late-Romantic Poetry of Emily Dickinson," *Symbiosis* 10.2 (October 2006): 93–114. A shorter version of chapter 4 appeared as

"Dickinson's Signature Conundrum," *The Emily Dickinson Journal* 16.1 (2007): 27–52. For their permission to reprint that material here, and for their editorial guidance, thanks are given to Leslie Eckel, Chris Gair, Roger Lundin, Cristanne Miller, Susannah Monta, and Joel Pace.

ABBREVIATIONS

Fr   Emily Dickinson. *The Poems of Emily Dickinson*. 3 vols. Ed. R. W. Franklin. Cambridge, MA: Harvard UP, 1998. Citation by poem number.

L   Emily Dickinson. *The Letters of Emily Dickinson*. 3 vols. Ed. Thomas H. Johnson and Theodora Ward. Cambridge, MA: Harvard UP, 1958. Citation by letter number.

INTRODUCTION

[W]e were rich *in conversation—*

—Emily Dickinson to Austin Dickinson, October 5,
1851, L54 (Dickinson's emphasis)

*How farcical it seems to sit here a writing, when another Sunday's
sun shall shine upon us all in each other's society, and yet thanks to
a being inventing paper and pen, they are better far than nothing!
By means of them indeed, 'tis little I can tell you but I can tell how
much I would if I could, and there's something comforting in it.*

—Emily Dickinson to Austin Dickinson,
November 16, 1851, L63

As a schoolgirl who already belonged to a Shakespeare club, Emily
Dickinson (1830–1886) appeared destined to select her own society
of letters.[1] The adult poet did just that. In "a room of [her] own," she
held "sessions of sweet silent thought" in which she read "ghostlier
demarcations" of other writers and heard "keener sounds" of their
oblique influence.[2] Encountering, at whatever remove, not only her
fellow-exemplars of belles lettres, as one would expect of her, but also,
surprisingly, such masters of expository prose as philosophers and scientists, she crossed the boundaries between, and generated new and
paradoxical amalgams of, various fields. Thus the Myth of Amherst
sojourned among the registers of diverse genius.[3]

This book, in one sense, is an extended meditation on E. D. Hirsch's
broad but discriminating and useful definition of "Literature" as
"everything worthy to be read, preferably the best thoughts expressed
in the best manner, but above all the best thoughts" (142). Hirsch,
for a change, subordinates "*les belles lettres,*" "the narrower, more
decadent conception of literature," to "*les bonnes lettres,*" "the grand,
broad, and noble conception" (140–41). Thus Hirsch welcomes to the
realm of letters what literati usually leave out, for example, philosophy, theology, or science. This book will explore belles lettres primarily through the poetry and prose of Anglo-American Romantics—the

lyrics of Dickinson above all—and the works of Moderns for good measure, and will explore bonnes lettres primarily through the empirically philosophical, empirically evangelical, and hard-core scientific prose of Dickinson's eighteenth- to nineteenth-century Anglo-American world. But the link is not hierarchical (bonnes, *pace* Hirsch, is not better than belles) but conversational. The Romantic- to Modern-era motif of this study draws support from Richard Gravil's *Romantic Dialogues: Anglo-American Continuities 1776–1862* (2000): among other things, Gravil gives new meaning to Coleridge's "*Conversation* Poems" (Coleridge's phrase; emphasis added) as a founding idiom of belles lettres throughout Romantic Anglo-America.[4] The philosophical and scientific themes of *Emily Dickinson's Rich Conversation: Poetry, Philosophy, Science*, moreover—"Theme alone can steady us down," as Frost reminds us (31)—aspire to the historical breadth and interdisciplinary ambition of Paul Crumbley's distinctive companion volumes on the political context of Dickinson's brand of dialogue. Crumbley's works and this book can together illustrate how Dickinson interacted stylistically as well as thematically with quite a varied and inclusive range of bonnes lettres.[5]

Sometimes by her design and sometimes through the detached but intriguing self-consistency of her Zeitgeist, Dickinson's speakers dramatically engaged with her precursors and contemporaries in literature as broadly and emphatically understood here as well as in Hirsch. When the sway was point blank, she found in that upstairs garret instant and plentiful fellowship among comparable imaginations and kindred minds. These more than just cyberspace-like soul mates animated her studying and composing quietude, and, however exclusively they represented her virtual reality, they succeeded in preventing her unrelieved isolation. They and their personae placed her and her speakers squarely enough in their good company, and vice versa, to make *companionable* or *sociable*, if not exactly *gregarious* or *Rotarian*, a label sufficiently plausible even for the Myth of Amherst. Of course, Dickinson's personae often disputed among themselves and with her signifying others. Still, they more or less willingly kept civil tongues in their heads, for they did not so much brandish uncompromising injunction as deploy poetic argument. Dickinson did not merely indulge in self-communion nor simply bet the family homestead on posthumous communication with however large a throng of readers. Quoting her language alongside that of her signifying others—frequently indenting her letters and poems and their poems and prose as if in dialogue form—can serve to suggest that this poet exchanged ideas through the usually indirect but always complex and not seldom direct process of cultural osmosis.

Here, for an introductory example of such parallel quotations, are lines from Wordsworth's high Romanticism, on the one hand, and from Dickinson's late Romanticism, on the other, both passages chosen, like all other such sets of purely belletristic dialogue scattered throughout this book, for their philosophical and even scientific implications. Wordsworth's empirical orientation to

> the world
> Of all of us,—the place where in the end,
> We find our happiness, or not at all!
> (*The Prelude* [1850] 11:142–44)

finds coiled match in Dickinson's:

> The Fact that Earth is Heaven -
> Whether Heaven is Heaven or not
> If not an Affidavit
> Of that specific Spot
> Not only must confirm us
> That it is not for us
> But that it would affront us
> To dwell in such a place -
> (Fr1435)

Dickinson and those among her signifying others like Wordsworth elected to plumb "the substance of things hoped for," and found in, this world (contrast Heb. 11:1).[6] Her distilled demarcations, however, can jolly well sound livelier than the works she read by her companion explorers of reality, whether sublunar or stellar. She knew this news would spread, expected her descendants to hear this earth-to-universe-and-back-again message, and then to join her select society of partners in literary, philosophical, and scientific tradeoff. For her and for her fellow-conversationalists, whether or not she was always aware of talking with them, and including whoever will ever enter this discussion, experience can feel as efficacious as experiment can prove dispositive. For this "us," at least, formative, pivotal experience can parallel experiment, the latter seen, in their collective view, less as reliable solace of predictability than as the natural grace of "What next?"[7]

So it was that Emily Dickinson grew "*rich* in conversation" (her words and emphasis) not just with such friends and loved ones as brother and soul mate Austin but with writers of belles and of bonnes lettres alike. Whether or not she typically agreed with what all these others "often thought," she of all people, perhaps, would have discerned their meanings behind their masks (compare Pope, "Essay on Criticism" [1711], line 298). In however mordant a fashion, she would undoubtedly have approved whatever all these others "well expressed" (compare Pope, "Essay on Criticism," line 298). Their language, clearly, possessed the power to please her. Thus, as though in common cause with such wordsmith-presences-in-waiting before the "inward eye" or "bliss" of her "solitude," and whether or not she always consciously contributed to such communal copy, Emily Dickinson presided especially over her own society of dead or living poets, philosophers, and scientists (compare Wordsworth, "I Wandered Lonely as a Cloud" [1804], lines 21–22). Even when her participation was subconscious, this imaginative, intelligent woman and these codialogists, figuratively and literally so called, relished how their metaphorical, epistemological, and scientifically methodical approaches to knowledge did not so much limit as release possibilities for well-being through understanding.

What did such an enigmatically happy achievement of this collection of talent, this Dickinson-culminated but cumulative concentration of the fully curious, mean, if not their delighted and profitable absorption in their shared stance of smart optimism? If only on the principle of the "invisible suffusion" of all these "afterlives" throughout her poems of their climate, Dickinson and these others mutually verified their faith in progress, their outlook of meliorism.[8] This group quest for known unknowns, unknown knowns, and unknown unknowns sustained her even in her most nonadventurous bouts of lassitude, thereby feeding her various personae of postexperience or of aftermath on her not-so-muted hope that humankind will survive and thrive in "the world / Of all of us."[9] The "unhope" of "waiting" less "for Godot" than for "the horror, the horror" or the "blood-dimmed tide" of Modern- to post-Modern-era nihilism or violence was what Hardy, Beckett, Conrad, and Yeats, respectively, began to express "Full soon" (this last phrase is Wordsworth's presciently lamenting adverbial).[10] The worldviews of these Moderns, however, were scarcely the same as that of Dickinson. For all the advancement of science in the century-just-passed, she and her age boasted more confidence in imagination, more robustness of sense-based reason, and more brio of sense-driven method than was ever to be evident in the paralyzed skepticism on her turn-of-the-twentieth-century horizon, notwithstanding the depressing aspect of mid-nineteenth-century Darwinism. Although Dickinson eerily foreknew the pessimism of the twentieth century, she nonetheless, to conflate her language with that of Wordsworth, "dwel[t] in Possibility - " (Fr466, line 1) of "something evermore about to be" (and about to

be good) in the late Romantic era.[11] With a little help from her counterparts in philosophy/science as well as poetry, she discovered that
hope-against-hope sufficed, if not for goodness, beauty, and truth,
then for all that she needed to know about her milieu, and perhaps
even for all that she could ever envision concerning reality itself.

The sort of dialogue to which these opening paragraphs have
referred enrich Emily Dickinson's art of knowledge, as distinct from
her "art of belief" (Roger Lundin's more religious than philosophical or scientific label for her poetry will receive the respect it is fully
due). With regard to belles lettres, in particular, please hear a word
at the outset about a major method of this book, a recurrent procedure that has already begun to operate. Dickinson would have been
familiar with many of the literary references and would have recognized many of the literary echoes woven throughout this book[12];
she foreshadowed all of the quotations of, and allusions to, Modern
literature. Consistent with the idea that each quotation, like each
allusion, forms part of Dickinson's dialogue, authors, titles, dates,
and line numbers will continue to be provided, except where they
would unduly clutter the text. Then, as has already been the case,
these full disclosures will appear in the notes, though authors' names,
for the convenience of readers, will usually remain in the text (if only
in parentheses). Allusions, by definition, will stay unidentified, but
readers can catch them, if only through Google. If readers can regard
the arc from Romantic to Modern as itself a huge but unified poem—
that is, as cultural poetics—then these quotations and allusions will
appear less taken out of their immediate contexts in belles lettres than
integral to grasping literary history as an organic whole.[13] This aesthetic kind of dialogue within Emily Dickinson's rich conversation,
as distinct from her no less stylistic for being purely philosophical or
scientific mode of exchange, will tend to situate her poetry closer to
Blake's than to Stevens's.

To be sure, just as the lavish sibilants of Shakespeare's "sessions
of sweet silent thought" rival those of "The Soul selects her own
Society - " (Fr409, line 1), so this latter line, from Dickinson's verse,
comprises her signature statement of choosing "her own company"
(Leiter 202)—that is, of "prefer[ring] not to" associate with other
people (Melville's phrase).[14] Nevertheless, as though her hundreds of
otherwise widely differing love poems all embraced the proverb "Love
is to be at one with one alone," "The Soul selects her own Society - "
can also signify, if only on a subliminal level, "the selection of a permanent earthly beloved" (Vendler 190).[15] Even more comprehen-
sively for present purposes of interpreting her art dialogically, these six

striking words can ultimately state that, if only through "the power of weak ties" (compare Ruef), not a few other individuals can well fill the circle of Emily Dickinson's acquaintance. Consider, for instance, what the speaker of this poem, as distinct from "The Soul" who "selects," observes—namely, that

> I've known her - from an ample nation -
> Choose One -
>
> (Fr409, lines 9–10)

Do these lines logically indicate that, besides sometimes selecting one beloved, "The Soul" sometimes picks out no one and sometimes taps more than two, as though her goal were to oscillate between solitude, however virtually populated, and community, however trending small? In any case, just as "red life" streamed in Dickinson's veins and her less "blood-dimmed" than blood-bright imagination saw "into the life of things" or of otherness (behold Keats, Yeats, and Wordsworth, respectively, standing at her side), so Dickinson's personae breathe in time to her inscribed but vital others.[16] And just as she held "sessions of sweet silent thought" in "a room of [her] own" at the Homestead, so she did this for the express rationale of sending out her "letter to the World" to come (Fr519, line 1), her poetry to emotionally and intellectually compatible readers then unborn.

For Emily Dickinson and her "cloud" of fellow-"witnesses" to the human condition, life was as significant for letters as letters for life (compare Heb. 12:1). Consequently, *the Myth of Amherst*—the "lady whom the people call the *Myth*" (Leyda 2:357; Mabel Loomis Todd's emphasis)—will henceforth refer less to Dickinson's diehard reputation as a recluse than to her legendary status as a poet for all seasons.[17] A large measure of her greatness as an author lay in the defining, creative sense, the conversational dynamic, in which she thought and wrote globally and for all times, as well as locally and at her time.[18] As her strategy for acquiring the fair guerdon of her proper renown, she won her gamble on her audience-connecting but challenging combination of less-is-more hymn form with deep but wide-ranging subject matter.

*   *   *

Can literature migrate from belles to bonnes lettres and back? Can poetry, philosophy, and science, though scarcely interchangeable, overlap? Can the common-sense writers in these three disciplines discern an obscure and tenuous but palpable and appreciable line that runs from things through thoughts to words and back? Can the poetry of Emily Dickinson at one extreme of this linguistic range of nuance and philosophical and scientific discourse at the other illustrate a single frame of reference? Can the aesthetic of her gemlike flame aspire to the condition of philosophy and science in the sense that metaphors and models alike generate knowledge from and seek truth through experience?

Addressing these fundamental questions, the remainder of this introduction can outline the case for certain master figures of belles and of bonnes lettres as leading but neglected members of Dickinson's cast of characters. For her, thanks largely to the direct as well as indirect influence of her partners in dialogue, "the unforced force of the better argument" would yield better poetry than any such all-too-humanly tempting but unsubtly conventional and woefully destructive command as "Stop in the name of the law!"[19] No more than poets of her world would philosophers and scientists of that world coerce. No less than philosophers and scientists in her world would poets there persuade. Just as Dickinson's precursors and contemporaries in literary history proved primary for her practice, if not all-important to her thought, so philosophers and scientists prominent, too, among her signifying others proved primary for her thought, if not all-important to her practice. Thus, even from the beginning of this book, close reading of Dickinson's key concepts can and should proceed in earnest with a particular view to whether or not and to how these presiding ideas filled the air of her select society "meetings."

Since a bard of Dickinson's undisputed stature deserves no less than placement in as broad a context as possible—that is, within the international atmosphere of her intersubjective achievement—a leisurely, if not lavish, overview of the historical, interdisciplinary argument to follow is in order. At stake throughout the delight here taken in this near-communitarian approach to her poetic innovation is whether or not her philosophically and scientifically as well as lyrically dialogical exchange is central to her art. It is. For the Myth of Amherst and her opposite numbers in belles and bonnes lettres, literature stands for experience and experiment alike. Thus, for instance, the metaphor- and model-producing power of her imagination aligns a sizeable category of her scientific speakers with the laboratory skills she strengthened in her garden and her greenhouse (a facsimile edition of her herbarium has recently appeared).

Dickinson entered into conversation, first, with exemplars of Anglo-American Romanticism, stipulated (consistent with the scope of *Nineteenth-Century Major Lives and Letters*) as stretching from the late eighteenth century to her time and place. If Blake, Wordsworth, Coleridge, Shelley, Keats, Carlyle, Tennyson, and Emerson caused Dickinson "the anxiety of influence" that named Harold Bloom's theory of literature (Bloom has just refined his terms in *The Anatomy of Influence* [2011]), the language of these deep denizens of belles lettres nonetheless lived in her high art. If such among her literary precursors and contemporaries as these eight authors of poetry or of belletristic prose or of both overburdened her at times with their less courteous and espousing than overbearing and perpendicular masculinity, she nonetheless rejoiced in and blessed their endowments of strength.[20] Their talents she deemed worthy of her own compound of androgynous—recall: "room of *one's* own" (emphasis added)—excellence in creativity. If the tender hearts of Blake, Emerson et al. intensified Dickinson's pleasure in aesthetic form, she nonetheless thrived on how their tough minds increased her profit from aesthetic content. This cherished benefit of her association with these gifted others underlay how Carlyle's picture on her bedroom wall copresided at her society gatherings in her room with a subtle view of the world.[21] Her toughness excelled that of her fellow-Romantics, for she showed scant sign of the sentimentality or humorlessness that from time to time beset, if not such high-to-late Romantics as these, then rhymesters in their orbits and their wakes.

Featuring sometimes Carlyle and sometimes other codialogists of his ilk at the head of her seminar table, Dickinson moderated debate centering on whether or not and on how the road of experience leads to the palace of wisdom. "Yes, it can, through the both/and logic, 'the everlasting nay and yea,' of life as well as of art, including the energy in the laboratory," tended to answer Dickinson and her select society of partners in belletristic conversation. It is as though they took their cue from Carlyle when it was his turn to speak. He explored throughout the clever prose of his *Sartor Resartus* (1831) his conundrum less of art-versus-life in decadent favor of the former than of the alternate nay and yea of art and of life alike. Among these others with whom Dickinson often enjoyed the mutuality, as distinct from always feeling the anxiety, of influence, she sought to describe the love of paradox, the passion of one's inner English major for life/art principles like "the everlasting nay and yea," as what best defines being human. To anyone who would listen, she said, "[A metaphor] won't bite. My dog Carlo now..." (L34).

For Dickinson and her peers in Anglo-American Romanticism, the A=B of metaphor—Wordsworth's Lucy *was* a "violet by a mossy stone"—and of model—Newton's light was a particle *and* a wave—illustrated how paradox was the simple produce of the common day, as well as of uncommon creative incandescence (compare Wordsworth, "She Dwelt among the Untrodden Ways" [1799], line 5). Like a Blake/Wordsworth composite, with which duo, however well acquainted she was with its works, Dickinson appeared to be in consultation, she understood that one's "Poetic Genius"—Blake's phrase for *inner English major*—lifted "the *burthen* of the mystery"—Wordsworth's magic (emphasis added)—without *dispelling* the mystery.[22] Like an embodiment of Shelley, whose less stylistic than thematic, yet whose striking and uncanny, parallels with Dickinson will form another motif here, she well acquainted herself with the liberating power of skeptical paradox at which he excelled (Pulos; O'Neill). Whether or not, like him, she exposed the "fraud" of rigid system, and whether or not, like him, she opposed the "woe" of oppressive authority, she nonetheless resisted, in both these cases of her Shelley-like mode of imagining and of thinking, the logic of either/or (compare Shelley, "Mont Blanc" [1816], line 81). Although she seldom ever predictably agreed with other members of her society of either belles or bonnes lettres, and although she could often beat them at their own game of paradox, the poet who chose "not choosing" (compare Cameron *Choosing*) preserved at least a remnant of freedom for all. To bring about this positive result of her game of riddling, she worked in tandem with all these other fellow-enthusiasts of enigma.

The poet for whom there was "no frigate like a book" (Fr1286, line 1) underwrote her society of belles lettres with the both/and logic of positive paradox. How she and these others comprehended contraries! Nay/yea, ignorance/knowledge, falsehood/truth, pessimism/optimism, despair/hope—all such binaries constituted the play of their earnestness and the seriousness of their fun. For Dickinson, it was less dialectic of and more oscillation between these tough and tender nodes or poles of human experience:

> Experience is the Angled Road
> Preferred against the Mind
> By - Paradox - the Mind itself -
> Presuming it to lead
>
> Quite Opposite - How complicate
> The Discipline of Man -
> Compelling Him to choose Himself
> His Preappointed Pain -
> (Fr899)

Perhaps Dickinson's suspension of meaning between the nihilism of indeterminacy and the Romantic-era possibility of guilelessness can yet keep options open for that not-so-select society of partners in dialogue called her posterity.

Although Dickinson coveted the aspiration of Blake, Emerson et al. to the ideal and otherworldly—that is, although she envied their philosophical and theological transcendentalism—she relished, above all, their epistemological savvy.[23] She acquired her love of paradox from their search for how to know. She watched their coalescence, thrilled at their interpenetration, of subject and object. This "Solution sweet" preserved subject/object independence, yet yearned for subject-object interdependence (compare Keats, "The Eve of Saint Agnes" [1820], line 322). Thus the role of mind in nature felt ambiguous to the Myth of Amherst, sometimes heady and sometimes vertiginous, precarious, unlikely, or ironic:

> Perception of an Object costs
> Precise the Object's loss -
> Perception in itself a Gain
> Replying to it's price -
>
> The Object absolute, is nought -
> Perception sets it fair
> And then upbraids a Perfectness
> That situates so far -
>   (Fr1103)

Dickinson's observer-participant conundrum foreshadowed that of Heisenberg but harked back to that of her Romantic-era forebears and fellow-laborers in the vineyard of knowledge and truth, energizing her creation of her similarly sense-substantial but even more precisely perception-calibrated art. The scientifically methodical as well as empirically philosophical contribution made by her Anglo-American Romantic heritage "gild[ed] the lapses of [her] time" (compare Keats, "How Many Bards" [1817], line 1). That is, she enriched her study and composition with belletristic exchanges concerning whether or not mind matters as lord of nature, or as part of nature, or as both.[24]

Although Dickinson would occasionally cotton to the intermittent predilection for the philosophical and the religious transcendental among the Anglo-American Romantics, she mainly emulated their more characteristic modulation from sense-procedural sophistication to precocious and prescient scientific savvy. The précis in appendix A of this book can indicate how previous installments in this ongoing series of volumes on English-language Romanticism described the collective effort of the Anglo-American Romantic imagination to reconcile philosophical and religious language. This book, though, yields to a difficult fascination with Dickinson's empiricism per se, including her scientific knowledge. A view to her philosophically and theologically transcendental idioms continues to obtain here, as a secondary commentary to keep the discussion dramatic—that is, as a subtext in the persistent spirit of inclusive conversation-in-perpetuity. Volume 7 in this series of arguments, tentatively entitled *Emily Dickinson's Rich Conversation: Poetry and Faith*, is planned, and will overhear her evangelical accent per se, as distinct from pursuing her role, if any, in the empirical/evangelical dialectic of Romantic Anglo-America. At present, however, somewhat unlike what Volume 5 said (Brantley *Experience*), and hence as a partial palinode, in the sense of one's dialogue with one's self, it appears that Dickinson separated her evangelical yearning from, and depreciated that obscure desire in favor of, her empirical voice of ascendant, up-from-the-grassroots authority.

Emily Dickinson's transatlantic significance, moreover, highlighted the philosophically interdisciplinary component of Anglo-American bonnes lettres. She matriculated at the Common Sense School of Scottish philosophy in "sessions of sweet silent thought" in father Edward's library, an influence in such clear scholarly focus that it need figure here only tacitly.[25] What is less well known is that Dickinson read *about* philosophy, too, and was aware of its English-language roots in the seventeenth century. She even knew of ancient Greek philosophy, as the next segment of this introduction will point out.

Here is a mouthful of what Dickinson's poetry in league with philosophy and science means. The rational empiricism of pioneer of British empiricism John Locke (1632–1704) discovered a circuitous but less roundabout than clearly marked route into Dickinson's works through the Locke-inflected influence of founder of British Methodism John Wesley (1703–1791) on the American evangelism of his transatlantic revival legatee Charles Wadsworth (1814–1882). Readers curious about Wesley's self-portrait as "a philosophical sluggard" at times more interested in the school of Locke than in being an itinerant minister, and hence about the philosophical/scientific nature of his intellectual influence, as distinct from his well-known role as a warm-hearted revivalist, may wish to peruse appendix B. Part I of this book will make clear that Dickinson read the Locke- as well as Wesley-tinged sermons of Wadsworth, a renowned clergyman whom she called, among her other honorifics for him, "my dearest earthly friend" (L807). Readers interested in the emotional as well as intellectual aspect of her love for Wadsworth, and perhaps even of his for her, are invited to consult appendix C, for one's inquiring mind may wish to entertain the possibility of their romance, however cerebral. The emphasis in the body of this book, however, without losing sight of the emotional content of their friendship or of a possible love interest, lies, fair warning, on the primarily intellectual basis of their long-term conversation. A comparison/contrast between Wadsworth's sermons and Dickinson's letters and poems will account for her less metaphorical/evangelical than model-driven/empirical approach to reality, and hence for her more naturally than spiritually experiential "poetry of earth" (compare Keats, "The Poetry of Earth Is Never Dead" [1817]).

Wadsworth, whom Dickinson also called "My Clergyman" (L790), wittingly as well as unwittingly served as Wesley's similarly well-known, equally protean, yet as such almost entirely unacknowledged protégé. These twin giants, the one of British and American Methodism and the other of the First and Second Great Awakenings in America, valued as well as spiritualized empiricism, for even for them "to write against something" was also for them "to take their bearings from it."[26] Their versions of evangelical faith proved as tough as tender, for neither of these leaders of the Anglo-American revival was anywhere near as concerned to use his private religion of the heart as a cushion against reason and the senses as one might think. Each was intent, instead, on welcoming sense-based reason as the starch-giving, stiffening agent, the method or method-ism, of his belief, and perhaps even as the suspending mechanism of his disbelief, however elusive actually seeing God turned out to be in each man's otherwise thoroughgoing religion. Each refreshed the formulae of his heart-religion through his state-of-the-art, all but scientific or proto-William James/anthropological understanding of empirical, outward, or "Earthward" experience of the soul.[27] Wesley's and Wadsworth's Locke-derived rational empiricism stayed up-to-date or ready on their naturally as well as spiritually experiential common ground to negotiate with their dominant evangelical witness to immediate and traditional revelation.

For Dickinson's part in this quasi-scientific, variety-of-religious-experience perspective on "faith" as "the *substance* of things hoped for," the "*evidence* of things not seen" (Heb. 11:1; emphasis added), Dickinson's empirical leanings did not so much come to terms with, or heighten, as do battle with her nostalgically evangelical yearnings. She interpreted Locke and Wesley through Wadsworth, and perhaps even through her other nearby, philosophically ministerial partners in discussion (who will receive further notice). In the end, however, she imbibed her empiricism neat, not necessarily in the sense that she read Locke all the time, yet certainly in the sense that her personae, with their trenchant empiricism, harked back to his views (recall "Experience is the Angled Road" and "Perception of an Object costs").

"He buys me many Books—but begs me not to read them—because he fears they joggle the Mind" (L261). So the poet wrote about her father to one of her best friends, her most highly literary "Preceptor" (L265), Thomas Wentworth Higginson. Less through Edward Dickinson, perhaps, than through her "dearest earthly friend" and most intriguingly religious counselor, Wadsworth, she thanked the ultimate empiricism of Locke for making her more philosophical, less religious. Her graduation from the Common Sense School had the same effect. Through Wadsworth's Locke- as well as Wesley-inspired prose, and through Wadsworth's emphasis on the empirical Wesley, Locke's *Essay concerning Human Understanding* (1690) gave subliminal, subtextual, subversive, and efficient sanction to Dickinson's outsized search for reason—as well as for sense-based metaphors and models of reality. With these images she countered and resisted, if only to keep in play, what she reluctantly but honestly came to think of as the experientially attractive but otherwise all too purpose-driven, in-the-dark-whistling theology of her still-esteemed, always-beloved clergyman.

Undoubtedly it pained Dickinson to parse Wadsworth's prose in any such pejorative way. But that possible interpretation of his sermons (however mixed with her abiding affection for them) will be an implication of this book. Although Dickinson admired Wadsworth's Locke-consistent, sense-based acts of genuine, this-worldly faith, she usually did not share (however often she tried to embrace, however much she was tempted by) his Wesley-derived, sense-analogized leaps of otherworldly, cloud-cuckoo faith. She was persuaded less by her fellow-intellectual-evangelical's kerygmatic appeal than by his skeptical streak. This Dickinson, counterintuitively speaking, richly became something of an agnostic-if-not-atheistic Christian, and, speaking in the same appropriately paradoxical manner, this Dickinson strangely turned into a Christian agnostic-if-not-atheist. Judging by her veiled reports in her letters and poems, and based on Wadsworth's own supple hints in his 75 published sermons, it was like preacher, like poet, both harboring not-so-secret doubts about the personality, power, justice, mercy, and existence of God, "The missing All" (Fr995, line 1). This exquisitely gerundive, participial, ambiguous epithet, to which chapter 1 (segment 7) will return in detail, was one of Dickinson's kinder, gentler, least sarcastic names for the Deity, whenever the poet's back was up.

A comparison/contrast between Dickinson's letters and poems and the writings of her clergyman and of his mentor Wesley can indicate, perhaps even more explicitly than her conversation with the Romantics, just how she valued sense-grounded reason for its own sake. She embraced empiricism probably with greater enthusiasm, and surely with less trepidation, than Wesley and Wadsworth, and hence with a pivotal, decidedly imaginative result for literary history. Of course, Dickinson was as far as possible from being polemical about philosophy-versus-faith. Still, from the standpoint of her flexible but proud empiricism, and with an attitude fitting for the forceful but unforced and unforcing openness of art, she conversed in more than just effect with these near-allied twin ministers of the transatlantic revival. Although the God who fled out of her door would come back, if only fleetingly, in her window, Locke nonetheless played Epicurus to her Lucretius (compare Greenblatt *Swerve*). Dickinson discovered anew, for her time and place, the relation between what is thought in philosophy and what is said in literature, and between what is thought in literature and what is said in philosophy (compare Steiner on just this subtly category- or genre-bending nexus during the twentieth century). Dickinson's rising faith in experience did not just talk with, and temper further, but even talked back to, and further tested, the falling remnants of her Experiential Faith.

Dickinson's transatlantic significance, finally, highlighted a *scientifically* interdisciplinary component of Anglo-American bonnes lettres, as chapters 1 and 2 will emphasize. For example, as just a single foretaste here, such a foremost British practitioner of "natural philosophy" (Locke's and Wesley's synonym for science) as evolutionary biologist Charles Darwin (1809–1882) ranked high within the poet's select society of partners in scientifically methodical inquiry. Darwin's admission to Dickinson's inner circle of fellow-artists and fellow-experimental intellectuals set up a major phase of her development in just how aesthetic thought can make common cause with empirical practice. If her interaction with such avant-garde science as Darwin's trended even more extraordinary than her truck with rationally empirical philosophy and empirically tinged evangelical religion, so be it. Darwin's impact on her works paralleled the fair treatment received by his *On the Origin of Species* (1859) in New England venues of debate. In New England journals to which the Dickinson family faithfully subscribed, and which embraced, with respect for the insecure feelings of otherwise well-informed traditional religious opinion-makers, an accurate understanding of natural selection as knowledge, if not truth, Dickinson, her brother, and her sister, Lavinia, eagerly read think-tank pieces about

Darwin (Eberwein "Outgrowing Genesis?"; Keane *Emily*; Kirkby "'We thought'"; Peel).

To anticipate the findings of part I in this regard, the poet reversed Wadsworth's subordination of Darwin's theory of natural selection to natural and revealed religion, and she appeared to know, notwithstanding Darwin's word *selection*, that his achievement does not so much assume agency as demonstrate randomness. In this respect, she probably disagreed (though unwillingly) with her friend Wadsworth. Notwithstanding Wadsworth's conservative inclination in the evolutionary controversy (shades here of the Wilberforce/Huxley confrontations during the 1860s) and in part because Wadsworth offered to that orthodox effect a stout stance in contrast with Dickinson's mounting receptivity to Darwin's science, Wadsworth lived in Dickinson's mind as well as in her soul and heart. She responded among her scientific as well as philosophical and literary codialogists to Darwin's intellectually wholehearted but emotionally fraught challenge to religion (his wife, Emma, after all, was an evangelical) by out-Darwin-ing Darwin, by emphasizing *his* terms as *her* means of trying Christian doctrine and of trying out evangelical experience. By counteracting Darwin's unintended but inexorable disenchantment of nature and of human life, she also parried his inadvertent but home-striking thrust at "poetic faith."[28] She consciously turned her inner-English-major guilelessness-plus-paradox-attunement into Darwin-savvy but still somehow lyrical and musical sallies of the imagination during her late-Romantic era. So she became at least as remarkably scientific as she has remained philosophically religious or religiously philosophical.

Anglo-American Romantic authors, rationally empirical philosophers, empirically oriented preachers, innovators of physical science, and pioneers of life science worked together, in effect, to broaden and to deepen the writings of Emily Dickinson. Her art, in turn, culminated and enhanced this heritage of belles and of bonnes lettres alike. All these signs of her personae, and of her others, agree that the imagination took its rise and footing from sense perception, and not so much from instinct, emotion, intuition, mysticism, the Holy Ghost, or the muse. Locke, Wesley, Wadsworth, and Darwin, too, possessed vision. The Romantics and Dickinson, too, schooled theirs in experience. In the Anglo-American setting, the Romantics, Dickinson, Wesley, and Wadsworth were scarcely more likely than Locke and Darwin to leave sense-based reason and the scientific method out of the writer's equation. They all went so far in their habitat as to sharpen their skills at language on their quasi-joint assimilation of precise laboratory procedures.

Their mastery of scientific method obtains, no matter how much late-Romantic Dickinson still had in common with the tradition of religious/prophetic vision and of scripture-revelation alike (compare Doriani). Preference for inductive observation over deductive logic applied as closely to the Romantics, Dickinson, Wesley, and Wadsworth as to Locke and Darwin. Dickinson's personae spoke in these terms, sometimes against and sometimes to or for her others. Her others, in this manner, contributed their multiple perspectives to her method-in-madness kind of sequestration—that is, to the cloistered but fully dust-and-heat-aware virtue of her aesthetic experience in her own room at the Homestead.

Did Emily Dickinson's lyrical monologues begin and end in dramatic dialogues concerning whether or not sense data can satisfy one's need to know what is naturally true? Yes, but no matter how much she and her attendant "cloud of witnesses" to the human condition doubted that sense data impinged on the spiritual sense, neither she nor her fellow-watchers-in-the-night ever pretended that such data could slake their thirst, quench their desire, for whatever might be spiritually true. Her poetic dialogists, in large measure because of their exchanges with these others, remained optimistic in their quest for knowledge, and rarely, if ever, did they give up their hope of truth, however elusive they all found truth to be. Dickinson and her fellow-writing prodigies made empiricism and science the foundation of their substance and of their appeal alike. The lead in her chorus, the obbligato over all her singers—consisting of her poetic self-projections and of those inscribed others as "*rich* in conversation" as she—was her empirical voice. This canonical idiom coexisted uneasily but fruitfully with her stubbornly persistent evangelical vernacular. Faith in experience and in experiment, in her case, though scarcely always in the instances of her others (at least for anywhere near as much of the time) overdrove the converse—namely, the experience and the experiment of faith.

This momentous modulation of the Myth of Amherst occurred over the course of her 30-year career and grew out of, and perhaps even happened because of, her interactive language. However "awash" was her age "in the sea of faith" (compare Jon Butler), her art of knowledge (compare her "art of belief") resulted from her group effort, as opposed to any group-think or to any solipsism on her part (compare Schulz on the collective as well as individual propensity of humanity to be wrong). The works of Wordsworth, Emerson et al., and of Locke, Wesley, Wadsworth, Darwin et al. declared themselves alongside hers. Wadsworth provided an especially conversational, two-way bridge from her social circle to her ever more select, yet still inclusive, society of Anglo-American master figures. "Master," significantly, looks prominent among her edgy but less irony-laced than laudatory designations for her men friends (Lease makes this point). Ghostly presences of belles and of bonnes lettres alike felt palpable to her.

What was true of high art, for Dickinson, was also true of expository prose, for her—that is, not just that substance and style are one and the same but that, as Harold Bloom has observed in another context, "[i]maginative literature [one would here stipulate belles and bonnes] is otherness, and as such alleviates loneliness. We read not only because we cannot know enough people, but because friendship is vulnerable" (*How* 1). As reader and writer, Emily Dickinson fit these interpersonal comments. She enjoyed conversation among, took a turn on the dance floor of dialogically inscribed and human-defining language with, "empiricists" like Wordsworth and Wadsworth and empiricists like Locke and Darwin.

This book is of a piece. It highlights dialogue throughout. It makes philosophy and science overt in part I and covert in part II. At the same time, it tries not to be as thesis-ridden as perhaps some previous arguments in the series were.

Part I will specify that by no means alone did Emily Dickinson gather knowledge from experience and draw near truth through experiment. Without losing sight of French rationalism and German idealism as influences on Anglo-American Romanticism, and while keeping the empirical/evangelical dialectic of Romantic Anglo-America in play, part I will concentrate on British empiricism and science as the transatlantic substance of Dickinson's dialogical expression and the transatlantic evidence of her appeal.[29] Nor, as part II will elaborate, did Dickinson ask entirely by herself what to make of, and how to cope with, those disenchantments of existence that follow experience gone awry and experiment at dead end. Accordingly, part II will acknowledge that the loss of others and of otherness in Dickinson's poems of postexperience or of aftermath was severe, and made her generic poet's perennial quandaries of disillusionment and disaffection especially excruciating dilemmas in her case. This daunting condition of Dickinson's art persisted, no matter how bravely she contrived to overcome it. Nothing stopped this poet, though. Even the self-reliance of her overall triumph, if not that of Emerson's, was in part other-directed.

Emily Dickinson's rich conversation about poetry, philosophy, and science can go on—that is, her art of knowledge can still address whether or not the creative imagination that once flourished primarily on religion-as-ground can in any brave new world of reason and the senses survive (witness public university STEM-subject mania). Her poetry is made up of voices defining "Wonder - " not only as "not precisely knowing" but also as "not precisely knowing not - " (Fr1347, lines 1–2). She declares this "condition" "bleak" but "beautiful" (compare Fr1347, line 3). Thus her canon constitutes curriculum vitae.

*   *   *

Did the personae of Emily Dickinson choose their sparring partners from among philosophically and scientifically inclined speakers in belles and in bonnes lettres alike? If so, as this book maintains, the others who proved significant to her would surely have agreed that she stayed front and center in their common enterprise. *Emily Dickinson*'s rich conversation contained the multitudinous voices of *her* dialogical art. If her poetry is one part *group* biography of *communal* knowing, it is another part embodiment of *her* aesthetic and intellectual life. Accordingly, before emphasizing how this poet combines the expressive function of her art with the pragmatic or audience-oriented hemisphere of her imagination—this blended purpose may well be the most original stylistic contribution made by her art of knowledge—one should first pay attention to her expressive function per se.

To be sure, one of Dickinson's personae is a male cigar smoker (Fr107). Others are characters buried alive (e.g., Fr448). Nevertheless, "Wild nights - wild nights!" (Fr269) intimates the poet's lesbian fantasy for her sister-in-law, Susan Huntington Gilbert Dickinson.[30] Thus the poet and her speakers can appear interchangeable. If at the core of her art of conversation is the flesh-and-blood poet as discussion leader, this book is right, *pace* New Criticism, sometimes not to distinguish between the speaker of a poem and this artist whose self-portrait is philosophically and scientifically as well as aesthetically delineated.

"When I state myself, as the Representative of the Verse—it does not mean—me—but a supposed person" (L268). Although this thumbnail version of Dickinson's aesthetic (disclosed to Higginson) can seem anything but autobiographical, "*When I state myself*" heralds her conviction that "the Representative of the Verse—" is *she*. The comma that follows "myself" violates the rule against separating the reflexive pronoun from the restrictive qualifier, slows the pace of the reading, and draws out Dickinson's insistence that her lyrics concern *her* condition. Her declaration signifies "not that her poems were totally free from autobiography but just the opposite—that there was more of her personal situation in them than she would care to have made public" or than meets the eye (see Shurr 130). Even "a supposed person" by that logic denotes a facet of her: the distinction between the real one who supposes and the fictional one who is supposed tends in the case of this poet to fall into abeyance or to rise into suspension. Although Dickinson can seem to maintain complete separation of life from art, she wants to know if her "Verse is alive" and to "think it breathed" (L260). As a "real woman, lineal indeed / From Pyrrha's pebbles and old Adam's seed," she and her others enliven her personae (compare Keats, *Lamia* [1820], lines 332–38). She suggests that artifice entails "yeasty" "*self*"-fashioning, to quote Gerard Manley Hopkins (emphasis added), as well as mere "self-*fashioning*," to quote Stephen J. Greenblatt (emphasis added), though with more Romantic-era self-apotheosis, on her part, than Hopkins's implication of Original Sin would countenance.[31]

The multivocal quality encouraging such paradoxical reading between the lines of Dickinson's art-versus-life conundrum finds excellent match in Robert Browning's similarly double-edged principle: "I'll tell my state as though 'twere none of mine."[32] Browning's formulation, too, would seem to highlight the difference between him and the "supposed person" of his "Verse—." His subjunctive mood, however, goes contrary to the fact of his poet-persona *identity: his* state is what his poetry tells his readers about. For Browning, again to use Dickinson's language, any "Representative of the Verse—" proves congruent with that speaker's poet-creator, as though there were an Iago in Shakespeare. The lack of such a possessive construction in Dickinson's dictum as Browning's word *mine* calls attention to the covert, subliminal, or subversive sense in which her art remains *hers*.

One thinks in this connection, albeit whimsically, of an ironic instance of popular culture, Miss Piggy's "*Moi?*" Although the Muppet's rhetorical question poses as her wry self-effacement, her trotter-on-sternum, eye-rolling gesture makes her fans receive her meaning loud and clear: "Yes, now that I think of it, '*Moi!*' with a vengeance, and, for that matter, '*Me, Myself, and I!*'" Dickinson's subjectivity, too, highlights wryness and sarcasm: unlike Miss Piggy, however, or perhaps even like her after all, the poet intends no uncertain degree of high-serious appeal. Just as Dickinson "withdraw[s] into the several isolations of her closet while ceaselessly soliciting the other" (Werner 36), so her composite of selfhood-and-dialogue constitutes her intellectual-and-cultural outreach.

The riddle of Dickinson's not-so-feigned, not-so-separate presence runs throughout her life/art conundrum, from her nominative "I" at one pole, through her intensive "myself" at the heart of her meaning, to her coyly objective but scarcely withheld "—me—" at the end of her statement. The *thin* disguises of her personae can thus reveal the contours of her selfhood. Yes, poets and their speakers can dwell apart, can occupy mutually exclusive, antipodal realms, and Dickinson's self-projections, too, can don the demeanor of art for art's sake. Yes, any given mode of her expression, her empirical voice included, can adopt the belletristic conceit of an autonomous, isolated character hermetically sealed from the inaccessible poet and her others, and Dickinson's readers, accordingly, may declare to her personae, "We know that you are scarcely the poet herself. We acknowledge you for yourselves alone, and not for your marks of either your creator's DNA or her expatiating consciousness." At the same time, though (and herein lies the chief, unabashed assumption of this book) her readers may exclaim to her speakers at no inconsiderable length,

> We recognize you as the loose federation of the lyric genius who rivals Wordsworth's egotistical sublimity. With apologies to the New Critical resistance to autobiographical significance, we can appreciate the fact that your creator, like Whitman, can "contain multitudes," and that her poetry, like Wordsworth's and Whitman's, can constitute her "own personal expanse" of intentionality and, for that matter, of self/other-referencing simultaneity.[33]

If this latter response seems unlikely, and perhaps even if it speculates to a fault, it nonetheless keeps faith with the vitality of Dickinson's art. Her speakers do not so much mediate as illustrate and lay bare her dialogue with the Romantics, Locke, Wesley, Wadsworth, and Darwin. The implicit "we" of her self-expression becomes, if anything, more intriguing than its explicit "I."

Charles Wadsworth will loom so large in Dickinson's "we" that in advance of comparing his prose and her poetry it appears advisable to survey the empirically inflected historical context and the cultural ramifications of their "marriage of true minds." First, the early-Enlightenment correspondence between the Rev. John Norris and Mary Astell adopted a Christian-Platonist, anti-Locke stance. Failing to "carve out a position" between Norris and "the Empiricism of Locke," Astell concluded that "Sensible Congruity" (Norris's phrase) between soul and body amounted to "materialism."[34] Then, during the 1720s and 1730s, the exchange between John Wesley and Mary

Granville Pendarves (later Delany) mapped out a pro-Locke route to experiential faith, and hence preserved a role for rational empiricism in Christian feminism.[35] After 1738, when Wesley's "heart was strangely warmed" and his American as well as British revival was aborning, Jonathan and Sarah Pierpont Edwards breathed in the Wesley/Pendarves atmosphere of religious "epistemology": George Marsden recognizes the spiritual-sense component of the transatlantic revival and of the Edwards' rich conversation.[36] Finally, former minister Ralph Waldo Emerson and his key discussion partner, Margaret Fuller, grounded their revival-modulated Transcendentalism in the revival-central but empiricism-analogized doctrine of the spiritual sense (Hankins). Wadsworth and Dickinson occupied a crowning position on this arc of social progress. In fact, especially considering that the nineteenth-century alliance between ministers and their women parishioners suffered a scandalous end during the 1870s, because of the affair between the Rev. Henry Ward Beecher and Elizabeth Tilton, Wadsworth and Dickinson climaxed the drama at its proper best.[37]

This historic series of intellectual conversations between Anglo-American divines and their protégées sheds light on the empirical as well as evangelical content of Dickinson's passionate esteem for the man whom she called, above all of her other glowing Wadsworth-designations, "My Clergyman" (L790). Wadsworth's sermons and Dickinson's poems culminated nearly two hundred years' worth of Anglo-American male/female dialogue about philosophical and scientific as well as religious methodology.[38] There was clearly something about the combination of rational empiricism and heart-religion—was it receptivity/openness to experience of all kinds natural as well as spiritual?—that proved conducive to advancement and enhancement of the more than merely cultural link between the sexes. Of course, Wadsworth and Dickinson were significantly religious writers, in his case especially so.[39] This book adds Arminian evangelicalism—the proexperiential emphasis on the doctrine of free will, on the soul's own role in, and responsibility for, its salvation— to what Alfred Habegger, Jane Eberwein, and others have written concerning the fraught relationship between Dickinson's poetry and predestinarian, non- or antiexperiential, Puritanism/Calvinist evangelicalism.[40] Still, consistent with how the works of Wadsworth and Dickinson bear witness to faith *and*, in her case more often than in his, profess faith in experience, his sermons include analogues to, and sources for, her concretely experiential, natural as well as spiritual vision. The 1,125 pages of his 75 published homilies serve in this book, in advance of further and more religiously oriented uses to be made of these sermons in a future study, to amplify Dickinson's empirical voice. She steeped herself in philosophy and science in a manner commensurate with, and perhaps even in large measure because of, his interests.[41]

Dickinson read Wadsworth less to seek the sense-related or sense-analogized ground of religion, whether natural or revealed, than to stand on the epistemological ground of sense-based knowledge. Their composite "heart [leapt] up" when it was strangely warmed by inward faith, but also "when [they beheld] / A rainbow in the sky"—that is, when the preacher and the poet read hope and promise in, into, contingencies (compare Wordsworth, "My Heart Leaps Up" [1802], lines 1–2). Anyone for whom sermon interpretation has formed an element of historical, interdisciplinary criticism would testify that Wadsworth's prose compares favorably with the readable Wesley's, outstripping the repetitious and convoluted Edwards's.[42] Wadsworth's prose made up a pleasing frame of reference for the grand end of "selving" in Dickinson's life of writing (compare Hopkins, "As Kingfishers Catch Fire" [1881–1883], line 7). Concerning more than just religion, Wadsworth's sermons placed the mind as well as the soul-and-heart of the Myth of Amherst in context.

To apply Emerson's language to the Wadsworth/Dickinson dialogue, and to underscore the most pertinent word of that language, Emerson's call for "every man to be so much an artist that he could repeat in *conversation* what had befallen him" ("The Poet" [1842] in Murphy 1:925; emphasis added) appealed, in effect, to this man and to this woman. One should adjust Emerson's gendered prose. In mutual language both comprehensive and comprehensible, the preacher and the poet directly and indirectly reported to one another on their natural and spiritual experience. His contribution to homiletics provides a foil for her art. Of course, the two could part company, and did so on more than one occasion. Still, the substance, style, and wit of Wadsworth's sermons can also animate one's approach to Dickinson's paradox of experience and faith. The sermons will comprise one of the most important strategies of this book, and of the next in the series—namely, establishing explanatory parallels to her language of experience. The Wadsworth glosses on her poetry— the method of reading her poems in the light of particular passages from his works—supply an intersubjective method for relating her spiritualized to her "naturalized imagination," and for emphasizing the latter.[43]

Understood as intellectual autobiography, Dickinson's art marks a path back to Locke and across to Darwin by way of the Romantics, and through Wesley and Wadsworth. The context from Blake to Wordsworth to Whitman can give meaning to the sincerity of her select society of partners in discussion. Just as her empirical voice echoes evangelical thought and practice, so she hums the "spilt religion" (T. E. Hulme's phrase) of Romanticism. Donne, Herbert, and Crashaw, too, grapple with "the new philosophy [science]" that "calls all in doubt" (Donne's language in *An Anatomy of the World* [1611], line 205), but the Romantics rank among Dickinson's nearby, and most temperamentally and aesthetically similar, partners in science. Her personae fashion themselves not as "sicklied o'er" with the "pale cast" of revival idiom but as colored with the blush of Romantic-era earth-poetry, for, to italicize and expand on her words, her speakers sound like "*Scientist[s]* of [Poetic] Faith" (Fr1261, line 12; emphasis added). Just as, among the ghostly but stirring presences of her art, *Words*worth counts as her chief literary dialogist, so *Wads*worth emerges as her main partner discussing Locke and Darwin. Wesley serves as her figurative partner discussing Locke; Darwin epitomizes her partners discussing science. The intersubjective thread of Dickinson's life-writing is thus the quality of mutual verification.

Empirically philosophical principles in league with scientifically methodical procedures make up prime topics of Dickinson's conversation with others. This dramatically dialogical aspect of her lyric mastery squares with John Emerson Todd's grasp of her "scenarios" or groupings of personae seeking to solve existential conundrums together. Subject/object coalescence or interpenetration and such scientific challenges to all and sundry denizens of the nineteenth century as how fossils illuminate natural selection can mean, for her, that two or more heads are decidedly better than one. The young discipline of cognitive science provides an analogy that stresses the think-tank dimension or "subtle para-conversations" of scientific pursuit.[44] Dickinson pioneers such collective genius, thereby meriting what Blake calls the "Enthusiastic Admiration" due to great art in general. Although that response might seem an insufficiently cerebral assessment of an art of knowledge, Blake's criterion of "Enthusiastic Admiration" nonetheless constitutes what he boldly proclaims as "the first principle of Knowledge & the last."[45] A definition of individual genius—namely, "instinctive and extraordinary capacity for imaginative creation, original thought, invention, or discovery" (*OED*)—serves well for Dickinson's mutual kind of genius except that to "instinctive and extraordinary" one might add a humbler but no less talent-acknowledging phrase: "yet also experience-based, methodical, and group-oriented."

A portrait penned in the mid-1860s by New York journalist and longtime friend of Dickinson Joseph Lyman cries out for explanation and interpretation in any claim of a social role for this lyric genius as the presiding member of her and her fellow-writers' philosophically and scientifically select society:

> A library dimly lighted, three mignonettes on a little stand. Enter a spirit clad in white, figure so draped as to be misty[,] face moist, translucent alabaster, forehead firmer as a statuary marble. Eyes once bright hazel now melted & fused so as to be two dreamy, wondering wells of expression, eyes that see no forms but gla[n]ce swiftly to the core of all thi[n]gs, very firm strong little hands, absolutely under control of the brain, types of quite rugged health[,] mouth made for nothing and used for nothing but uttering choice speech, rare thoughts, glittering, starry misty figures, winged words. (Qtd. in Sewall *Life* 2:425)

Lyman's tone would seem to make Dickinson's works sound like anything but brainy seminars or forensic chorales. Her "choice speech, rare thoughts, glittering, starry misty figures, winged words" appear to signal narrowly, privately lyrical soaring, from solitude into some vague stratosphere of the empyrean perpendicular. She is scarcely as ethereal or, for that matter, as diminutive, however, as Lyman's portrait makes her out to be: just as she knows that he takes her measure, so he must know that she takes his, desiring not his gaze but their mutual understanding. Whether or not Lyman responds "correctly," others can, in the conversational, dialogical spirit of her select society.

The "choice speech" of Lyman's Dickinson and of the Dickinson of this book is an emblem of "rugged health" in the sense that her poetry incarnates, amplifies, and augments the protean human landscape, communicating with her hearers and readers less about politics, sex, and religion, for a change, than about literature, philosophy, and science. Thus to dwell between the lines of Lyman's word-picture is to discern that Dickinson's unseen exists not "in here" or "up there" but within humankind and matter. Lyman's compound/complex comprehension of his "subject" matter and of her subject matter draws on her interior "wells of expression" and intimates her twin cores— namely, her tender mind and her liberated spirit. Consistent with Shelley's "unremitting [and all but dialogical] interchange / With the clear universe of things around," however, Lyman also unwittingly, or wittingly, discloses for all to see and participate in, the surgical precision of the poet's hand-to-eye coordination—that is, her tough mind or robust empiricism plus laboratory skills (compare Shelley, "Mont Blanc" [1817], lines 39–40).

The lyric pragmatism of Emily Dickinson, the deeply felt message of her philosophical and scientific imagination ("emotional thought" was the first label given to her published works) inheres in the signature poem of this outreach—namely, "Experiment escorts us last" (Fr1181).[46] This first line of the poem alone, to say nothing of the whole lyric until the discussion of it in chapter 2 (segment 2), encapsulates how her art of knowledge transports "us," including her select society of twenty-first-century partners in conversation, to the point of realizing that trial and error blessedly define humanity. As if in reply to Wordsworth, for whom "our destiny, our being's heart and home" can in certain of his moods be otherworldly "infinitude" or the "invisible [transcendent] world," Dickinson pins her hopes on "Experiment" instead, as though this personification were her ultimate partner in dialogue (compare Wordsworth, The Prelude [1850] 6:602–04). The only ten other words of this miniature poetic manifesto of her outlook will suggest, if a crucial part of chapter 2 succeeds, that her speakers and their others tread softly, if at all, from means to ends, case to conclusion, and humble method to arrogant system.

Although the poet listens and adjusts to other voices coming to her from other rooms, and although she respects these among her personae, Dickinson's empirical voice sings over, as well as in harmony with and with dissonance against, her chorus of literary figures, philosophers, ministers, and scientists. She remains a recluse only in Wordsworth's sense. The Recluse: or, Views of Nature, Man, and Society (1798–1850), unfinished at Wordsworth's death, retreats from the world not to escape the world but rather to gain distance from it, the better to acquire and offer perspective on it (note well Wordsworth's other proto-Dickinson word: Society). The experience-philosophy in Dickinson's background, and the physical and life science of her time and place, carry her and her readers along the road to knowledge, and this "us," this cultural history in league with reader-response to her poetry, keeps accumulating wisdom, and so goes on growing in stature.

On the one hand, Dickinson's cryptic statement of purpose, "My Business is Circumference" (L268), can signify that her rounds encompass rarefied endeavor or fierce, otherworldly aspiration. Just as Jesus "must be about [his] father's business" (Luke 2:49), so the Myth of Amherst must be "out opon Circumference" between yearning for transcendence and attaining it (Fr633, line 7).[47] Her lyrics sometimes say that what her eyes fall short of perceiving exists as reality slanted toward her from a world elsewhere. Harking back to some of Shelley's personae, some of her speakers, too, can

> dart [their] spirit's light
> Beyond all worlds, until its spacious might
> Satiate the void circumference.
>   (Shelley, "Adonais" [1821], stanza 47, lines 454–56)

Like Shelley's speakers in certain moods of theirs, moreover, some of hers can rise to be "pinnacled dim in the intense inane," the cobalt dynamic of empirical "transcendence" or astronomical science (compare Shelley, *Prometheus Unbound* [1820], act 3, scene 1, line 204).[48]

On the other hand, notwithstanding how Dickinson's poems of astronomy will form a focus of chapter 1, her personae tend to arrive at such distant goals of inquiry more rarely than Shelley's. Perhaps even Shelley, whose transcendentalism mixes with skepticism (Notopoulos; Pulos), would agree with Dickinson that the certainty of the absolute and of the science of the stars differs from, and not only can but probably should yield to, the slant truths of sublunary contingency. Dickinson's relatively small number of purely religious poems, whether unworldly or this-worldly in their orientation, figures in this book. "My Business is Circumference" means above all, however, that the industriousness of her habit of composition negotiates the philosophical and scientific spheres of her experience and influence.

To be sure, the poet acknowledges that "[p]hilosophy don't know" (Fr373, line 6) and, with equal doubt about the scientific method, admits that "[t]his timid life of Evidence / Keeps pleading - 'I dont know' - " (Fr725, lines 15–16). Nevertheless, she can seldom stop "[p]luck[ing] at a twig of Evidence - " for material knowledge (Fr373, line 3). She would preserve a core of realism. She would rarely jump to conclusions about the afterlife for which she hungers but in which she refuses to take unexamined, unwarranted consolation. If the religion of father Edward accompanies her at the point where her knowledge ends, it does so belatedly, inconstantly. Her speakers, with her ascendant criterion of experience eclipsing the waning moon of her faith, can sound Job-like, defiant, and, if in the margin of her works theology whispers, echoing her nostalgic religious concerns, it feels rearguard there, beleaguered. Her personae, more often than not, emanate from her naturalized imagination, confidently but subtly deploying their collective sense perception in paradoxically subject/ object interchange, colloquy.

After the manner of Matthew Arnold, Dickinson's philosophy- and science-minded speakers and their conversational counterparts in belles and bonnes lettres of the Anglo-American world exercise their keen observation in the laboratory of their free mental play. To conflate the second epigraph of this chapter with a meta-poetical lyric of hers, Dickinson's "paper and pen" proves "better far than nothing" (L63) at "tell[ing] all the truth," however "slant" or nuanced (Fr1263, line 1), to her loved ones, friends, fellow-writers past, present, and future, and readers then and now. Her verbal self-projections tell some of the direct truth *about* these various addressees. That is, her insight into motivation (see John Cody) becomes acute enough to make her a psychological as well as philosophical and scientific discussion leader. Her personae and those of her others, however, make up, above all, an all but externalized community that takes phenomena in stride and sometimes at face value. Insofar as her ideas of sensation and her models of reality mingle with those of her epistolary and poetic recipients, the personal and the interpersonal, for her and for them, are not so much the political or the religious as the philosophical and the scientific.[49]

Dickinson's elevation of the pragmatic (read: audience-oriented) and the expressive (read: autobiographical) functions of art over its mimetic, near-realistic, and objective, purely aesthetic functions justifies her reputation for originality.[50] For Anglo-American Romantics like her, aesthetic innovation has more to do with recombining already-existing elements than with creation ex nihilo. Of course, her philosophical and scientific interests preserve and concretize her mimetic urge and inform and enhance her formalistic finesse. Still, her power to amalgamate these offices—mimetic, pragmatic, expressive, and objective—and her emphasis on the expressive and the pragmatic, reinforce her all-seasons prowess as conversation starter par excellence. Her inner-than-the-bone lyric selfhood issues in the centrifugal force of her dialogical aesthetic (compare Fr334, line 14).

Although Dickinson's style can seem obscure—one might well ask: how can this poetry pass for conversation?—her goal of finding "fit audience... though few" turns out, counterintuitively, to please at least those general readers who like conundrums (compare John Milton, *Paradise Lost* [1674] 7:31). Her enigmas invite solutions— that is, one can scarcely too often bring to mind her round reminder of one's all too timid inner English major that "[A metaphor] won't bite" (L34). The give and take of her riddles exceeds her devising. Her life-writing is her gregarious form of empirically minded problem-solving. Her initiates can respond to her puzzles as sensibly as her contemporaries.

To borrow a metaphor from astronomy, then, Wordsworth, Emerson, and Dickinson et al. pull Locke, Wesley, Wadsworth, and Darwin et al. into singularity, and vice versa. These literary figures, philosophers, ministers, and scientists suffer scant loss of either light or energy on either side of the equation, perhaps even when one side appears to be absorbed into the other. The next two chapters will pay equal attention to masters of belles and of bonnes lettres. Part II will say less about empiricists, evangelists, and scientists, and more about Dickinson's fellow-authors on the Romantic to Modern arc, yet will answer *yes* to whether or not the well-earned optimism and wise hope of her reliance on experience and on experiment can survive in her postexperiential category of poems. Thus, even where (ironically) tacit in her rich conversation, bonnes lettres stays operative there, too, like the one half of a binary star system only temporarily occluded.

In the conclusion of this book, finally, Locke, Wesley, Wadsworth, and Darwin et al. will reappear explicitly. They will do so again alongside the Romantics, as in part I. Insofar as the creative imaginations of such masters of bonnes lettres possess as much authority as those of such masters of belles lettres, the former group holds "lamps unto the feet" of the latter, and "light[s] the path" of the Myth of Amherst in particular (compare Psalm 119:105). As her doubt about Experiential Faith increases, and because of this growing skepticism, she recasts her faith in experience. She thereby offers to those among her partners in dialogue still holding fast to their idea of Experiential Faith her reaffirmation of their select society's fundamentally rational, sense-based epistemology.

In sum, Emily Dickinson engages written language, to put it mildly. Of course, if "dialogism" entails "the spoken world of folk consciousness," so does her dialogical art, though the sung world of hymns, too, is audible in her mix of oral culture.[51] Still, as background to novel-writing, "dialogism" scants the inscribed world that her lyric imagination also reflects and enlarges.[52] Many of her speakers, like the less reclusive than communicative author herself, internalize, echo, answer to, and reply to printed voices of elite and popular culture.[53] She proves *"rich* in conversation" with all these fellow-lovers of language who are most vital to her in their published forms of belles and of bonnes lettres alike. This love of books obtains, perhaps even when she thinks of Shakespeare's dialogical characters as her partners in an almost more oral than written kind of traditional conversation, for, like a good Romantic, she reads Shakespeare in her room, does not see him on the stage. Literary figures, philosophers, and scientists grow prominent, more than ministers, among members of her "Royal" Society, New England chapter.[54] Sometimes belles lettres and sometimes bonnes lettres characterize philosophy and science, for her, for she encounters these latter disciplines directly, and as they (a) impress her from between the lines of her literary precursors and contemporaries and (b) toughen the theological prose in which she elects to immerse herself.

PART I

GATHERING EXPERIENCE

CHAPTER 1

PROCLAIMING EMPIRICISM

Why did Charles Lamb label Wordsworth's poetry "natural methodism"?[1] Perhaps Lamb's low-key, lower case orthography meant less that Wordsworth was Methodist than that the warm-hearted this-worldliness of Wordsworth's personae borrowed authority from John Wesley's this-as-well-as-otherworldly heart religion. So, too, could Emily Dickinson's perspective on the transatlantic revival be low-key, lower case, and at the same time alert to poetic possibility in the genius of the revival for the here and now, for spiritual-yet-temporal immediacy. Almost as though she knew that Wesley's emphasis on spiritual experience built on his understanding of sense perception (Brantley *Locke* 37–102), the Myth of Amherst reversed his process and turned her Experience of Faith, intermittent, into her faith in experience, trademark. Her lyrically dramatic expression of herself in relation to her others and in the presence of nature harked back to Wordsworth's down-to-earth adaptation of the Methodist brand: she bequeathed to her readers an art less of belief than of knowledge and more of epistemological/scientific witness than of revival testimony.

If Emily Dickinson's late-Romantic version of "natural methodism" muted the voice and secularized the message of heart religion, her poetry for that reason proved all the more decidedly admirable for its credibility and all the more mutually verifiable for its authenticity. She could mix experience and faith scarcely better than she could reconcile them. She could balance experience and faith rather more readily than she could subordinate the former to the latter. Even when she enjoyed faith, as she did on occasion, she gave the last word to experience. She capitalized "Experiment" not so much because she managed somehow to locate pure and simple transcendentalism in the concept—far from it—as because she trusted, honored, venerated, and engaged—personified—the contingent but complex and satisfying, the as-if-interpersonal, reality of this world (compare Fr1181, line 1; see also the discussion of "Experiment escorts us last - " in chapter 2). Reluctantly, at first, but with greater and greater cultural maturity and with more and more intellectual honesty, she comprehended the big difference between what Elizabeth Barrett Browning would have called the "childhood's faith" of high Romanticism and the "lost saints" of late-Romantic adulthood (compare Barrett Browning, *Sonnets from the Portuguese*, 43 [1845–1846], lines 9, 11). Perhaps Dickinson associated this very idea, this very language, with the picture of Barrett Browning on her bedroom wall. Dickinson did not acquiesce in that big difference but spun the straw of that transcultural trend of gradual desiccation, that descent from the strange warming of the up-leaping heart to its dry salvages, into the liquid-lyric gold of an even more thoroughgoing "poetry of earth" than Keats's or Wordsworth's (compare Keats, "The Poetry of Earth Is Never Dead" [1816]).

This chapter and the next are offered in a spirit of tactical recantation of the faith-favoring emphasis in all five previous installments of this series of arguments. Did the evangelical expression of Anglo-American Romanticism outdo the empirical language that also resounded there? The provisional answer here is *probably not*. The series has hitherto made the empirical thesis perhaps overly dependent on the evangelical antithesis of Romantic Anglo-America's stab at synthesizing experience and faith, not so much through the magical powers as through the sleight-of-hand of the creative imagination. This book, for its part, moves from the strategy of dialectic to the quite possibly more aesthetically defensible, the certainly more modestly imaginative, position of dialogical explanation. Yet mystery remains, for Dickinson's lesson that "[a] metaphor...won't bite" (L34) entails less systematic interaction between poles of materialistic determinism than oscillating interplay among incandescent prospects of this world. The rich conversation of Emily Dickinson's art allows experience its fighting chance against, its efficacious alternative to, faith, notwithstanding this poet's nostalgia for, nay, her love of, her evangelical heritage.

The fifth volume of the series—namely, *Experience and Faith: The Late-Romantic Imagination of Emily Dickinson* (Brantley 2004; paper 2008)—assumed that her poetry subsumes philosophy and science under religion. That theory remains explanatory, but the present book, without necessarily taking the opposite for granted either, yet for the sake of fresh argument nonetheless, explores the practically critical results of shifting focus among Dickinson's less dialectical than oscillating and dialogical interdisciplinary interests. In the present volume, the full series-set of critically analytical terms (from empiricism to evangelicalism) endures but with her religious concerns as distinct subset this time (and for a change). In this sixth installment of the series, emphatically lower case "natural methodism," if "emphatically lower case" poses no very insurmountable challenge of indigestible counterintuition, abides to describe her late/belated Anglo-American Romanticism as made up of only one part Experiential Faith, perhaps, but of two parts philosophy-science.[2] Her "natural methodism" reconsidered the transatlantic revival less by choosing epistemology and the laboratory, rather than spiritual discipline or religious training, than by weighing the latter in the light of the former. She achieved this realistic reassessment of her religious heritage without entirely losing sight of faith as in itself an oscillating/dialogical subelement of her imagination. Her "natural methodism" did not so much reduce the role of the transatlantic revival in Romantic Anglo-America as make sense-based reason the test of a poetic faith modeled on, but not in any final sense beholden to, experiential faith (no capitals).

According to the check of her case conducted throughout the remainder of part I, Dickinson was the better poet, though not the more flamboyant or the more relentless writer, for soft-pedaling her inner synthesizer. She recognized, with Keats (whose words follow here), that "the fancy cannot cheat so well," cannot square contraries so efficiently, "[a]s she is fam'd to do, deceiving elf" (compare "Ode to a Nightingale" [1819], lines 73–74). Nor, perhaps, by her overall implication, if not by Keats's, should any other-directed as well as self-respecting, tough as well as tender Romantic-era author even try. The properly hard-driving marks of this poet's imagination were two in number. First, the both/and logic of her perspective on paradox meant that her all but salutary stance of faith in experience overmatched, if only by a technical knock-out, her would-be-saving experience of faith. Second, the I/thou dynamic of her appeal to conundrum spread the word of Experiment, albeit with serpentine wisdom as well as with dovelike harmlessness.

As this book took shape, the word processor made a very good point every time it tried to correct Lamb's lower case. Even *methodism* uncapitalized, after all, plays on the name of John Wesley's revival, and so occupies pride of *religious* place in Lamb's adjective-noun combination. Thus *natural methodism* can still call for, can yet justify, a judicious, selective, and subtle interpretation of Wordsworth's poetry as religiously transcendental-izing in impulse, if not in tendency. Can this locution of Lamb's, despite his reinforcing of its earthward direction through his joining of the word *natural* to the word *methodism*, work across the ocean to fix the religious in the empirical, thereby bidding fair to span the traditionally unbridgeable gulf between experience and faith? Whatever the answer, Lamb's concept can continue in these religious as well as philosophical and scientific terms to tantalize the student of Romanticism as the boldly evocative, thoroughly expounding metaphor that it will likely remain for as long as one can foresee. Whether or not *natural methodism* is to be so regarded—that is, as delicately upper case in effect, as well as deliberately lower case in fact—Anglo-American Romanticism in general and Emily Dickinson's in particular will whisper throughout even this empirically oriented volume as a literature of experience both natural and spiritual.

This chapter and the next, accordingly, do not presume to preclude a future go of the series to the exclusively religious aspect of Dickinson's Romanticism, for, after all, the series was "doing religion" long before the post-9/11 turn-to-religion-in-academe proclaimed by Stanley Fish. This book, in fact, anticipates just such an installment. Perhaps Volume 7 will ask less how Dickinson's evangelical idiom relates to, and supersedes, her empiricism, than in what sense, if in any, this idiom stands alone, worthy of analysis in its own right.[3] Such a sally of practical criticism could even yet discover that evangelical faith of the eighteenth and nineteenth centuries accounted for a distinct quality, a pure idiom, of this poet's witness to the truth, in contrast with her testimony of wisdom. Her "art of belief," apart from however often it conducted dialogue with empirical philosophy and scientific method, could yet appear to stand alone again, as it has not so long ago done throughout Roger Lundin's understanding of Dickinson's religious poetry in its twentieth-century as well as immediate theological context.

That having been said, it is proper to emphasize Lamb's e. e. cummings-like lowercasing, Lamb's Rudolph Bultmann-like demythologizing, of the Methodist Movement. Like all other previous volumes in this sequence of arguments, the first, *Wordsworth's "Natural Methodism"* (Brantley 1975), strongly misread the initial *m* of Lamb's word *methodism* as upper case. The current book, if not the long run of this skein, takes Lamb at the face value of his low-key, lower case orthography, applying his phrase to Dickinson's poetry as she would, by back-grounding the religious and foregrounding the philosophical and scientific concerns of her personae. Just as Lamb's phrase "natural

methodism" appears to signal his admiration for Wordsworth's philosophical and scientific acumen, as distinct from his religious yearning,
so any lingering religious implication of Wordsworth's "natural methodism" need scarcely entail honorific assessment of Wordsworth's
thought and practice. With some justification, after all, Francis, Lord
Jeffrey, long ago called Wordsworth's poetry "the mystical verbiage of
the Methodist pulpit" (14), and Jeffrey's proper usage of the capital
letter intended no compliment to this poet. Even when read as lowercasing with a vengeance, *natural methodism* can seem too oxymoronic, too epistemo-*religious* or *religio*-epistemological, for its own
good. Lamb's implicit boast of experience/faith gap-closing, however
subliminal it might remain, appears a consummation stoutly to be
resisted, feeling neither likely in the great scheme of things nor, considering, say, the prudence of church/state separation, desirable in
this real world of potential fanaticism.

Without too closely reading two words, the forms and contents of
Anglo-American Romanticism, especially Dickinson's, can yet shine
in the light of Lamb's uncannily articulated though uncapitalized
and idiosyncratic expression for a cross-culturally defining compound
trait. Lamb's down-to-earth, epistemology- and science-sounding
adaptation of the Methodist marque applies even more tellingly to
the naturalizing contribution of Dickinson's late-Romantic perspective on the transatlantic revival than to her chief high-Romantic-era
precursor Wordsworth's. Make no mistake, Dickinson muted the
voice and secularized the message of heart religion in the name and
to the benefit of art. Her eye altering thus altered all. The empirical
warp, as opposed to the evangelical weft, of her tightly woven inter-
connections with other weavers of the Anglo-American Romantic
web highlighted the texture of her works, and changed the pattern
of literary history.

Dickinson's empirical voice acquired edge and volume from belles
lettres but, more surprisingly, from bonnes lettres, or the arc from
intellectual history to popular and elite culture connecting John Locke
and John Wesley to Charles Wadsworth, Dickinson's "dearest earthly
friend" (L807), and Charles Darwin. Although sense-based reason
and the scientific method figured in transatlantic evangelism, the
rational empiricism of Locke and the evolutionary biology of Darwin
challenged religion. Locke and Darwin disenchanted poetry to the
point where Dickinson could at times appear more philosophical and
scientific than literary! Wadsworth's Wesley-inspired use of the proto-
scientific language of Locke, his view of experience as the best means
of knowing what is naturally and spiritually true, resonates with, and

sounds most like, Dickinson's empirical tone. Wadsworth's sermons represent the least-studied aspect, constitute the least-studied context, of her dialogical art of knowledge.

Dickinson's conversation with Wadsworth asked not just to what extent the poet stood on the preacher's solely evangelical ground but, more importantly, how her and his empirical procedure or faith in experience checked their evangelical yearning or experience of faith. The intellectual and cultural arc that extended from Locke and Wesley to Anglo-American writings of many kinds, ended with prose stylist Wadsworth and lyric master Dickinson, as historic a pair in the way of their world as Locke and Wesley in the way of theirs. Reveling in the claim-testing swagger of constructive skepticism, Wadsworth and Dickinson kept their options open, including choices made through sense perception, as well as through faith and imagination. Their free will evangelicalism pertained to rational empiricism in concert with scientific method. In dialogue with Wadsworth, yet with greater tough-mindedness, Dickinson found enough paradox in nature alone to remystify the universe and the earth. Perhaps she even thereby enjoyed her generous portion of the existential given, and perhaps, too, she even thereby received secular grace from the world of thoughts and things. Finally, she attained these values while at the same time maintaining her less heady than dignified posture regarding physical and life science. The poet talked with, and back to, the preacher about the spectrum from steam technology, through geology and astronomy, to the healing arts and natural selection.

This chapter will respect the trend among some scholars to connect the empirical language of mid-nineteenth-century authors primarily to the advancement of science at that immediate time. For example, Robert Scholnick's pioneering essay on Walt Whitman's immersion in state-of-the-art science, and Robin Peel's complete study of Emily Dickinson's, have shown how these poets turned out to be methodologically up to date not only in their metaphors of earth but also in their models of reality. In such a spirit of historical nearness, this chapter will suggest that Dickinson's conversation with Wadsworth formed a vital but unexpected part of her informal education in both the philosophy and the science of her day. Perhaps this intellectually biographical/dialogical motif can supplement and broaden what is already known about the focus and the cutting edge of her formal scientific education at midcentury. This chapter will also emphasize, however, that no less than her conversation with Wadsworth, her lively interchange with Wordsworth (and company) kept her in touch with, and inspired her to reimagine, the eighteenth- as well as nineteenth-century, philosophical as well as scientific tradition of sense-based reason in the Anglo-American world.

* * *

As a very young woman, Emily Dickinson showed herself to be a well-informed though not necessarily a just-yet-empirically-vociferous aficionado of philosophy. At 14, writing to fellow-student Abiah Root, she recognized the distinction between Plato and the chief persona of his dialogues: "We'll finish an education sometime, won't we? You may then be Plato, and I will be Socrates, provided you won't be wiser than I am" (L5). At 20, writing to her brother, Austin, and replaying the pairing of Plato with Socrates, she spoke of philosophy-cum-mythology, if not of philosophy-cum-religion, in the same breath, in this flurry of sentences: "I had a dissertation from Eliza Coleman a day or two ago—I don't know which was the author—Plato, or Socrates—rather think Jove had a finger in it" (L57). Thus satirizing Coleman for subordinating philosophy to religion, and thus expressing regret regarding her friend's shortcomings as a partner in philosophical discussion, the latter comment suggests how schoolgirl Dickinson would one day become the Socratic-satirical gadfly-poet. Relative to Plato's philosophy, Locke's *Essay Concerning Human Understanding* (1690) lies proximately behind Dickinson's love of philosophy in general and the epistemology of sense-based reasoning in particular. In terms consistent with poetry, her tradition of empiricism calls the *plays* of her "fine mental chaos," to borrow a richly *ludic* as well as faintly scientific phrase from how British Romantic novelist Thomas Love Peacock thought of the high-Romantic aesthetic (qtd. in Swingle 71). As though coordinates on the arc from Locke and Wesley to Wadsworth and Dickinson comprise a cultural poetic, this segment will set up a sounding board for the empirical voice heard throughout the Dickinson interpretation in this chapter and in the next. Before devoting the remainder of part I to close reading like this, it may be helpful to encapsulate the historical, interdisciplinary, and biographical reasons (arising from belles and bonnes lettres alike) for describing Dickinson's imagination as philosophical and scientific in background and in outlook.

With regard to bonnes lettres, first (as being first in time for this study), the founding document of British empiricism contends that simple ideas or ideas of sensation form the mind's account of what the senses bring, and so solve experiential problems of mundane existence. Locke asks, modestly, can one know, and if so, how and what, or does one simply believe philosophically in preference to religiously? Locke travels the road to knowledge by trusting the reasoning component of his sensationalist epistemology. Grounding the mind in sense-data, his set of stages would present the working opposite of French rationalism and of German idealism, both of which were beginning, in the seventeenth and in the eighteenth century, to declare the mind's independence of, and superiority to, sense impressions. Locke's rational empiricism contrasts with the pure rationalism of Plato, as well as of Descartes, and, for that matter, differs from such staples of Kant's philosophy as his sense-suspicious disposition. On the other hand, despite Locke's inductive procedure, his *Essay* not only assumes, but also engages in, considerable lordship of mind over universe. Without deducing, or leaping to, world-transcendence, he soars to the point of it, as where his masterwork savors just how much more the mind can comprehend than his contrasting but equally characteristic view of mind's limitation by the senses would seem to allow:

> Nor let anyone think [simple ideas or ideas of sensation] too narrow bounds for the capacious Mind of Man to expatiate in, which takes its flight farther than the Stars, and cannot be confined by the limits of the World; that extends its thoughts often, even beyond the utmost expansion of Matter, and makes excursions into that incomprehensible Inane. (Locke *Essay* 2.7.10; Nidditch 131)

Dickinson's seven-word version of these fifty-four words, "The Brain is wider than the Sky - " (Fr598, line 1), captures Locke's expansive content in laconic form and, evoking less vertical than horizontal vastness (contrast "wider" with "farther than the Stars"), beats Locke at his game not of transcendental but of empirical philosophy.

Significantly, Locke's governing concept of tabula rasa rolls trippingly off the tongue of über-Methodist Wesley:

> For many ages [Wesley writes], It has been allowed by sensible men, *Nihil est in Intellectu quod non fuit prius in sensu.* That is, "There is nothing in the understanding which was not first perceived by some of the senses." ... [T]his point has now been thoroughly discussed by men of the most eminent sense and learning, and it is agreed by all impartial persons, that although some things are so plain and obvious, that we can hardly avoid knowing them as soon as we come to the use of our understanding, yet the knowledge even of those is not innate, but derived from some of our senses. (Jackson 7:231)

Thus Wesley reconfirms his sometimes recessive but stubbornly reassertive heritage of straightforward and straight empiricism. From

June 5, 1782, through June 30, 1784, in 30 issues of his serial, *The Arminian Magazine*, he devoted 91 pages to his extracts of 28 passages from Book One and from Book Two of the *Essay* and gave 6 pages to his remarks on 24 excerpts from Book Three and from Book Four (see the table of reference in Brantley *Locke* 224–25). This remarkable detail should ever renew Wesleyan scholarship: a contemporary analogy would arise, if, a big if, the Reverend Rick Warren were to expect his flock to read his very own edition of Martin Heidegger or of Emmanuel Levinas! Wesley, for his part, reported on Locke's ideas of sensation to his "parish," "all the world" (Wesley's words qtd. in Hurst 141), and this world extended in time and place, accordingly, to the philosophical and scientific, as well as to the religious, climate of the Myth of Amherst.

Wesley's Locke-inspired philosophy, in brief (but recall also appendix B), ranged from his sense-based reasoning to his educational theory and practice. With respect to the former, first, he concludes:

> No sooner is the child born into the world, than he…feels the air with which he is surrounded, and which pours into him from every side, as fast as he alternately breathes it back, to sustain the flame of life; and hence springs a continued increase of strength, of motion, and of sensation; all the bodily senses being now awakened, and furnished with their proper objects. (Wesley *Sermons* 176)

Thus Wesley's ideas follow Locke's *Some Thoughts concerning Education* (1693). The preacher, in tribute to the philosopher, held that the design of an ideal pedagogy counterbalanced the bias of nature. Locke's very wording, in fact, appeared in Wesley's written rules for his Kingswood School, an empirically philosophical experiment in Christian education.[4] In the fourth year of the curriculum there, Wesley appropriately, if somewhat startlingly, required Locke's *Essay*, which, as the second title in this series argued (Brantley *Locke*), underlay his experience-oriented—that is, his sense-tested, as well as merely sense-analogized—heart religion.[5]

The Locke-derived foundation of Wesley's experiment at Kingswood merits further attention in light of Samuel Pickering's *John Locke and Children's Books in Eighteenth-Century England* (1981). That root grew educational stem and flower in the nineteenth century, with Dickinson's theme of intellectual development a prominent blossom. The 14-year-old girl's "thoughts concerning education" in her letter to Abiah Root are ultimately Locke-relevant, as well as possibly Plato-centric.

Just as Wesley preached Locke-understood ideas of sensation to his flock, so Wadsworth's sermons evoked Locke: "Sensations," Wadsworth writes, "are the image, or form, of a thing in the mind" (*Sermons* [1869] 23). Wadsworth even recalled the arcana of empirical philosopher and Bishop George Berkeley: like Berkeley, Wadsworth holds that "a complete idea must also be the image of a whole thing, and not merely one of its parts" (*Sermons* [1869] 23).[6] The suggestion that ideas were somehow both independent mental entities and the products of shaping forces lent weight to the revival-doctrine of soul-competence in the world. Such philosophical fare was a more bracing tonic for Wadsworth's flock than would have been, say, a rather passive evangelical teaching of the post-post-Modern world— that is, that Jesus likes to find parking places for shoppers.[7] The both/ and logic of Wadsworth's subject/object subtlety (his *image* in the mind, after all, is a *thing* there) harks back through Wesley to Locke: "Ideas," Locke writes, "are Perceptions in the Mind" *and* "modifications in the Bodies that cause such Perceptions in us" (*Essay* 2.8.7; Nidditch 134). Wadsworth's echoing parallels Romantic-era reimagining of paradox.

To be sure, the attitudes that Wadsworth and Dickinson shared could seem anti-intellectual in their wickedly antiprofessorial bias. Using an antiexperiential, if not a rather anti-Locke, Presbyterian diction, Wadsworth complains of "Scholarship," viewing it, "by a dread necessity, as *predestined* to be valetudinarian" (*Sermons* [1884] 231; emphasis added). "Nay," he continues, reflecting, incidentally, Wesley's insistence that the clergy be red-blooded men, a scholar "must be a creature of the delicate frame-work and the unbronzed cheek and the lily fingers, and... like heavy ordinances, such an intellectual will recoil on its mounting and shatter a puny frame-work" (*Sermons* [1884] 232).[8] One thinks in this connection of Theodore Holland, son of Dickinson's friends Elizabeth and Josiah Gilbert Holland (please recall, in this regard also, that these parents may have served as intermediaries for Dickinson's correspondence with Wadsworth).[9] When Dickinson hears that Theodore has passed his oral examination at Columbia University Law School, Dickinson is delighted, writing, "I am glad if Theodore balked the Professors— Most such are Mannikins, and a Warm blow from a brave Anatomy, hurls them into Wherefores—" (L901). If one would expect her to take issue with what smacks of Wadsworth's sexist language here, one would be mistaken, for though she was an early feminist (Bennett) she and Wadsworth appreciated humor based on stereotypes of manhood (she sometimes called herself "Uncle Emily" [e.g., L315]).

Nevertheless, although Dickinson agreed with Wadsworth on the superiority of robust men to effete academics, she also concurred with his theory of education, which harked back not simply to Wesley's Kingswood but even to Locke's *Some Thoughts concerning Education*. Wadsworth defines "*education*," in Locke's terms, as "simply a *drawing-forth*, a development, not knowledge or erudition *forced into* the mind, but the mind itself, quickened, strengthened, trained unto thoughtful, practical activity" (*Sermons* [1905] 231; Wadsworth's emphasis). In a manner reminiscent of Dickinson's teenaged aspiration to "finish an education sometime," Wadsworth declares that "there is none whose education is," or by his implication ever should be, "finished" (*Sermons* [1869] 331). He proclaims that "[e]very man to whom God hath given an intellect should have enough self-knowledge to understand thoroughly its peculiar powers" (*Sermons* [1869] 14). He laments that "[m]any men practically ignore their intellectual faculties," that "some...never think at all," and that these "live among feelings," "prefer[ring] to buy thought as they buy groceries, second-hand and diluted" (*Sermons* [1869] 114–15). Consonant with Wadsworth's views, Dickinson asks of her literary preceptor, Thomas Wentworth Higginson, "How do most people live without any thoughts [?]," adding, "There are many people in the world (you must have noticed them in the street)[.] How do they get strength to put on their clothes in the morning[?]" (L342a).[10] Thus, in 1870, a year after Wadsworth has, Locke-like, lambasted people who purchase their thought secondhand, she, Locke-like, too, advocates earning thought firsthand, and surely she appreciated the rhetorical flair that comes across in Wadsworth's conclusion: "So the popular press roars and foams a grand Niagara of sentiment and water!" (*Sermons* [1869] 115).

So Dickinson's readers can gain a clear sense of the kind of empirical thought that attracted her by comparing her writings to those of philosophically sage, empirically savvy Reverend Wadsworth, whom she could have met, one may recall, through her partner in philosophical discussion, Eliza Coleman.[11] As the rest of part I will continue to indicate, Dickinson subscribed to Wadsworth's Locke- as well as Wesley-like standard for clergy and for laity alike. Locke, Wesley, Wadsworth, and Dickinson thought that all people should heartily endorse sense-based reasoning and faithfully strive for up-to-date knowledge of empirical philosophy and of science, wherever this sort of intelligence might lead. Who knows, these four horsemen of evangelical empiricism or of empirical evangelicalism, however welcome or unwelcome they would have found the oxymoron of such a label, might just have accepted even those findings of twenty-first-century climate science that appear to threaten science-averse evangelicals.

At any rate, Dickinson's down-to-earth, downright empirical instructors taught her well, in part, no doubt, because of the reception granted to empiricism by such simultaneously normative and trend-setting proponents of religious values as Wesley and Wadsworth. At Amherst Academy, Mount Holyoke Female Seminary, and Amherst College, where she may have attended lectures by Dickinson family friend and eminent professor of natural history and divinity, later president, Edward Hitchcock, Dickinson, like other young women of her locale, benefited from scientific training.[12] Thanks to the legacy that her teachers of science inherited from the empiricism of Locke, as well as due to their own strengths and virtues, these preceptors of the poet-to-be eschewed pedantry, intellectual pride, overly refined game-playing, and the ascetic, sterile will-o'-the-wisp or bugbear of mind/body dualism. As a result, her education never ceased, nor did she ever lessen her respect for empirical procedures. To say little here of the other pole of her late-Romantic exposition or expedition—namely, the experiential faith that Dickinson struggled constantly to reach—her experiential philosophy and her science made a crucial difference to her image-making power, as distinct from her spiritual sense fore-shadowed by her sense-based reason.

The rest of part I will continue to indicate, as well, that a sample of Dickinson's poetic personae carries their education forward step by step. Many, if not most, of these lyric speakers advance their education from strength to strength. This combination of exaltation and humility, of headiness and earthward-ness, is of the very essence of this poet's Anglo-American sense, as distinct from any mere sensibility on her part. That sense of hers is anticipated in the first instance by what one ought to think of as the exalted humility of Locke and of Wesley, too. And that sense of hers is in the end paralleled by the paradoxically earthward headiness of Wadsworth, on one hand, and of her fellow-Romantic-era authors, on the other.[13]

Consider, as the final background to Dickinson's thought and practice, and as a foretaste of her almost more than merely metaphorical conversation with her Romantic- to Modern-era fellow-writers, how Percy Bysshe Shelley relates to John Locke. For one thing, in a clear allusion to the first of the two passages from Locke's *Essay* quoted earlier, Shelley boasts of "darting [his] spirit's light / Beyond all worlds" and into the "intense inane."[14] For another, as the other *Essay* passage implies through subject/object paradox, Locke may have approved, too, of Shelley's "clasp" of the "pendulous Earth."[15]

Of course, Dickinson's dramatic dialogists can sometimes venture (her words) "out opon Circumference - " of selfhood, world, and universe (Fr633, line 7). Such speakers of hers can become as exalted as the long Romantic Movement could inspire them to be. Still, like the other, humbler aspect of the Locke/Shelley composite, her inscribed self-projections can often approach the "intense inane" as mere "speck[s] opon a Ball - " (Fr633, line 7), and then they may well prefer to come back down to earth (compare Robert Frost, "Birches" [1916]).[16] Thus, like the empirical imaginations of Locke, Wesley, and Wadsworth, and like those developed in their wakes by such high- to late-Romantic exemplars as Wordsworth and Emerson, Dickinson's, too, sometimes cherishes and impels and sometimes underwrites, with the modesty that Anglo-American Romanticism can also model, the sense-based means of epistemology. That same exalted humility applies likewise to the corresponding sense-driven method of science in the Anglo-American eighteenth and nineteenth centuries.

Without losing tender-minded overtone, as in Platonic or French rationalism, German idealism, or, for that matter, the evangelical faith embedded in her Anglo-American context, Dickinson's empirical voice demonstrated the richest payoff of her experience-laden worldview—namely, her almost scientifically tough-minded tone. Her spirit of experiment prevailed even on the interpersonal level of her existence. Her poetically reasoned transposition from sense-based means to sense-driven method transformed her ideas of sensation and reflection into "finely explicit" (Bloom *Shakespeare* 7) models of reality—that is, poeticized hypotheses for physical and life science. Thus reaching back to Locke, the late-Romantic paragon of Anglo-American letters did not simply "dwell in Possibility - " of empirical truth (Fr466, line 1). She also realized the facsimile of scientific knowledge.

Of the "Anglo-Saxon" age in which he and Dickinson thrived, Wadsworth exclaims, "We live in the harvest time of mind and thought," adding, "The development of the mental follows the law of material development" (*Sermons* [1869] 292). In his celebration of mechanical inventiveness, Wadsworth rejoices that the telegraph "has demonstrated the great possibility. And to Anglo-Saxon thought, a great possibility is a great *certainty*" (*Sermons* [1869] 293–94; Wadsworth's emphasis).[17] His down-to-earth as well as ethnocentric philosophical optimism suggests that Dickinson's words "I dwell in Possibility - " can refer to the pause between an idea of sensation or reflection and the thing it produces, as in how the Romantic-era imagination is believed to yield the thing imaged. According to this brash duo's reading of history, and despite how quaintly this binational predilection now strikes the ear, "a great possibility is a great *certainty*" for better, not worse, in Britain and the United States.

Do the words "I dwell in Possibility - " signal "totally self-contained experience" (Walker 21)? Does this signature sentence of Dickinson's life of writing imply the either/or choice between existence and aesthetics, as though Dickinson's imagination were "deadlocked" and her life/art dilemma "irresolvable" (Robinson 34)? Does this saying of hers struggle between "a Poeian constriction" "I *dwell* in Possibility - " and "an Emersonian expansion" "I dwell in *Possibility* - " (29)? If "Paradise" in line 8 of Fr466 is "the farthest space conceivable," and if the poet's "mind can expand to include it" (Juhasz *Undiscovered Continent* 19–20), her not so enclosed earthly garden can also encompass the Anglo-American setting for human advancement in both knowledge and well-being. With something of Wadsworth's triumphalism, she gloried in steam technology, and with something of his strangely humble exaltation, yet with little—or none—of his at times complacent theology, she approached geology and astronomy.[18] Finally, if scarcely with as much sky-wide brain as she could bring to bear, and with only outdated support from her literary, philosophical, religious, and scientific *traditions,* she struggled to sustain her epistemological brio in the face of *modern*-era medicine and of *modern*-era evolutionary biology. Through it all, and more incisively than even the mordant Romantics, on one hand, and the mordant Locke, Wesley, Wadsworth, and Darwin, on the other, Dickinson believed that the realm of observation and reflection, no matter how dubious the progress or dehumanizing/dispiriting the message, rendered superfluous the "pure serene" as a false lure. That phrase of Keats's from "On First Looking into Chapman's Homer" (1816, line 7) is honorific in context, a way for him to name the transcendent realm of literary discovery, but can serve here pejoratively to prefigure Dickinson's growing disdain for the tender excess of axiomatic rationalism and of top-down idealism alike.

*   *   *

Wadsworth's praise of steam technology, first, can sound unmistakably like Dickinson's. At the same time, however, his tribute can serve to throw her genius for substantive and stylistic condensation into especially bold relief. "Steam—that fantastic shape that played aerial and useless before the eyes of old dreamers—" has become in Wadsworth's modern vein "man's Titanic servant everywhere: chained in the dark caverns of the earth, fettered to the wheels of great machinery" (*Sermons* [1869] 292). Wadsworth marvels, in particular, at steam "harnessed on the thoroughfares of traffic; rushing through the valleys; leaping on the mountains; marching on the seas—God's own wingèd wind unto man's chariot, bearing him over all the brute forces and forms of nature, in imperial dominion conquering and to conquer" (*Sermons* [1869] 293). Dickinson's 12-word paean to all kinds of steam power, similarly, envisions virile engineering. Her persona suitably hisses the message of fire-generated energy (her *f*'s and *l*'s, and even her *v*, too, embody flapping, licking flame):

> For*ce* *Fl*ame
> And with a B*l*onde pu*sh*
> O*v*er your impoten*ce*
> *Fl*its *s*team.
> (Fr963, lines 9–12; emphasis added)

This enthusiasm for steam power, like Wadsworth's, evinces no anticipation of the post-Titanic-disaster irony that marks the hubris and the nemesis of the Modern world (see Howells).

To be sure, some such complexity enriches Dickinson's ode to the steam locomotive:

> I like to see it lap the Miles -
> And lick the Valleys up -
> And stop to feed itself at Tanks -
> And then - prodigious step
>
> Around a Pile of Mountains -
> And supercilious peer
> In Shanties - by the sides of Roads -
> And then a Quarry pare
>
> To fit its sides
> And crawl between
> Complaining all the while
> In horrid - hooting stanza -
> Then chase itself down Hill -
>
> And neigh like Boanerges -
> Then - prompter than a Star
> Stop - docile and omnipotent
> At its own stable door -
> (Fr383)

The speaker's social consciousness, after all, intimates that the train by no means necessarily brings good things to life. Nevertheless, though

Dickinson's more than merely two-handed engine can seem to pose obscure but palpable threat, her liking of it still comes through loud and clear. Despite the satirical undertone here, the admiring tone rings.

Just as Wordsworth's "Steamboats, Viaducts, and Railways" (1841) gives rails pride of place among products of cultural poetics, so "I like to see it lap the miles - " is meta-poetical, for Dickinson's lines speak of poetry-in-motion as a work of art. Turner's train comes to mind more readily than even Lincoln's rail line litigation. Dickinson's prophetic train, her "Son of Thunder" or preacher of rumbling progress, exemplifies, for better or worse, the evangelically tinged Romantic-era imagination of the Anglo-American world. Wordsworth's just referenced sonnet, surprisingly and rather uncharacteristically, proclaims "Railways" as Imagineering advancement. More closely than the attention that Wordsworth divides among three different Isambard Kingdom Brunel-like engineering marvels of the late-Romantic industrial message, however, the subject matter or empirically tinged late-Romantic prophecy of Emerson's "Nature" (1836), too, applies to Dickinson's poem. "What new thoughts," Emerson writes (though not explicitly claiming prophecy), "are suggested by seeing a face of country quite familiar in the rapid movement of the railroad car!" (Murphy 1:845–46). Dickinson's train, likewise, defamiliarizes valley, mountain, hill, and star, though less through the bells and whistles, the wheels within wheels, of wild-eyed Romantic progress prophets, if such ever purely existed, than through the sheer good description, the robust empirical imagination, of the midcentury Turner-train vision before her not-so-lying eyes.

As though the trained, disciplined physical eye is all artists need for defamiliarization (Russian formalists, unite), Dickinson's empirical voice takes on the form, boasts the power, of a more than merely Wadsworth-related, an equally Anglo-American Romantic endorsed or sponsored concentration on the rise, complexity, and progress of the Industrial Revolution. Speaking of Wadsworth, though, "I like to see it lap the Miles - " signals the poet's strikingly Wadsworth-related pride in her father, who, as director of the Amherst and Belchertown Railroad, brought the world to Amherst, and vice versa (see L72). Wadsworth's comparison of a man like Edward Dickinson with a train like the one in Dickinson's poem applies to the poet's industrial art.

Patience and earnestness, conservatism and progress [Wadsworth writes]. These must be found together in the character of the truly successful man. These qualities are not opposites; they are only different manifestations of perseverance. They answer respectively to the steam power and the brakes of a train. Without the first life has no movement at all; without the last it moves only to disaster and destruction. (*Sermons* [1905] 182; Wadsworth's emphasis)

The fact that Dickinson's train moves has as much to do with the earnest and progressive spirit of her father and of the Industrial Revolution as with the "sexual advance" of the "male" (Philip 74–75). The fact that Dickinson's train halts has as much to do with the patient conservatism of her father and of his Whig Party's stop-and-start, slow-but-sure plans for moderate American expansion as with the "symbolized...journey of death" (Downey 28).

"I like to see it lap the Miles - " might be "about poetry and about itself" or might concern "the differences in traditional masculine and feminine consciousness in the nineteenth century" (William Freedman 31). Pertaining to the latter possibility, dominating "locomotive" versus "landscape subject" comes through (Wendy Martin 134–35) to complicate Dickinson's conversation with Wadsworth (does her poem take issue with his Anglo-American bluster?). This well-known poem, however, can best be understood as addressing certain straightforward, sturdy values of the nineteenth century or what Wadsworth would call "different"— that is, antiphonal more than opposing—"manifestations of perseverance," be they progressive, conservative, personal, or cultural.

*   *   *

Did Edward Hitchcock influence Dickinson's attention to the new science of geology, as Richard B. Sewall has argued (*Life* 2:452–53)? Yes, but Wadsworth also wrote about geology in ways parallel to her views of this protoevolutionary methodology. With a little help from friend Wadsworth, perhaps, she balanced the vast reaches of geological time with the pressing needs of her brief span of life. Without diluting facts, she came to terms with, and made the best of, the harshly impersonal force of this physical science.

In a surprisingly tough-minded, refreshingly prescient grasp of geological issues, Wesley had asked, "What is at the center of the earth?" and "What, for that matter, does one know of its surface?" (Jackson 13:492–93). Wadsworth built on the empirical interrogative posed by his religious forebear. Dickinson's "dearest earthly friend" asks and answers other geological questions.

For tell me where, either in Creation or Providence, God thus hurries to conclusions? How many ages were consumed in the slow progress whereby this planet became fitted for human habitation? Why, the very fuel consumed in your houses is the slow product of countless years. And the tiny gem of your adornment was crystallized only in an immensity of generations! Jehovah's law of work is no hurrying or headlong progress. He wins slowly, and in circles of immense sweep! A thousand years are but as a day in the majesty of his movements. And in all this quiet and slow progress how truly Godlike he seems! (*Sermons* [1869] 14)[19]

Dickinson's "Business" of "Circumference" (L268) is in part to explore, though without as much divine reference as Wadsworth indulges in, the "circles of immense sweep" wherein earth takes time to crystallize gems.

Here is a poem in which Dickinson, like Wadsworth, suggests that later is better as eons go forward, for spiritual as well as natural reasons:

> The Day that I was crowned
> Was like the other Days -
> Until the Coronation came -
> And then - 'twas Otherwise -
>
> As Carbon in the Coal
> And Carbon in the Gem
> Are One - and yet the former
> Were dull for Diadem -
>
> I rose, and all was plain -
> But when the Day declined
> Myself and It, in Majesty
> Were equally - adorned -
>
> The Grace that I - was chose -
> To me - surpassed the Crown
> That was the Witness for the Grace -
> 'Twas even that 'twas Mine -
> (Fr613)

The second stanza recalls a passage in which Wadsworth's geological language supplies him with an analogy to sacred life: "The value of a gem is not in its composition, but in its crystallization. Even the diamond is composed mainly of carbon, and differs from the black coal of our furnaces only in this mysterious transfiguration...But the spiritual man has through gracious crystallization become a gem, reflecting Divine light, and thus fitted for a diadem" (qtd. in Sewall *Life* 2:452–53). In line with Wadsworth's analogy, as Sewall acknowledges, the poem engages in a more than simply geological colloquy with his prose. One recognizes, for instance, the speaker's "ritualism reminiscent of New England baptism" (Rowena Revis Jones 40).

For the poet, if not for the preacher, though, just as carbon changes into diamond, so plainness becomes beauty of otherworldly holiness and of this-worldly love alike. Is the "Crown" more emphatically hers for being as real as symbolic? Perhaps, for the final stanza can appear to say this to the point of making those difficult but fascinating lines look like they are about an actual "marriage" as much as they can concern an allegorical one. "The Day that I was crowned" appears to transpose Wadsworth's chord of spiritual loveliness into the welcome and affecting but true to life and minor key of natural grace. Dickinson's both/and logic here can come across as the have your cake and eat it, too, vision of a marriage made in heaven but for the earth. Thus, just as later is better in Wadsworth's geological prose, so in Dickinson's poem plainness grows earthy, attractive. Although, as Rowena Revis Jones implies, Dickinson's persona paradoxically values inner social meaning more highly than she rates the external symbols and trappings of her new bond of love (40), the focus of the poem entails an alternately, even a simultaneously, religious and romantic interconnection. Geological science hovers as secular seal on this intimation of two-way attachment.

"The Day that I was crowned" appears more than merely "the heretical assumption of autonomous being" (Keller *Only* 290). The psychosocial and the psychosexual, if mutually consenting, tinges of this contribution of Dickinson's earth-real as well as spiritual discussion can feel palpable to readers of this poem. Whether or not, in Locke's terms, her speaker entertains a simple idea or, what may be more, an idea of sensation concerning Wadsworth's persona, she "was chose - " as much by human as by spiritual agency, if only in the realm of virtual reality. In light of the physically scientific imagery of the poem, "was chose - " shines as an oddly backwoods, homespun, down-to-earth predicate that signals for the poet's self-projection here how the personal is scarcely ever as much the religious or the political as the philosophical and the scientific. As though it were somehow scientifically methodical to do so, she understands geology rather tenderly. Toughness remains in her implication, however, of a more than merely religious marriage—that is, in her inconvenient but deeply desired truth of a marriage in fact, if not through sacrament.

*   *   *

With Dickinson's poetic use of astronomy the views of Wesley vibrate. The clergyman commits himself to empirical analysis of the stars, in a manner consonant with his theological inquiry.

> The omnipresence or immensity of God, Sir Isaac Newton endeavours to illustrate by a strong expression, by terming infinite space, "the Sensorium of the Deity." And the very Heathens did not scruple to say, "All things are full of God." Just equivalent with his own declaration— "Do not I fill heaven and earth? Saith the Lord." How beautifully does the Psalmist illustrate this! "Whither shall I flee from thy presence?" (Jackson 6:388; compare Ps. 33:5; Jer. 23:24; Ps. 139:7)

The divinity symbolized by, or equivalent to, Dickinson's Northern Lights may seem less present than Wesley's God, but her god, the ultimately astronomical object of her veneration, and hence the pantheistic rather than theistic character of her belief here, remains as mysterious as Wesley's God.[20]

> Of Bronze and Blaze -
> The North - tonight -
> So adequate - it forms -
> So preconcerted with itself -
> So distant - to alarms -
>
> An Unconcern so sovreign
> To Universe, or me -
> Infects my simple spirit
> With Taints of Majesty -
> Till I take vaster attitudes
> And strut opon my stem -
> Disdaining Men, and Oxygen,
> For Arrogance of them -
>
> My Splendors, are Menagerie -
> But their Competeless Show
> Will entertain the Centuries
> When I, am long ago,
> An Island in dishonored Grass -
> Whom none but Daisies, know -
> (Fr319)

What Wesley and Dickinson have in common between his passage and her poem, the former in part a tribute to chief astronomer Newton and the latter wholly an ode to the Aurora Borealis, is the quality of humility, Wesley's spiritual and Dickinson's natural.[21] Just as the persona in Wesley's prose sounds reverential rather than apotheosized, so his tribute to God's astronomy foreshadows the reduced, secularized idiom through which Dickinson's speaker can sound more modest than heady.

Can Dickinson's poetic use of astronomy, here, in any sense pass for orthodox humility, in the opening and closing lines of the poem? Perhaps, for if her praise of the Aurora Borealis is less conventionally religious than Wesley's hymn in prose, it is also no less filled with awe and even more filled with fear. Denominating the Northern Lights as "adequate," a shrewd, understating choice of words meaning not so much sufficiently inspiring as abundantly sublime, impressively "distant," she implies that these lights can recall and derive authenticity from the remote, serene, and inaccessible God of Deism. "[P]reconcerted," "sovreign," the Aurora Borealis also evokes, for the poet, the predetermining, inscrutable God of Calvinism. Since Dickinson's Northern Lights, to borrow the language of Keats, can stay "far above" "All breathing human passion" ("Ode on a Grecian Urn" [1819], line 28), her persona's self-abasement before natural sublimity can compare with Wesley's humility before his infinitely superhuman God. No more than Dickinson, after all, is Wesley predictable, for he oscillates between his usual Arminian deity of dialogical interaction and his other, Calvinist God of aloof, inviolate majesty. Confessing that her poems sink to the level of trick-performing circus animals when compared to the pinnacled brilliance of celestial bodies, to say nothing of any further-off Reality that might transcend even stellar/universal appearance, Dickinson adopts a tone of "dust and ashes" like Job when prostrate before the Creator of Leviathan (Job 42:6).

On the other hand, the speaker can contemplate and even perceive reality, no matter how large, as though she takes reality on, becomes and affects it. This heady trait leaves her initial, near-religious humility behind, and goes for the egotistical sublimity at the heart of this poem.[22] After "the North - tonight / Infects" the persona's spirit with disdain for all below, she can appear chummier with the stars than Wesley was in his most astronomical dreams. Is this familiarity peculiarly American, notwithstanding that Briton Wordsworth invented egotistical sublimity? Perhaps, for compare Emerson, who writes of "that wonderful congruity which subsists between man and world; of which he is lord, not because he is the most subtile inhabitant, but because he is its head and heart, and finds something of himself in every...fact of astronomy" ("Nature"; Murphy 1:854). Dickinson's singer, similarly, however divine Northern Lights have seemed to her to be, and however divine they may appear to her to be again, subordinates them, in the middle stanza, to *her* I AM THAT I AM.

The word *Infects*, though, anticipates the persona's return to human earth in the closing lines, where she falls with such finality that she goes all the way underground forever, heady no more. Hers is now humility naturalized, of the earth, and, albeit partaking of the dignity inherent in the common fate ("Death is the distinguished thing," said Henry James), this humility is nonetheless still without any of the spiritual leavening to be found in Wesley's. With regard to lower case reality implicit in the last lines, Dickinson's alternate word for "Daisies" (the six-feet-under speaker will push them up) is "Beetles" (see Franklin's variorum), which capitalizes as horrifyingly chthonic her Humiliation: if there is a god of nature, he/she/it loves teeming beetles best. Thus, just as lowly beetles might seem a joke on the speaker and even on the exalted stars, so Dickinson's diction of "alarms, "Men," "Oxygen," Grass," "Daisies," and "Beetles" is tough-minded, stays a far cry from any complementary but rather too glibly comforting notion of benign or benevolent transcendence, whether theological or philosophical. When one reads "Of Bronze and Blaze - " in the philosophical and scientific terms that this book regards as Dickinson's predominant models, then the speaker emerges as much more fearless-objective than overreaching-subjective, more unswervingly empirical than idealistically deluded, and more psychologically and creatively dead-ended than egotistically sublime. Her science thus tells her what is, not what ought to be. If "their" (line 15) refers to the Northern Lights, then the persona's poems are as "dishonored" as the poet, and even if "their" refers to her poems, the poet remains defunct and would surely, Woody Allen–like, prefer to have achieved immortality by not dying than to have realized it through her works.

It remains a question whether or not the humble, Wesley-like tone or the arrogating, Emerson-like overtone of "Of Bronze - and Blaze - " proves the more attractive feature of the hymn. Either way, Dickinson's range of attitudes here enriches her speaker's response to astronomical truth. Her oscillating persona "expatiates farther than the Stars" and "makes excursions into the incomprehensible Inane" but also submits, equally Locke-like, to these very forms and forces of external reality (the planet on which she lives is not just constellated but oh, so local). Thus her empiricism naturalizes her idealism and secularizes her reverence. Her identification with the Aurora Borealis constitutes an all the more memorable instance of Anglo-American Romanticism for being at once and paradoxically inebriated and sober. Even the egotistically sublime Emerson writes that "the stars awaken a certain reverence, because though always present, they are always inaccessible" ("Nature"; Murphy 1:826; please note the naturalized Arminian/Calvinist distinction). The desacralized but deep humility in "Of Bronze - and Blaze - " accords with that same emphasis among many of Dickinson's works, including such not-so-well-known poems of astronomy, properly to be considered in this context, as "She went as quiet as the Dew" (Fr159).

The poem calculates a deceased woman's worth, alludes to French astronomer Jean-Joseph Leverrier, who "discovered" the planet Neptune, in 1846, and develops philosophical perspective on mortality through a precise understanding of astronomical imagery[23]:

> She went as quiet as the Dew
> From an Accustomed flower.
> Not like the Dew, did she return
> At the Accustomed hour!
>
> She dropt as softly as a star
> From out my summer's eve -
> Less skillful than Le Verriere
> It's sorer to believe!
>
> (Fr159)

Charles Wadsworth, without exactly being in dialogue with this speaker, unknowingly (in this case) provides a context for Dickinson's poem, and perhaps even a framework for disputing it, observing philosophically and scientifically that "[t]he old Astrology...hath ripened into a grand practical science, till our Astronomy [Wadsworth means by "our Astronomy" how such British practitioners as William and Caroline Herschel enhanced astronomical concentration within the scientific emphasis at Amherst College] elevated the race into the region of *most useful philosophy* and loftiest *knowledge* of God" (*Sermons* [1869] 292; emphasis added).[24] By contrast with Wadsworth's point, and as if in debate with it, Dickinson's version of the mathematically exact science of astronomy fails to "elevate the race" but instead situates her speaker's wisdom on the uncelestial but self-respecting and even honorable level of a tragic conundrum. That is: the all too useful, the tough rather than tender, philosophy of precious but ephemeral life. The new astronomy of which Wadsworth writes, with emphasis on the cerulean (not the object of scientific experiment so much as the emblem of divine certainty), would seem to disclose first one and then another sidereal entity, but never to subtract any. Dickinson's impermanent woman, on the other hand, dropped out of the sky in almost more than a manner of speaking, for she is as cancelled as Dickinson's astronomy says a star can be.

To be sure, Dickinson's quietly going woman (it is not that, like Icarus, she proudly presumes on sublimity) bids adieu to generations of readers for as long as they can endure. Nevertheless, the no less scientifically accurate for being psychologized astronomy of "She went as quiet as the Dew" demonstrates only that she was "here today, gone tomorrow."[25] Does the speaker stay consistent, here, with the sharply observing character, the closely observed result, of Anglo-American empiricism in its astronomical mode? Yes, more than Wadsworth's star-gazing does, for, though in fairness it could be said that his view is more comprehensive, while hers offers only half a loaf, hers wears better, is less formulaic, is edgier, more emotionally intelligent.

More or less vividly in all these respects, yet as one poet appeals to another even more powerfully than Emily Dickinson reaches out to "My Clergyman" (L950), "She went as quiet as the Dew" recalls, finally, Wordsworth's most anthologized elegy on Lucy (1800), which reads:

> A slumber did my spirit seal;
>   I had no human fears;
> She seemed a thing that could not feel
>   The touch of earthly years.
>
> No motion has she now, no force;
>   She neither hears nor sees;
> Rolled round in earth's diurnal course,
>   With rocks, and stones, and trees.

On the one hand, Wordsworth's lyric and Dickinson's resemble one another in their respect for empiricism as the proclamation of what counts. Since Lucy "neither hears nor sees"—that is, since she has lost everything immediate, vivid, worthwhile, and human—Wordsworth's speaker mourns her; he is far from being in any heady mood to identify either himself or her with long-running stars as grand figures of persistent existence. In Dickinson's case, similarly, the tangible regularities of dew and flower that come and go comprise her high premium on sense experience as life itself, and her corresponding recognition of the absence thereof as death on a cosmic scale parallels her perspective on stars as ever disappearing, never recoverable. On the other hand, the two elegies differ, for, though both deploy astronomic imagery, Wordsworth's does so for consolation, Dickinson's to express grief. Rolling "round in earth's diurnal course," Lucy illustrates permanence according to the first law of thermodynamics, and her pluperfect status (witness the past participle *rolled*) makes this Everywoman decidedly constellated—that is, almost as mythically as naturally ongoing. By contrast, just as the woman who "went quiet as the Dew" leaves no more trace than an extinct star, so astronomy serves the persona here, all too instructively, all too astringently, only to register oblivion.[26]

* * *

As though the sublimity of astronomy "cannot cheat so well / As [it] is fam'd to do, deceiving elf" (recall Keats), and as though the impersonality of technology and of geology were finally unpoetic, Dickinson turned the attention of her empirical imagination to life science. She was "toll[ed]...back" from Aurora Borealis not to her "sole self," which would be expected procedure for any Romantic-era writer indulging in the "usual suspect" of subjectivity, but to the relatively disenchanted but salutary, the increasingly disenthralled, topic of the lowly place of humankind on earth (compare Keats, "Ode to a Nightingale" [1819], line 72). The most individually applicable version of her eighteenth- to nineteenth-century empirical heritage, first, was the healing arts. Dickinson sought out the remedies of medical science in the spirit of Wesley and of Wadsworth—that is, with a mixture of skepticism toward, and gratitude for, what doctors, with variable results but improved method (Bynum), were patiently contributing to the pragmatic sum of human knowledge.

Just as Wesley faults "the four Greek sects, the Platonic, Peripatetic, Epicurean, and Stoic," for not making "any considerable improvement in any branch of natural philosophy," so he ranks empiricism as the facilitator of medical progress (Jackson 13:483). With a Locke-like twist on the search for scientific language (recall Wesley's abridgment of Book Three of Locke's *Essay*), he writes: "When physicians meet with disorders which they do not understand, they commonly term them nervous; a word that conveys to us no determinate idea, but it is a good cover for learned ignorance" (Curnock 5:496). Wesley's cheaply printed *Primitive Physick* (1747) joined the dozen or so most widely read books in England and America from 1750 to 1850 (Rousseau). Wesley's title signifies not outdated or crude supposition but foundational common sense based on observation. His blunt preface praises Greek doctors in the scientific terms of the British Enlightenment: "The Trial was made. The cure was wrought. And Experience and Physick grew up together" (vii). Although the preface deplores medical practices in general (these often "set Experience aside"), it rejoices that "there have not been wanting from Time to Time, some Lovers of Mankind…who have laboured to explode out of [physick] all Hypotheses, and fine-spun Theories, and to make it a plain intelligible Thing, as it was in The Beginning: Having no more Mystery in it than this, 'Such a Medicine removes such a Pain'" (ix). When Wesley asks, "Has not the Author of Nature taught us the use of many…Medicines?" he invokes theism in the process of scientific inquiry (xi; Locke's empiricism, for that matter, invokes theism, too [Spellman; Waldron], and it is also worth remembering that "empiric" is an eighteenth-century [post-Locke] synonym for "doctor" [*OED*]).

In explicit homage to Wesley's medical ideas, albeit without applying them as much to religion, Wadsworth recommends a principle of *Primitive Physick*: "We do not wonder that that most sagacious and Scriptural man, John Wesley, declared that '*cleanliness is next to god-liness*'" (*Sermons* [1905] 169; Wadsworth's emphasis). Wadsworth's wit is diverting:

> That this science is, as yet, imperfect and uncertain, the truest physician is himself the first to acknowledge…In other words, the [false] physician is very much like Walter Scott's Irishman, who, coming to a street where there was a great row, seized his stick, and looking up to heaven, cried, "*The Lord grant I may take the right side!*" And rushed in and laid about him. (*Sermons* [1905] 170; Wadsworth's emphasis)

Despite this criticism, Wadsworth warns against too much levity directed doctors' way.

> This is, just now, rather the popular view of the matter [Wadsworth writes];…but…Medical science, if as yet imperfect, is immensely important, *upon the first principle of experiment and induction*. (1) It has mastered the anatomy, or whole mechanism, of the body. (2) *Physiology*—all the functions of the organs and tissues. (3) *Materia Medica*—the effect of every drug on all conditions of diseased organs; and *Hygiene*, whose laws of health are as reliable as gravitation. By thousands of years of patient observation it has done all this; and if there be a practical lunatic on earth, it is he who confounds the true physician with the quack, and true medicine with nostrums. (*Sermons* [1905] 170–71; Wadsworth's emphasis)

"Men in this generation," Wadsworth concludes, "ought to outlive the old patriarchs," adding, "First, because the use of machinery relieves them of most of the wear and tear of labor, and secondly, because medical science enables them to set many diseases at defiance" (*Sermons* [1905] 158). Wadsworth's keynote of Wesley-derived confidence in medical science comes through in these lengthy but revealing quotations, though Wesley would not have made the point at the expense of the patriarchs.

To be sure, Dickinson recognized that what Wadsworth called "medical science" was in an infant state even as the nineteenth century was drawing to a close. In 1881, the death of William Stearns, the consumptive son of Amherst College president and Mrs. W. A. Stearns, dashed his loved ones' hopes for his high-altitude cure at Colorado Springs, Colorado. Nothing remained to be done but for Dickinson to pen, in May of that year, one of the most compassionate among her exquisite letters of condolence (see L694). Later, in August of 1884, bitterness colors her comment on her own terminal illness (she died on May 15, 1886, at 55, perhaps of Bright's disease): "The doctor calls it 'revenge of the nerves,' but who but Death had wronged them?" (L907). Thus, like Wesley, she rejects medical mumbo jumbo, attributing her illness instead to losing beloveds, including Wadsworth two years before (he died on April 1, 1882). Nevertheless, generally resisting the temptation to condemn medical practice, Dickinson endorsed the experimental effort of her mother, Emily, in 1856, and of her good friend Samuel Bowles, in 1861, to find relief from hypochondria and sciatica through the "water cure" of a Dr. Dennison of Northampton, Massachusetts (L182, L241). One thinks with pity in this regard, yet surely with no present-ism, of Keats and of Tennyson, in whose lives the "water cure" figured painfully (Motion 312; Robert Bernard Martin 137).

Dickinson prized what Wadsworth called "great principles of experiment and induction" in medical science. Her rigorous and skeptical but descriptive and positive attitude toward doctors comes across in an 1851 letter to Austin:

> I am glad to know you are prudent in consulting a physician; I hope he will do you good; has anyone with neuralgia, tried him, that recommended him to you? I think that warmth and rest, cold water and care [well-observed remedies in *Primitive Physick*], are the best medicine for it. I know you can get all these, and be your own physician, which is far the better way [his advocacy of this "better way" is why Wesley the

eighteenth-century WebMD made the basics of medicine available for every man and woman to be his or her own Empiric, again to use the Locke-resonant *OED*-synonym for doctor]. (L66)

Thus, if Dickinson's stance seems not quite scientific, her suspicion nonetheless appears prudently empirical. When she questioned prescription, she did so with open-minded, receptive tones of trial and error. She even exemplified quiet scientific cooperation with the doctor in a mutual search for the cure. From her mix of medical observations and reflections, she rarely precluded potential benefits.

No triumphantly ironic attitude qualifies Dickinson's genuine sorrow over the death, in 1880, of Dr. David P. Smith, a lecturer at the Yale University Medical School who was frequently consulted by the Dickinson family. Dickinson writes to Elizabeth Holland, "—[I] grieved for Dr. Smith, our Family Savior," adding enigmatically, "living Fingers that are left, have a strange warmth—" (L683). The image of the dying Dr. Keats's still-"living hand" comes to mind, for as Keats prophesied on his deathbed in a manner consistent with the conflation of his physician/ poet roles,

> This living hand, now warm and capable
> Of earnest grasping, would, if it were cold
> And in the icy silence of the tomb,
> So haunt thy days and chill thy dreaming nights
> That thou wouldst wish thine own heart dry of blood
> So in my veins red life might stream again,
> And thou be conscience-calmed—see here it is—
> I hold it towards you.
> ("This Living Hand" [*ca.* 1819])

Keats was one of Dickinson's favorite poets (Diehl *Dickinson* 15–19), and it is tempting to think not only that she learned from the dashes and the 85 percent quotient of lucid monosyllables here, but also that she imputed the sentiments of these very lines to "our Family Savior." She wished to see Dr. Smith alive again, and pressed home the unbearable poignancy that Dr. Smith's fingers, cold in death, would evermore lack their scientific, as well as perhaps Christ-like, power to keep the hands of others warm, living.

Like Wesley and Wadsworth, Dickinson sought out "true medicine" and "the true physician." For several months of 1864, her quest succeeded. Even after her reclusive tendencies had set in, around 1860, she sojourned in Boston as the patient of an early ophthalmologist, Dr. Henry W. Williams. If he did not improve her condition, he nonetheless did her some good, and he caused her no harm (Guthrie).

* * *

What was Dickinson's attitude toward whether or not, and how, she and her fellow human beings fit into Charles Darwin's method of natural selection? Her lyrics run the gamut of emotions from bemused hope and precariously controlled insouciance through despair to calm acceptance. First, however, again after the manner of Wesley and of Wadsworth—Wesley being especially prescient in this regard—she showed herself capable of meditating on evolutionary biology as a species of rather surprisingly joyful wisdom.

As observer-participants in Methodist heritage know (Collier 34–35) but as few, if any, mainstream academic historians have recognized, Wesley prepared ground for Darwin's theory, as odd as that might sound to anyone familiar with the ongoing resistance to Darwin's legacy among early-twenty-first-century evangelicals of an American stripe. Like Darwin, except for the religious reference, and as a foreshadowing of his evolutionary biology, Wesley's substantial abridgment of Charles de Bonnet's *Contemplation of Nature* (1764) emphasizes that God gradually but progressively develops nature through organic and human forms (Barber 74–77).[27] Thus, in the long run-up to *On the Origin of Species*, Wesley's natural philosophy figured more prominently than one might expect, perhaps even from such a scientifically cutting-edge evangelical as he turned out to be. This fearless aspect of his primarily religious leadership needs to be much more widely acknowledged, and far more often contemplated.

As though reflecting and building on Wesley's bold but secondhand and somewhat naïve conflation of divine agency with an early version of natural selection, Wadsworth's attitude toward evolutionary biology feels in a "New Englandly" manner (compare Fr256, line 15) blithe but more than a little defensive. Affecting a relaxed and humorous tone concerning the then-explicit issue of Darwinism, mid-nineteenth-century Wadsworth pauses in his homiletic defense of Christianity just long enough to joke that "[i]f any man will continue to believe that he is only an improved beast, we will not quarrel with his genesis, but only wish him joy of his grandmother" (*Sermons* [1884] 2).[28] One thinks here of the Huxley-Wilberforce exchange during the 1860s, which rather misleadingly centered on the sense in which human beings were more akin to apes than to angels.[29] "The humor that pleased Mark Twain" when he heard Wadsworth preach "was close to the 'roguery'" that Dickinson "cherished" in Wadsworth, and "often indulged in" herself (Sewall *Life* 2:251–52). The preacher and the poet would no doubt have shared a response to Darwin genuinely bemused, and amusing, but also more than a little nervous.

Dickinson's Wadsworth-like squib "Science is very near us—I found a megatherium on my strawberry" (Prose Fragment 102, L927) familiarizes Darwin's theory but retains an element of the ominous threat posed to humanity by natural selection. On the one hand, since a megatherium is "a huge extinct sloth" (L927n), its disappearance is solacing, as if to say that a gigantic identical sloth, homo sapiens, survives as yet, if not as a large bug that attacks her flowers, then as the gardener who plants but imperfectly tends them. On the other hand, notwithstanding her smile at Darwinism, the poet's megatherium also implies the frightening prospect of extinction for humankind. "Science is very near us" indeed—that is, all too close for comfort. Thus, if Dickinson's empirical voice can sound anything but concerned about evolutionary biology, she can also appear quite worried about it. In her book, the tough-minded Darwin ultimately proves a scarcely intimate partner in discussion, and perhaps even a powerfully inauspicious, not to say foreboding presence, as far as her poetic faith and her fundamental optimism were concerned.

Despite the underlying Darwinian method of "A Science - so the Savans say," this poem illustrates the lighthearted mood with which Dickinson is sometimes capable of taking Darwin in stride, and sounds as delicately lyrical as this poet practically ever declares herself to be:

> A science - so the Savans say,
> "Comparative Anatomy" -
> By which a single bone -
> Is made a secret to unfold
> Of some rare tenant of the mold -
> Else perished in the stone -
>
> So to the eye prospective led,
> The meekest flower of the mead
> Upon a winter's day,
> Stands representative in gold
> Of Rose and Lily, manifold,
> And countless Butterfly!
>   (Fr147)

Like "the meekest flower of the mead," "countless Butterfly" tempers toughness established by stanza one, for as these lines progress, the speaker turns her eye toward living species.[30] The "representative flower (perhaps herself) stands, after the Emersonian manner of each and all, as typal synechdoche of the whole of nature" (Keller "Alephs" 310–11); thus the monodrama exemplifies in its dialogical manner the most upbeat, most carefree quality of Dickinson's lyric program or Romantic-era agenda.[31] The poem remains no less sweet for Dickinson's having "surely learned [from Edward Hitchcock] her lesson" in the protoevolutionary science of "geology and fossil findings" (Wolff 196–97).[32] To the name of Hitchcock one would add those of Wesley and Wadsworth, whose lessons of an evolutionary kind, owing to the robust epistemology and constructive skepticism of British empirical philosophy, as well as to their Christian faith, in one sense need disturb no one's equilibrium. Just as Wesley anticipated the truths of evolutionary biology with sangfroid, and just as Wadsworth contemplated them with nerve and blithe spirit, so the Dickinson of "A Science - so the Savans say," as of Prose Fragment 102, on one level of its meaning, stays at once evolution-minded and relatively untroubled. For this Dickinson, the age of Darwin coexisted with late-Romantic lilt, as though the latter could withstand the former.

Another Dickinson, however, who wrote Prose Fragment 102 at the other level of its meaning, recoiled from Darwin's science, alarmed by, and struggling with, whom or what Tennyson discovered at the source of harsh particulars—namely, "Nature, red in tooth and claw / With ravine" (*In Memoriam* 56:15–16).[33] Dickinson's cry that "Darwin does not tell us" "*Why* the Thief ingredient accompanies all sweetness" tells us *that* it does so for reasons of Darwin's science (L359; emphasis added). Although Darwin's science by no means turned out entirely irreligious (Brown), that science reduced God, at best. As Emerson laments, with a proto-Dickinson blend of sarcastic blasphemy and sorrowful anger, "Providence has a wild, rough incalculable road to its end, and it is of no use to try to whitewash its huge, mixed instrumentalities, or to dress up that terrific benefactor in a clean, white shirt and white neckcloth of a student in divinity" ("Fate" [1852] qtd. in Whicher 333). In the form of natural selection, Darwin's science applied Ockham's razor to God's very existence. The cryptic, caustic comment that Dickinson made to her late-life love-interest Judge Otis P. Lord, with whom she shared a skeptical streak (Guthrie), leaps to mind as central to her grasp of just what Darwin signified for the second half of the nineteenth century and thereafter: "Mrs Dr Stearns called to know if we didn't think it very shocking for [former Union General and candidate for Massachusetts Governor

Benjamin F.] Butler to 'liken himself to the Redeemer,' but we [Emily and Lavinia? Emily and Austin?] thought Darwin had thrown 'the Redeemer' away" (L750). Thus if, as the result of evolutionary biology, God is dead, then Butler's apotheosis of himself, though only in the heat of political campaigning, represents the sole kind of divinity still feasible in the late-Romantic period, no matter how much this development might have scandalized "Mrs Dr Stearns."[34] Dickinson could never kill God off lightly, for she might agree with Dostoyevsky that without God, all is permitted, but, with a touch of bitterness, she rather waggishly enjoyed, and even relished, Darwin's intended or unintended discard of Jesus as divine.

Many of Dickinson's empirical personae grew quite shocked by their recognition that Darwin spells the death of God, and hence the end of Redemption. This Darwin-haunted speaker, for instance, faces galling disenchantment:

> The missing All - prevented Me
> From missing minor Things.
> If nothing larger than a World's
> Departure from a Hinge -
> Or Sun's Extinction, be observed -
> 'Twas not so large that I
> Could lift my Forehead from my work
> For Curiosity.
>
> (Fr995)

"The distinctive feature of this poem," Sharon Cameron writes, "is its impersonality, the largesse with which departure characterizes not only psychological reality but also physical and natural fact" (*Choosing* 170–71). One could well replace "largesse" with "chill." "The real subject of the poem," Heather McClave writes, "is the continuing sense and the definitive act of *missing*"; "clearly," she adds, "this is what sets the terms of [the speaker's] existence, so that the mind has some choice in the drama of happenstance" (4–5; McClave's emphasis). The choice that the mind has, however, yields cold comfort. To conflate Dickinson's words with those of Dylan Thomas, after the death of "The missing All," or God, "there is no other death," for all would then be death already (compare "A Refusal to Mourn the Death, by Fire, of Child in London" [1937], line 16).

A serviceable sort of redemption may be implied in the intensity with which the speaker remains absorbed in her creative work of composing poems. She recalls the tradition of work as efficacious. This heritage extended from Aristotle's Nichomachean Ethics and the

Book of Ecclesiastes to Byron's *Childe Harold's Pilgrimage* (1814), as in Byron's well-known words: "'Tis to create, and in creating live / A being more intense" (*CHP* 3:46–47). Melville provides an analogy, where Ishmael dispels despairing, suicidal thoughts of morbidity and of godless nihilism, by doing what he does—that is, by going to sea, no matter what (see the discussion in Delbanco 136). Ishmael can match even the droll, antic disposition of Dickinson's concentration on her work, as indicated by her poem "The missing All - prevented Me."

The disappearance of species in "The missing All - prevented Me" and, for that matter, the vanishing of worlds in this poem, seem bad enough. The extinction of God, however, looms worse still.[35] In the poet's mind, even wholesale loss of any other kind would feel less cataclysmic. Dickinson's nonchalance marks her undertone of gallows humor. She intimates her horror at the prospect of anything-but-kinetic vacuum. "The missing All," with lower case m and upper case A, occupies limbo between insignificance and awe, but hollowness spreads, if "missing," as gerund, belongs to the speaker's lassitude.

The deliberated, upper case importance of "Me," in the phrase "prevented Me," can well disturb the peace of readers. The capitalized pronoun appears to arrogate godhead. Does the persona, like General Butler, self-apotheosize, substituting her own creativity for that of a God now gone, now dead, and buried with the fossils? If *yes*, then she does so without pride, and with discreet, touching gesture, averting her glance from cosmic disaster. Just as Dickinson desired the God of her father, so this speaker would rather not be God. Her stance, though plucky or full of aplomb, lands the poem 180 degrees away from Wesley's *mot*, "The best of all is, God is with us" (qtd. in Hurst 141), and Dickinson's *Deus Absconditus*, or Deity Moribund, makes all other departures negligible. As she memorably observes elsewhere, "Parting is all we know of heaven, / And all we need of hell" (Fr1173, lines 7–8), but, without God's presence, all seems absent anyway, or so Dickinson implies, in her signature response to the most ominous implications of Darwin's science.

Grace seldom leavens Dickinson's poems of evolutionary biology. What one might call her *acquiring grace*, a paradoxical combination of claiming merited favor (recall her Arminian heritage) and receiving, however intermittently, unmerited favor (witness the Calvinist tradition) is fitfully evident in "The Day that I was crowned," already discussed, and in some poems to be considered in part II. It remains a distinct possibility, however, that this concept is nothing more theologically precise than a secularized version of grace; her poems of evolutionary biology, in any case, perplex and retard anything like what Wesley understood as the prevenient grace of an always already present God. In these poems, as in Darwin's *Origin*, species just are, while they last, and no divine whitewashing can alleviate, either through what these personae can make happen or through what happens to them, this cold, brutal fact of existence. This canon-within-the-canon of Dickinson's art of knowledge by no means equates to all she wishes to learn, yet appears to be "all / [She] knows on earth" and all there is to know (compare Keats, "Ode on a Grecian Urn," lines 49–50). As the result of composing these poems, of burning through "the fierce dispute" between Darwin's science and "impassioned clay," did she entertain the likelihood that Darwin bore as much responsibility for the decline of poetic as of religious faith, as he himself might have acknowledged (compare Keats, "On Sitting Down to Read *King Lear* Once Again" [1818], lines 5–6)?[36] To repeat Tennyson's language, for it is the best of all poetic encapsulations of evolutionary biology, Darwin's "Nature, red in tooth and claw / With ravine" relegated Dickinson's lyric impulse to the "bittersweet" (compare Keats, "On Sitting," line 8).[37] In Keats's terms, Darwin taught her, forced her, to "leave melodizing" on the "wintry day" of his astonishing, yet scarcely all that welcome, range of life-science discoveries, thereby giving her the nineteenth-century means of becoming a realist poet of Shakespearean proportions (compare Keats, "On Sitting," line 3).

For Dickinson, the natural law of Darwin's evolutionary biology defeated any haughty regard, on her and on her readers' part, for the role or position of humankind in any larger scheme of things. The relentless and irresistible force of natural selection, as far as she and her select society of tough-minded fellow-searchers and -researchers were concerned, beat human measures against, say, the rodent kind, for, in her natural law, as in Darwin's, even the despised rat occupied a strangely ineluctable place of legitimacy. Notice how resignedly one of her poetic laboratory reports can forbear to punctuate the equilibrium of the rat, no matter how strongly the speaker might appear to wish to do so (Stephen Jay Gould understood evolutionary biology as "punctuated equilibrium"):

> Hate cannot harm
> Foe so reticent -
> Neither Decree prohibit him -
> Lawful as Equilibrium
>   (Fr1369, lines 7–10)

And even a phylum so alienated from, and so much at enmity with, humankind as the detestable, rebarbative fly failed to alter or dislodge the poet's brave acceptance of scientific reality as all the more ultimate for differing from any human-centered concept of rightness or fairness.[38] "Of their peculiar calling," she declares of flies in her not so much studiedly neutral as grudgingly respectful tone, "Unqualified to judge," adding, in not-so-subtly attenuated Calvinist idiom, "To Nature we remand Them / To justify or scourge" (Fr1393, lines 13–16). Thus Dickinson described species as meticulously, and with as little regard for human agendas of interpretation, as Darwin depicted the objects of his life-form attention on Galapagos, or as David Hume critiqued causation. Perhaps she did so, above all, as Wesley, the follower of Locke as well as of Jesus, showed his all but Darwin-like, and by now not-so-surprising, reverence for science.

By way of concluding this segment, here follows Wesley's most striking passage of an empirically philosophical, scientifically rigorous kind, one with which Dickinson would have agreed:

> I endeavor [Wesley affirms] not to account for things, but only to describe them. I undertake barely to set down what appears in nature; not the cause of those appearances. The facts lie within the reach of our senses and understanding; the causes are more remote. That things are so, we know with certainty; but why they are so, we know not. In many ways, we cannot know; and the more we inquire, the more we are perplexed and entangled. God hath so done his works, that we may admire and adore; but we cannot search them out to perfection. (Jackson 14:301; compare Eccles. 3:11)

Although Dickinson appeared scarcely so "certain" even that "things are so," much less "why they are so," these words of Wesley's anticipate her Darwin-informed worldview. Wesley here rebukes, before the fact, the anti-intellectualism of much twenty-first-century American-evangelical creationist discourse, there being, it bears repeating, little such British expression nowadays. Like Wesley as well as Darwin, Dickinson wrote things down, respected them apart from the writing down, and, without assuming causation, reached nonirritably for an array of possible explanations for all these natural and, as often as not, living things. Like other Romantic-era authors of the Anglo-American world, and like Locke, Wesley, Wadsworth, and Darwin, Dickinson acknowledged the perplexity, viscosity, and entanglement of truth, yet knew it would "hold - " (Fr343, line 10). "The Truth," as she told it slant but wise and whole, "is Bald - and Cold - " (Fr343, line 9), but she took both the violent mutability and the plodding sameness of the world in stride—that is, with composure and poise, if not with a grain of salt. Casting her objective eye on life, on death, she passed on, started over. She set the example of heroic imagination and of courageous intellect alike.

* * *

To come full circle, the "natural methodism" of Romantic Anglo-America, as distinct from Natural Methodism there, inspired Emily Dickinson to subordinate spiritual discipline, for which Methodism and the two Great Awakenings are well known, to the intellectual discipline of Locke and of Darwin alike. Among her protean shapes, the mature poet assumed the guise of a philosopher, not so much of a "transcendental realist" kind, as David Van Leer understands Emerson to be, as of a rational empiricist kind, as Brantley (*Coordinates* and *Anglo-American*) understands Emerson to be. In effect, Dickinson took Charles Lamb's point: she would have found in his low-key, lower case phrase a gentle rebuke of, a modest corrective to, nineteenth-century transcendentalism, whether literary, philosophical, or religious. As recorded throughout this chapter, her empirical voice sings of knowledge based on natural experience, as opposed to faith based on intuition, mysticism, traditional revelation, or spiritual experience (immediate revelation). Thus, like her fellow-writers in English-language belles lettres, the Myth of Amherst held to the truth of imagination.

To be sure, more often than in Dickinson's poetry "natural methodism" in the rest of Anglo-American Romanticism can inflate to Natural Methodism. This distinction points to her *late* Romanticism. Nevertheless, her poetry was scarcely without resource, recourse, inasmuch as she turned Natural Methodism upside down, or, to shift the language to imported (but more usual) phrasing, she returned to earth the Transcendentalism, the Natural Supernaturalism, of Coleridge, Carlyle, or Emerson. She conceived of "natural methodism" as the best part—that is, as the sense-based foundation—of Anglo-American Transcendentalism of whatever kind, for, perhaps even better than her co-Romantic-era participants in "the free play of the mind," she came to understand that "ideal form" begins, and ends, in sense perception.[39] If one may alter Coleridge's formula, she suspended little disbelief, because she cultivated much skepticism.[40] As a result, her art of knowledge can feel more creditable than her art of belief can appear credible. This distinction holds—no matter to what degree these hemispheres of her imagination subsisted on her select society of conversational sparring partners, belles as well as bonnes. The sonority of belles lettres, in particular, augments the historical, interdisciplinary "audition" of her singing—that is, her dramatically lyrical self-projection as "*Scientist* of Faith" within a chorus of such others (Fr1261, line 12; emphasis added).

Dickinson did not profess as much poetic faith, then, as one might expect from the lyric genius that she remained. In company with her others, yet more intrepidly, she found "what to make of a diminished thing" (compare Robert Frost, "The Oven Bird" [1916], line 14). More consistently than these others, with relatively restrained, less blue-nostalgic-sad than boldly minimalizing resort to the formulaic supernaturalism of her religious culture as a whole, she mainly generated art from nature. With no false modesty, she concluded (a) that her "poetry of earth," too, was anything but a reduced form of art and (b) that, also like Keats's, hers more than sufficed as art. Of course, her letters and poems were sometimes intuitional or mystical. Her idioms, moreover, included not just the sound of revealed religion but even the spiritually experiential emphasis of the transatlantic revival, and hence the immediate-witness mood of Romantic Anglo-America's Natural Methodism (if not of her "natural methodism"). Still, as Lamb must have thought was the case with Wordsworth's language, Dickinson's granted privilege at once to the role of mind in nature and to the influence of nature on the mind. Whether or not she ever chose matter over mind—"Theme this but little heard of among men"—her tough, not-so-subjective Romanticism would have resisted the Euro-continental drift that approximated all Romanticism to Descartes's French-rationalist elevation of mind over matter, or to Kant's insistence on the German-idealist perpendicularity of Natural Supernaturalism (compare Wordsworth, Prospectus to *The Recluse* [1814], line 67).

To be sure, the leap that this chapter has taken across space and time could look, to say the least, anachronistic. Nevertheless, the Anglo-American "sense" for which Locke and Wesley alike qualified as prime movers proved a subtler near influence on Wadsworth and on Dickinson alike than even his Presbyterian allegiance and her Congregational affiliation. The Reverend Phineas Densmore Gurley of the New York Avenue Presbyterian Church, Washington, DC (visited by President Abraham Lincoln) represented a counterpart to the Presbyterian faith of Gurley's just as well-known contemporary and fellow-Presbyterian Theological Seminary graduate Wadsworth. According to Ronald C. White, Jr., Gurley straddled the fatalism of

John Calvin and the evangelical New School's emphasis on free will, an Arminian rather than Calvinist development within nineteenth-century Presbyterianism. Wadsworth's paradoxically quasi-Methodist faith, too, derived from the free will theology that Wesley learned from Arminius, and then passed on to the Second Great Awakening, in which Wadsworth and Dickinson participated, and which, in its spiritual *sense*, corresponded to the reliance of philosophical empiricists on experience and of scientists on experiment.

In sum, just as the capital letters often used by Emily Dickinson would seem to contradict, yet really paradoxically respected, Charles Lamb's instigation of lower case modesty in literary persuasion, so her ballad- and hymn-like stanzas ironically lent formalistic authority to her inchoate, and most un-hymn-like, data base. Of course, her art of knowledge remembered the fleeting philosophical transcendentalism of Wordsworth's lyrical ballads and the dominating religious transcendentalism of the Wesley brothers' hymns. Still, although the religious emphasis of Wesley and of Wadsworth remained their paramount concern, and although Dickinson's spiritual subtheme stayed audible in, as well as subsidiary to, her philosophical and scientific leanings, natural philosophy burgeoned from Locke and Wesley through the Romantics to Wadsworth and Dickinson. The arc from eighteenth- and early-nineteenth-century natural philosophy to mid- and late-nineteenth-century science ("natural philosophers, after 1833,...were to be called scientists" [Gaull "Conjecturing" 68]) described, for instance, the discovery of transatlantic weather, "the birth of Anglo-American meteorology" (Gaull "Conjecturing" 68). Thus Dickinson's version of "natural methodism" did not so much evoke the otherworldliness of the transatlantic revival or of Romantic Anglo-America as sanction and triangulate the here and now of British empiricism, Anglo-American Romanticism, and evolutionary biology. Not just like Wadsworth the "natural methodist," as distinct from Wadsworth the Natural Methodist, but even like Wesley the "philosophical sluggard," as distinct from Wesley the "itinerant Preacher" (Telford 2:68), Dickinson the philosopher-poet became something of a scientist, too. Her imagination trusted in induction. She paid homage neither to the mind alone nor to a world elsewhere so much as to her home-ground of thoughts and things.

Chapter 2

Guiding Experiment

British Romantic philosopher William Godwin's rededication to his nationally cultural birthright of sense-based epistemology constituted a dramatic palinode, for him, and aptly prefigured the "New Englandly" intellectual position of his descendant Dickinson (compare Fr256, line 15). In 1797, four years after he had espoused French rationalism, in *An Enquiry Concerning Political Justice*, Godwin reaffirmed British empiricism, in *The Enquirer*: "We proceed most safely [Godwin writes], when we enter upon each portion of our process, as it were, de novo...There is danger, if we are too exclusively anxious about consistency of system, that we may forget the perpetual attention we owe to experience, the pole-star of truth" (*Enquirer* vi, viii). Dickinson, similarly, dwelled on the possibility of empirical findings but, hastening to no rash judgment, avoided overconfidence in predicting them. Not only like the imagination of Godwin but also, as Elizabeth Dolan has recently and thoroughly shown, like those of his wife, Mary Wollstonecraft, of his and Mary's daughter, Mary Shelley, and of Charlotte Smith, Dickinson's was both empirically philosophical and scientific. Perhaps even more than this British quartet of writers, yet without forgetting the insight, as expressed by Nietzsche, that "[a]s the circle of science grows larger, it touches paradox at more places," the Myth of Amherst expected experiential and experimental discoveries to approximate truth, however unwelcome, as well as knowledge (see *The Birth of Tragedy* [1872] qtd. in Putnam 12).

"We cannot hope for truth, only for ever richer (humanly created) meanings," post-Modern anthropologist Clifford Geertz declares, adding, "indeed, an embarrassment of meanings; for such is the indeterminacy of the signs we use, uncontrollably proliferating meanings are present in the slightest, least considered utterance" (qtd. in Tallis 3). Entertaining, in riposte, the not necessarily untroubled but nonetheless hardy perennial idea of "a fundamental attunement between the human mind and the universe," skeptical reviewer Raymond Tallis asks of Geertz, "What is the truth status of the assertion that truth has dissolved into meaning?" (4). "Doubtful," Dickinson would answer. From her and her dramatic dialogists' thought-and-word experiments, adjustment of mind to the universe—that is, the promise of realizing brain/world coalescence and of conceiving intellect-cosmos interpenetration—can arise as testing of stable truth, and not merely as recording of changeable and bare, albeit teeming, meanings. Thus, perhaps even as Dickinson sidesteps naïveté (she never found the stable truth), she can "march breast forward," can strive and thrive, and so, in the hope of arriving somewhere real (though not without the strain of getting there), fights on (compare Robert Browning, "Epilogue to *Asolando*" [1890], lines 11, 19).

To be sure, as chapter 1 has already indicated, Dickinson's technological, geological, and astronomical forays "out opon Circumference" and "into the intense inane" were nagged by such bouts of her recurring pessimism as her medically and biologically forced descent back down to earth again. Moreover, as part II will everywhere and consistently acknowledge, Dickinson's pre-Modern mode can often render the constructive skepticism of Locke, Berkeley, Hume, and Shelley-influencing William Drummond destructive, whether or not her optimism survived in the end, and however often her hope did triumph (compare Pulos; Swingle). Nevertheless, just as chapter 1 has balanced her post–Civil War, post-Darwin gloom with her ebullient, pre–Civil War atmosphere (Lundin first made this useful distinction), so this chapter will show how she displayed neither paralyzed skepticism nor static states of unbelief but, instead, maintained equal measures of dynamic and salutary, though astringent, naturalism. This poet stayed afloat.

The previous chapter concluded that Emily Dickinson held in equipoise and kept in play the natural philosophies and the scientific imaginations of the Romantics, Locke, Wesley, Wadsworth, Darwin et al. Dickinson's devotion to sense-based reason and the scientific method captured and capped the "*philosophy* of enthusiasm" ascendant in the temporal experience of Wordsworth, Emerson et al. and the spiritual experience of Wesley and Wadsworth.[1] Thus, whether she encountered people face-to-face, on the page, or "inner than the bone" of her binational DNA (compare Fr334, line 14), Dickinson reinforced her partners in conversation and her readers to favor the explanatory powers of experiential philosophy and of the laboratory over the testimonial witness and the new-evangelical song of Experiential Faith. This chapter will emphasize (a) her signature lyric of empiricism, "Experiment escorts us last - " (Fr1181); (b) her prime example of subject/object oscillation, "On a Columnar Self - " (Fr740); and (c) her miniature poetic manifesto of philosophical and science-driven theology, "Apparently with no surprise - " (Fr1668). Thus, adding to the practical criticism in the last chapter and climaxing with her trademark contribution to the august tradition of theodicy, this chapter is intent on formulating some hitherto only implicit historical, interdisciplinary, and biographical principles of interpreting Dickinson's poetry henceforth.

The next segment will feature a close but wide-ranging reading of "Experiment escorts us last - " (Fr1181). The third will contrast "On a Columnar Self - " (Fr740) with German idealism, thereby bringing out the Anglo-American quality of Dickinson's grounded subjectivity. Finally, in the fourth segment, a larger than eighteenth- to nineteenth-century perspective on Dickinson's impulse to theodicy will emerge—that is, a broad, global approach to her dilemma of reconciling physical and moral evil with the time-honored view of a God who "so loved the world" (John 3:16) that He saves it. The chapter will fill out the group sketch begun in chapter 1, with Dickinson remaining at the center and her others forming, through the auspices of her select society, the composite, presiding, inward, and outward genius of "the dogged aggregation of phenomena." This meaty, mouth-filling phrase, as opposed to "abstract reasoning" or "complicated mathematics," can serve, here, to characterize Dickinson's group effort to acquire as much knowledge as possible, and perhaps even to approach, if not the truth itself, then what may well be strangely more, the truth of the collective imagination.[2]

*   *   *

Dickinson personifies the scientific method thus:

> Experiment escorts us last -
> His pungent company
> Will not allow an Axiom
> An Opportunity -
>   (Fr1181)

To paraphrase: Like the sense-based means of epistemology, the sense-driven method of science can stay by our sides long after all our other props have fallen into abeyance, and proven as chimerical as our tragic predisposition to closed-system, sense-superior abstraction. By substituting method for system (Dickinson would have it so), "Experiment" can guard against such theoretical extremes as how "the economics profession," nowadays, "devotes itself to the mathematical modeling of delusional harmonies" (Gray 29). "Experiment escorts us" suggests that laboratory procedure (a) points out what we might not otherwise observe; (b) attends us like a mentor and as protection against deductive, syllogistic reasoning; and (c) like a loving friend or true lover delivers proof against falsehood. Thus, in the predicate "escorts us last - ," *last* signifies that "Experiment" will be there, for us, all the way out to the edge of doom.

It is not that "Experiment" will help us only *at* last, as in grudgingly, perfunctorily, belatedly, or as a mere afterthought. Nor is it the inference here that it is *about* time, *high* time, that "Experiment" helped us, at *long* last. Rather, in the context of Dickinson's empirical voice as a whole, the piquant, spicy, "pungent company" of "Experiment," curiously strong, makes us *visionary*, in the concrete, *eyesight-specific* meaning of this word, as though the poem transposes into a secular key the "visionary" chorus, the *spiritual* "company," of Bunyan's *Pilgrim's Progress* (1678). "Experiment escorts us last - " can teach Dickinson's fellow-dialogists, *avant la lettre*, that even the empirical quintessence of logical positivism need sacrifice no subtlety, mystery, or enchantment to the demands of sense perception.[3] Instead, like imagination in this poet, "Experiment" in this poem can appear to her "us" as more credibly creative for being Vulcan-like, sweaty, even naturalized not spiritualized.

To be sure, the poem can seem to constitute pejorative characterization of empirical procedures. Dickinson's alternate word for "escorts," after all, is "accosts" (see Franklin's variorum), suggesting that empiricism can be threatening and that Darwin's science can assault one's self-esteem. In not allowing "an Axiom," personified, "An Opportunity," typified, to join the dance of "*all* the [embodied] Truth - " (compare Fr1263, line 1; emphasis added), "Experiment," only-too-humanized, can seem intolerant, exclusionary, as though scientific method owed no dialogical courtesy to either rationalism or idealism as a way-of-knowing legitimate in its own right and up to a point. Nevertheless, these layers of negative valence prove secondary, relating mainly as devil's advocates to this speaker's primary, favorably presented, and highly recommended composite of sensationalist epistemology and scientific method. The "voice of seasoned skepticism," heard by Richard B. Sewall in "Experiment escorts us last - "

("Teaching" 49), is a far cry from scientism. The poem means less that the scientific method is the only justifiable access to the truth than that test sites provide the best of all possible "*slant[s]*" on the truth (compare Fr1263, line 1; emphasis added). Science, personified, develops into the rather modest winner of the competition for intellectual acceptance bestowed by the select and adjudicating society of "us" in the world of thoughts and things. To modify Sharon Cameron's phrase for Dickinson's love of paradox, the poet does not so much "choose not choosing" either the word *accosts* or the word *escorts* as give the nod to the latter for reasons of its positive import, its gallant effect (see *Choosing Not Choosing*).

Of course, "escorts" in Dickinson's time by no means so readily connoted the salacious, the scandalous. Still, Dickinson recognized and considered the downside of science, as though she were aware of a twofold implication, first, that laboratory results can be for sale and, second, that they can be no more repeatable, and perhaps even no more respectable, than one-night stands. "Experiment," after all, can seem to behave like a jealous, possessive lover, in not allowing "An Axiom" to dance with "us," and can appear to act like that out of an almost psychological sense of the insecurity of his own position. Thus, Dickinson can seem to ask: Is scientific method as seductive, as deceptive in its way, as the overweening, all-too-heady systems of rationalism and of idealism? Or, on the other hand—and much more in keeping with the argument here—does she think of the scientific method as the president, so to speak (honorifically), of her Royal Society of fellow-researchers? The latter interpretation, on balance, stays primary here. We can keep the former in view, however, as this chapter proceeds—if only to keep things honest (just as any PhD defense committee might include members outside the department in question, for the corrective purpose of their different, opposing, or complementary points of view).

"Experiment escorts us last - " conveys the untheoretical, down-to-earth, and anything but destructively skeptical outlook of a poet-persona as loyal to the one who brought her to the dance as "Experiment" remains faithful to her and her philosophically and scientifically receptive others. The poem implies that despite being reductive, despite doing violence to the widespread perception of humankind's importance in the grand scheme of things, rational empiricism and science alike can resist tender-minded rationale for hermetic thought, whether logical or illogical. This experiential and experimental brand of reasoning and of imagining can keep in play, and perhaps even can include, the mathematical, rationalistic, intuitive, or idealistic strain of knowing, yet surely cannot tolerate the pseudoscientific, speculatively psychological, top-down political, fanatically religious, or hothouse-aesthetic way of "knowing." The face value of "Experiment escorts us last - " denotes concisely and in no uncertain terms that what one sees is what one gets, whether one knows it or not. This speaker brings into focus how other such Dickinson dialogists are to be overheard, or heard and conversed with. As this self-projection of the poet would acknowledge, "Experiment" can prove limited in scope and in outcome, but Dickinson's breathing of trial and error here, like the "voice" of Shelley's "great mountain," retains power (again to apply Shelley's words to her case) "to repeal / Large codes of fraud and woe."[4] It is no accident that the very poem (Fr256) in which Dickinson announces her perspective as "New Englandly" (line 15) acknowledges the simultaneous and consequent possibility that her outlook is Anglo-American: witness the all but self-fulfilling fantasy in line 8, "Were I Britain born."

As a global means of broadly reading this signature lyric of Dickinson's empirical voice, it remains to survey this persona's philosophical and literary heritage from Locke to Emerson, with special reference to their scientific idiom. It may be helpful to quote the words of Locke, Emerson et al., the better to dramatize their dialogical relation to Dickinson. The background of empirical philosophy, first, tilled ground for the scientific emphasis of a poem like "Experiment escorts us last - ," the carefully chosen language of which can carry the freight of this venerable tradition. Locke's *Essay* says that solidity, resistance, inertia, extension, figure, shape, and divisibility can stay accessible to, though independent of, sense perception (see Brantley *Locke* 73–77); thus Locke's confidence in correspondence between matter and mind rests on his subscription to primary qualities as the rock-solid reality that Dickinson's "*Experiment*" persona also perceives. "*Experiments* and historical observations we may have," Locke warns, "from which we may draw advantage of ease and health, and thereby increase our stock of conveniences for this life; but beyond this I fear our talents reach not, nor are our faculties, as I guess, able to advance" (qtd. in MacLean 137; emphasis added). Despite the earlier-quoted *Essay* passage on making excursions "far beyond the Stars" and into "the incomprehensible Inane," Locke would have approved of Dickinson's modest but firmly trusting means of carrying her education forward (recall chapter 1, segment 2) by questing for the sake of questing, and with scant expectation of arrival. One may read "Experiment escorts us last - " in just such a low-key, yet keen, manner.

Wesley, too, foreknew "*Experiment* escorts us last - ": "Reason and *experiment*," he writes, bring about "gradual improvement of natural philosophy," for "not single persons only, but whole *societies* [note well the Royal- as well as Methodist-Society implications of this perhaps more science- than religion-related, and certainly this Dickinson-appropriated, word], apply themselves carefully to make *experiments*, that, having carefully observed the structure and properties of each body they might the more safely judge of its nature" (Jackson 13:483; emphasis added). "All we can attain to," Wesley concludes, "is an imperfect knowledge of what is obvious . . . enough to satisfy our need, but not our curiosity" (Jackson 13:496). However, Wesley's salutes to telescopes, microscopes, burning glasses, barometers, thermometers, air pumps, diving bells, and diving machines disclose his working assumption that the senses, if extended, yield the base of knowledge (Jackson 13:487). Dickinson's tribute to microscopes in

> "Faith" is a fine invention
> For Gentlemen who *see*!
> But Microscopes are prudent
> In an Emergency!
> (Fr202)

comes readily to mind in this bottom-line, sense-trusting regard. And in like manner "reason and experiment" in "Experiment escorts us last - " do so.

The foreground of Anglo-American Romanticism, moreover, tilled the ground for the new-empirical song chanted in "Experiment escorts us last - ," the carefully chosen words of which can carry the freight of fresh belletristic heritage. Late-Romantic Carlyle, for his part paralleling Dickinson's pairing of science and mystery, emphasizes that "the man who cannot wonder, who does not habitually wonder (and worship), were he President of innumerable Royal Societies, and carried the whole Mécanique Celeste and Hegel's Philosophy, and the epitome of all Laboratories and Observations with their results, in his single head,—is but a pair of Spectacles behind which there is no Eye" (*Sartor Resartus* [1831] qtd. in Shelston 104). "I have the fancy," writes Emerson to Carlyle (in a manner resembling Dickinson's implied elevation of concrete content over near-decadent form), "that a realist is a good corrector of formalism, no matter how incapable of syllogism or continuous linked statement" (qtd. in Slater 122). Since Emerson encapsulates the point by remarking that "[n]ature does not like to be observed," he practices the "wise passiveness" with which

Wordsworth epitomizes Locke's wisdom for the high-Romantic, English-speaking setting, and with which Dickinson in "What mystery pervades a well!" (Fr1433) does, too, for that same setting in its late-Romantic phase.[5] On middle, British and American ground between form- and sense-drive, Emerson writes, with an attitude toward mathematics similar to that of Dickinson in "Experiment escorts us last - ," "We may climb into the thin and cold realm of pure geometry and lifeless science, or sink into that of sensation. Between these is the equator of life, of thought, of spirit, of poetry—a narrow belt" ("Experience" [1844] qtd. in Murphy 1:950). The Anglo-American duet of Carlyle and Emerson harmonizes so closely with Dickinson's empirical voice that, to mix the music metaphor with an image from painting, a mere brushstroke of the trio can depict the philosophical and scientific worldview of Anglo-American Romanticism as efficiently as possible. Dickinson's empirical voice can chime with Carlyle's and Emerson's, for hers lends obbligato to theirs, though partly by way of the proximate voice of Charles Wadsworth's empiricism, which italicizes his tribute, worth repeating here, to "*experiment and induction*" as "*the first principle*" of all mental and material progress whatsoever (Wadsworth *Sermons* [1905] 170; Wadsworth's emphasis).

Carlyle the defender of British empiricism against French rationalism (see Brantley *Coordinates* 43–75), not Carlyle the importer of German idealism (contrast Cazamian), not-so-modestly wins the competition for chief muse of Dickinson's "Experiment escorts us last - ." To evoke the intuition-idiom of neo-Euclidean Descartes, and to paraphrase the assumption underlying "Experiment escorts us last - ," French rationalism relies too heavily, and too complacently, for Carlyle's and Dickinson's developing tastes, on the glibly advocated, downright spurious doctrine of self-evident truth.[6] One hears overtones here of Thomas Jefferson's unpragmatic, if not oddly un-American, mood of Francophiliac rationalism. Carlyle the empiricist aspires "toward those dim infinitely-expanded regions, close-bordering on the impalpable Inane" (*Sartor Resartus* qtd. in Shelston 108), and thereby adds to Locke's "incomprehensible Inane" and Shelley's "intense inane" an enthusiasm for the ultraobjects of the universe that rivals Dickinson's for edge-of-natural-reality "Circumference"—that is, for "far off" but less retro-Transcendental than neo-immanent being (compare, respectively, Fr633, line 7, and Fr740, line 11). According to Carlyle's alter ego Teufelsdröckh, "Science" never proceeds "in the small chink-lighted, or even oil-lighted, underground workshop of Logic alone," for the rationalism of such French mathematicians as Lagrange and Laplace is "the head screwed off, and set in a basin to keep it alive" (*Sartor Resartus* qtd. in Shelston 103). Despite Dickinson's adeptness at mathematics (Sewall *Life* 2:336–64; compare Fr78, Fr99, Fr670, Fr980, and Fr1725), the reliable, steadfast prop called sensationalist epistemology comes to her aid—in part through Carlyle's mediations—for the acute, keen companionship of the scientific method helps this poet to spurn the advances, and to counteract the blandishments, of pure logic alone. "Experiment escorts us last - " should serve, henceforth, as the caption for Emily Dickinson's picture of Carlyle, in its place of honor on her bedroom wall.

To "speak in philosophy," for the moment, rather than in the religious dialect or in the literary-critical vernacular that an emphasis on empiricism must also respect, Dickinson's empirical values preclude, on the one hand, the "coherent, independent, subordinate, and deductive" principles of rationalism or idealism and, on the other, the agendas of materialism. Thus Jonathan Culler's description of Frederick Harrison's rationalism, if not of Harrison's idealism, contrasts with Jeremy Bentham's materialistic utilitarianism (Culler 158–90, esp. 161), and provides the means of placing Dickinson the empiricist somewhere between these philosophical extremes. Though on what Coleridge calls the "dread watchtower" of the "absolute self" ("To William Wordsworth" [1807], line 4; compare Hab. 2:1), the not-so-solipsistic Dickinson associates matter with mind, and vice versa. At the same time, however, she (a) forswears subject-on-object coercion and (b) parries object-on-subject violence. Without either descending into mere confusion or diffuseness, and without overreaching to either facile reconciliation or coalescence, her empiricist's to-do list ranges from (1) balancing to (2) interacting with to (3) interchanging to (4) interpenetrating thoughts and things. Dickinson's procedure proves unsystematic, yet by no means unmethodical.

* * *

The following 52 words of palpable obscurity can sound as tonally superior to sense impressions as any rationalist/idealist Romantic work, English-language or other, and so these lines can put to the test any claim that Dickinson's primary voice is empirical:

> On a Columnar Self -
> How ample to rely
> In Tumult - or Extremity -
> How good the Certainty

> That Lever cannot pry -
> And Wedge cannot divide
> Conviction - That Granitic Base -
> Though none be on our side -
>
> Suffice Us - for a Crowd -
> Ourself - and Rectitude -
> And that Assembly - not far off
> From furthest Spirit - God
> (Fr740)

As Dickinson writes to Higginson, "There is always one thing to be grateful for—that one is one's self & not somebody else" (L405n).[7] The poem counts as her "culminating expression of self-confidence and self-reliance as an intellectual female" (Leder and Abbott 50–51). Is the speaker so far from professing humble, tough faith in experience that she veers all the way toward the other pole of transatlantic Romanticism, the tender headiness of faith in intuition, conscience, spirit, "soul-competence," or egotistical sublimity?[8] No, it is a subject/object balance.[9] Whether or not the speaker can still sing the old sweet song of empiricism, Dickinson's spirit of experiment prevails on her plane of existence in this poem. Despite the apparent autonomy of self-projection here, the diction of *tumult, extremity, lever, wedge,* and *base* features sense-relation, as though these three stanzas, after all, stay grounded in externality.

To be sure, the thesis statement of the poem—namely, "On a Columnar Self - / How ample to rely / In Tumult - or Extremity - " —constitutes Dickinson's incandescent version of Kant's categorical imperative. These three lines might well qualify as her "German" perspective on the larger Romantic movement for which Kant deserves considerable credit as forerunner. Although philosophical approaches to Dickinson's poetry have hitherto remained rare, Frederick L. Morey argues from Zeitgeist that she echoes Kant from time to time.[10] Dickinson's language in "On a Columnar Self - " can certainly seem as self-contained, and perhaps even as self-satisfied, as Kant's can sound. Nevertheless, to add the concept of influence to that of Zeitgeist, the British as well as American accent of Dickinson's empirical voice invites homegrown philosophical interpretation of her texts, this lyric included. If the "Columnar Self - " seems psychologically withdrawn, philosophically subjective, or morally upright, then this self also becomes independent, unselfconscious, modest, and engaged (one may refer to this self, and to the speaker of the poem, as "she," though each is as human, in every respect, as the poet is androgynous).

The persona of the poem holds within her English-speaking precincts not Kant's communion with pure reason alone so much as Shelley's "unremitting interchange / With the clear universe of things around" ("Mont Blanc" [1817], line 141–42). Indeed, to conflate the concepts of Emerson, Coleridge, Locke, and perhaps even Darwin, "the opposing strengths of me and not-me" in "On a Columnar Self - " express Dickinson's undertone of thought/thing dynamic, and hence her intimation of the sense-based means of epistemology and of the sense-driven method of science (see the discussion in Juhasz "Tea" 149).

For Sewall, the reality principle of "On a Columnar Self - " concerns the transcendent otherness of God. The poem, Sewall argues, "comes close to reconciling these two disparate phases of [Dickinson's] being: her love of the God of her fathers and her belief in herself" (Sewall *Life* 2:390). The strangely Puritan-polytheistic God of the poem proves welcome as one of its palpable obscurities. Its concluding quatrain melds monotheism and a multitudinous divine selfhood equally real and mysterious. On the other hand, as Suzanne Juhasz observes, "The point of the poem is the self relies upon itself, not God," who, whether Puritan or polytheistic, or somehow both, "becomes secondary to where power resides" (Juhasz "Reading" 220–21). This psychological point does not necessarily come at the expense of the poet's attractive paradox of Puritan polytheism, for such religious oxymoron can represent healthy cultural development,[11] but, given her subjectivity-turned-objectivity here, there are more things in the heaven and earth of the lyric than theology. Equal to the "solitary beliefs" of the "Columnar Self - " are "forces external to it" (Juhasz "Tea" 148), and these appear more philosophical than religious. Dickinson's balance of me and not-me lies between this speaker's psychological and religious combination of internal with external, anchoring the dynamic of these lines in outright empiricism.

Surprisingly, in light of his heritage of intuition-emphasizing German idealism, Søren Kierkegaard's Danish philosophy of Christian existentialism provides an instructive analogy to Dickinson's experience-based, other-directed self-reliance, so notably expressed in "On a Columnar Self - ." Kierkegaard's dialogue with the dialectics of Hegel takes a step away from adherence-to-idealism, as though moving toward the *grounded* intuition of Dickinson's poem. In vibration with its empirical voice and against Hegel, Kierkegaard writes that "a life-view born of experience is more than a totality or sum of principle maintained in its abstract indeterminacy. It is more than experience, which as such is always atomistic. It is in fact the transubstantiation of experience; *it is an unshakable security in oneself won from all experience*."[12] These last

11 words appear to distill Dickinson's 52, in which "Conviction"—
"Wedge cannot divide it"—deepens over time, almost because time
passes. The solipsism of Hegel's synthesis, as Kierkegaard would have
understood it, exceeds even the degree of self-consciousness in "On a
Columnar Self - ." With thoroughgoing idealism, and with no simple
idea, no idea of sensation, anywhere in sight, Hegel's "spirit knowing itself as spirit," his "Speculative Idea of Absolute Knowledge,"
devalues the role of the world in human development (Hegel qtd. in
Leib 38). As Kierkegaard might have recognized, the world acquires
an active role during the course of this initially hermetic lyric. As her
"Columnar Self - " sings from stanza to stanza, Dickinson progresses
from certainty and undividable conviction to open assimilation of, and
entire absorption by, "far off" but not vertical being.

Dickinson's subject/object oscillation here, like Kierkegaard's
spiritual/natural quest, negotiates the Scylla of Hegel-like "spirit
knowing itself as spirit" and the Charybdis of materialism. Close to
her thinking, though, is Emerson's, according to which, "[l]ife is not
dialectics" ("Experience" qtd. in Murphy 1:948). "In these times,"
Emerson adds, "we have had enough of the futility of criticism and
thought. Our young people have thought and written much on labor
and reform, and for all that they have written, neither the world nor
themselves have got on a step" ("Experience" qtd. in Murphy 1:948).
The impersonality and predictability of Marx's dialectical materialism, as Kierkegaard would have known, appears too pat to explain (an
overly systemic Marxist approach would tend only to explain away)
Dickinson's intimate wildness.[13] *Dialectics* emerges from Kierkegaard's
quarrel with Hegel as too technical a term to apply to Dickinson (or,
for that matter, to any other literary talent worth his or her salt). She,
for her aesthetic part, scarcely signs on to read even Kierkegaard, as
though she were some sort of philosophy major, for, like Kierkegaard
and like Emerson, she would have rejected the synthesis-driving relentlessness and the antiliterary rigidity of inflexible terminology. That
said—thanks in part to the near influence of Wesley and Wadsworth
and their combination of orthodoxy with empiricism—the speaker
of such an otherwise fully self-conscious poem as "On a Columnar
Self - " carries on a rich conversation between "spirit knowing itself
as spirit" and "far off"—read: natural/horizontal—being. This partly
religious and poetically subtle, yet by no means entirely unphilosophi-
cal lyric, awards a leading role to the world in Dickinson's drama of
human development, or, rather, in her paradoxical self-dramatization
of that development, with her speaker as everyman and as everywoman alike.

Finally, just as "On a Columnar Self - " progresses from the personally perpendicular to the decidedly objective, so the poem begins to function as Dickinson's signature lyric of reader liberation. On a sociological level, the speaker telescopes women's history from Wollstonecraft to the present. This persona travels at light-speed from "feminist" to "female" to "free" (no "feminine" here; compare Showalter). "On a Columnar Self - " realizes the possibility that Locke, perhaps even more than Wesley, calls for.[14] Locke advocates political equality for women, whereas Wesley merely lets them preach.[15] On the philosophical and scientific note sounded throughout this book, though, the "Columnar Self - " goes beyond sociological self-esteem and psychological self-reliance to "make excursions into the incomprehensible Inane" as quite the rational empiricist. Thus her more dual than dueling purpose of suspending subject and object releases both into freedom. Dickinson's career-spanning alternation from one perspective to the other jibes with the play of the mind and sanctions the both/and logic of the very best art of knowledge and of paradox alike.

* * *

The age of Darwin could scarcely reconcile the fact of suffering with belief in God as just and powerful, if not loving. For example, since natural selection fragmented the theological world-picture of Emily Dickinson, she wrote theodicy (from *theo-dice*, God plus justice) only in fragments or as fragmentary, such truncation sufficing for her spiritual pilgrimage in the latter day. If she did not exactly pursue the questioning/answering dialectic of this most skeptical sub-category of traditional religious thought, she at least master-minded the interrogative mood of her quarrel with God. She gravitated toward "obstinate questionings" not only of "sense and outward things" but also of God Himself (compare Wordsworth, "Ode: Intimations of Immortality" [1802–1804], lines 141–42). Just as Blake's miniature poetic version of theodicy consists entirely of such prying questions as "Did he who made the Lamb make thee?" ("The Tyger" [1794], line 20), so Dickinson's in-process poems of unfrozen-in-amber theodicy denote for the ongoing age of Darwin the inquisitive gambit of this well-tempered but go-ahead kind of interdisciplined imagination.[16]

To be sure, such a fellow-poet of Dickinson's as her contemporary Tennyson also grappled with the faith-challenge posed by the convergence of geology and evolutionary biology. Nevertheless, notwithstanding her high regard for the laureate's musical ear (Gravil "Emily"), Dickinson would undoubtedly have found complacent the all too systematically religious accounting for physical and moral evil in certain passages of *In Memoriam* (1850). For instance, where the opening lines address "Strong Son of God, immortal Love" and declare that somehow not for worse but for better "Thou madest Life in man and brute" (lines 1, 6), Tennyson responds, in effect, to Blake's cheeky query, doing so from the outset on willful grounds of willed orthodoxy. It is almost as though theodicy-after-Darwin would appear necessarily formulaic, pious, and closed-off, and perhaps even tossed-off, intellectually dishonest, and artistically unsubtle. Of course, authors long before Darwin and as otherwise various as the writer of the Book of Job (450 BCE?) and Milton in *Paradise Lost* (1674) wrought well their theologically well-worked-out but satisfyingly complex and imaginatively cogent explanations of suffering. Still, as her poetic strategy in the face of natural selection suggests, Dickinson left her theodicean's task deliberately uncompleted, making a virtue out of the necessity of excelling at the questioning form, as opposed to the answering content, of this literary as well as theological subgenre. Dickinson defined the problem of suffering not by seeking religious solutions in glib systems but, shades of Shakespeare's Cleopatra, by hurling open-ended and near-blasphemous interrogatives at the God not so much of orthodoxy, whether Calvinist or other, as of nature in the rawness of its violence. Thus leaning away from closure, she became the poetic experimenter par excellence, some of whose most tough-minded lyrics alternately embodied the only remaining possibility of, and toyed with the oddly liberating impossibility of, justifying the ways of God to humankind.

According to Patrick J. Keane, on whose recent study of Dickinson's reimagined theodicy this discussion aims to build, the signature poem of her perspective on "divine design and the problem of suffering" appears "less hopeful than many readers...would seem to prefer" (Keane *Emily* 30):

> Apparently with no surprise -
> To any happy Flower
> The Frost beheads it at it's play -
> In accidental power -
> The blonde Assassin passes on -
> The Sun proceeds unmoved
> To measure off another Day
> For an Approving God -
> (Fr1668)

The poem resists "any facile conception of either a painless natural theology or a providential Design" (Keane *Emily* 130). "By the breath of
God," Job declares, "frost is given" (37:10); thus, if Dickinson thinks
of the luminously beautiful "blonde Assassin" as divine in origin, she
nonetheless takes a dim view of the frost-God as *pale* rider, *ash* blonde,
"an agent of the destruction of beauty" (Keane *Emily* 129, 140). The
speaker of the poem remains appalled that God would wish, or will,
such waste.[17] Whereas Jesus's theodicy interprets a grain of wheat in
the ground as a metaphor for earthly death that leads to heavenly fruit
(John 12:24), Dickinson's bid can find no such divine purpose in the
literal, natural death of "any happy Flower." "By making the symbolic
'victim' of violence floral rather than human" (Keane *Emily* 28), she
takes a cosmic view. She rejected such human-centered theodicy as
that people can suffer (a) when they abuse the divine gift of free will or
(b) as part of God's omelet-creating but egg-breaking plan of ultimate
redemption. The 53 pages given over to this 36-word lyric constitute
Keane's thick description of how Dickinson attempts in good faith,
yet fails at, and then disdains, theodicy full blown.

"Apparently with no surprise - " sarcastically gives up on God and triumphantly spurns Him without either denying that He existed, at least
in the past, or waiving the right to speak with Him again. Keane's close
reading brings Dickinson's word *accidental* from the root-theological
connotation of fortunate fall, *ad-cadere*, to fall, to the fast-developing
nineteenth-century meaning of randomness, chance (Keane *Emily*
121). One thinks of Emerson's near-dismissal of his son Waldo's death
as "caducous" ("Experience" [1844]) and of the "Crass Casualty" in
Hardy's "Hap" (1866; line 11). Dickinson's poetry would appear to
include more of Blake's "dull round" or of Stevens's "malady of the
quotidian" than of any coherent plan, "genuine dialectical change," or
"Kantian or Darwinian purposiveness without purpose" (Keane *Emily*
140). One may add Keane's sharp detail to Richard Gravil's argument
(*Dialogues*) that Dickinson's relation to her high- to late-Romantic
precursors and contemporaries remains more dialogical than subversive (for Dickinson's relation to these Romantics as more subversive
than dialogical, see Diehl *Dickinson*; Homans).

With further regard to how Dickinson's unrealized desire to
reach the elusive goal of theodicy relates to her position on the
arc from Romantic to Modern, she keens a Romantic-era song of
suffering perhaps not as secularized as, but even grimmer than,
Wordsworth's theodicy. Of course, Dickinson twice alluded (L315,
L394) to Wordsworth's "Elegiac Stanzas" (1807), and she acquired
her own Wordsworth-like "poetic realization of the inevitability

and universality of loss and suffering mingled with hope" (Keane *Emily* 190). Still, the stubbornness of her questioning, as distinct from any pre-Darwin theodicean's insouciant solution, marks her late Romanticism as less hopeful, more tragic, than Wordsworth's darkest songs of suffering.[18] Darwin, for his part, could not share the benign theism of Wordsworth's *Excursion* (1814), in which "darts of anguish" "*fix* not" in the Wanderer's flesh (*The Excursion* 4:12–22; Wordsworth's emphasis; see Keane *Emily* 183–90).[19] Neither could Dickinson, for, in "There's a certain Slant of light - ," "Heavenly Hurt" wounds her persona deeply, permanently:

> We can find no scar,
> But internal difference -
> Where the Meanings, are -
>   (Fr320, lines 5–8)

Dickinson parted company, in effect, with the Wanderer's bland stoicism, doing so, paradoxically, on somewhat Calvinist grounds.

Although the "Romantic crisis" is "the dichotomy between the world of scientific laws—cold, indifferent to human values—and man's inner world" (Milosz 94), Dickinson's perspective on suffering as a variety of religious experience craves at least a rearguard "defense of divine holiness and justice in respect to the existence of evil" (see the definition of *theodicy* in the *OED*). At the same time that Dickinson sings "the dark under-song of Romanticism," laments "the cleavage between the human and the natural" (Keane *Emily* 125), the sundering of the human and the divine makes her Romanticism three-dimensional. Her poetic effort to complete theodicy for her time corresponds to various works by Wordsworth, Emerson et al., but can contain more theological rigor than their only theodicy-*like* substitution of hope-without-an-object for God (compare Coleridge, "Work without Hope" [1825], line 14). Whereas Wordsworth huffs and puffs, "I must think, do all I can," that "there was pleasure" in the flower ("Lines Written in Early Spring" [1798], lines 11–12), Dickinson grows sure, witness her "Apparently with no surprise - ," that, *pace* Wordsworth, *not* "every flower / Enjoys the air it breathes" ("Early Spring," lines 19–20). Unlike Wordsworth's "poetic faith" (Coleridge's phrase), which for all Wordsworth's pre-*Excursion* genius could be complacent in its less theistic than pantheistic moorings, Dickinson's could wonder in a traditional vein of theological questioning whether this was the best of all possible created worlds, the worst of all possible godless universes, or, somehow, both.

In one sense, Dickinson agreed with Thomas Jefferson's characterization of the early-nineteenth-century God of Calvinism as nothing more than "a daemon of malignant spirit" (qtd. in Charles Taylor 804n59). In this sense, she joined Shelley's attack on this God (see *Queen Mab* [1813]). As she confronted her tormentor God, she became less thankful or inspired, and more "dismayed or denunciatory" (Keane *Emily* 40). On the other hand, she scarcely embraced Jefferson's conclusion that "it would be more pardonable to believe in no God at all" than to acknowledge the existence of the malignant daemon (qtd. in Charles Taylor 804n59). The discarded, dead, or even deadening God who haunts Dickinson's art is the inscrutable Calvinist Deity whom she "alternately believed in, questioned, quarreled with, rebelled against, caricatured, even condemned, but never ceased to engage" (Keane *Emily* 36). If Dickinson could not quite credit this God, she nonetheless brought her case before Him, and appealed to His nobler nature. Equally like Job, she also brought her case against Him:

> "Heavenly Father" - take to thee
> The supreme iniquity
> Fashioned by thy candid Hand
> In a moment contraband -
> Though to trust us - seem to us
> More respectful - "We are Dust" -
> We apologize to thee
> For thine own Duplicity -
>
> (Fr1500)

Such bold, if not wickedly irreverent, poems as "'Heavenly Father' - take to thee" (the deflating quotation marks here are heavily ironic) turn back on God His prejudgment of human beings as guilt-ridden dust (Gen. 3:19), worms (Job 25:2–6), and embodiments of sin, of depravity (Exod. 20:5).[20]

Dickinson's reply to Paul's rhetorical question "If God be for us, who can be against us?" (Rom. 8:31) is saucy, bitter: "but when he is against us, other allies are useless—" (L746).[21] According to Paul's theodicy, "the whole creation" has been groaning "until now" (Rom. 8:22); such divine delivery from suffering, however, failed to assuage Dickinson. Keane sums up flatly: "Dickinson's omnipresent deity is personal, though more likely to be an antagonist than a friend, exercising his power unpredictably and often cruelly" (*Emily* 74). Dickinson's Calvinist God was more inscrutable than personal. As far as Dickinson was concerned, except perhaps in some poems, where her deity appears more Arminian, more free will-granting, loving, and joy-inspiring, than Calvinist—that is, predestinarian, forbidding, and dour—and hence more friendly than antagonistic, God stays so far from solving suffering as to constitute the problem (compare Brantley *Experience* 19–20, 162–63, 197–98).

Dickinson's sympathetic portrait of Jesus as fellow-sufferer came as close to finished theodicy as she ever got, but, from her late-Romantic vantage point, she could depict no smug extreme of theological closure, perhaps even in her Christological reflection. "To be human," she writes, "is more than to be divine, for when Christ was divine, he was uncontented till he had been human" (L519). Thus she admits that Jesus existed "before Abraham was" (John 5:58), but she honors his flesh and blood, and, since her Jesus is no longer God, his suffering complicates, renders futile, the religious approach to the problem. Dickinson's Jesus echoes Schopenhauer's, also the emblem of suffering humanity, and parallels Nietzsche's crucified Christ (this Christ, Nietzsche says, is the only true Christian [compare Keane *Emily* 93]). Dickinson reasons that the exclusively human Jesus's agony speaks well for him, for, as the spiritual song has it,

> Nobody knows the trouble I've seen,
>   Nobody knows but Jesus,

and his *passion*, from *pateo, patēre*, to endure, has appealed to the suffering ages. In Dickinson's view, however, Jesus's sorrow yielded no satisfying solution to the theodicean's dilemma, for "the resurrection was to Dickinson testimony of the humanity of Jesus," and "Christ's suffering and death registered," with her, "more powerfully than the resurrection" (Keane *Emily* 93).[22] As the poet proclaims, in just 11 of her breakthrough words,

> 'Twas Christ's own personal Expanse
> That bore him from the Tomb -
>   (Fr1573, lines 3–4; emphasis added)

—that is, Jesus is remembered not for his agency of God's salvation but because so courageously did he live in danger that he came out on the other side of it, as in *ex-perior*, to go through danger. Thus, the extravagant claim of Jesus as God, and the modest concept of him as God's surrogate, alike flunk the scientific test of Dickinson the empirical poet, for she "raises a possibility never dreamed of" before (Keane *Emily* 36–37) even by liberal theologian Henry Ward

Beecher—namely, that "Darwin had thrown 'the Redeemer' away" (Dickinson's words that bear repeating in this chapter [L750]).

For Darwin and Dickinson alike, the game of cat and mouse imaged truth, however bald and cold and with whatever character, whether natural or divine. Consider Darwin's 1860 letter to his friend and fellow-scientist Asa Gray, for whom evolutionary biology and intelligent design stayed somehow commensurate:

> I had no intention [Darwin discloses] of writing atheistically. But I own that I cannot see as plainly as others do, and as I should wish to do, evidence of design and beneficence on all sides of us. There seems to me too much misery in the world. I cannot persuade myself that a beneficent and omnipotent God would have designedly created the Ichneumonidae [assassination wasps] with the express intention of their [larva] feeding within the living bodies of Caterpillars, or that a cat should play with mice. (Darwin 2:105)[23]

For her part in this mid-nineteenth-century dialogue between science and religion, the Huxley/Wilberforce shades of which have come down to cloud this very day, Dickinson also signaled her acknowledgment of, and horror at, cat-and-mouse cruelty, what Tennyson called "Nature, red in tooth and claw / With ravine" (*In Memoriam* 15:15–16).

> The cat [Dickinson writes] reprieves the mouse
> She eases from her teeth
> Just long enough for Hope to teaze -
> Then mashes it to death -
> (Fr485, lines 5–8)

Like scientist, like poet, the cat-and-mouse, state-of-the-art-biological, God-of-Calvin-dominated model of existence demanded the theodicean's inquiry.[24] As Keane observes of Dickinson's stance, she, like Ivan Karamazov, "was no atheist but a challenger who, in her own oblique way, never ceased asking the same questions: Why does evil strike so meaninglessly? Why do the innocent suffer? How can a purportedly omnipotent and loving God approve of such an apparently random, brutally violent process?" (*Emily* 72). Just as no "divine resolution," in the otherwise devout Dostoyevsky's judgment, can justify "the tears of a single tortured child" (Keane *Emily* 72), so answers can, and should, elude the faith-attracted, yet always thinking, Dickinson's persistent interrogations.

Suffering is well and simply clarified as the fallout of natural selection, and therefore need not represent a mystery to be explored in relation to God's ways with, or tender mercies toward, humankind. The empirical voice within Dickinson's protean range of personae, however, plumbs a residual form of theodicy, a term coined by Leibniz, in 1710, to label the time-honored, difficult fascination of suffering/faith settlement. Just as Darwin yearned for such understanding, so Dickinson struggled toward it, staying as far as possible from any slick-but-superficial outcome of a Dr. Pangloss, and abjuring the unearned result of any easy victory.[25] Far from throwing up her hands and taking refuge in agnosticism as Darwin did, Dickinson neither let God off the hook nor let Him up off the mat, for with "Wrestling Jacob," to evoke here one of Charles Wesley's most highly regarded hymns (see Brantley "Charles"), she vowed, "I will not let thee go except thou bless me" (Gen. 32:26).[26] Her quarrel with God was based on her acceptance of Darwin's science but also paralleled Melville's quarrel (see Thompson; T. Walter Herbert, Jr.) and harked back to Job's in Job 14, 19. Of course, her impassioned as well as intelligent stab at the all but God-denying problem of physical and moral evil arose from the "upheaval" of her near-philosophical as well as scientifically grounded "thought" (compare Nussbaum). Still, her theodicean's initiative dwelled more in the theological realm than on the cusp of evolutionary biology. Even her scientific investigation found more faith in honest doubt than in half the creeds.

Dickinson's challenge of God never received an answer, either directly, in the form of theophany (as in Job 29–31), or indirectly through the vatic, self-apotheosizing voice of Romanticism: contrast the alternating of divine authority in *Paradise Lost* to Milton's own godlike utterance throughout his sometimes proto-Romantic epic. Thus, although Dickinson's inability to finish theodicy, her Bartleby-like preference not to do so, bears religious overtones, even her context of the Book of Job can appear scarcely comedic, however large a role the Bible plays in the origin of comedy. Even the religious quality of her theodicean's impulse is tragic enough to imply a godless universe. Although her pessimism can anticipate Yeats's "Gaiety" that "transfigures all that dread," all that gloom (compare "Lapis Lazuli" [1936], line 7), she resisted any view that "poetic faith" can be advantageously untroubled. By analogy, by what Keane calls "mutual illumination" (3) as well as through direct influence from the works of others to hers, and vice versa, the theodicy-like aspect of her poetry describes a near-tragic arc of Anglo-American Romanticism.

Because Darwin's science called Dickinson's religious frame of reference into doubt, her theodicean's imperative can feel rather less full-throated than that of the equally brainy, yet less Darwin-haunted, Hopkins (see the latter's *Wreck of the Deutschland* [1875] and his "terrible sonnets"—that is, his divine-terror-filled, divine-terror-inducing poetic sequence [1885–1889]). Dickinson's suffering-themed poetry of emotionally cerebral God-talk, however, looks forward. It yet grabs those for whom shoring fragments against their ruin remains their first-aid means of survival. "Better an ignis fatuus," she tells them, "Than no illume at all - " (Fr1581, lines 8–9), but, she would also say, better still to brave the bald, cold truth that holds (compare Fr341, line 9; for the immediate nineteenth-century recognition of the materialism and atheism inherent in evolutionary biology, see Kirkby "'[W]e thought'" 13–17).

It is not necessarily that Dickinson's philosophical and scientific perspective on theodicy, and hence her reservations about this venerable form of theological disquisition, to the point of abandoning it, means that she is not, after all, in any central sense a religious poet. For her, on the contrary, "Faith is *Doubt*" (L912; Dickinson's emphasis), and, in an accordingly counterintuitive manner, the constructive skepticism of her controversy with God kept Him as hearer of something like her prayer.[27] Would she have agreed with Harold Bloom's harsh stricture against anyone who indulges in theodicy (Bloom regards theodicy here as excessively, hubristically, intellectualized luxury)?

> Theodicy [Bloom writes] is a mug's [a seemingly sophisticated but actually naïve or easily deceived person's] game: no humane individual could bear to justify God's ways to man. Nazi death camps, schizophrenia, cancer do not yield to ideologues who assert they speak for God. In old age, I rebel against moral idiocy. Job, rejecting his horrible comforters, speaks to and for me until the Voice out of the Whirlwind ("storm" in the Hebrew) silences him in shocked awe at the audacity of the Creation; after that I go back to his superbly laconic wife: "Curse God and die." (*Shadow* 199–200)

That is to place anyone immersed in the theodicean's pursuit, fascinated by the theodicean's heritage, from Habakkuk, Jeremiah, and Job, through Jesus and Paul, to Milton, Blake, Coleridge, and Tennyson, under a rather dark cloud of suspicion.[28] Dickinson, however, would have agreed with Bloom to some extent. She, too, would have denounced self-satisfied justification of God's ways. No more than Bloom, however, would she ever, even for a moment, have found such complacency in this Job- and Milton-proud tradition at its skill-fully aesthetic best.

Perhaps Dickinson's prayer, as unanswered, entailed her hope for the unforced force of a better dialogue in heaven, where never is heard the command to stop in the name of the law. Perhaps her "Flood subject" of "Immortality" (L319) was not so much about pie in the sky as about her coming day in God's court of justice, where she would be less a criminal in the dock than a plaintiff expecting an award of heavy damages. "Then call, and I will answer; or let me speak, and do thou reply to me," Job pleads, as he imagines talking to God in an afterlife (Job 13:22). The result of such an exchange, for Dickinson, would be "Some new Equation, given - " by God (Fr403, line 11) to satisfy "Man that is born of a woman" (Job 14:1)—that is, everyone—with why the unjust and the just alike must endure affliction on this earth. Who knows, for no traveler has ever returned from that bourn, but her hope of explanation and of judgment in favor of her and of her select society of fellow-petitioners might, just might, have proved adequate to keep this failed theodicean at her present time a vindicated one in prospect.

Did Dickinson's desire for conversation with God grow from Royal Society as well as from Methodist Society roots? Did the "double consciousness" that led Darwin to make an "ideal argument held in his own mind" (Barrett 90) parallel Dickinson's model of produc-tive, philosophical, and scientific as well as religious, dialogue? As Gillian Beer writes, "Darwin's reading is always a process of *conver-sation*, marked by ripostes scribbled on the page as well as rumina-tive notes recorded alongside. And beyond that, he engages in active silent *dialogue* in which the reader slides into the place of the writer and yet presses back into his or her own person too" (180; emphasis added). Thus, especially for Dickinson the theodicean, the sight of the face is sufficient, yet not necessary, for communion. Her verbal, inscribed masks do not belie, deny, or militate against, but, rather, enact engagement with, verbal, printed personae, of which the one in *On the Origin of Species* (1859) is prominent indeed. The combination of her speakers with such others represents a transcultural moment of her select society of partners in philosophical and scientific (as well as religious) dialogue about the problem of suffering (as about almost any other topic of conversation one can conceive of).

*   *   *

To recapitulate part I, at some length, although Dickinson's personae can range from Jesus-loving hopers through no-hopers to near-nihilists, many breathe philosophy and project science. These can sound watchful rather than self-contained, reflective instead of self-satisfied, reliable different from predictable, inductive athwart deductive, and open-minded not abstract. They may search for the historical Jesus as "the light," but they "see the light" shed by sense perception on what to think and on how to live. To borrow a phrase from Wordsworth, in a not-so-different context, and to apply it to Dickinson's personae in this framework, their "master light" of all their seeing is rational empiricism (compare "Ode: Intimations of Immortality," line 154). Imagination, reason in conjunction with the senses, underlies her art of knowledge.

To be sure, as Patrick J. Keane argues in another book of his (comparing Wordsworth and Emerson), Wordsworth's "master light of all our seeing" can equate to the "intuitive reason" that Kant construed as the distinguishing faculty of mind. Kant, after all, buzzed in English-speaking circles of art, from the dawn of the nineteenth century to the fin de siècle and after. Wordsworth's boon companion Coleridge and University of Vermont president James Marsh imported German idealism into their respective countries as though with a long-run view to the idealistic pragmatism of John Dewey.[29] Nevertheless, the signature metaphor of Wordsworth's epistemology, "the master light," can move away from "intuitive reason," and back onto the experiential common ground of the British Enlightenment, in the first instance, and Anglo-American "sense," English-language seeing, in the next. His "master light" derives not as much from his "shadowy recollections" as from his "first affections" ("Ode," lines 150–51). Does his "master light," as sense-based reason, even signal continuity between Locke the progenitor of the British Enlightenment and such late-Romantic duumvirates of Anglo-American literature as Carlyle and Emerson (compare Brantley *Coordinates*) and as Tennyson and Emerson (compare Brantley *Anglo-American*)?[30] If so, then, for reasons of British more than German philosophy, Dickinson absorbs into her American identity Emerson's "tide of being, which floats us into the secret of nature," until "the advancing soul has built and forged for itself a new condition, and the question and the answer are one" ("The Over-soul" [1841] qtd. in Murphy 1:918). The en*light*ened Romanticism of England and the United States arced to her latter-day but not belated version of faith in experience and sufficed for her knowing much.

Dickinson enters into, possesses, reinvigorates, and imparts her naturalized, naturalizing British heritage of philosophy. Whenever she gives priority to this homegrown as well as cross-pond empiricism, she seeks equilibrium between thick substance and broad appeal. By teaching Americans, in particular, not to sell their birthright of tough mind, she makes pilgrims of experiment. Apart from her "Flood subject" of "Immortality" (does she paradoxically find even immortality at hand, on earth, where "Paradise is of the option" [L319]?), she sojourns in Wordsworth's

> world
> Of all of us,—the place where in the end
> We find our happiness, or not at all!
> (*The Prelude* [1850] 11:140–42)

When she acknowledges that "Philosophy, dont know," whether or not "[a] Species stands beyond - ," she not-so-simply means that philosophy is not yet, but someday might be, certain that heaven is as real as, say, evolutionary biology (Fr373, lines 2, 6). Above all, though, these lines signify that philosophy should avoid the besetting sin of knowingness. Empirical epistemology can do no better than "see through a glass, darkly," an afterlife like the life Dickinson knows she loves in the here and now, whatever glibness she hears may be true or untrue of some putative world elsewhere (compare I Cor. 13:12).

Dickinson the empiricist remains sure of only one aspect of her flood subject. "Earth is Heaven - / Whether Heaven is Heaven or not" (Fr1435, lines 1–2). Although her personae hunger for that world elsewhere, they sustain wonder at this world. They sharpen and add to what they know by interrogating how they know it, as Wordsworth does, through constructively skeptical, "obstinate questionings / Of sense and outward things." To the extent that the poet calls even sense into question, she allows for an afterlife, though unseen. Because she mainly questions by means of sense, however, she doubts that she ever will "stand beyond" this life. Dickinson the empiricist does not cling to the self-centered goal of eternal life (one thinks here of those colossally egomaniacal pyramids of the pharaohs) but progresses on earth, without dubious "intimations of immortality."

In the spirit of Matthew Arnold's willingness to change his mind on occasion, the Dickinson phase of this series on Romantic Anglo-America has, in this second installment of it (compare Brantley *Experience*), devoted separate analysis to her search for knowledge through sense perception. From the series' usual combination of empirical philosophy and evangelical faith, part I of this volume has stepped back, to focus on her empirical milieu, temperament, and expression. Her faith in experience so religiously follows the rational highroad of her senses into a clearing of secular epiphanies that her empirical voice deserves as reverent a hearing as her new-evangelical song. She leans away from the Calvinist, Puritan, predestinarian, and antiexperience thesis of Anglo-American evangelism, and toward its Arminian, Wesleyan, free will, and pro-experience antithesis, for even Presbyterian Wadsworth tilts like this. Her experience of faith as indicated by her hermeneutic circle—"understand in order to believe; believe in order to understand" (Ricoeur 27)—is a disciplined, muted assessment of Jesus, and a sense-tested, clear-eyed measurement of God. Insofar as her rational empiricism overrules the nonrational witness that she intermittently but memorably registers, Locke's reasonable Christianity wins out during the long years of her thought.[31] The philosophical and scientific manifestation of her poetic genius harks back, across time and the Atlantic, to renew Locke's temporal kind of externalized seeing as a more than adequate substitute for the inward light of intuition and of the soul. If the sense-based means of epistemology, the sense-driven method of science, can serve the spiritual sense on the common ground of experience, and if Dickinson's empirical voice can lend credibility to the sometime summons of her faith, then that voice can also terminate that call, replace that art of belief.

Dickinson generates mystery from, finds joy in, her evangelical empiricism (compare the history of joy [Potkay]). She recommends observation and reflection as the bifold means to "all / Ye know on earth" and, even more forcefully, "all ye need to know" (compare Keats, "Ode on a Grecian Urn" [1819], lines 49–50). Besides adding a religious dimension *to* empiricism, as though suggesting that faith in "the world / Of all of us" analogizes to, overlaps with, strengthens, and blends with faith in a world to come, her poems can feel evangelical *about* empiricism. For instance, her unattenuated awe of Locke-inspired scientific method entails her bipartite, near-explicit imperative, Trust in Experiment! Test Religion! Thus, if her spiritual sense aspires to otherworldly faith, it does so guardedly. If her sense-based reason qualifies as empirical procedure or even as scientific method, it does so rigorously, with expectation of result. Finally, if this dynamic of her creativity coexists with the hymn-form and -content of her nostalgia for, and reenactment of, evangelical life, her empirical voice sings solo. The dominant sound of her art proves worthy of an audition by itself, and not necessarily in two-part harmony with her new-evangelical song.

Since Dickinson's evangelical empiricism can yield imagination, perhaps more than the other way round, her poetic incarnation of truth reconstitutes simple ideas and ideas of sensation, and also not unlike

Locke's philosophy, her art can make way for ideals. Precisely because of her touching capacity for childlike belief, guileless enchantment, she can trace her pedigree of cerebral engagement to a no-nonsense, flexible tradition that her words can incarnate, can give back. Her empirical voice thus becomes as important to historical, interdisciplinary criticism of her works as her religious concerns have been hitherto. This poet regards grounding in the senses as the most indigenous, appropriate, and authoritative corrective of any of the most subjective, intuitive, or fanatical extremes to be found among even her otherwise most cherished traditions of faith. To add literary history to the history of ideas, her late-Romantic hope boards the ark back and forth across the Atlantic to the British Enlightenment and its liberating standard of imagining as well as of knowing all things. Accordingly, although she can espouse tender-mindedness, her rational empiricists proceed from their wise and well-earned optimism to their anything but foolish disinclination to believe any longer in six impossible things before breakfast. Through the Locke-like aspect of Wesley's and of Wadsworth's experiences of faith, Dickinson's works describe the arc from *An Essay Concerning Human Understanding* to the almost scientific tough-mindedness of Anglo-American Romanticism, as distinct from its voice of idealism.

The late-Romantic imagination of Emily Dickinson draws on Locke's *Essay* as much by way of the "natural methodism" in Romantic Anglo-America as by means of the more empirically methodical than hard-shell Methodist ingredient of the transatlantic revival. No longer thinking of methodism as capitalized, one can redefine *natural methodism* not as a religious concept but as empiricism practiced with religious fervor. Dickinson derives from *les bonnes lettres* and from *les belles lettres* of England and the United States an empirical voice all the more distinctive for its evangelical inflection, even as that voice is also all the more satisfying for its Romantic-era modulation.

Sense-based reason and scientific method of a neoclassic as well as Romantic stripe kept the head of the Myth of Amherst on straight. Her avoidance of abstracted, self-administering excess meant that her rational empiricism shaded into passion and attachment. Like Wordsworth and company, and like Locke, Wesley, Wadsworth, Darwin et al., she schooled her mind in ideas of sensation and developed knowledge and definitions based on keen, sophisticated observation. Far from positioning the mind elsewhere, her empirical imaginings thus realized scientific findings.

Through the fundamentals of the Industrial Revolution, the saga of geology, the arcana of astronomy, the basics of physic, and the shock of Darwin's science, in particular, Dickinson nurtured joyful wisdom. She understood that vitality can be economic, that change must be as temporal and spatial as moral and spiritual, that cosmic sublimity whispers oblivion (but what a way to go), that hope for well-being can survive well-founded, that struggle of species reinforces "the one Life within us and abroad" (compare Coleridge, "The Aeolian Harp" [1796], line 26). Whether at a reach "farther than the Stars" or on the "dull round" of the celestial mill, or whether paradoxically embracing both stances toward astronomy at once, the living, breathing truths of empiricism, on the one hand, and its bald, cold truth, on the other, all carried over to the poet.[32] From the philosophical and scientific as well as religious and literary perspective of Anglo-America, and hence with the exalted humility and imaginative verve of empiricism and of evolutionary biology alike, Emily Dickinson beheld the world steady and whole, and what mystery yet pervades the deep well of her truth!

Dickinson might well have distilled the argument of this book something like this (her words): "Common Sense is almost as omniscient as God" (L922). This prose fragment, number 68 of 124, plays on the Scottish Common Sense School on father Edward's shelves but alludes, by way of Anglo-American lettres bonnes and belles, to Locke's primal senses. On the one hand, this signature aphorism of her proverbial mode boasts superhuman depth and breadth of reference. As Keats writes, in something of a cocky Cockney manner: "Knowledge enormous makes a God of me" (*Hyperion: A Fragment* [1817] 3:117). On the other hand, Dickinson's miniature prose manifesto of her poet's empirical voice implies that recognition and understanding emerge slowly but surely from the procedure of the laboratory. As Dickinson also writes, and also in prose (albeit poetically, metaphorically), "truth like Ancestors' Brocades can stand alone—" (L368), which says, inter alia, that whether or not love can match death, wisdom can grow sturdy on experience.

Like Wordsworth, Dickinson visualizes the "light that never was, on sea or land" (she twice alludes to these words of his) but "see[s] into the life of things" (she makes this predicate of his her own).[33] Her outward experience does not just balance but checks her inner life. The empirical tone of her letters and poems overrides their religious overtone. Dickinson the empiricist, as distinct from the legatee of her evangelical heritage, oscillates between exaltation of mind over matter, and the humility of matter over mind.[34] Thus her Anglo-American grounding explains the rich strangeness of her sense perception. Dickinson's philosophical and scientific underpinnings make her art broad and nuanced alike.

If the ideal, tender character of British and American Methodism and of America's First and Second Great Awakenings could cushion the soul and heart of the Myth of Amherst, then the tough, sensate element of this binational religious movement could also stiffen her mind. The thick substance of her imagination can traffic with a spiritual sense not merely analogous to the physical senses but conspicuously arrayed with them on the natural to spiritual continuum of experience. Dickinson's writings can vibrate with Locke's *Essay*, as this influential masterpiece of British empiricism remains undistorted, though retrospectively colored, by the sense-oriented component and the spiritual-witness emphasis of the transatlantic revival.

Dickinson's words can compare to "the subtler language" of the Romantics, as well as to the perhaps less subtle, yet no less telling, words of Locke, Wesley, Wadsworth, and Darwin (compare Wasserman *Subtler*). That is, belles lettres, too, upholds the integrity, and underwrites the efficacy, of sense-based reason and the scientific method alike. The "natural methodism" of Romantic Anglo-America, Wordsworth's "language of the sense," contributes the secular authority of the creative imagination to Wesley's sanction of empirical tradition, thereby clearing a field for Dickinson's "naturalized imagination," her confidence in experience as test of fidelity, to take root (compare "Tintern Abbey," line 108; recall Stillinger's phrase).

Of course, the need to distinguish between empiricism as an epistemological philosophy and simple keen observation as a poetic methodology can scarcely be greater than in the case of Emily Dickinson's modus operandi/vivendi. Still, since the words of Locke can bond with Anglo-American Romanticism, as well as bind to transatlantic revivalism, she can sing the senses electric without ever losing (say rather, scarcely ever losing) her status as a proper aesthete. Dickinson's empirical voice can call on "the better angels of our nature" to preserve our birthright of salutary realism.

To emphasize the words "Philosophy" and "Science" in the subtitle of this book—"Poetry" will occupy front and center in part II—here, conclusively, is how a more empirical than evangelical strain can run the gamut from Locke to Dickinson. Since Wesley's *Essay*-inspired expression of spiritual experience can leave room for natural experience to ascend in Wadsworth's British background, the experiential ground of philosophy and faith underlies Dickinson's transatlantic givens, too. Whether or not her poems, regularly included in her correspondence, influenced Wadsworth's sermons, which she read, his sermons can figure as the most immediate "preceptors" of her "independent study" in empiricism. Consistent with the twofold fact that Locke, like Wesley and Wadsworth, was widely known, and that Wesley and Wadsworth, like Locke, were philosophical, this intellectual and social as well as literary history casts empirical rationalism in the starring role of her philosophical drama, shedding its light on her experiential aesthetic. Thus, regardless of where England and the United States can stand philosophically now, late-seventeenth- to mid-nineteenth-century empiricism can register in her art in Amherst. Dickinson's practical philosophy, in turn, logically comes down to her sense of laboratory discovery, no less binationally sanctioned and, above all, Darwin-informed, or, to put it more generally and less historically, her outlook does not shade, but shades into, the truth of nurture over nature.

At the risk of too many intellectual and mid- to high-cultural contexts, then, yet in the hope of just enough, the first half of this book has sought to broaden out fully from Dickinson's Homestead. Although criticism has often favored local and biographical atmosphere (Wadsworth, too, breathes there), she radiates from her village to the globe, and from her present to the past and future. Thus, cultural poetics have sought to illuminate how her empirical leanings turned her inner philosopher into her inner scientist. An aesthetically alert as well as sociologically ramifying combination of empirical *method* with *Methodist* discipline (a pun on the binary opposition is earnestly hereby intended) affects her writing. A philosophically and scientifically up-to-date strain of belles lettres exerts an equal impact on her web-like connections with transatlantic authors. The arc from Locke's *Essay* to Wesley's and Wadsworth's prose to Anglo-American Romanticism to her empirical values hums with science and, serving to differentiate between her art of knowledge and her art of belief, promises to reintegrate these antipodes of her late-Romantic imagination. Perhaps Emily Dickinson's rich conversation can even pivot "the world" to which she sent her "letter" (Fr519, line 1).

The fox and the hedgehog, finally, can join forces. Foxlike, *Experience and Faith: The Late-Romantic Imagination of Emily Dickinson* ranged over British and American terrain; like a hedgehog, moreover, the book tried to home in, as well, on dialectics. Now, *Emily Dickinson's Rich Conversation: Poetry, Philosophy, Science* can skim the surface of the subject, yet can also burrow, perhaps deeper than its companion volume did before, into the empirical thesis. The sweep can remain, insofar as this book has to this point, at least, succeeded in locating the poet's concerns on the philosophical and literary as well as scientific curve from the eighteenth to the nineteenth century.[35] As though "the empirical/evangelical dialectic of Romantic Anglo-America" were too big an idea, were too totalizing, for critical specificity, however, this book has sought, above all, to modify the phrase by changing *dialectic* to *dialogue*, to *conversation*, or to *oscillation*. It has concentrated on empirical glosses that border on, yet do not strain to reconcile, evangelical contexts. It has not intended to reach irritably after system, program, project, or closure, yet has attempted to suggest that empiricism "wins out," however provisionally, in the exchange. Combining equal measures of dynamic and salutary realism with her fine mental chaos of contingent truths, Dickinson's breadth and depth of thought make her aesthetic minimalism into a major force to reckon with, a great name to conjure with, in this and for all seasons.

In sum, "Retrospection is Prospect's half - / Sometimes, almost more - " (Fr1014B, lines 7–8) can capture Dickinson's counterintuitive message of reminiscence that brings rebirth. Through a sometimes direct, yet more often indirect and rather complex, process of cultural osmosis, her "retrospective" imagination can renew her literary, philosophical, and scientific heritage. Thus, just as her oeuvre can reverberate from Amherst to London to Grasmere and back, so she can turn milieu into timelessness. Dickinson's empirical voice proves richer for the bitter-sweetness of its would-be-evangelical inflection and of its Romantic-era modulation alike. It remains for part II to overhear whether or not, and if so, how, that voice can still resound in her pre-Modern mode, her post-Modern intimations.

PART II

EXTENDING EXPERIENCE

CHAPTER 3

GAINING LOSS

"Even to write against something," including whenever "something" turns out to be one's very own position, "is to take one's bearings from it." As an example of this variation on Denis Donoghue's useful insight into creativity (see his *Third Voice* 18), the difference between Emily Dickinson's poetry of experience (recall part I) and the "post-experiential perspective" of her poems of "aftermath" (for thorough discussion of this canon-within-the-canon, see Pollak *Anxiety* 202ff.) is one of degree. Yes, "After great pain, a formal feeling comes" (Fr372, line 1) goes from trauma to feigned emotion, but does this line as well as the poem of which it serves as title also suggest the re-form-ation, the salutary disciplining, of the however-much-traumatized senses? Does the line hint of something positive not so much in hardwired as in deep-structured-by-life emotion, hence "a formal *feeling*," as distinct from merely going through the motions of emotion, hence a "*formal* feeling"? Some cockeyed optimist might, just might, catch here the whisper of pretraumatic feeling now refined or revised and extended as though happy days were here again, as though Post-Experience, personified, could somehow, as in paradoxically, renew The Promise of Experience Past.

To be sure, "After great pain, a formal feeling comes" can mean that the speaker grows numb. Nevertheless, these signature words of Dickinson's subcategory of postexperience can signify, too, that her suffering does not preclude, does inspire and empower, her taut but impassioned and explosive idiom of death-in-life come back to life, as in "A wounded deer leaps highest" (Fr181, line 1). The Dickinson of postexperience remains the poet of experience in that her language of aftermath is act outperforming deeds, as in whenever Thomas

Jefferson's words about equality outlive his slaveholding days. In Dickinson's outcries of seeming paralysis, yet real movement, little or nothing is ever quite all said or done, if only because her saying still lives, still breathes, as in "The smitten rock...gushes" or "The trampled steel...springs" (Fr181, lines 5–6). It is as though, as far as the Myth of Amherst is concerned, not anything is ever quite over and done with, and certainly not her life that defeats quietus, as when enlargement attends agony: "Power is only pain" (Fr312, line 10).

As counterintuitive as it all may sound, Dickinson's "post-experiential perspective" does not so much lull and suppress as preserve and spread out experience. For one thing, her "great pain" lasts. For another, though without fully reimagining her empirical voice of rich conversation about poetry, philosophy, and science, the Dickinson of aftermath cleanses the doors of her perception, and so equals Blake in refreshing the senses.[1] Unfreezing effort, restoring expectation, replenishing desire, and reopening dialogue with her selfhood, as well as with her others living or dead, this Dickinson, too, honors the ranks of the Romantics, who were distinguished for their "poetry of experience" (see Langbaum *Poetry*). Although Dickinson's "post-experiential perspective" scarcely anticipates the ebullience of a Theodore Roosevelt or of a Rotary Club president or of any other kind of a cheerleader, her poems of aftermath nonetheless struggle to salvage the troubled but resilient faith-in-experience that Anglo-American Romanticism and her art of knowledge alike so well profess. The Dickinson of postexperience especially rivals Keats—that is, she values process as "[her] own and man's chief good," and, short of foreclosing actual/ideal oscillation, regards any transcendental element of dialogical or dialectical explanation as a false lure (recall Stillinger on Keats).

The pessimism of Dickinson's aftermath not only prefigures posteverything post-Modernism but also balances with, and yields to, the perennial remnant of traditional optimism. Of course, this pessimism is prescient, for it forebodes the fin de siècle lassitude of Hardy's belated "gloom," foreknowing that "Modernism's...true name's Despair."[2] Still, this pessimism is also traditional, for it sharpens the Romantics' already-heightened foretaste of posttraumatic stress disorder.[3] The Dickinson of postexperience, without necessarily reliving the Romantics' heart leaps of immediate joy, harks back to, and intimates, Wordsworth's own postexperience-sounding "hope that can never die."[4] This Dickinson recounts the twofold experience of holding despair at bay and of keeping hope-against-hope, though not quite hope full blown, alive. Thus, to repeat her lines perhaps most worth repeating of all her lines, just as "Retrospection is Prospect's half - / Sometimes, almost more - " (Fr1014B, lines 7–8), so her late-Romantic imagination survives in, and survives, her pre-Modern mode, for especially her poems of aftermath can look backward on the arc from Romantic to Modern.[5] Two prose fragments and two letters can serve at the outset of this chapter to elaborate the thesis of part II—namely, that however contradictory it might seem, even Dickinson's "post-experiential perspective" does not so much spurn as detach itself from, and then test/(recapture?), the experiential vision of Romantic Anglo-America.

"Did we not find (gain) as we lost," Dickinson writes, "we should make but a threadbare exhibition after a few years."[6] This drollery suggests (a) that experience leaves us naked and delivers us to death and (b) that gain and loss nonetheless work together for good to those who still love life. "I 'have gained a loss,' or *by* the loss," writes Byron in a similar vein (Byron's emphasis).[7] Losing gain but gaining through loss, Dickinson's speakers of aftermath harbor scant illusion about, yet yearn for, return of gain, and their latter-day-Blake version of "More! More!" is the cry of "Man" and "Less than All cannot satisfy" ranks as experience more intense for being felt and uttered in postexperience (compare Blake, *There Is No Natural Religion* [b] [1788], Principle V).

A second prose gloss also interprets Dickinson's poems of aftermath as the coincidence, the serendipity, of loss and gain: "Tis a dangerous moment for anyone [Dickinson writes] when the meaning goes out of things and Life Stands straight—and punctual—and yet no content(s) (signal) come(s). Yet such moments are. If we survive them they expand us. If we do not, but that is Death, whose if is everlasting."[8] The first two sentences acknowledge the devastation of emptiness, and the second part of the fourth sentence suggests that each loss scares us to death. Thus experience is ineffectual, violent. The third sentence, however, speaks of hope-against-hope, and perhaps even of hope-after-hope, though not quite of hope itself (her "if" is big): "If we survive [dangerous moments] they expand us" parallels Nietzsche's "What does not kill us makes us stronger."[9] If survival "expand[s] us," if "the meaning of things" never entirely "goes out of things," then "post-experiential perspective" (is this phrase something of a misnomer, after all?) neither bids adieu to, nor curtails, but entails and heralds, experience. Although aftermath might seem closer to T. S. Eliot's "hollow men" than to Wordsworth's "Happy Warrior," "mighty Poets," the Dickinson of postexperience nonetheless renews her lease on life and on imagination alike.[10] Tipping the balance between gain and loss in favor of regression from the former to the latter, and of progression from the latter to the former, this

Dickinson takes a two-way street back to near-cancellation and forth to reconfirmation of experience.

"Emerging from an Abyss, and reentering it—that is Life, is it not, Dear?" asks Emily Dickinson of her "Sister Sue" (L1024). The pessimistic aspect of this rhetorical question compares closely with Shelley's version of aftermath, his tragic vision of modern love:

> When the lips have spoken,
> Loved accents are soon forgot.
> . . .
> From thy nest every rafter
> Will rot, and thine eagle home
> Leave thee naked to laughter,
> When leaves fall and cold winds come.[11]

Relentless in their harsh detail, these lines match Emerson's for postexperiential determinism. "Every roof," Emerson writes, "is agreeable to the eye, until it is lifted; then we find tragedy and moaning women, and hard-eyed husbands, and deluges of lethe, and the men ask, 'What's the news?' as if the old were so bad" ("Experience" [1844], in Murphy, ed., 1:947). Emerson adds, "Our relations to each other are oblique and casual" (Murphy, ed., 1:947). Emerson concludes that "the plaint of tragedy which murmurs" from the failed search "in regard to persons, to friendship and love" derives from the abandoned quest for a "lasting relation" between "intellect" and "thing" (Murphy, ed., 1:947). Thus the pointed quality of Dickinson's rhetorical question, her bitterness, suggests the troubled past of her relationship with Susan, as well as indicating her premonition of death, for the poet's final illness had begun.

On the other hand, if Dickinson's question scarcely balances pessimism with optimism, if her interrogative hardly chooses the latter over the former, it does more than merely negate her experience, for she emerges from, as well as reenters, "an Abyss." The next sentence sets up her complimentary close, "Lovingly—": "The tie between us is very fine, but a Hair never dissolves" (L1024). Like the just-cited verse of Shelley and like the just-quoted prose of Emerson, her poems of aftermath neither negotiate the strait between experience and faith nor synthesize experience and faith but, rather, affirm the former as tough epistemology. To epitomize the Romanticism from which Dickinson conjures her world-grounded ability to generate hope from despair: "It is only by touching the abyss that the soul [of the British Romantic poet] comes to recognize its power" (Swingle 77).

"The things of which we want the proof are those we knew before—" (L334). On the one hand, this letter to Susan speaks of absence, of postexperience, pessimistically, for, insofar as *want* means lack, whatever we used to possess has disappeared without a trace. Such loss looms so inevitable that even what we have seems gone. On the other hand, since *want* can mean desire, we scarcely forfeit that for which we yet seek evidence, and we rarely give up on anyone for whom we yearn. We rejoice

> that in our embers
> Is something that doth live,
> That nature yet remembers what was so fugitive!
> (Wordsworth, "Ode: Intimations of Immortality"
> [1802–04], lines 129–31)

The actor Timothy West read these lines at the wedding (2005) of Prince Charles and Camilla Parker Bowles, giving heart to those of a certain age whose experience-in-postexperience, aftermath, has made them sadder-but-wiser folks whose hope does not so much triumph over past experience as subsist on/rekindle because of afterglow. No sooner does Dickinson appear to second Keats's "Fled is that music" ("Ode to a Nightingale" [1819], line 80) than she would embrace for the very reason of her loss Wordsworth's posttraumatic but far from paralyzed or ascetic quadrilateral of values: "Effort, and expectation, and desire, / And something evermore about to be" (*The Prelude* [1850] 6:68–69).

To be sure, death in Dickinson's postexperience can dominate her perceptions there. Tennyson's great poem of aftermath, *In Memoriam* (1850), feels the same "awful sense / Of one mute Shadow watching all" (30:7–8). Emerson's postexperience, in equal prefiguring of Dickinson's, offers an antiexperiential reason for not writing autobiography, the genre most compatible with experience. "Our life looks trivial," Emerson writes, "and we shun to record it" ("Experience," in Murphy, ed., 1:943). "Nothing is left us now," he adds, "but death" (Murphy, ed., 1:945). Emerson concludes, "We look to that with grim satisfaction, saying, there at least, is reality that will not dodge us" (Murphy, ed., 1:945). Nevertheless, in keeping with the lighter mood of Tennyson or of Emerson—namely, the optimism or the "soul-competency" of their Anglo-American Romanticism—even the Dickinson of aftermath can move "downward to darkness" with lyrical lilt.[12] Thus the Myth of Amherst reconstitutes experience as hope-against-hope in, as hope-after-hope for, the here and now.

The precedent for Dickinson's symbiosis of postexperience/ experience is Romanticism. Of course, her withdrawal from social life has something to do with the "alternate joy and woe" of her love for "Sister Sue" and for Wadsworth, and her posttrauma attends her implicit interpretation of Darwin's science and the Civil War as twin omens of Modern-era diminishment and shell shock.[13] Still, her "post-experiential perspective" derives not only from these emotional and these intellectual reasons for her reclusive tendency but, more optimistically, from the spiritual dedication from which she makes a not-so-cloistered virtue of her Tiresias-/Homer-/Milton-like eye- trouble, thereby preserving herself as "daughter of prophecy" who well and truly sees.[14] Wordsworth's "abundant recompense" for "such loss" as the "aching joys" and "dizzy raptures" of his "boyish days...all gone by"—namely, "the still, sad music of humanity," the "years that bring the philosophic mind"—offers Dickinson's speakers of aftermath a not-so-muted mitigation of it.[15] Insofar as the natu- ral grace of Dickinson's poetry of experience, her art of knowledge, becomes the unvarnished, astringent truth that her "post-experiential perspective" curiously welcomes and strongly recommends, her pre- Modern mode develops residually Romantic-era consolation for faded "splendor in the grass" and for lost "glory in the flower" (com- pare Wordsworth, "Ode: Intimations of Immortality" [1802–04], line 180).

*   *   *

To confront, first, the pessimism of Dickinson's aftermath, and to give it its due, here is a signature poem in point, lines resistant to any ame- liorating exegesis:

> The difference between Despair
> And Fear - is like the One
> Between the instant of a Wreck -
> And when the Wreck has been -
>
> The Mind is smooth - no Motion -
> Contented as the eye
> Opon the Forehead of a Bust -
> That knows - it cannot see -
>   (Fr576)

Of course, this fear-turned-despair finds alert style, "the complex- ity that analogy and parallelism often achieve" (Juhasz "'To Make a

Prairie'" 16–17). Still, the poem says that aftermath and numbness/ paralysis are the same and permanent. The poet sent the poem to Susan. Thus, in the physical absence of the beloved, the speaker waits on Godot. To repeat what bears repeating as one reads this poem, "Tis a dangerous moment for anyone when the meaning goes out of things and Life stands straight—and punctual—and yet no content(s) (signal) come(s)."

A poem of two lines is so pessimistic as to constitute an antiaubade, a perverse subversion of the hopeful dawn-poem genre:

> To Whom the Mornings stand for Night,
> What must the Midnights - be!
> (Fr1055)

Instead of substituting for, or replacing, nights, and rather than compensating for loveless nights by eliminating, reducing to just proportions, intense darkness indeed, the speaker's mornings symbolize loveless nights. These mornings, in fact, become these nights, for, by Dickinson's implication, aubade that follows nonepithalamium proves scarcely worth distinguishing from the dead of night, from night's barely alive, merely undead companions.

Dickinson's longest statement of postexperiential pessimism merits full quotation here, and also calls for an assessment of, a contribution to, the most pertinent critical conversation about the poem:

> It would never be Common - more - I said -
> Difference had begun -
> Many a bitterness had been -
> But that old sort - was done -
>
> Or - if it sometime showed - as 'twill -
> Opon the Downiest morn -
> Such bliss - had I - for all the years -
> 'Twould give an easier - pain -
>
> I'd so much joy I told it - Red -
> Opon my simple Cheek -
> I felt it publish - in my eye -
> 'Twas needless - any speak -
>
> I walked - as wings - my body bore -
> The feet - I former used -
> Unnecessary - now to me -
> As boots - would be - to Birds -

I put my pleasure all abroad -
I dealt a word of Gold
To every Creature - that I met -
And Dowered - all the World -

When - suddenly - my Riches shrank -
A Goblin - drank my Dew -
My Palaces - dropped tenantless -
Myself - was beggared - too -

I clutched at sounds -
I groped at shapes -
I touched the tops of Films -
I felt the Wilderness roll back
Along my Golden lines -

The Sackcloth - hangs opon the nail -
The Frock I used to wear -
But where my moment of Brocade -
My - drop - of India?
                                    (Fr388)

Joanne Feit Diehl's idea that the poem qualifies as "paradigmatic expression" (Diehl "'Ransom'" 170–72) finds a counterpart in Maryanne Garbowsky's placement of these lines at the center of Dickinson's "poems of aftermath" (Garbowsky 128–29). Cristanne Miller, too, addresses the meta-poetical dimension of a lyric that "tells a Cinderella story in which the speaker is her own fairy godmother. She turns herself from a 'Common' woman into a poet, and her magic gift and husband Prince are all words" (147–49, 151). Shira Wolosky and Alice Fulton acknowledge that the poem is about poetry, but they highlight the poet's fall from, rather than her access to, verbal power. "The poem," Wolosky contends, "perhaps merely describes the passing of poetic inspiration" (*Emily* 155–57).[16] Fulton concludes that here "a woman confronts literary effacement" (43).

Cynthia Griffin Wolff emphasizes the ebb of the speaker's ebb-and-flow of verbal prowess. "The ever-shifting balance of power between the creative forces and the forces of destruction swings against the poet, and the effort to impose order must begin again" (217–19, 383, 529). Thus, although the poet-speaker ranks high as an artist, she ends on a note of aesthetic timidity. The final line laments the loss of her "drop - of India," her thick, black ink for the lettering of her works. Dickinson's pen has run dry.

To be sure, Ben Kimpel holds that Dickinson's poems of aftermath, including "It would never be Common - more - I said - ," describe "occasions in her life out of which her religious response occurred" (245). Emily Miller Budick, too, sees this poem as religious. Nevertheless, as Budick makes clear, this speaker's experiential temper limits the success of her religious aspirations. "The attempt to characterize heaven in ordinary symbolic language can only result in a disappointment and loss that are both proximate and ultimate" (71–73). The third, fourth, and fifth stanzas entertain such miraculous transcendence that they have nowhere else to go but toward a correspondingly intense, postlapsarian tone, in the sixth, seventh, and eighth stanzas. Dickinson comes across here as more pessimistic than optimistic, more naturally than spiritually oriented.

One of the most skillful effects of "It would never be Common - more - I said - " concerns the poet's use of dashes in the sixth stanza to mark the transition from first love to forlorn devastation. In the seventh stanza, where the speaker reports that she "felt the Wilderness roll back / Along my Golden lines - ," Dickinson psychologizes the New England/Puritan "Errand into the Wilderness."[17] The myth of the golden age, as Shelley dilutes it in "The World's Great Age Begins Anew" (1822) and as Joni Mitchell further attenuates it in "We've Got to Get Ourselves Back to the Garden" (1971), proves equally apropos. Although Dickinson's persona, in the final stanza, puts behind her the "Sackcloth" of bitterness, her "Frock" of young love's hope and promise recedes, too. She stands alone, in a daze, looking backward, wondering what hit her.[18]

"After great pain, a formal feeling comes - " explores how the "formal feeling" stays so far from functioning as a palliative that it can, and probably will, kill the sufferer:

> The Feet, mechanical, go round -
> A Wooden way
> Of Ground, or Air, or Ought -
> Regardless grown,
> A Quartz contentment, like a stone -
>
> This is the Hour of Lead -
> Remembered, if outlived,
> As Freezing persons, recollect the Snow -
> First - Chill - then Stupor - then the letting go -
> (Fr372, lines 5–13)

As Jane Marston observes, "The event that has caused pain is not named; thus, pain may be understood as either loss or physical pain, the one prefiguring grief, the other, death…The speaker cares about effect, not cause—about what it is like to live out the aftermath of pain" (114). "The poem," Garbowsky writes, "suggests the panic attack where the individual is numbed with anxiety and fear, feeling as if death has come" (134–35). Vivian Pollak's insight that Dickinson's "pain signifies a loyalty to frustrated aspirations, which is both heroic and dysfunctional," qualifies as an equally psychological, no less tough-minded approach to the poem (199, 206–11).

Formalistic understanding of the poem and of its post-Modern intimation of formalistic disconnection emerges from John Robinson's conclusion that the "orderly and analytic" message here "is dramatically enacted in terms which challenge that control and even threaten the message" (126). In a historically aware as well as formalistically sophisticated observation, A. R. C. Finch writes that "as the meter of the past poets overtakes the poem, the poet uses iambic pentameter to present an image of helpless, frozen stupor" (167). Wolff drops a formalistically radical, almost post-Modern bombshell: "themes of violation and disorder" in the poem mean that Dickinson's poetry as a whole "has been fatally wounded by the pain of its creator" (154). Thus Dickinson foreshadows such Moderns as Yeats, Eliot, Frost, and Stevens.[19] As Linda J. Taylor puts it, "After great pain, a formal feeling comes - " helps "to establish a place for [Dickinson] in the mainstream of…post-romantic poetry in England" (253).

The poem also helps to align Dickinson's postexperiential pessimism with the high- to late-Romantic version of pessimism, for the tough-minded side of Anglo-American Romanticism provides a solid model for both the "great pain" and the "formal feeling" of her aftermath. "In the death of my son [Waldo], now more than two years ago," Emerson writes,

> I seem to have lost a beautiful estate,—no more…[I]t does not touch me: some thing which I fancied was a part of me, which could not be torn away without tearing me, nor enlarged without enriching me, falls off from me, and leaves no scar. It was caducous. I grieve that grief can teach me nothing, nor carry me one step into real nature. ("Experience" in Murphy, ed., 1:944)

This attitude, as Barbara Packer recognizes, appears both "self-lacerating" and filled with "casual brutality" (117). "We can imagine a voice that says all these things with bitter irony," she adds, but we can also imagine "a voice as toneless and detached as that of a witness giving evidence in a war crimes trial" (117). Another analogy to the latter voice, in Packer's view, inheres in the "wasted and suffering" discharged soldier whom Wordsworth questions in Book 4 of *The Prelude* (1850):

> In all he said
> There was a strange half-absence, as of one
> Knowing too well the importance of his theme
> But feeling it no longer.
> (Lines 442–45; qtd. in Packer 120)

Packer thinks that "the casual brutality of the sentence in which Emerson introduces the death of his son *as an illustration* is unmatched by anything I know of in literature, unless it is the parenthetical remark in which Virginia Woolf reports the death of Mrs. Ramsey in the 'Time passes' section of *To the Lighthouse* [1927]" (120; Packer's emphasis). Packer thinks, as well, in this regard, though far back in time, of Sir Thomas Browne's *Hydrotaphia* (1681): "There is no antidote," Browne laments, "against the *Opium* of time" (qtd. in Packer 129–30). Most significantly for present purposes, though, Packer mentions Dickinson's "After great pain, a formal feeling comes - " as an especially memorable example of postexperiential pessimism from Wordsworth to Emerson to Woolf (Packer 132).

* * *

On the other hand, Aliki Barnstone offers an optimistic reading of Dickinson's poems of aftermath—that is, that such a poem as "After great pain, a formal feeling comes - " illustrates "the Nirvana principle of abandonment to nothingness, which is a release and a liberation, the necessary state for revelation" (142–43). This observation seems too religious to suit the poem. The poem, though, is more than a psychological case study. It prescribes a strangely positive procedure for even the worst experiences of aftermath—namely, survival training for this "World of Pains and troubles" (compare the letter from Keats to George and Georgiana Keats, February 14–May 31, 1819).

"After great pain, a formal feeling comes - ," accordingly, emerges as a more late-Romantic than pre-Modern poem. Consider, in this regard, Edward Fitzgerald's perspective on the lowest moments of *In Memoriam*. "I felt that if Tennyson had got on a horse and ridden 20 miles, instead of moaning over his pipe, he would have been cured of his sorrows in half the time. As it is, it is almost 3 years before the Poetic Soul walks itself out of darkness and Despair and into Common Sense" (qtd. in Ricks 214). But Fitzgerald undervalues how

Tennyson's hope "*comes from* darkness" (Kincaid 83–84; Kincaid's emphasis). Even the empirical voice of *In Memoriam*, to say nothing of its voice of faith, moderates the poet's desolation over the death of Arthur Henry Hallam (for both voices of *In Memoriam*, see Brantley *Anglo-American* 33–50). Dickinson's empirical voice, like Tennyson's, lends vitality, if not exactly untroubled robustness, to her late-Romantic version of aftermath. Instead of ever having backed off, with an attitude of "Do I dare to eat a peach?" the persona has welcomed "frequent sights of what is to be borne," and so sustains liberating abandonment to nothingness.[20] Recall: "then the letting go - ."

In Dickinson's poems of aftermath, the premium placed on survival training reflects her hard-won optimism, and hence her empirical, if not scientific, values, as distinct from her defense mechanisms identified by such a psychoanalytic approach to her works as that of pioneer psychological critic John Cody. Yes, the "Languour" or "Drowsiness" that equates to "Pain's Successor - " "Envelopes [Dickinson's] Consciousness - " (Fr552, lines 1, 3, 5, 7). And yes, her postexperience turns out to be an even more ominous portent of her death than her first sharp outcry of pain.

> The Surgeon - does not blanch at pain -
> His Habit is severe -
> But tell him that it ceased to feel -
> The Creature lying there -
>
> And he will tell you - Skill is late -
> A Mightier than He -
> Has ministered before Him -
> There's no Vitality
>   (Fr552, lines 9–16)

However, as psychologically and linguistically acute as Dickinson's most pessimistic understanding of aftermath can be, she concludes in these poems as a group that even the worst of postexperience fulfills the late-Romantic function not so much of spiritual discipline as of stoic endurance.

Dickinson's hope paradoxically comes from the darkness that sometimes encompasses her.

> There is a pain - so utter -
> It swallows substance up -
> Then covers the Abyss with Trance -
> So Memory can step

Around - across - opon it -
As One within a Swoon -
Goes safely - where an open eye
Would drop Him - Bone by Bone -
(Fr515)

Pollak is under no illusion about the lingering effects of affliction as it
is presented in these lines. "Extreme pain destroys the memory of its
occasion... The soul cannot bear too much reality and commands a variety of amnesiac responses which blank out pain, all of which prefigure
the ultimate amnesiac, death" (209). Garbowsky's clinical interpretation of Dickinson's poetry, as agoraphobia, goes further than Pollak in
capturing whatever ameliorative properties these lines may display. "This
description of the trance-like effect of depersonalization brought on by
the panic attack accurately describes its release function and the protec-
tive purpose it serves. By cutting the victim's feelings off, depersonalization prevents him or her from a more serious breakdown" (123). Thus
the speaker of the poem does not so much forget his or her suffering
as use trance to remember it gingerly, and, as distinct from sleepwalk-
ing to oblivion, he or she "Goes safely - ," does not burn with a hard,
gemlike flame but lives in some security. If Dickinson's poems of aftermath sometimes include the near-suicidal mood of the third chapter of
the Book of Job or of Hopkins's "No Worst, There Is None" (1885),
poems like this one, and indeed especially "There is a pain - so utter - ,"
nonetheless provide the setting for her reemergence.

What might seem to be Dickinson's defense mechanism of denial
can turn out to be the natural grace of her recuperative powers (recall
the discussion in chapter 1 of her almost scientific faith that every man
or woman can be his or her own physician):

A Doubt if it be Us
Assists the staggering Mind
In an extremer Anguish
Until it footing find -

An Unreality is lent,
A merciful Mirage
That makes the living possible
While it suspends the lives.
(Fr903)

Barbara Mossberg sums up the poem. "While the voice of the poet
is anguished, it is operative" (29). Pain no longer envelops this

consciousness. Dickinson's speaker appears more pragmatic than solipsistic, more experience-hungry than inwardly tortured.

The most autobiographical among Dickinson's less pessimistic than optimistic poems of aftermath merits, like "It would never be Common - more - I said - " (perhaps the most pessimistic of these poems), full quotation and careful moderation, modulation, of the received critical dialogue:

> I tie my Hat - I crease my Shawl -
> Life's little duties do - precisely -
> As the very best
> Were infinite - to me -
>
> I put new Blossoms in the Glass -
> And throw the Old - away -
> I push a petal from my Gown
> That anchored there - I weigh
> The time 'twill be till six o'clock -
> So much I have to do -
> And yet - existence - some way back -
> Stopped - struck - my ticking - through -
>
> We cannot put Ourself away
> As a completed Man
> Or Woman - When the errand's done
> We came to Flesh - opon -
> There may be - Miles on Miles of Nought -
> Of Action - sicker far -
> To simulate - is stinging work -
> To cover what we are
> From Science - and from Surgery -
> Too Telescopic eyes
> To bear on us unshaded -
> For their - sake - Not for Our's -
>
> Therefore - we do life's labor -
> Though life's Reward - be done -
> With scrupulous exactness -
> To hold our Senses - on -
>
>   (Fr522)

This aftermath, it is true, seems grim enough, for "life is represented [here] as fury coming to terms with sexuality, and both are subject to the efforts of repression" (Cameron "'A Loaded Gun'" 431). While Dickinson's readers might identify with her uncharacteristically pejorative use of an empirical metaphor—"Dickinson's fear that the inner

world would be looked into is surely connected with the development of science, particularly the telescope" (Uno 98)—her desire
to keep the subconscious repressed might strike them as unhealthy.
Nonetheless, "the speaker's admission that the bomb is calm now
reveals that the panic attacks are in remission, and although the bomb
is still intact, she is in a state of relative ease, trying to appear nor-
mal" (Garbowsky 126). Thus "time is meaningless to [Dickinson]"
at a subjective level, but "objectively, it continues to organize her
behavior" (Pollak 204). In other words, "I tie my Hat - I crease
my Shawl - " concerns "a life in which control is the only meaning
and meaning the only control," and this conundrum suffices (Dickie
Lyric 131). Since the poem "allows us a sight of Emily Dickinson
presenting herself to the eyes of other people and sustaining herself
by the fact of that observation" (John Robinson 97), the formalism
of her postexperience contributes to, and perhaps even constitutes,
her very survival. Dickinson, to give the last word on this poem to
an especially optimistic conclusion arising from the criticism of it,
does not just speak here of the "trivial duties that must be done" but
even "remains in firm control of her poem" by "choosing figures"
that do not exaggerate but "understate" her "dilemma" (Patterson
Emily 112).

By corollary, finally, these more optimistic poems of Dickinson's
aftermath can remain in firm control of content as well as of form.
Of course, to understate her dilemma can be to condense, abridge,
shorten, or curtail experience. Still, these sadder but wiser words comprise no mere summary, abstract, or selection of essential facts. They
deepen experience, as well. Perhaps these speakers even gain distance
on the present through hindsight, the second self of foresight.

Make no mistake: Dickinson's poems of aftermath can dwell on the
past. This harking back, however, is an almost desirable, as well as an
inevitable, result of losing what, or whom, she cherishes most.

> Pity - the Pard - that left her Asia!
> Memories - of Palm -
> Cannot be shifted - with Narcotic -
> Nor suppressed - with Balm -
> (Fr276, lines 10–13)

The leopard remains "somehow involved in the central idea of love as
tropical heat, vitality itself" (Patterson *Emily* 151). Thus "Pity - the
Pard - that left her Asia!" sympathizes with a zoo-confined animal
deprived of rich experience in her native land, for "the Pard" is a

surrogate for the postexperiential poet in her unshakable, pointblank remembrance of exotic, bygone persons, places, or things.

The speaker of "I held a jewel in my fingers - " looks back with the bittersweetness of nostalgia, as well as in anger at herself:

> I held a jewel in my fingers -
> And went to sleep -
> The day was warm, and winds were prosy -
> I said "'Twill keep" -
>
> I woke - and chid my honest fingers,
> The Gem was gone -
> And now, an Amethyst remembrance
> Is all I own -
>
> (Fr261)

Although blankness here means "Dickinson's fear of losing her ability to create," and although "jewels appear often in Dickinson's imagery as emblems for the poet's self, or more specifically, for her artistic genius," her pet name for her "dearest earthly friend," Charles Wadsworth, is "Dusk Gem."[21] Dickinson uses the "gem metaphor to heighten the sense of the preciousness of her friends" (Simpson 38). Just as this poem defines poetry as "the reclamation or repossession of absence," so these lines exemplify the lyric genre as "the owning of loss," as "the owning *up* of loss" (Gelpi "Emily Dickinson's Word" 44; Gelpi's emphasis). In Dickinson's case here, it is perhaps more the latter.

"Where I have lost, I softer tread - " provides a blueprint, not only of the postexperiential Dickinson's balance between pessimism and optimism, but also of her tipping the scales from the former to the latter:

> Where I have lost, I softer tread -
> I sow sweet flower from garden bed -
> I pause above that vanished head
>   And mourn.
>
> Whom I have lost, I pious guard
> From accent harsh, or ruthless word -
> Feeling as if their pillow heard,
>   Though stone!
>
> When I have lost, you'll know by this -
> A Bonnet black - A dusk surplice -
> A little tremor in my voice
>   Like this!

Why I have lost, the people know
Who dressed in frocks of purest snow
Went home a century ago
    Next Bliss!
       (Fr158)

The lyric poses the where, who, when, and why of parting in general and of bereavement in particular. As the poet would later observe, in lines worth repeating here if only because of how they have captured the imagination of the present age (compare Harry Crews's title),

Parting is all we know of heaven,
And all we need of hell.
    (Fr1773, lines 7–8)

To the extent that "When I have lost, I softer tread - " cannot answer these journalistic questions, these four stanzas merely own *up* to loss—as "I held a jewel in my fingers - " does primarily—as death-in-life that defines antiexperience. Thus only those who now see face to face in heaven could explain why she has lost (compare I Cor. 13:12). Her funereal sorrow when she loses proves her only certainty. To the extent that the lyric can answer such questions, however—and here is where the tone emerges—these lines own loss. Perhaps even within Dickinson's "post-experiential perspective," they represent her ongoing experience.

To illustrate how "Where I have lost, I softer tread - " owns loss, consider a parallel between the second stanza, beginning "Whom I have lost," and the fourth and fifth stanzas of a more familiar poem, "My Life had stood - a Loaded Gun - ."

And when at Night - Our good Day done -
I guard My Master's Head -
'Tis better than the Eider Duck's
Deep Pillow - to have shared -

To foe of His - I'm deadly foe -
None stir the second time -
On whom I lay a Yellow Eye -
Or an emphatic Thumb -
    (Fr764, lines 13–20)

On the one hand, the speakers of both poems lead "impoverished and inadequate" lives (Margaret H. Freeman's language [262] for the persona of Fr764), for the one grieves over the literal or figurative death of her beloved, and the other suffers from jealousy. For the poet, on the other hand, "knowledge of the world is *formed* by an experience of the world" (Freeman's emphasis), for, despite her life of reduced circumstances, each poem, that is, Fr158 as well as Fr764, embodies Dickinson's wisdom.[22] "Where I have lost, I softer tread - ," in particular, locates wisdom in fidelity, suggesting that Dickinson's desire to see Charles Wadsworth again, though certainly not her expectation of beholding him in heaven, is as strong as death, and perhaps even keeps him near her.[23]

Dickinson's withdrawal from society does more than signal either her posttraumatic stress disorder or her fugitive, cloistered, unpraiseworthy virtue. Her reclusive tendency signifies, as well, fullness of time. Her aftermath, as it appears from the pages of this chapter, can go from lesson learned, to gist grasped, to concentration intensified, to watchfulness restored, to imagination unwearied. Can faded friendship and lost love, for her, open heartfelt access to the divine, as opposed to exacerbating destructive skepticism, on the one hand, and paralyzed *aporia*, on the other?[24] Whether or not the answer is *yes*, and even if her reputation as a recluse is well founded, the experience of being one, for the Myth of Amherst, shades into being one with experience.

*   *   *

At their lowest moments of distress and hopelessness Dickinson's aesthetic self-projections manage to salvage, against all odds and in their best and worst of all possible worlds, the constructive skepticism and the lyrical lilt of her late-Romantic imagination. The "perpetual attention" that her poems of aftermath pay "to experience, the pole-star of truth" (to press William Godwin's crucial language into service again) glosses the sensationalist epistemology, if not the Experiential Faith, of Romantic Anglo-America. Her "post-experiential perspective" has more to do with Wordsworth's "wise passiveness," his deliberate survival training verging on spiritual discipline, than with defense mechanisms.[25] Her poems of aftermath, like the contemplative dimension of Keats's art, foster "being in uncertainties, Mysteries, doubts, without any irritable reaching after fact & reason" (Keats's words can scarcely be too often brought to bear on Anglo-American Romanticism).[26] Dickinson's version of "*Negative Capability*" remains as far from nihilism as his.

To move from Dickinson's high-Romantic precursors to a late-Romantic contemporary, the more optimistic than pessimistic poems

of her aftermath vibrate more sympathetically with Carlyle's version of postexperiential suspension than, say, with Eliot's Prufrock.
According to "The Hero as a Man of Letters" (1841), Carlyle's
"skepticism is not an end"—that is, it is not an acquiescence in static
doubt after strong faith "but a beginning"; it is not "the decay of old
ways of believing" but "the preparation afar off for new and wider
ways" (Shelston, ed., 253). Also pertinent to hearing Romanticism
in Dickinson's postexperiential combination of pessimism with optimism is Carlyle's hard-won but nowhere near exhausted definition of
doubt as constructive skepticism. "Doubt," he writes, represents "the
mystic working of the mind, on the subject it is getting to know and
believe" (Shelston, ed., 253). Though perhaps of the very essence
of aftermath, doubt remains a key to purposive process, and, in this
sense, Carlyle's portrait on the wall of Dickinson's room keeps her
spirits up, especially at the very center, at the near-sacred inner sanc-
tum, of her postexperience.

Dickinson's assimilation of the open quality of Tennyson's and of
Emerson's skepticism, furthermore, obtains in the free space of her
aftermath. On the pessimistic side, Tennyson's implication of doubt
as postexperience can sound like Dickinson's, though she is rarely as
glib in her God-talk as *In Memoriam* can be:

> And falling with my weight of cares
> Upon the great world's altar-stairs
> That slope through darkness up to God,
>
> I stretch lame hands of faith and grope,
> And gather dust and chaff, and call
> To what I feel is Lord of all,
> And faintly trust the larger hope.
> (*In Memoriam* 55:14–20)

On the optimistic side, Emerson's implication of doubt as postexperience can sound even more Dickinson-like, for her language, as
this chapter has everywhere tried to show, is usually as philosophically
acute, and is usually as soft-pedaled in God-talk, as this passage from
his "Experience" (1844): "For, skepticisms are not gratuitous or law-
less, but are limitations of the affirmative statement, and the new philosophy must take them in, and make affirmations outside of them, just
as much as it must include the oldest beliefs" (Murphy, ed., 1:955).
Emerson adds, "Out of unbeliefs a creed shall be formed" (Murphy,
ed., 1:955). Dickinson would say, "Out of aftermath a new beginning shall be willed," for she absorbs and makes her own the radically

skeptical but eminently constructive stance of such Romantics, if only in their mode of postexperience, as Wordsworth, Keats, Carlyle, Tennyson, and Emerson.

Dickinson goes "White - unto the White Creator - " (Fr788, line 7), but does her candor (from *candidus*, white) signify innocence of experience,[27] as though, at the end of her life, she were "blank" (from *blancus*, white), like the clean slate or tabula rasa of John Locke? No, for her personae speak from experience, and those of aftermath, in particular, not so much sweet and guileless as frank and direct, have turned their experience into wisdom.[28] Dickinson's wisdom, accordingly, is not only the tougher for following upon, but perhaps even the more efficacious for reconstituting, her experience. In her book, especially from its postexperiential perspective, going "White - unto the White Creator - " signifies not so much having existed timidly or palely, seeking refuge in retreat, as having lived life to the fullest, burning through it not to its ashes but to its calcined form of near-spiritual purity.

Dickinson's candor means, finally, her incandescence—that is, the glow with which her personae of aftermath retain, reimagine, and rekindle the white-hot heat of experience, albeit in the crucible of a highly creative postexperience (compare her metapoetic "Dare you see a Soul at the 'White Heat'?" [Fr401]).[29] To conflate her language with that of Wordsworth, himself a poet both of experience and of postexperience, her aftermath constitutes, if not her "spontaneous overflow of powerful feeling," then her "emotion recollected in tranquility," making "internal difference - / Where the Meanings, are - ."[30] The whiteness of her aesthetic self-projections—that is, her presence-of-all-color, as opposed to either her unstained purity or her point-blank nihilism (whiteness/blankness can connote, after all, nothingness)—signals an existential authenticity, a perdurability that, for better or worse, yet "burn[s]," in her, "with a hard, gem-like flame" indeed (compare Pater, Conclusion to *Leonardo da Vinci* [1873]). Thus she aligns herself with what Shelley means by Mont Blanc, "a vacancy that nevertheless holds in itself the potentiality of all that is," as distinct, say, from Ahab's apprehension of void in the whiteness of the whale, or as distinct from Arthur Gordon Pym's horror in the snows of Antarctica.[31] The whiteness of Dickinson's postexperience betokens further, fresh experience, dynamic possibility (recall "I dwell in Possibility - ") of near-death experience, of "the white radiance of Eternity," and, for that matter, of gloriously, mind-blowingly aesthetic/cinematic white-out.[32]

Dickinson's poems of aftermath, then, do more than just illustrate the "post-experiential perspective" of her pre-Modern mode and the antiexperiential bias of her post-Modern intimations. This strain of her genius, if only by fits and starts, reactivates the natural and spiritual dialogue of Romantic Anglo-America. Her experience of postexperience features the yet-viable role of friendship and of love in her "internalized quest romance," thus turning loss into the gain of gold on the page.[33] Is her "post-experiential perspective" consonant with her poetry of experience? Yes, for, besides equating to disastrous consequences, Dickinson's poems of aftermath entail outcome, and perhaps these personae even augur harvest in this world again.

CHAPTER 4

DESPAIRING HOPE

As the letters and poems of Emily Dickinson seek to understand it, the human condition integrates despair and hope. The same woman who lamented "the hollowness & awfulness of the *world*" (Leyda 1:213; Dickinson's emphasis) testified that "I find ecstasy in living—the mere sense of living is joy enough" (L342a).[1] As though her despair could regularize her hope and her hope could celebrate her despair, each of her opposing stances dramatizes the other at any given point of her life of writing.[2] To complicate for Dickinson studies an affirmation lately appropriated by the US "culture wars," her despair and her hope alike, paradoxically at the same time, can let her "choose life" (compare Deut. 30:19). Thus, the pessimism that recurs throughout her career can cultivate the very seed of her perennial resilience.

As though *simple* hope could bestow only chaste satisfaction, Dickinson's personae prefer *despairing* hope, albeit at some risk of their merely seeming to indulge, thereby, in overclever oxymoron. Whenever they can avoid that kind of hazard (this chapter will imply that they often do), then, even if their despair does not exactly *yield* their hope, it can nonetheless yield *to* their hope. Dickinson's "despondency," to borrow Wordsworth's word, her "dejection," to redirect Coleridge's, can serve here as the catalyst not so much to her rarefied, muted, and detached hope, as to her uncloistered, articulate, and engaged hope.[3] One thinks in this connection, by way of comparison/contrast between her despondent hope (so to speak) and the even more dejected quality of Lord Byron's, of this pertinent lyric (1814) by him:

> They say that Hope is happiness—
> But genuine Love must prize the past;

And Mem'ry wakes the thoughts that bless:
They rose the first—they set the last.

And all that mem'ry loves the most
Was once our only hope to be:
And all that hope adored and lost
Hath melted into memory.

Alas! It is delusion all—
The future cheats us from afar:
Nor can we be what we recall,
Nor dare we think on what we are.

The despairing hope of Emily Dickinson rarely, if ever, sinks this low. Whether or not the inextricable intertwining of her despair with her hope is a witting antidote to Byron's legacy of near-hopelessness in the deceiving guise of, in the mere name of, hope, this chapter will attempt, at any rate, to make clear, nonetheless, that her despairing hope constitutes *her* happiness. Thus, while her very despair could outhope her hope, she can prevail: she can come out on the other end of times when even her hope would appear to be outdespairing her despair.

To be sure, Dickinson's love for her "dearest earthly friend" (L807), Charles Wadsworth, on the one hand, and her love for her sister-in-law, Susan Dickinson, on the other, would seem to have equated to hopelessness itself. Vivian R. Pollak suggests that the geographical distance between Charles and Emily (Wadsworth lived for a time, 1864–1867, in San Francisco) and the emotional distance between neighbor Sue and Emily (so near, yet so far) contributed narrative tension and dramatic conflict to Dickinson's hundreds of love poems. "Poems for Master" and "Poems for Sue" (these are Judith Farr's labels for this manifold category of Dickinson's verse) emerge from Pollak's psycho-biographical criticism as more tragic than many readers might expect love poetry to be. Dickinson's philosophy of friendship and of love alike can turn skeptical enough to darken her poetic tone. Perhaps the discipline with which the poet learned to do without Wadsworth (did he know how much she loved him?) mirrored something of his Presbyterian doctrine of self-denial: he declared, for instance, that "[t]he grand secret of contentment is found, not in increasing our supplies—but in diminishing our necessities" (*Sermons* [1869] 266). Wadsworth's use of a dash appears here as a Dickinson-like element of this rather dour homiletic aphorism. Just as Byron's dashes can also seem proto-Dickinson, so Wadsworth's punctuation parallels her way of indicating the emphatic quality of

her habitual minimalism—that is, the sometimes pronounced emptiness of her poetic content, as well as the sometimes deliberate paucity
of her poetic form.

Nevertheless, as a not-so-one-sided understanding of Dickinson's
outlook in general and of her views on friendship and on love in particular, this chapter will specify that the modest goal of contentment
set forth by Wadsworth's instruction contrasts with Dickinson's signature conundrum—namely, "*sumptuous* Destitution - " (Fr1404, line
7; emphasis added). This enigma does not merely fluctuate between
seeming opposites: Byron's phrase "love's alternate joy and woe"
comes to mind as not quite apposite here (see "Maid of Athens, Ere
We Part" [1812], line 7). Rather, Dickinson jumbles antitheses. She
might counter Wadsworth's dictum with Blake's maxim: "Without
Contraries is no progression" (Blake, *The Marriage of Heaven and
Hell* [1790–1793], Plate 3). As novelist Kathryn Harrison observes in
quite another context, "Desiring to not desire, after all, is itself a new
form of desire" (922). Dickinson's "less" proves strangely rich, hence
"more," as though her idea treats despair and hope in the same way,
in tandem. Such both/and logic, in the case of William Wordsworth,
can emphasize the former—as in

> We Poets in our youth begin in gladness;
> But *thereof* come in the end despondency and madness.
> (Wordsworth, "Resolution and Independence" [1807],
> lines 48–49; emphasis added)

—whereas Dickinson's poetic reasoning, as this chapter maintains, can
reverse the progression, drawing gladness out of despondency.

The signature lyric of Dickinson's "sumptuous Destitution - "—that
is, the poem in which this phrase appears—puts sorrow and joy in the
same breath, as though such opposites, such paired stances, were to
coalesce, to interpenetrate, in the speaker's inspiration:

> In many and reportless places
> We feel a Joy -
> Reportless, also, but sincere as Nature
> Or Deity -
>
> It comes, without a consternation -
> Dissolves - the same -
> But leaves a sumptuous Destitution -
> Without a Name -

Profane it by a search - we cannot -
It has no home -
Nor we who having once waylaid it -
Thereafter roam.

(Fr1404)

The lower case "sumptuous" and the upper case "Destitution - " that exemplify Dickinson's adjective-noun combinations address the mystery of life and recognize "the hollowness & awfulness of the *world*" but forgo joy no more willingly than the persona loses either the natural anchor of, or the divine presence in, her theism. The absence of these two doctrinal mainstays from her unorthodox thought here could constitute her joylessness, and any effort, on her part, to rediscover joy here, whether psychological or spiritual, could oversimplify the intrigue of the original experience. Dickinson's having had joy, however, squares with her still having it, perhaps even before the extraordinary times when she effortlessly receives back what she has had to resign. To say nothing of her "ecstasy in living," her "mere sense of living is joy enough," because "sense of living" counts as abundant life of the imagination, only one remove from "living" as ordinarily understood. According to Jean McClure Mudge's ironic reading of these lines, "Joy's sincerity parallels Nature's and God's; that is, it is untrustworthy, for both cosmic forces betrayed [Dickinson]" (223–24). The happiness of the speaker, however, fades by degrees, and scarcely dissipates, as though lack of consternation were to ease transition from joy to "sumptuous Destitution - ," and as though joy, alloyed but implicit in "sumptuous," could stay relatively genuine, after all.

The previous chapter began to modify mainstream supposition of Dickinson's pessimism. Now, further to do so, this chapter emphasizes that the "post-experiential perspective" of her "poetry of aftermath" still includes posttraumatic despair but coexists with, and features, hope as "the thing with feathers- ," "a strange invention - ," or "a subtle Glutton - ."[4] Such an inexhaustible lyric as "After great pain, a formal feeling comes - " (Fr372), interpreted to some extent in the last chapter, can sound here even less like sheer outcry over disastrous consequences, can look here even more like renewed witness to outcome auguring further harvest. At the risk of smoothing out Dickinson's three-steps-forward, two-steps-back kind of progress (Job's, too, can scan thus ragged), this chapter samples these poems out of chronological sequence, the better to highlight her power to resume optimism. If she forgets that "the thing with feathers" is "perhaps...every human's potential for music and poetry, brave stays against the brooding dark" (Wolff 248), she remembers in the dark. The ongoing renewal of hope among her speakers of postexperience, and not just the persistence of their hope-against-hope, their hope-after-hope, demonstrates the upholding strength of her "Columnar Self - " (Fr740, line 1). The pluck of her speakers of aftermath discloses as much about *her* as about her *artistry*.

Although the psycho-biographical perspective on Dickinson's poetry of aftermath remains of interest here, the relation between her postexperiential perspective and the natural as well as spiritual vision of Romantic Anglo-America is of even more concern here. Her context in philosophy, faith, and science forms the subtext of this literary-historical emphasis. John Locke, John Wesley, Charles Wadsworth, and Charles Darwin, despite their contrasting emphases on inference (Locke/Darwin) and direct knowledge (Wesley/Wadsworth), seek access to, and assurance of truth, and they imply between the lines a foil to Dickinson's crisis of confidence in such empirical/theological procedures. Literary history, though, can explicitly measure her hard-won reaffirmation of these very criteria. If the pre-Modern visage of her Janus-face looks on individual and collective trauma as historically prescient despair, her late-Romantic visage surveys just how cultural, as well as personal, aftermath can fortify traditional hope. Dickinson escapes the midcentury limbo of aesthetic transition. She finds positive new meaning in Romantic-era versions of postexperience as experience.

Like the previous chapter, yet even more often, this chapter will allude to, quote, and parallel Anglo-American writers of belletristic prose, fiction, and poetry. As explicitly as possible, yet in the short-hand manner of Matthew Arnold's "touchstones" of literary quality (compare Arnold, "The Study of Poetry" [1880], paragraphs eight and nine), the method for marking Dickinson's more late-Romantic than either Victorian-American or pre-Modern place on the arc from Romantic to Modern can build on Nicholson Baker's homage to John Updike in *U and I* (1991). Just as Baker's closed-book, self-administered testing of his loving memory of Updike's novels alludes to, and quotes, only what he recalls, so the present discussion can draw largely on such scattered bits of Anglo-American literature as spring to mind in this context. Thus, without betraying density, the chapter aims at a pastiche, a mosaic, of allusive, conversational argument, in the conviction that the best-written, most substantial literature lodges in the mind (compare Frost, "The Figure a Poem Makes" [1949]), and through the observation that the cultural poetics of Dickinson's art can thrive especially on her immersion in belles lettres.

* * *

Although Dickinson's speakers of "sumptuous Destitution - " can suffer terribly from loss, absence, and rejection, and although gain, presence, and embrace can frequently elude them, seldom do they settle quietly into contentment or desperation. On the contrary, their posttraumatic stress disorder can arrive at cognition. They can learn from, as distinct from merely dwelling on, or coping with, abandonment, or deprivation.[5] Reeling from, but able to speak after, their throes, they can proceed, only by stops and starts, toward intellectual, spiritual, and imaginative solutions to problems faced by humankind in general, and by themselves in particular (thus they reenact Job's advancement from self-absorption to empathy). Above all, they can lead lives of strenuous abundance, for, as befits their origin in gladness, and by way of perpetuating this joy, they can accumulate spiritual wealth. "Redeem[ing] the time" of their postexperiential existence, "glory[ing] in [their] tribulations," they can keep up appearances—can recover not just splendid expression of selfhood but even powerful representation of others and of otherness.[6] And they can do all this despite, if not in part because of, having been forsaken, deserted, and robbed, for Dickinson's aftermath—the muddled but not-so-belated middle of her experience—does not so much set despair off against hope as, Shelley-like, spark hope from the ashes of despair.[7]

To be sure, one of Dickinson's earliest poems of aftermath can seem full of so much more despair than hope as to sound entirely hopeless:

> I breathed enough to take the Trick -
> And now, removed from Air -
> I simulate the Breath, so well -
> That One, to be quite sure -
>
> The Lungs are stirless - must descend
> Among the cunning cells -
> And track the Pantomime - Himself,
> How numb, the Bellows feels!
> (Fr308)

Nevertheless, Dickinson relishes clarity here: her postexperiential perspective in general, if not in this poem in particular, harks back to the by no means entirely hopeless procedure of Tennyson's aftermath, as in the well-known section 54 of *In Memoriam* beginning

> O, yet we trust that somehow good
> Will be the final goal of ill,

and ending:

> but what am I?
> An infant crying in the night;
> An infant crying for the light,
> And with no language but a cry.
> (Lines 1–2, 17–20)

At this "grim center of *In Memoriam*," Timothy Peltason writes, "we are characteristically given no single moment of greatest despair, but a pattern of related moments, a virtuosity and variety of despair. And this despair, like the charged and changing grief of earlier lyrics, is both the evidence and the cause of imaginative activity, an incitement to us to re-chart the poem's course" (84). As though virtuosity of despair somehow yields the good, even "I breathed enough to take the Trick - " advances in firsthand, almost scientific language the scarcely hopeless proposition that airlessness, lunglessness, comprises the working model, the metaphysical conceit, of suspended animation.

"If we place the agoraphobic syndrome at the center" of "I breathed enough to take the Trick - ," according to Maryanne Garbowsky, "we gain a deeper insight into the physical discomforts the poet documents, as well as into the nature of the psychic disturbances that fueled them" (89). This criticism proves more helpful than narrowly expert, or reductively clinical. Garbowsky's insight blends with Peltason's. Dickinson's insight into "psychic disturbances" and into "physical discomforts" does not shrink back from facing the truth, whatever it might be. "I breathed enough to take the Trick - " constitutes "a virtuosity and variety of despair" that signify "imaginative activity," and hence hope.

Dickinson's "post-experiential perspective," as "Too happy Time dissolves itself" can illustrate, poses riddles for her readers to puzzle over, or be diverted by.

> Too happy Time dissolves itself
> And leaves no remnant by -
> 'Tis Anguish not a Feather hath
> Or too much weight to fly -
> (Fr1182)

Residue of happiness, by turns, can appear like dissolved sugar, or like a bird either newly featherless or grown too heavy to leave the ground.[8] The poet, in another such poem of aftermath, has learned enough from her experience to articulate what Blake calls "Proverbs of Hell," on the one hand, and to substitute them, on the other, for the outmóded, greeting-card-like sentimentality of such conventional wisdom as "time heals all wounds."[9]

> They say that "Time assuages" -
> Time never did assuage -
> An actual suffering strengthens
> As Sinews do, with Age -
>
> Time is a Test of Trouble -
> But not a Remedy -
> If such it prove, it prove too
> There was no Malady -
> (Fr861)

In the mid stages of her postexperience, the speaker here claims to know little. She conveys ambiguity concerning whether her suffering gets worse or whether she grows stronger the worse her trial becomes. To apply to Dickinson's case the language of Shelley, and of Dylan Thomas, she remains sentient enough "to repeal / Large codes of fraud," if not of "woe"—that is, to gut cliché by means of her "craft, or sullen art."[10]

To read between the lines of "They say that 'Time assuages' - ," Dickinson knows that, to use Hopkins's words, her "cries" have become "a chief- / woe, world-sorrow" (compare Hopkins, "No Worst, There Is None" [1885], lines 5–6). To think of "Too happy Time dissolves itself" and of "They say that 'Time assuages' - " as companion pieces, her chief woe has matured, as the world-sorrow of Wordsworth did, in "Thoughts that do often lie too deep for tears" (compare Wordsworth, "Ode: Intimations of Immortality" [1802–04], line 203). She might now pore over, and even might assimilate, Wordsworth's own vein of fierce self-correction.

> Through what power [Wordsworth writes],
> Even for the least division of an hour,
> Have I been so beguiled as to be blind
> To my most grievous loss!
> ("Surprised by Joy" [1815], lines 16–19)

Dickinson the late-Romantic poet of aftermath would no longer even want the facile consolations of nostrums about the passage of time.

As though her postexperiential perspective were a "dark night of the soul" phase of her spiritual as well as natural autobiography, she prefers the hard truths of her blended despair and hope. Thus Dickinson's darkness, like that of St. John of the Cross, is a good thing—that is, at once the occasion for meditation and the cause less of blindness than of insight, and perhaps even of revelation.

To be sure, the apathy, or at best the aimless, obscure searching, of Dickinson's aftermath, can appear more corrosively cynical than either ironic or straightforward:

> From Blank to Blank -
> A Threadless Way
> I pushed Mechanic feet -
> To stop - or perish - or advance -
> Alike indifferent -
>
> If end I gained
> It ends beyond
> Indefinite disclosed -
> I shut my eyes and groped as well -
> 'Twas lighter - to be Blind -
>   (Fr484)

Kenneth Stocks emphasizes the historical importance of this poem, which "extends beyond the purely personal and subjective into the consciousness of the age" (97). This consciousness, according to Douglas Novich Leonard, proves to be pre-Modern: "The absurdity of life, the unknowableness of its purpose, and sheer fatigue overwhelm the speaker and leave her in a state of spiritual apathy" ("Emily Dickinson's Religion" 337–38). Cynthia Griffin Wolff expresses the nihilistic implications of these lines: "'Blank' is almost a totemic word in Dickinson's work to identify a course of human affairs that has been stripped of larger significance. Now ... there are no defined beginnings or endings to be acknowledged or rejected. Even the structure that the drive toward death had imposed has been lost" (473). Shira Wolosky, too, acknowledges the pessimism of "From Blank to Blank - ": "When space has no definition, [seeing and not seeing] become functional equivalents—except that blindness raises no doomed expectations. Blindness is therefore chosen, but as a darkness which remains itself: an incomplete dialectic un-synthesized into any all-inclusive divine light" (*Emily Dickinson* 23–24). Nevertheless, as though remembering the positive dimension of darkness in the annals of Christian mysticism,

Wolosky emphasizes, besides the blank despair of the speaker, her continued deliberation, if scarcely her robust activity. As Leonard also acknowledges, knowing, by implication, that much worthwhile is even yet being written on the dark tablet of Dickinson's soul in postexperience, "[t]he very blankness of the poem becomes a kind of vision, its own reward for the heroic seeker after light" ("Emily Dickinson's Religion" 338).

Again within the stark confines of Dickinson's postexperiential perspective, and with no irritable reaching, on her part, after renewed experience, her poetry shows itself capable of more than tenebrous, if not clear-sighted, cognition. For instance, to assume a psycho-bio-graphical aspect to a lyric that looks back on summer, the following exemplar of her personae of "sumptuous Destitution - " so vividly recalls "the Affairs of June" (shades of a lost beloved) that she now plumbs new depths of love:

> Like some Old fashioned Miracle
> When Summertime is done -
> Seems Summer's Recollection
> And the Affairs of June
> ....
> Her Memories like Strains - Review -
> When Orchestra is dumb -
> The Violin in Baize replaced -
> And Ear - and Heaven - numb -
>   (Fr408, lines 1–4, 13–16)

"We learn it in Retreating," declares another speaker, "How vast an one / Was recently among us - "; this persona then adds, with exquisite paradox,

> A perished Sun
>
> Endear in the departure
> How doubly more
> Than all the Golden presence
> It was - before -
>   (Fr1045)

Dickinson's postexperience appears of itself able to advance new understanding of Charles, of Sue, of both.

The poems discussed in this chapter have generally received insufficient critical attention, because, notwithstanding their emphasis on loss, even they can sound too upbeat for post-Modern taste. In the

subtlest, if not the most profound, of these relatively unfamiliar lyrics, Dickinson suggests, in keeping with the laws of optics, that her
clear vision of one of her others departing (again, perhaps, a beloved)
depends on his or her having moved out of the poet's sight ("wick"
implies his).

> By a departing light
> We see acuter, quite,
> Than by a wick that stays.
> There's something in the flight
> That clarifies the sight
> And decks the rays
>   (Fr1749)

Thus "None can experience stint / Who Bounty - have not known - "
(Fr870, lines 1–2). At the same time that such lines do not necessarily clarify whether the relation between then and now is good
or bad, Wolosky is right to observe of "By a departing light" that
"Recompense is posited here" (*Emily Dickinson* 82). After all, "decks"
could mean "adorns," as well as "covers," or "floors" (as in "knocks
down"). Wordsworth's positing of "Abundant recompense" as the
payoff of his postexperience—that is, his awareness of the more hellish
than heaven-bound partings to be endured in death-in-life—comes
to mind as an analogue to the way Dickinson's poetry of aftermath
acquires strong aesthetic vision even, or perhaps especially, in reced-
ing light (compare Wordsworth, "Lines Composed a Few Miles above
Tintern Abbey" [1798], line 88).

   An unusually comprehensive account of Dickinson's experience
of postexperience contrasts the speaker's wounded and imprisoned
condition in the beginning ten lines and in the ending six, with her
moments of relief, release, freedom, and ecstasy in the middle eight:

> The Soul has Bandaged moments -
> When too appalled to stir -
> She feels some ghastly Fright come up
> And stop to look at her -
>
> Salute her, with long fingers -
> Caress her freezing hair -
> Sip, Goblin, from the very lips
> The Lover - hovered - o'er -
> Unworthy, that a thought so mean
> Accost a Theme - so - fair -

The soul has moments of escape -
When bursting all the doors -
She dances like a Bomb, abroad,
And swings opon the Hours,

As do the Bee - delirious borne -
Long Dungeoned from his Rose -
Touch Liberty - then know no more -
But Noon, and Paradise -

The Soul's retaken moments -
When, Felon led along,
With shackles on the plumed feet,
And staples, in the song,

The Horror welcomes her, again,
These, are not brayed of Tongue -
(Fr360)

Of course, the speaker's horror of living in a metaphorical prison, absence from the beloved, perhaps, never entirely dissipates, and indeed returns with the uppercase vengeance of annihilated love, as well as of enervated life (Joseph Conrad's Modern-era personification of evil/nihilism/atheism also comes to mind). Still, what is original about this poem of aftermath, what is not often "brayed of Tongue - ," is its realization that while the alpha-and-omega of postexperience is death (the ultimate posttraumatic stress disorder), the muddled middle of aftermath need not be either death-in-life (lovelessness) or "The Horror" of death itself. Rather, Dickinson's "post-experiential perspective" can include—can frame with realism, and hence can set off all the more dramatically—the imagined ideal, the virtual but very present help in trouble, of joy through love, and vice versa.

Does Dickinson here use "the traditional distinction between female powerlessness and male aggression" (Wendy Martin 120)? Undoubtedly, but surely the aggressor is not "The Lover," whether male or female, but the usurping "Goblin" of death, and the speaker's feeling for "The Lover," in any case, remains powerful and empowering. "The ability of the speaker's 'Soul' to flip between images of lover and goblin is unnerving. To depict desire as always vulnerable to control by death equates desire with threat" (Budick 374–75). However, not even this death threat of desire can take away the jouissance of stanzas three and four, which match any other passage of sustained optimism in Dickinson's works, for, precisely because life does not last, one kisses. "The tone of these stanzas on manic release overpowers even the reader's judgment to the point that one

regrets the psychological bomb's forced return to captivity and horror" (Eberwein *Strategies* 125). Yes, but since one's regret registers
power in the speaker's idiom of release, one might replace "manic"
with "ecstatic," for, even in her opening lines of postexperiential
pessimism, such language as "the very lips / The Lover - hovered -
o'er - " can seem more than spiritually—can appear lustily—autobiographical. If "The Lover" may refer to the Wadsworth of Dickinson's
imagination, then there occurs no more joyous an expression of her
transporting, redeeming esteem of him, perhaps especially during
the long years of his physical absence from her, than in stanzas three
and four.

Dickinson's "moments of escape" within the walls of her postexperiential prison testify to the persisting possibility that her love will
continue to sustain her long after she has seemed to lose it. That
explains why "A Prison gets to be a friend - ," "A Geometric Joy - ,"
to the point that "the Liberty we knew" of, is "Avoided - like a
Dream - " (Fr456, lines 1, 16, 29–30). As Wordsworth put it, in
1807, "Nuns fret not at their convent's narrow room." Freedom also
appears to exist only within, if not because of, the prison walls of
Beethoven's *Fidelio* (1805), of Byron's "The Prisoner of Chillon"
(1816). Dickinson's four citations of Byron's "Prisoner," not so incidentally, make this hopeful poem of high-Romantic aftermath the single most-mentioned Romantic work in all of her letters and in all of
her prose fragments (see L233, L249, L293, L1042).[11] Since one of
these citations occurs in a "Master" letter (L233), Dickinson appears
to have associated Romantic-era postexperience with just such a lost
beloved as Wadsworth.

In Dickinson's definition, *freedom* emerges as her choice to do
something, anything, on the assumption that even within the pen-
umbra of her aftermath, the fact of her doing trumps the question
of whether or not her doing can ever grow meaningfully, truthfully
effectual.[12]

> At leisure is the Soul
> That gets a staggering Blow -
> The Width of Life - before it spreads
> Without a thing to do -
>
> It begs you give it Work -
> But just the placing Pins -
> Or humblest Patchwork - Children do -
> To still it's noisy Hands -
>
> (Fr683)

These lines concern "the woman in her dealings with Power" (Wendy Martin 65), but the woman in quest of, and with residual faith in, the abiding power of action, however unspectacular, speaks here, as well. "At leisure is the Soul" suggests, by corollary, that the fact of doing can constitute faith, perhaps even if the doing can appear ineffectual. "Yet go," Tennyson writes, in similar vein,

> and while the holly boughs
> Entwine the old baptismal font,
> Make one Wreath more for Use and Wont,

for Tennyson parallels Dickinson's insight that staying busy, simply going through the motions, fills in for faltering faith (*In Memoriam* 29:9–11).

"The Soul / That gets a staggering Blow - " says nothing. Thus, Dickinson's intimation in "At leisure is the Soul," that the fact of doing trumps the question of whether or not language proves effectual, can appear to benefit, however ironically, however paradoxically, from Carlyle's vaunted preference for deeds over speech:

> The cloudy-browed, thick-soled, opaque Practicality, with no logical utterance, in silence mainly, with here and there a low grunt or growl, has in him what transcends all logic-utterance: a Congruence with the Unuttered. The Speakable, which lies atop, as a superficial film, or outer skin, is his or not his: but the Doable, which reaches down to the World's centre, you find him there![13]

Of course, Dickinson is not cloudy-browed or thick-soled. Still, like Carlyle, and like Keats before him, the persona of "At leisure is the Soul" all but explicitly places fine doing above fine writing.

The tension between Tennyson's "practice…expert / In fitting aptest words to things" (*In Memoriam* 75:5–6) and his logic of silence also comes to mind here. What makes Tennyson more late-Romantic than either high-Victorian or pre-Modern is the force of his preference for life over art, his faith in experience. Thus Bloom rightly concludes that "the Tennyson who counts for most is certainly a Romantic poet, and not a Victorian anti-Romantic resembling the [belated] Arnold of 'Merope' or the straining Hopkins of 'The Wreck of the Deutschland'" (*Modern Critical Views* 9). Bloom adds, with telling, if amusing, near-redundancy, that Tennyson "is a major Romantic poet" (*Modern Critical Views* 9). Emerson's late-Romantic faith in experience, likewise, parallels the ironically *stated* preference for acts over speech: "Central Unity [Emerson writes] is…conspicuous in actions.

Words are finite organs of the infinite mind. They cannot cover the dimensions of what is in truth. They break, chop, and impoverish it. An action is the perfection and publication of thought. A right action seems to fill the eye, and to be related to all nature" ("Nature" [1836] in Murphy, ed. 1:843). The relation between what Emerson says here, though not the voluble way he says it here, and the laconic style of the Myth of Amherst constitutes a sense in which his imagination haunts hers. Dickinson's thus Emerson-linked conviction that "Publication - is the Auction / Of the Mind of Man - " (Fr788, lines 1–2) can mean that genuine publication is not popular, sell-out, poetry, but the unbought, unbuyable, deliberately chosen, and ultimately readable inwardness that precedes, accompanies, and ensures literature of cohesive, lasting, and infinite truth.

The final quatrain of "I can wade Grief - " provides perhaps the best opportunity to drive home the presiding idea of Dickinson's as well as of Nietzsche's postexperience—namely, that what does not kill her makes her stronger:

> Give Balm - to Giants -
> And they'll wilt, like Men -
> Give Himmaleh -
> They'll carry - Him!
> (Fr312, lines 13–16)

"Here Dickinson identifies power with pain, because, by means of one's own discipline, one can possess it" (Juhasz "Reading Doubly" 58). "Here Dickinson explicitly argues against accepting any surrogate: permit no one to suffer in your behalf, the poem entreats, for when you seek to evade sorrow, you only relinquish the means to strength. Even God's mercy can be castrating" (Wolff 214–15). Thus in "I can wade Grief - " "pain strengthens and provides a stimulus to extraordinary action, whereas prosperity debilitates and renders ordinary" (John Cody 15). Pain that makes the Myth of Amherst stronger resembles the painfully posttraumatic effort that goes into the acquired and accruing strength of Atlas. To make the point in religious terms, the pain of Dickinson's aftermath proves tantamount not so much to her natural grace as to what Wesley might describe as her "responsible" grace—that is, the strenuous role that she elects to play in her own salvation.[14] Her balance between choosing and being chosen—that is, her inquiring and acquiring grace—boasts in common with Wesley's responsible grace "The Fascination of What's Difficult" (Yeats's title [1910]) about the experience of postexperience (the

Christian myth of the fall of man, after all, is the founding example of aftermath in the West).

The fact that action turns out to be possible "after," and in part because of, as well as during, "great pain," yields sublime, transcendent nobility.

> Superiority to Fate
> Is difficult to gain
> 'Tis not conferred of any
> But possible to earn
>
> A pittance at a time
> Until to Her surprise
> The Soul with strict economy
> Subsist till Paradise.
>   (Fr1043)

Here, it is true, Dickinson "challenges the idea of having objectives and seeking to reach them, of judging life by targets which are or are not attained. Such purposefulness...makes someone vulnerable to circumstance, whereas her hope...is that someone who manages in different terms may be liberated" (Robinson 22). Nonetheless, besides being oddly embedded in the past, as opposed to sounding forward-looking, the quality of Dickinson's hope lingers in the presence of difficult circumstances.

Lest one go too far toward imputing stoical, static stance to the speaker of "Superiority to Fate," Douglas Leonard reminds readers that "[t]he poem is faithful, even in its equivocation, to Emerson's concept of self-reliance...The paradox still intrigues her: fate, necessity, and chance are present and inescapable, yet the soul can achieve its own will by constant striving" ("Emily Dickinson's Religion" 340–41). The poem modulates from philosophical to religious language. The Calvinist/Arminian controversy of the eighteenth and nineteenth centuries, like the theological tendency of "Superiority to Fate," pits predestination against free will, and perhaps even tilts toward the latter.[15] The "arminianized Calvinism" of Dickinson's day—that is, the paradoxically strong-armed imposition of human choice on foreordination—"softened the fundamental Calvinist dogma asserting depraved man's total dependence on God for salvation by allowing for a person's cooperation in the work of salvation through exercise of free will" (Eberwein review 98). The Arminian, freewill ascendancy in Dickinson's thought and practice, as in Wadsworth's, would be well worth revisiting, if any scholar should ever feel so inclined, or if the next volume in this series ever gets written.[16]

* * *

Insofar as the speaker of these lines,

> Paralysis - our Primer dumb
> Unto Vitality -
> (Fr284, lines 7–8)

and her fellow-sufferers from aftermath (witness "our"), are "*dumb /
Unto Vitality - ,*" Dickinson's postexperience represents mute death-
in-life. To inflect these lines a different way, however, and to imply
paradoxical progression from the stunned silence to the determined
reticence to the eloquent incisiveness of the poet's "post-experiential
perspective," the persona and her others—for rich conversation
resumes here—are "dumb / *Unto Vitality* - ." Insofar as these six
words, "Paralysis - our primer dumb / Unto Vitality - ," make up
the signature lines of the aftermath-subcategory of Emily Dickinson's
works, even the "Paralysis" of aftermath can comprise a schoolbook
for living on, and so fits crucially, after all, into her experiential art of
knowledge as a whole.

The species of vitality specific to Dickinson's experience of postexperience can look at once natural and spiritual:

> Before I got my eye put out -
> I liked as well to see
> As other creatures, that have eyes -
> And know no other way -
>
> But were it told to me, Today,
> That I might have the Sky
> For mine, I tell you that my Heart
> Would split, for size of me -
>
> The Meadows - mine
> The Mountains - mine -
> All Forests - Stintless stars -
> As much of noon, as I could take -
> Between my finite eyes -
>
> The Motions of The Dipping Birds -
> The Morning's Amber Road -

For mine - to look at when I liked,
The news would strike me dead -

So safer - guess - with just my soul
Opon the window pane
Where other creatures put their eyes -
Incautious - of the Sun -
                                    (Fr336)

Whether or not these lines can seem increasingly intuitional, can appear residually sense-based, or somehow both, one would not wish to overestimate the optimistic outlook of the speaker. The poet's chief loss here remains "the faithless beloved" (Patterson *Riddle* 44). Equally downbeat, the "metaphorical (and perhaps occasionally literal) blindness in this poem" functions, harking back to Sophocles, "as a castration metaphor" (Gilbert and Gubar 595–96). By implication, the persona sorely misses the direct physical sight of whom she once knew, still loves. But Dickinson also suggests here that "the superiority of insight over visual sight is given in the claim that she now sees more when blinded than she did sighted" (Robinson 65–66). Whichever kind of vision wins out, the speaker saw much before, and continues to see much, through natural/spiritual double-ness.

Thus the "sublimities of the household seer" come across as "more authentic" than the sublimities she knew before (O'Hara 176–78). The "two kinds of perception" implied by "Before I got my eye put out - "—namely, the experiential visual and the nonexperiential intuitive—emerge as "ambiguities deliberately left unresolved" (Greg Johnson 8–9). Despite, or in part because of, the conditional mood of the middle stanzas, their intensity illustrates the poet's new dispensation of spiritual experience. And these 13 lines virtually restore Dickinson's world of sense experience.

The best paraphrase of Dickinson's "sumptuous Destitution - " has come from Douglas Anderson. Anderson understands that Dickinson's postexperience is well attuned to natural and spiritual vitality. With special sensitivity to "Before I got my eye put out - ," he argues that "the condition of perception that Dickinson describes...is both something less and something more than ordinary human power" (220–21). To clinch his balanced view, Anderson concludes: "To maintain its poise between the remembered fact and the present miracle of memory is the poet's chief objective" (222). The chief glory of the poem, Dickinson's hopeful tone, grows out of, and depends on, the perennial miracle of memory.

Dickinson's poems that follow upon her loss of Charles or of Sue or of both, or of someone else such as William Smith Clark (Ruth Owen Jones) or Judge Otis Lord (Walsh), or of something equally momentous (natural religion? faith in God?), evince paradoxically an emotion quite like happiness, if not beatitude. "Transport's mighty price is no more than he is worth" (L359). Dickinson suggests here that ecstasy grows more valuable for its fleeting quality. The residue of ecstasy (she implies) substitutes for the experience. One thinks, in this connection, of Wordsworth's "emotion recollected in tranquility," or, as Keats would say, since joy ever bids adieu, bursting its grape can extend its savor.[17] Dickinson's Wordsworth- and Keats-like philosophy or science of aftermath excels Frost's later nostalgia-inducing view that "happiness makes up in height what it lacks in duration" ("The Figure a Poem Makes" [1949]). Dickinson's postexperience by no means starves her, and perhaps even sustains her. If what remains to the Myth of Amherst turns out to be only a strategy of survival or of spiritual discipline, this plan transcends any mere defense mechanism against manic depression or, for that matter, against just plain depression.

Do Dickinson's close encounters of this remnant kind revive her late-Romantic soul? Do her high-Romantic "Superior instants" (Fr630, line 1), when her heart, like Wordsworth's, leaps for joy (compare "My Heart Leaps Up" [1802]), extend to the late Romanticism of her aftermath? Quite possibly, *yes* to both questions, for, from moment to moment, and not simply from time to time, the poetic personae of her "sumptuous Destitution - " can illustrate the paradox of their posttraumatic hope. Though fallen from the grace of experience, it is felix culpa, for these speakers expect the world to lie all before them, anyway. Thus, they can bear the resonance of, can aspire to the animated suspension between, despair and hope, not unlike John Milton's postlapsarian couple.

The lingering effect of Dickinson's loves equates to abundant recompense for her losses. As her contemporary Tennyson declares, in perhaps his keenest anticipation of her works,

'Tis better to have loved and lost
Than never to have loved at all.
(*In Memoriam* 27:15–16)

"Quoted by now into meaninglessness," observes Peltason of these lines, "they evidence an important new understanding. The end of experience is not the sum of experience or the only source of meaning.

The poet has loved and he has lost, but the second of these has not canceled out the first" (61). The epilogue to *In Memoriam* rejoices that "love is more / Than in the summers that are flown" (lines 17–18). Tennyson adds,

> I myself with these have grown
> To something greater than before. (Lines 19–20)

Even the Tennyson who has loved and lost, and not just Tennyson in his ecstasy, assumes the efficacy of natural, if not spiritual, experience. In like manner, even the Dickinson of aftermath, and not just the Dickinson whose heart leaps high, cultivates the faith that time and experience can define character. Time and experience can make us know our selves, as Wordsworth implies, in

> the world
> Of all of us,—the place where in the end
> We find our happiness, or not at all!
> (*The Prelude* [1850] 11:142–44)

—and let us commit these 20 most Dickinson-pertinent words that Wordsworth ever wrote to memory.

In short, Emily Dickinson's poems about "post-experiential perspective" include experience. George Bernard Shaw, as though he, too, thought of writing as living, had an answer for those bemused by the fact that his love for actress Ellen Terry consisted entirely of his 25 years' worth of letters to her: "Let those who may complain that it was all on paper remember that only on paper has humanity yet achieved glory, beauty, truth, knowledge, virtue, and abiding love" (qtd. in Peters 159). Dickinson's poetry of aftermath, at any rate, contributes a greater degree of dramatic urgency than of either/or logic to the perennial debate between art and life. As evidenced even in these lyrics, as well as in the darkest hours of her letters and of her prose fragments, her ongoing "afterlife" can stay far from being merely unalloyed grimness. It can become, if not exactly an overrunning cup, then new life, at least.

On the evidence of Dickinson's set pieces of aftermath, specifically, the physical absence of Wadsworth and of Susan Dickinson enhances their ghostly power in the poet's imagination. Notwithstanding Pollak's persuasive view that Emily Dickinson's loss of the two great relationships of her life creates an "awful Vacuum" in her art (Fr887, line 3), Dickinson's continuing, if only imaginary, experience of

Charles and of Sue proves almost more than merely metaphorical, and perhaps even partly positive (Pollak *Anxiety* 190–221). In fact, all manner of others and of otherness abides in her imagination, not just as anticipation or sustaining memory, but even as presence or revivifying force. An *awe*-filled vacuum, after all, signifies, if not the fulfilled potential of Dickinson's optimism, then the mysterious possibility held in reserve for her by her hope. Whatever "fallings from us," whatever "vanishings," she might appear previously to have incurred, including her strained but enduring friendship or star-crossed love for Charles or for Sue, the poet whose life seems to have passed her by appears yet to enjoy her life (compare Wordsworth, "Ode: Intimations of Immortality," line 143).

Dickinson's "sumptuous Destitution - ," like her late-Romantic imagination, resounds with her mimetic as well as expressive conviction that, as Emerson prefigures it in his own blend of the ideal and the actual, "[m]y book should smell of pines and reverberate with the hum of insects" ("Self-Reliance" [1842] in Murphy, ed., 1:899). Just as Emerson's "smell of pines" pertains to Dickinson's "old house under the pines" (Bianchi *Life and Letters* 27), so the rich strangeness of this aroma serves to evoke the nonverbal or preverbal aspect of her continuing experience. Just as Emerson's "hum of insects" reverberates as the "spectral Canticle" of Dickinson's lines entitled "My Cricket" (Fr895, line 11), so this entomological music signals the verbal and aesthetic character of her continuing experience. Contrary to the solipsism of her times, and of Modernism and post-Modernism, Dickinson's signature conundrum of "sumptuous Destitution - " views the external world as more than a window on her soul—that is, as an objective correlative to her desire and to her cognition.

Striking a balance between comparison and contrast, Jed Deppman's take on Dickinson's foretelling of post-Modernism allows for her active, connected subjectivity. While "post-Modern theory makes visible important aspects of her work," Deppman points out, she "played more seriously, engaged more sharply with...vocabularies, and had more all-around faith in the agency of the writer than does your average post-Modern" (*Trying to Think* 87). Dickinson's poetry of aftermath, accordingly, scarcely prevents her from reexpressing, with however subtle or muted a tone, the perennial Western belief that life remains well worth living and perhaps even quite full of promise. By reopening personal access to otherness through others, and vice versa, even Dickinson's postexperiential perspective revamps, in particular, the foundational strategy whereby the naturalized imagination of her poetry in general grasps what Tennyson calls the mystery of "all in all" (compare Tennyson, "Flower in the Crannied Wall" [1869], line 5).

Despite whatever traumas of aesthetic crisis, flawed epistemology, challenged faith, or fading friendship have crossed her mind, soul, and heart, Dickinson's paradox that less of one thing means more of another, and perhaps even an ongoing version of that one thing, reflects and re-sounds the ultimate Western conundrum of felix culpa. Her strangely maximal minimalism—that is, the harder her fall, the more her grace—emerges from, entails, and augurs her experience, as well as that of the 34 poetic personae presented in this chapter. Notwithstanding such destructively and deconstructively skeptical poems in this category as "I like a look of Agony" (Fr339) and "Severer Service of myself" (Fr887)—to read them is to weep—her art of aftermath bids scant farewell to her life. On the contrary, although the Dickinson of postexperience "see[s]," with Wordsworth, only "by glimpses now," "the hiding-places of [her] power," like those of Wordsworth's, "Return upon [her]" nonetheless,

> enshrining,
> Such is her hope, the spirit of the Past
> For future restoration.
> (*The Prelude* [1850] 12:279, 281, 284–86)

Such harking back links the present to the past, and the present and the past to the future. Her definition of "Retrospection" as "Prospect's half, / Sometimes, almost more - " (Fr1014, lines 7–8) fits the "definition" of her poetic definitions as "the universal, structural, and essential aspects of an experience" (Deppman "'I Could Not'" 53). That is, a given definition expressed even during Dickinson's aftermath represents not just her inward life—not just "the consciousness of the one involved in the experience," whether "the one" be Dickinson herself, her aesthetic self-projection, or her reader—but also such outward circumstances as those that exist in memory and in expectation (53).

The lyric in which Dickinson's language of prospective retrospection explicitly occurs proves conclusive with regard to understanding both her own experience of postexperience and that of the others in her social circle:

> This was in the White of the Year -
> That - was in the Green -
> Drifts were as difficult then to think
> As Daisies now to be seen -

Looking back, is best that is left
Or if it be - before -
Retrospection is Prospect's half,
Sometimes, almost more -
                (Fr1014)

Dickinson sent this poem to her Norcross cousins in 1865; it probably refers to the deaths of their father and mother. The poem scarcely
glosses over the challenge posed by pessimism. "The *d* alliteration and
the short syllables suggest the difficulty which her thought strives to
express, and the auxiliaries are used for their contribution to the [bro-
ken or mournful] effect she is expressing" (Scherrer 40). On the other
hand, Dickinson's description of retrospection as prospective allows
Frances and Louise Norcross some consolation. If only through the
green thoughts of green shades that spring, following the winter of
grief, can offer, the poem intimates natural, if not spiritual, immortality. The capitalization in the penultimate line suggests that the only
seemingly receded earthly lives of the Norcross parents "roll round"
in the white-and-green of "earth's diurnal course" (Wordsworth's language), and perhaps even appear in the rayless, presence-of-all-color
light of the stars, "pinnacled dim," that is, in Shelley's astronomically
transcendent "white radiance of Eternity."[18]

*   *   *

If Wadsworth's aphorism "The grand secret of contentment is found,
not in increasing our supplies—but in diminishing our necessities"
was food for Dickinson's thought, she played with this notion in
her own way. For example, her arrival at "Quartz contentment, like
a stone - " (Fr372, line 9) reflects Wadsworth's modest goal, but
the signature lyric of aftermath in which these words of hers occur—
namely, "After great pain, a formal feeling comes"—does so more
imaginatively. Dickinson rarely makes more than a reluctant, uneasy
peace with any such strict injunction against self-indulgence, for even
such an otherwise similarly destitute poem of aftermath as "I felt a
Funeral, in my Brain" (Fr340) can appear to fall on the hopeful side
of "sumptuous Destitution - ." Of course, the last words of "I felt a
Funeral"—namely, "I . . . finished knowing - then - "—can mean that
the speaker is cut off, obliterated by death. Still, this speaker's cryptic
bow-out can also signify his/her "Finished"—that is, accomplished/
perfected (as well as truncated)—"knowing" at the end of life (line
20). Does Dickinson thus write "finis" to her alternately, nay, her at

once, experiential and postexperiential art of knowledge, as though her infinite yearning were at long last satisfied and the rest were silence? Is this wise speaker-from-the-grave ready, now, for revelation in his/her afterlife, as though there were such a restrospective prospect in store for him/her, after all?

Although Dickinson's "dearest earthly friend" counsels his congregation that straitened circumstances can build character, the poet would go further than the preacher. For Dickinson, less of one person or thing, however unwelcome the diminishment, signifies expectation—signals presence—of someone or of something else, purified by adversity. Her unfulfilled need leads, meanwhile, to surprising compatibility between material want/physical desire and moral/spiritual community. As philosopher Gaston Bachelard concludes, as though in dialogue with Wadsworth/Dickinson, "The attainment of the superfluous causes a greater spiritual excitement than the attainment of necessities. Man is a creature of desire and not a creature of need" (qtd. in Donoghue "Discreet Charms" 91). Dickinson would agree, for her "sumptuous Destitution - " alleviates misgivings of "blank desertion" (compare Wordsworth, "Ode: Intimations of Immortality," line 144). Dickinson's choice of renunciation cultivates deep hopefulness. Thus, as opposed to merely illustrating the experience of being a recluse, the Myth of Amherst embodies experience.

Dickinson's gnomic equivalent to high-Romantic inference of intimation from recollection—that is, her definition of "Retrospection" as "Prospect's half, / Sometimes, almost more - "—culturally as well as personally equates looking backward and looking forward. Her faith in progress deepens as her looking backward yields a sense of historical immediacy and prophetic foreknowledge. Not even her speakers of aftermath, aware as they are of collective human experience, finally commit the collective sin of pure nostalgia, the enemy of hope. Rather, their "historiography" outhistoricizes Hegel. That is, Dickinson avoids the nemesis of cyclical monotony. To echo Hobbes, she understands time and experience as naturally inexorable, if not spiritually efficacious. This Dickinson, as this chapter has tried to show, appears all the more dynamically paradoxical for becoming Anglo-American Romantic in hindsight, as well as pre-Modern in foresight.

As much as anti-Romantic signs of Victorian-American belatedness, and as much as ominous fragments shored against pre-Modern ruins, Dickinson's most prescient poems prove to be remnants saved by late-Romantic hope. To quote Robert Langbaum's phrase for the lyric expression that began in the early nineteenth century and extended far into the twentieth, "the poetry of experience" jibes with, and includes, Dickinson's poetry of aftermath, as well as the more straightforwardly experiential poetry sampled in part I of this book. Especially the last phrase of John Updike's statement of novel-reading goals—"What we seek, gropingly, in fiction, is enlargement, a glorification of the furtive and secret and seemingly trivial, *a valorization of human experience*" (108; emphasis added)—applies, as well, to the entire body of Dickinson's lyrical works. Thus, although even the best moments of her "post-experiential perspective" scarcely rival the "Superior instants - " of her poetry of full-blown experience (Fr630, line 1), her poetry of aftermath nonetheless earns well the not-so-muted optimism of outcome that augurs further harvest. These personae, too, share Wordsworth's deliciously vague sense of "something evermore about to be," of an imminence that includes, in Dickinson's case, not just auspicious engagement with past and present but even the prospect of an afterlife perhaps more vivid than Wordsworth's "intimations of immortality" themselves. Dickinson's poetic personae of "sumptuous Destitution - " play on, and hence they also keep in play, the religious as well as philosophical and scientific coordinates of her art of knowledge.

Although the double perspective of Dickinson's late-Romantic imagination achieves her strongest combination of natural models with spiritual metaphors, and although this counterintuition champions both the androgynous ideal of her nineteenth-century feminism and her provisional belief in immortality, her "post-experiential perspective" riddles with special skill, including a unique grasp of oxymoron. Notwithstanding the decidedly un-sumptuous enervation of their pre-Modern mode and the relentlessly antisumptuous anomie of their post-Modern intimations, her speakers of "sumptuous Destitution - " reap the bracing harvest of bald, cold truth, and revive her hope-against-hope, if not precisely Wordsworth's hope-after-hope. Though without ever quite professing Experiential Faith, and though only sometimes reengendering her all-seasons as well as late-Romantic dialogue between joyful wisdom and spiritual wealth, Dickinson's personae of aftermath yet "dwell in Possibility - " of abundant life.

The rich conversation among Dickinson's aesthetic self-projections, her literary precursors and contemporaries, and her friends and loved ones occurs perhaps *especially* in her poems of despairing hope, defining intriguingly, and against the odds, the possibility of personal access to others through otherness, and vice versa. Yes, Dickinson can form a party of one, like Milton's Abdiel. She rarely parties alone, however, not even through her only seemingly noncommunitarian poetry of aftermath. Thus, like the speaker of "The Soul selects her own

Society - ," she can "Choose One," that is, can pick not just herself alone, and not just one other person besides herself, but a "Society" of at least two others besides herself (see Fr409, line 10, and please recall the discussion in the introduction to this book). That latter, larger society is—even within the realm of her postexperience—made up of multitudes that she contains—namely, her personae and those of many real people besides. Thus, just as Dickinson's word *society* pertains to Locke's social contract and Wesley's societies alike, while at the same time harking back to the Royal Society, so this key term embodies her philosophical and scientific, if not spiritual communion, perhaps all the way through her works, and not just in her poetry of experience.

The frequent literary references in this chapter have suggested, then, that Dickinson knew Romantic-era authors well, and, in any case, these quotations, as dialogue with her letters and poems, have surely proved telling here. The desirability of juxtaposing, say, Shelley's love poetry with hers, inheres in the common frames of tonal and thematic reference that have by now become clear between the Romantics and the Myth of Amherst. True, among the master figures of Anglo-American Romanticism whom this chapter makes primary, Blake, Coleridge, Shelley, and Carlyle receive no mention in her 1,049 letters (she wrote many more, though) and 124 prose fragments (so much, then, for any significance to Carlyle on her wall?).[19] And yet, the letters name Tennyson four times (L23, L243, L320, L616) and Emerson eight times (L30, L330, L353, L457, L481, L486, L750, L962). The letters and prose fragments quote Wordsworth three times (L96, L315, L398), Byron three times (L233, L249, L293), Tennyson four times (L353, L486, L506, L801), and Emerson five times (L436, L794, L823, L1004, PF116), as well as alluding to Wordsworth once (L400), Byron once (L1042), and Emerson twice (L269, PF10). Her poetry of aftermath, like her works in general but more subtly, participates in Romanticism with particular affinities for Wordsworth. For instance, this important subcategory of her work, like a major strain of Wordsworth's verse, resolves itself into

> joy! That in our embers
> Is something that doth live,

and so makes interiority and language integral to experience (compare Wordsworth, "Ode: Intimations of Immortality," lines 129–30).

Dickinson's personae of "sumptuous Destitution - ," accordingly, go beyond mere intuition of familiar near-nihilism. They aspire to the more than simply "poetic" faith espoused among the most optimistic of her speakers. Her late-Romantic, anti-Victorian art differs from Arnold's anti-Romantic, high-Victorian

> Wandering between two worlds, one dead,
> The other powerless to be born.
> (Arnold, "Stanzas from the Grande Chartreuse"
> [1855], lines 85–86)

Dickinson's "postexperiential perspective" revives one world in order to grace the other's "growing gloom" (compare Hardy, "The Darkling Thrush" [1900], line 24).

In sum, according to this occasionally ironic but rarely anti-Romantic reading of Dickinson's poetry of aftermath, this canon-within-the-canon sometimes nearly regains the very paradise that the poet's more tender singing almost never loses.[20] Dickinson's pre-Modern mode, if not her post-Modern intimations, in fact, overlaps her late-Romantic imagination at the very point, perhaps, where her faith in experience resets her experience of faith (but this is largely a matter for the future book to look at). On the one hand, her *"formal* feeling" of "great pain" connotes closed-system, nothing-outside-the-text nihilism, thereby denoting the slough of her pre-Modern despond wherein, metaphorically speaking, she wonders stiffly whether or not to eat a peach. Her bleaker confession of this feeling presounds, if not the Modern to post-Modern cry of Sisyphean futility, then "the atonal banshee of the emerging egomania called The Modern" (A. N. Wilson 12). On the other hand, to inflect her phrase differently, the "formal *feeling*" that follows "great pain" might, just might, relieve it, as well as constitute heartache, uncertainty, doubt, or silence. Her grander confession of *this* feeling, even according to the set pieces of aftermath considered throughout this and the previous chapter, plays again, re-sounds, the old, sweet, Romantic song of love, joy, and hope. Dickinson's "postexperiential perspective" defamiliarizes itself, opens her very aftermath from within, to wise, well-earned, and anything but foolish optimism, alert to the intimation of undying hope.

CONCLUSION

To recapitulate: Emily Dickinson's rich conversation with her precursors and contemporaries in Anglo-American belles lettres, first of all, counts as her dialogical inspiration. In effect, she took her cue from the lower case orthography and the inductive modesty of Charles Lamb's scientific label for William Wordsworth's poetry: "natural methodism." Accordingly, she turned down the volume of Ralph Waldo Emerson's revival idiom and grounded his Transcendentalism in the senses. More succinctly than her counterparts in Anglo-American Romanticism, she laid the strengths and weaknesses of sifting and weighing data ("I ponder, and I cannot ponder," as William Blake's Thel puts it) alongside subjective and intersubjective values for doing so ("yet I live and love," as Blake's Thel adds; compare *The Book of Thel* [1789], Plate 5, line 6). Thus, before Wallace Stevens, Emily Dickinson discovered "what will suffice"—that is, again to apply the language of Blake to her case, she found religion "Too much" and science just "Enough!"[1]

Emily Dickinson's rich conversation with the likes of John Locke, John Wesley, Charles Wadsworth, and Charles Darwin, moreover, enriched her art of knowledge, as distinct from her "art of belief." At a distance, she took her cue from Locke, for, notwithstanding her poet's natural headiness, she defined thoughts as inseparable from, and as in partnership with, sense perception. She harbored nostalgia for the sense-favoring faith of Wesley and of Wadsworth, but, as opposed to keeping that faith whole in the "holiness" of her "heart's affections,"[2] her bracing realism traded the transatlantic revivalists' will to believe in the supernatural, the miraculous, for the uncertainty and mystery of experience. Her admiration for Darwin, whose evolutionary biology scourged religion (despite his reluctance to have done so), confirmed her toughness.[3] Consistent with the Higher Criticism of sacred texts, Dickinson's empirical voice called the Bible to account, and into question.[4] She brought the presiding idea of the transatlantic revival—namely, the spiritual sense—closer to science than Wesley and Wadsworth did. Since she could not at the same time rely on experience and profess faith, and since she could not compartmentalize the two (as though they were "non-overlapping magisteria"), she tended to choose the former over the latter.[5] Yet empirical philosophy and physical and life science yielded freer play among the subjects of her poetry than all the forms of faith in her English-language milieu.

Dickinson's methodical imagination, then, did not envision things unseen but searched out things seen in the company of Experiment, the guide of all natural enthusiasts like her. The signature poem of her art of knowledge, "Experiment escorts us last - " (Fr1181), puts *searching out things seen* at the top of her readers' lists of procedures to apply at will, and to good effect. Her word *us* means those among her partners-in-discussion who would follow not the "wise passiveness" but the wise activity of Emily Dickinson herself. The poem suggests that Anglo-Americans from the Enlightenment to the Romantic era would have echoed, perhaps even as her readers still can, the four indelible words of that savvy first line (and title) of this lyric. In agreement with the "pungent company" (Fr1181, line 2) of her literary, philosophical, religious, and scientific ancestors and coevals, Dickinson enlisted the hard truths of sense-based reason and of sense-driven method on the side of aesthetic complexity and satisfaction. She appeared braver than the visionary company she kept in England and in New England. Far from being as rootless as, say, an orchid, the "Columnar Self - " on which she "amply rel[ied]" (Fr740, line 2) was well grounded in her English-speaking milieu, steeped in reason and the senses as these British Enlightenment faculties modulated into Romantic Anglo-America. Especially richly did she converse with Keats, whose "*Negative Capability,*" whose "condition of being in uncertainties, Mysteries, doubts, without any irritable reaching after fact & reason," intensified how she dwelt in the possibility of all things natural, while at the same time holding out hope of some things spiritual.

"Experiment escorts us last - ," significantly, declares Dickinson's dialogical intent. Through her "common" sense, reporting her experience and learning from the experience of others, her concept of science as group effort adumbrated Modern- to post-Modern-era cooperation among cognitive scientists in particular.[6] Her poetry invites readers less to put things to the test than to try them out, and hence to answer the call of "Love" "to the things of this world," not in bland reconciliation of these things, but with "sustained tension, without victory or suppression, of co-present oppositions."[7] At the same time that Dickinson's imagery feels rich and strange, she would have "us" realize that her metaphors stay natural, or, as Rainer Maria

Rilke puts it, just as though he were summing up a presiding idea of Emily Dickinson's art,

> To see landscape thus, as something distant and foreign, something remote and unloving, something entirely self-contained, was necessary, if it was ever to be a medium and an occasion for an autonomous art; for it had to be distant and very different from us, if it was to be capable of becoming a redemptive symbol for our fate. It had to be almost hostile in its sublime indifference, if it was to give new meaning to our existence...For we began to understand Nature only when we no longer understood it; when we felt that it was the Other, indifferent toward men, which has no wish to let us enter, then for the first time we stepped outside of Nature, alone, out of the lonely world. ("Concerning Landscape" [1902], qtd. in Rilke xxv)

Thus, although Dickinson and Wordsworth would perhaps have found Nature no less mysterious for being somewhat less alien, if not more sociable, than Rilke's, she would have "us" rest content, like Wordsworth and like Rilke, with "see[ing] into the life of things" (compare Wordsworth, "Lines Written a Few Miles above Tintern Abbey" [1798], line 49). Dickinson could only infrequently embrace the religious explanation, the solace, which Tennyson tended to parrot. Unlike some of her companions in dialogue, Dickinson could not justify the ways of God to man as much as she would have liked. She would have applied the principle of natural *selection* as a means of separating out the timid from her *society*, theodicean chapter.

Dickinson's poetry of philosophy and of science would have toughened the minds of her favorite and otherwise kindred belletristic authors of the Anglo-American world, for it is uncannily as though she read all works by Blake, Wordsworth, Coleridge, Shelley, Keats, Carlyle, Tennyson, and Emerson, and they hers. Her core strategy of realism constituted her countermove to their temperamentally tender gambit. In accord with Wordsworth's signature predicate, she could "see into the life of things" with the best of them. However, she drew back from the pathetic, anthropomorphic fallacy committed by the Romantic era—that is, "the treatment of inanimate objects as if they had human feelings, thoughts, or sensations," as in "the sea is angry at us."[8] Does Wordsworth's word *life*, as applied to *things*, falsify the nonhuman world, and flatter human-centered agendas in it, as Dickinson appears to ask him? And as she appears to wonder, in response to his six-word imperative *see into the life of things*, do inanimate objects only *seem* to possess life, by leave not so much of Wordsworth's egotistical sublimity as of his delusions of grandeur? Finally, are lifeless things, on the one hand, and living beings who are dying, on the other, unpoetic, as Dickinson appears to query Wordsworth?

Dickinson brightened and sharpened the sepia of Wordsworth et al., though she would have recognized, with Kipling, that such a romanticized, brownish tint was "a sweet material to work with" (see the definition of *sepia* in the *OED*). For her repertoire of realism, she heightened the particularism of the Romantics. She tempered their elevation of the human. Despite some evidence to the contrary, like the opening, yet not the closing, lines of "Of Bronze - and Blaze - " (Fr 319), she rejected their apotheosis of humankind, except that her Darwin-like assessment of "Retrospect" and "Prospect" (Fr1014, line 7) intensified the somber dignity of *Homo sapiens*, however ironic Darwin-"Prospect" might appear. In effect, she returned her literary precursors and contemporaries to their homegrown, grounded vision, eradicating the air-plant of their borrowed French rationalism and of their imported German idealism. She reaffirmed her heritage of imagining that mind mattered more for not being the location of all reality. Her "natural methodism" wore as well as, perhaps even better than, Wordsworth's. If "she had the best mind of all our poets, early and late," she could outthink him, and perhaps even outobserve him (compare Bloom *Western Canon* 300).

"Experiment escorts us last - " signifies, above all, that Dickinson's poetry of philosophy and of science edges out her more religion-poised lyrics. The latter seek the evidence of things not seen, yet finally fail to find it: like the all-penetrating eye of Wordsworth, and of Darwin, too, the former can "see into the life of things," well and truly. "The force that through the green fuse drives the flower / Drives [Dickinson's] green age," to coopt the language of Dylan Thomas, yet scarcely dwells above her (compare Thomas, "The Force that through the Green Fuse Drives the Flower" [1934], lines 1–2). Without necessarily calling all unseen things into doubt (to "see into the life of things," after all, can be to look for something vital, yet hidden, behind, beneath, or within things), Dickinson's verbal self-projections submit system and creed to the point blank, piercing test of experience. This Dickinson kills, puts out of its misery, what was already moribund.

Dickinson's Wordsworth-like "language of the sense," in consequence, rivals that of Locke, Wesley, Wadsworth, Darwin et al. (compare Wordsworth, "Tintern Abbey," line 108). Her imagination directed Ockham's razor to the empirically charged, experiment-attuned model of spiritual experience devised by Wesley and developed by Wadsworth. Her close-shaven art scarcely emulated the fuzzy plenitude of the Anglo-American religion of the heart. However much he wished to join the congregation, Hardy's persona, too, could neither share what those people appeared to feel, nor see what they seemed to envision (compare Hardy, "The Impercipient (At a Cathedral Service)" [1898]). Neither biblical testimony nor spiritual witness, however desired or desirable, either could soften or was even needed to cushion the rough paradise of the world gathered for her select society by the narrow but wide-ranging hands of the Myth of Amherst.

Of course, the skip from sense base to sense analogy might conceivably have closed the gap between experience and faith. Still, the abrupt sleight-of-hand fell short, as far as Emily Dickinson was concerned. Her art of knowledge subsisted on, and consisted of, experience eschewing the leap of faith. Her "art of belief" remained apart, despite her yearning to reconcile her empirical voice with her evangelical vernacular. The former augmented, and the latter waned, as her career progressed. In the end, she resisted the temptation to synthesis. Did her faith in experience outlast her religious belief? Whatever the answer, her experience of faith visited her works by fits and starts, like Shelley's inconstant "Power" in "Hymn to Intellectual Beauty" (1817).

To be sure, Dickinson's poetry of experience could yield to her poetry of postexperience, of aftermath, which preempted, and tried with some limited success to solve in advance, the Modern-era poet's dilemma concerning "what to make of a diminished thing" (compare Frost, "The Oven Bird" [1916], line 14). Before Hardy, Dickinson felt "growing gloom," for, philosophically speaking, she foresaw that *"the experience of the real hinges on a constant preparedness to distrust experience"* (Pfau 21; Pfau's emphasis). Religiously speaking, similarly, her "lost saints" prefigured "fragments" and "ruins" of the Modern soul's world.[9] Scientifically speaking, she anticipated what Roland Barthes would soon enough come to say—namely, that "Method, too, is a fiction" (qtd. in Thirlwell 28). The Romantic to Modern colloquy in which Dickinson's poetry spoke, in both directions, included her pre-Modern mode, her foreboding of attenuated epistemology, desiccated spirit, and illusory knowledge. Nevertheless, though it represents her most pessimistic mood and an eye-catching, now-fashionable subset of her poems besides, even her poetry of postexperience, of aftermath, reflected the vitality of her poetry as a whole. Thus, although her testimony that "I find ecstasy in living" (L342a) can seem to whistle in the dark, her wisdom that "The mere sense of living is joy enough" (L342a) contributed "abundant recompense" to her imperfect, flawed knowledge, and perhaps even ample consolation for the loss of her childhood saints (compare Wordsworth, "Tintern Abbey," line 88). This wisdom survived in her aftermath, where her fading but persistent sense of joy could no longer simply drown her sorrow, yet where it still preserved, however barely, both her optimism and her hope.

Yes, the Romantic to Modern colloquy in which Dickinson's poetry played a leading role—how decisively she weighed in on this conversation!—came late to anxiety about science. Robert Burton's *Anatomy [or Science] of Melancholy* (1621), after all, foreshadowed how, in the works of Donne, Swift, and Johnson, the "new philosophy [science] calls all in doubt" (Donne's language). Consistent with the nineteenth-century genius for doubt, however, Dickinson's disquiet signaled as much of a crisis of faith in empiricism as of a crisis of faith in faith or, for that matter, of a predicament of love. She always exercised enough trust in science for Experiment to check her on-again, off-again religious belief. And Knowledge Avenue, for her, intersected with Aftermath Byway. On that smaller road, if only near that important junction, she came to view nostalgia for her "lost saints" as misplaced, unhealthy emotion, the enemy of hope. Notwithstanding the numbed senses, the paralyzing effect, of her pre-Modern mode, her poetry of postexperience, of aftermath, offered a remnant of sense-based reason, saved a share of sense-driven method. Dickinson's personae of postexperience could therefore join her speakers of experience at the nerve center of a Romantic to Modern choral company that sang of philosophical effort and of scientific expectation alike.

Perhaps the biggest payoff of Dickinson's retro/pro position on the arc from Romantic to Modern is the complex, aesthetically satisfying quality of her optimism, her hope. At least as decisively as Coleridge embraced melancholy (Eric G. Wilson reads him thus), Dickinson rejected "the willed and willful, feel-good optimism" of Benjamin Franklin and of "the Prozac nation" that sought, and still seeks, to drive all unhappiness out of consciousness, and into Disney-fied lobotomy-land.[10] Although her enchanting lack of guile can substitute for simple happiness, "the true path to ecstatic joy" for Dickinson, as for her literary precursors, contemporaries, and heirs, lay through what Wilson calls the "acute melancholia" of all these writers (compare Eric G. Wilson *Against* 146). As opposed to the mere happiness that tries to stand alone, "the deep power of joy" dwells with, and within, "world-sorrow," or so Dickinson appears to have thought, as though, in a stroke of genius rivaling the British Renaissance invention of tragicomedy, she conflated Wordsworth's phrase with Hopkins's term.[11]

To typify her conversation with Keats, and to locate her melancholia in his (as well as in that of her Modern to post-Modern descendants), her "sumptuous Destitution - " "glut[s]" her sorrow "on a morning rose," drowns her sorrow in joy.[12] Her "sumptuous Destitution - " more than merely wallows in the lugubrious Victorian mindset, nor does this signature conundrum, proto-Modern, just shore fragments of existential richness against the ruins of her bereaved psyche. Rather, Dickinson's role in the Romantic to Modern colloquy focuses, too, on her traditional (not just prescient) melancholia that paradoxically keeps Romantic-era hope for the here and now alive, however barely.

Dickinson's late-Romantic imagination, finally, overlapped her pre-Modern mode and her post-Modern intimations, and thus the Romantic to Modern arc described continuity as well as contrast. Her recognition of doom and gloom, perhaps even as this pessimism of hers originated in the era of high Romanticism, matched her reminiscence of high-Romantic hope and progress, perhaps even enough to extend her optimism in attenuated form to the Modern era. Of course, Dickinson's despair bears on Modern-era hopelessness. Still, her epistemological robustness and scientific brio not only thrived on Romantic-era optimism but also survived in Modern-era hope-against-hope (this wan emotion struggled against Great War horror and reeled from Titanic/iceberg convergence).[13] Dickinson's faith in experience hovered near her poetry of postexperience insofar as her bald, cold truths held as tightly in her pre-Modern mode as her clothed, warm truths in her late-Romantic imagination. Accordingly, as though Dickinson agreed with Tennyson's (by this point even more) familiar sentiment that

'Tis better to have loved and lost
Than never to have loved at all,

the continuing presences or afterlives of Susan Dickinson and of Charles Wadsworth in Dickinson's poems of aftermath leavened the poet's pessimism there. Thus, as distinct from lamenting lost friends and loved ones as high-Romantic Beethoven did in *his* mood of aftermath—hear his "*An die Ferne Geliebte*," "To the Distant Beloved" (1816)—some of the most mournful words of Dickinson's poems of postexperience can define new bounds of love.[14] Even these lyrics can promise meaning, and perhaps even knowledge and truth, as distinct from foreboding meaninglessness.

Can sons and daughters of Anglo-America still hear the woes, yet echo the sighs, of Dickinson's personae of aftermath? Can her posterity reflect, affect retroactively, the living embers of her hope, as expressed in these poems of her postexperience? Whether or not, in the spirit of her rich conversation, the answer to both of these questions is *yes*, her theme of aftermath can nonetheless illustrate her most mine-able ore at the present time. Its less-is-more subject matter can appeal to Modern- and post-Modern-era minimalism, at the same time that the metaphorical half-life of her poetry of postexperience can temper, relieve, and perhaps even substitute for, the literal-mindedness of now rampant fundamentalism. Such a potential benefit of dialogue with the Myth of Amherst can live in, and revive, one's dreams.

Can Dickinson's fellow-feeling for her literary precursors, contemporaries, and heirs contain the seed of one's own resilience? George Steiner epitomized so much of what this book has tried to argue that extensive quotation from his *Errata: An Examined Life* (1999) is needed here. First, like Dickinson, Steiner poses the question of optimism and of hope, despite, or in part because of, his understanding of pessimism and of despair:

> An irrefutable realism [Steiner writes] empowers the archaic Greek postulate whereby "It is best not to be born and next best to die young," old being, with so very few exceptions, a malodorous waste, an incontinence of mind and body made raw by the remembrance of the unfulfilled. What, then, is the well-spring of our ineradicable hopes, of our intimations of futurity, of our forward-dreams and utopias, public and private? ... [F]rom where rises the high tide of desire, of expectation, of an obsession with sheer being defiant of the pain...? (94–95)

Then, as though saying what Dickinson sings, Steiner answers his own questions, Wordsworth- as well as Dickinson-tinctured (and Steiner's lyrical brief can serve, for that matter, as higher education policy for the care and promotion of language arts departments):

> [T]hese liberations from the constraints of the physical, from the blank wall of our own death and a seeming eternity of personal and collective disappointment [Steiner continues], are in crucial measure linguistic. Bio-socially, we are indeed a short-lived mammal made for extinction, as are all other kinds. But we are a language-animal, and it is this one endowment which, more than any other, makes bearable and fruitful our ephemeral state. The evolution in human speech—it may have come late—of subjunctives, optatives, counterfactual conditionals and of the futurities of the verb...has defined and safeguarded our humanity. It is because we can tell stories, fictive or mathematical-cosmological, about a universe a billion years hence;...it is because "if"-sentences...can...deny, reconstruct, alter

past, present, and future, mapping *otherwise*. It is in these determinants of pragmatic reality that existence continues to be worth experiencing. Hope is grammar. The mystery of futurity or freedom—these two are intimately kindred—is syntactical . . . [T]he available vocabulary will comprise a wealth of exact discrimination, of psychologically, materially, and socially recognized density and shading . . . The riches of experience, the creativities of thought and of feeling, the penetrative and delicate singularities of conception made possible by the polyglot condition are the preeminent adaptive agency and advantage of the human spirit. (97–100; Steiner's emphasis)[15]

In the company of her masters of belles lettres, Dickinson's sublunary rage less for order than for wonder and awe could bless us in our worst of times. The very depth of her premonitory despair can sound the mystic chord of our lyrical lilt or lift. Her *avant la lettre* dialogue with Pater, Hardy, Frost, Yeats, Woolf, Stevens, Bishop, Rich, Wilbur et al. can hark back to Romantic-era relish of moments as they pass, despite how disjointed, destabilizing, or ominous such moments could be to Romantics, as well as to Pater or Eliot (and as well as to us). Dickinson's voice in the Romantic to Modern colloquy, as distinct from her conversation with Locke, Wesley, Wadsworth, and Darwin, highlights to this day the dialogue between her literary heritage and her literary posterity.

*   *   *

Like the five previous volumes in this series, this book has tested E. D. Hirsch's extension of the concept of literature from *les belles lettres* to *les bonnes lettres*. Of course, Dickinson's oeuvre remained more than sufficiently aesthetic. At the same time, however, her verse stayed broad, scarcely decadent. She consciously or subconsciously included not only Wordsworth, Emerson et al., but also Locke, Wesley, Wadsworth, Darwin et al., in literal or figurative colloquy with one another and with herself. The surprisingly belletristic sermons of Wadsworth signal the fact that her fellow-lover of Romantic-era literature was himself a poet (Sewall *Life* 2:444–62) whose especially dialogical, philosophical and scientific (as well as theological) prose provides Dickinson with perhaps her widest bridge to Anglo-American letters, belles and bonnes.

To be sure, the not-so-exclusively introspective art of Emily Dickinson echoes the oral tradition of revival testimony and of hymnody. The spoken and sung words of folk consciousness hummed in the background of her dialogical aesthetic. Nevertheless, her personae prove "*rich* in conversation," too, with the written words of others (Dickinson's emphasis). Although optimism and hope came hard for her, and although she could not as readily put on as many powers with her knowledge as these others did, she scarcely inscribed her poems at home alone. Her speakers spoke their piece to their virtual but lively, their metaphorical but genuine, companions, who, for all practical purposes of literary criticism, spoke theirs back to her, and so on up to the limits of her readers' imaginations. She and her counterparts in belles and bonnes lettres exchanged their views on the imagination as it worked for poets, philosophers, divines, and scientists alike. For her, and for these associates in literary and intellectual history, the model-producing faculty of the collective consciousness of popular and elite, if not folk, culture, arose from, and transmuted, sense-based reasoning. She thereby enjoined her select society of partners in discussion to undertake the common pursuit of freedom for all hearts and minds, and perhaps even for all souls.

The more written than oral sense in which Dickinson's poems can sound dialogical finds belletristic illustration in the philosophical and scientific aspect of her colloquy with literary history. Blake, Wordsworth, Coleridge, Shelley, Keats, Carlyle, Tennyson, Emerson, and other such luminaries of the Anglo-American Romantic milieu appealed to her in no small measure because of the rationally empirical strengths and glories of their respective visions. Like the especially proto-Darwin scientific prowess of Wordsworth, Keats, or Emerson, in particular, hers meant that she home-grounded the Euro-continental perpendicularity that dominated even her (occasional) philosophical idealism (compare Morey). Of course, her more than occasional evangelical idealism can appear dialectically to supersede both her immersion in rational empiricism (please review appendix A) and her concentration on evolutionary biology. Still, her late-Romantic imagination rather entertains oscillation than drives toward synthesis; the former strategy, after all, is closer than, say, any warmed-over method of Hegel's, to her conduct of rich conversation between the aesthetic temperament and the scientific understanding of all her partners in Anglo-American discussion.

In concert with the likes of Wordsworth and Emerson, in particular, Dickinson worried about how a poet can cope with the reduced circumstances of being human in a nature unrelated to spirit. In a world such as that (to adapt to her case Jack Stillinger's language for Keats's "naturalized imagination" or for Keats's "poetry of earth"), "process" would appear "[Dickinson's own] and man's chief good" (compare Stillinger 99–118, esp. 100). Transcendentalism of any kind, therefore, whether belletristic, philosophical, religious, or pseudoscientific, would constitute "a false lure" (100) for any would-be artist. This book has attempted, from the standpoint of Dickinson's literary heritage, to give a full account of what Dickinson came strongly to believe. That is, a high-Romantic poet should conclude, and a late-Romantic poet must conclude, that truth lies only near, and perhaps even dwells primarily in, experience and experiment alike, and that this condition is not only what can suffice for, but also what can assure, any art at all worthy of the name.

Like her forerunners and peers in the English-speaking realm of belles lettres, Dickinson gave up none of the difficult fascination with subject/object paradox and observer/participant overlap that made philosophy and science not so much an exercise as an embodiment of the creative imagination. Her relationship with these fellow-authors personified the depth of her international draw. She faced reality even more forthrightly than they. Just as her empirical language grew sturdier than their empirical idiom, so her evangelical idiom tapered off from their evangelical language. She thereby avoided the maudlin defensiveness with which they could parry fact. She thereby escaped the self-seriousness with which they could stiffen spine. Despite her belated, pre-Modern position on the high- to late-Romantic arc, however, her heart did resemble the irrepressible hearts of Romantic-era writers, and her senses, like theirs, too, much of the time, did assert themselves as irrefutable, for they could all scarcely disbelieve their own lying eyes. Though with an empirical leaning, on her part, that flinched at few realities, and though with her biting, trademark apprehension of incongruity on the road to whatever wisdom she could muster in this best and worst of all possible worlds, the Romantic-era drama of her tough and tender imagination ensued.

The more written than oral sense in which Dickinson's poems can sound dialogical finds biographical illustration, finally, in the philosophical and scientific aspect of her colloquy with religious tradition. The rational empiricism of Locke informed the spiritual sense of Wesley. Wesley, in turn, inspired the eighteenth- to nineteenth-century, intellectual as well as emotional transatlantic revival in which Dickinson's "dearest earthly friend," Wadsworth, participated. Unlike their opposite numbers in twenty-first-century America (please do not forget that there remain few evangelicals, intellectual, emotional, or otherwise, in England), Wesley and Wadsworth accepted empiricism. In the context of this book, it can scarcely too often be said that "[e]ven to write against something is to take one's bearings from it" (Donoghue *Third* 18). But Wesley and Wadsworth also theologized empiricism. And Dickinson, with respect for, but in resistance to them, did not.

The historical, interdisciplinary, and biographical method of this book has described Dickinson's conversation not just with Wordsworth, Emerson et al., but even with Locke, other empirical/pragmatic philosophers of the Anglo-American world, Wesley, Wadsworth, other empirically minded ministers of that world, and that domain's pre- to late-Romantic-era scientists. A salient fact of Wesley's career, that he was a self-described "philosophical sluggard," should seldom, if ever, go missing from accounts of his influence (please review appendix B, if not Chapter 1 through Chapter 3 of Brantley *Locke!*). Wadsworth, as chapter 1 of this book has attempted to bring out, acknowledged Wesley's empirically philosophical, medically scientific contribution, and, as vividly as Wadsworth lived in Dickinson's heart (please recall, for good measure, appendix C), he and Wesley through him haunted her mind and her imagination (just as part I has made cumulatively evident her familiarity with his sermons). Not only Locke and Wesley, but also Darwin, peopled Wadsworth's prose, and hence Dickinson's art of knowledge, as distinct from her "art of belief," and she read about (then read in?) Darwin's *On the Origin of Species* (as part I has emphasized). More consistently than Wesley and Wadsworth and with a fresh result for literary history, Dickinson valued sense-based reason and sense-driven method alike—that is, British empiricism and a range of science from technology to evolutionary biology. With an open-ended tone appropriate to art but with something of a polemical edge to her empirical voice, her faith in experience and in experiment talked with, tempered, tested, and talked back to Experiential Faith—that is, transcendentally capitalized Natural Methodism. Therefore, the likes of Locke and Darwin played composite Epicurus to her protean Lucretius, notwithstanding that the God who fled out of her door sometimes came back in her window (a phenomenon reserved for consideration later in the series).

Part II has answered *yes* to whether or not Dickinson's philosophical and scientific imagination can sustain, in the age of Darwin and the US Civil War, a robust and mutually verifiable outlook. Even her pre-Modern, supposedly crypto-hermetic and pessimistic poems of aftermath or of postexperience, like the lyrical but colloquial lilt of her late-Romantic resilience, evinces hopeful "dialogism"—that is, interpersonal warrants of "continuity in the midst of change" (if not intersubjective reaffirmations of dynamic joy).[16] If a fiction writer's voice thrown "in chorus," "in a dialogue," tends toward optimism and toward hope, the same holds true for this lyric writer's stance in whatever mood of her career, and more credibly for her tragic awareness.[17] This expressive pragmatist, whose blend of intellectual autobiography with a sense of like-minded audience pinpointed her academically inflected (as well as accessibly presented) originality, enlisted communal power on the side of comic knowledge. Thus her lyric monologues contain multitudes. Or rather, her lyric dialogues about poetry, philosophy, and science heed the less dueling than dual watchword implicit throughout her writings—namely, that "life is meeting" (if only in books, and in anticipation) and that meeting is knowledge (if not truth).[18]

Dickinson's literary world, on the one hand, and her philosophical and scientific world, on the other, especially as she encountered the latter on the horizon of the religious prose she preferred, crossed paths in her manuscripts. Sally Bushell's compositional criticism of Dickinson's poems, along with those of Wordsworth and of Tennyson, scrutinizes not the "teleological movement from early stages to finished product" but "a textual field that extends backwards and forwards between avant-texte and text" (35). Bushell follows Jerome McGann's watchword that "social forces and communal activity... bring the text into being" (Bushell 12; Bushell's paraphrase). Those forces and that activity are especially evident in how Dickinson's manuscript variants add aesthetic nuance to her philosophical emphasis on un-decidability, thereby redefining "the nature of understanding" (Bushell 210) and pushing Locke's *Essay* to the limit. Bushell acknowledges that Dickinson's openness "*also* emerges from a far more ancient, self-enclosed sense of spiritual identity, behind which lies the presence of God as supreme Author" (211; Bushell's emphasis contra Roland Barthes). Dickinson's undecidability functions as a mark of her religious humility, for instance, in such manuscripts as Dickinson's four-stanza version of "No other can reduce" (Fr738)—see Bushell's discussion of Houghton Library, Harvard, MS97a (211–14). On a more philosophical, scientific level, though, Dickinson foresaw Hans-Georg Gadamer's concept that the "dialectic of experience has its proper fulfillment not in definitive knowledge but in the openness to experience that is made possible by experience itself" (qtd. in Bushell 210)—specifically, by dialogical experience in "the world / Of all of us" (Wordsworth's resonant language).

Dickinson's personae and her select society of partners in discussion reasoned together, with a fresh result for the collective sense perception—the compounded visionary imagination—of her Anglo-American milieu of lettres belles and bonnes. Whatever the hardness of the truth they all found in league with one another, even she made every effort to cultivate optimism. Even she maintained the kind of muted but reasonable hope that bent not with the remover to remove. Her pursuit of natural truth, though scarcely winning near the goal, arrived not so much at the poetic faith as at the poetic knowledge that might, just might, yet release her readers into *their* free play of the mind.

Just as Dickinson submitted system and creed to the test of experience until faith either deepened or reeled (or both?), so she offered optimism and hope to those among her partners in discussion who would imbibe instruction from Experiment. She realized that scientific method replicated results only imperfectly—her poems on technology took this cold truth to heart—and that Nature, her metaphysical sparring partner par excellence, evinced only scant obligation, if any, to return straight answers to her "obstinate questionings / Of sense and outward things" (recall Wordsworth's language). Her empirical voice, however—her incisive version of Negative Capability—can yet set her readers free from claptrap and from cant. She defined "Hope" in reductive, scientific terms as "electric adjunct," yet commended its "unremitting action" and so capitalized it as a poetic but naturalized transcendentalism (Fr1424, lines 3, 5). She refused to take refuge in the Christianized empiricism by which her evangelical forebear Wesley and her evangelical friend Wadsworth sanctioned the experience of religious conversion and through which her literary associates claimed creative, if not spiritual, renewal. Her Congregational-inflected works fashioned and sponsored response to literary figures, philosophers, ministers, and scientists whose ideas of sensation and whose laboratory skills heralded her distillation of knowledge felt on the pulses as distinct from the uncertain trumpet of her sometime experience of faith (her faint heart-religion). These stakes of her lyrical calling proved modest but high: Dickinson's sense-liberated brain grew wider than the transatlantic sky under which she and her international society of significant others breathed.

Dickinson understood experience as knowledge, and, in no uncertain terms of art, she said so. Theodore Roszak, similarly, limits "experience" to "that which is not a report but knowledge before it is reflected in words or ideas: immediate contact, direct impact, knowledge at its most personal level as it is lived" (57). Dickinson would have taken the point. She, too, connected the preverbal with experience and with knowledge. If, however, like Roszak, she was not so interested in the preconscious, then, unlike Roszak, she was as fascinated as Emerson by "a report" of experience, and not just by experience per se. She would have gone further than Roszak, however, for she would have declared that words and the ideas to which they pointed (here is Locke's theory of language in a nutshell) ranked, too, as experience and as knowledge, and this latter point takes a step beyond Locke.[19] Language and concept, for Dickinson, could provide "immediate contact, direct impact," in the sense that words and ideas became interpersonal—that is, her "report" does not mediate but incarnates, perpetuates, her human interchange (to refute again, if refutation were needed, her so-called reclusiveness).

Much of what and how Emily Dickinson felt and thought, then, like much of who she was, derived less from the evidence on which the high argument of her poetry stood, and less from the logic of its assumptions, than from people. Her lyric genius boasted a dramatically dialogical as well as introspectively autobiographical dimension. If Wadsworth belonged among her cohort of beloveds, so did Wordsworth. The mutuality of teaching and learning, which she often encountered at a subliminal level that harked back in time, changed her sense of traditional presence to her spirit of skeptical counterinterpretation. What she understood from, and imparted to, her reflective cadre of partners in productive discussion, virtual and real, she passed along, in turn, to her posterity. She can still build up in her readers their equal measures of dynamic and salutary realism.[20] She believed that empirical procedure can make life rich and strange, knew that scientific refinement can make art strong and true. Her method, in consequence, can countervail ignorance—that is, her personae and their others can win through to the finish of knowing, and to the prospect of what next.

*   *   *

Of the sometimes childlike poet Dickinson, one might almost say what Wordsworth writes of "a Child Three Years old"—namely, that

> solitude to her
> Is blithe society, who fills the air
> With gladness and involuntary songs.
> ("Characteristics of a Child Three Years Old"
> [1811], lines 12–14)

The etched sibilance of "The Soul selects her own Society - " signals Dickinson's preparation for choosing a soul mate, for reaching an audience, or for both. The line signifies, as well, however, that her "Soul" seeks to converse with a "select" few kindred spirits other than, prior to, along with, and following after her distant beloved(s) and her letter-poem, poem-letter readers.[21] Her will in the world was renunciation of the world paradoxically for the purpose of channeling, of contributing to, the best of what had ever been, would ever be, thought or said in the world. Her renunciation began and ended in her desire to correspond with elected but numerous, not merely metaphorical company, from whom even she had much to learn, and to whom (paradoxically) she had much to say (however laconically).

Dickinson's sometimes real and sometimes metaphorical dialogue with the living and the dead favors voices over soliloquy, the efficacy of engagement over the lonely pursuit of truth. Joan Kirkby invokes Freud and Derrida to explain how Dickinson keeps the dead alive in her conscious experience: "When the death of a friend occurs [Kirkby writes], the friend remains within us, but, where classic psychoanalysis has said that we must resist this uncanny tenant, Derrida, like Dickinson, says that we must remain in dialogue with him and thereby dialecticize death" ("A Crescent" 135). Jonathan Bate's new history of English literature, accordingly, substitutes "*conversation* between living and dead authors, and authors and their readers," for the "canon" of an "inert traditionalism" (*English Literature* xiv; emphasis added). Hence the method of this book has been to juxtapose the words of Dickinson and those of her counterparts not only in belles lettres, but also in bonnes lettres. Her "Ecstasy of Influence" (compare Lethem) has appealed here, in effect, to Emerson's authority, as in "By necessity, by proclivity, and by delight, we all quote. It is as difficult to appropriate the thought of others as it is to invent" ("Quotation and Originality" [1876]).

To be sure, the difficulty of Dickinson's poetry might perplex and retard the dialogical aim of her art, and so might be cause for concern, rather than for celebration. The attention span of readers, after all, is now much reduced, and the audience for literature in general is diminishing at almost as fast a pace as poetic illiteracy in particular is growing. Nevertheless, in keeping with her advice to her readers—that is, "[A metaphor] won't bite" (L34)—consider how Douglas Leonard, for one, rises to the challenge of thinking with Emily Dickinson, of turning one of her most inscrutable anti-images into a sharp picture of wisdom, and perhaps even of truth. Leonard argues that her "Dome of Abyss... / Bowing into Solitude - " (Fr327, lines 18–20) betokens a sunset "slant of light," an experience-won perspective "on death and grief" (128). Even though the "Dome of Abyss," to say the least, might yet seem a hermetic metaphor, the sunset image evoking the near-religious fear that begins wisdom echoes down the decades, speaking to Dickinson's partner-in-discussion Leonard. Please recall, from the appropriate segment of chapter 1, the rich conversation between Emily Dickinson and her others about astronomy in general, and hence about the sunset image in particular. Dickinson's sunset slant of experience-won perspective encompasses the philosophical and scientific truth contemplated not only by her and her precursors and contemporaries in belles and bonnes lettres but also by her and her descendants in the world of academe. Her outlook has thus contributed to knowledge mutually aimed-at in the present.

Will ever more devotees choose, feel compelled to join, the select society behind, around, and within Dickinson's canon? Will they form The Gathered Church of Truth and of Otherness from Where Emily Dickinson and Her Significant Others Stand? Yes and yes: Her ostensibly monologist lyric writing shades into dialogue of such broad appeal that, against all odds "in these bad days" of declining literature enrolments (compare Matthew Arnold, "To a Friend" [1849], line 1), she will win increasing interaction from such readers and writers as can surely always survive. Her participation in belles lettres can even taste as other-directed as drama was, until that of Samuel Beckett, whose dramaturgy took on something of Dickinson's introspective subjectivity but little of her ability to sing and still less of her courtesy to the audience. Since Dickinson's poetry-motivated withdrawal from society allowed her to scorn delights, live laborious days, and attain excellence, and since people have therefore remained curious about the Myth of Amherst, her reputation has grown apace, ever since the 1890s, when three separate collections of her lyrics sold well and pleased critics. Do her poems fly off the shelves at least as quickly as those of best-selling former American poet laureate and Dickinson's twenty-first-century partner in literary discussion Billy Collins? Whether or not the answer is *yes*, Dickinson's standing is now unparalleled among poets (see Coghill and Tammaro; Gardner) as well as among scholars.[22] Insofar as this book has succeeded in signaling how her poetic idiom occupies the midpoint of a cross-cultural continuum that joins her experience to that of her readers, it can admit new members to the eighteenth- as well as nineteenth-century circle of her signification.

One of the best poets in Europe after 1950, Paul Celan translated Dickinson's verse and wrote, in German, the sort of undeceiving poetry that she did. Celan's watchword, "He speaks to truth / Who speaks the shade," harks back to Dickinson's slant truth (see the discussion in Felstiner, ed., trans., xix–xxxvi). Although John Felstiner does not systematically compare Celan and Dickinson, a series of his

insights into Celan evokes (and the last of these insights refers to) her
salient characteristics (and squares with the findings of this book).

> * Paul Celan's writing touches [men and women] like no other: clears
> their vision, fires their hope, braces their pain. (Felstiner xxii–xxiii)
>
> * Celan's most compelling, inspiriting poems presuppose duress and
> distress. (xix)
>
> * Celan's voice was intense, precise, sometimes monotone, grave yet
> resonant, registering nuance and emotion without excess. (xxxii)
>
> * Celan is a touchstone—for his life-and-death lyric seriousness, his
> uncompromising verbal honesty, and his courage in...driving language
> to the verge of unexpected revelation. (xxiii)
>
> * In Emily Dickinson, vastly removed though she was, Celan found
> kindred voicings of mortality and theological skepticism. (xxx)

Of course, the word *monotone* scarcely describes Dickinson's late-
Romantic, far-from-benumbed (far-from-Holocaust) empirical voice.
One might want to stipulate, as well, that her "theological skepticism"
is a function of her scientific method. Still, the affinity that Celan finds
between his poetry and hers suggests how the Myth of Amherst yet
brings the highest talent within the dialogical purview of her philosophical issues and of her scientific complexities.

To be sure, as even the author of *Emily Dickinson and the Hill
of Science* (2010) points out, such poems as "'Arcturus' is his other
name" (Fr117), "I never saw a Moor" (Fr800), and "Soto! Explore
thyself!" (Fr814) reject "the authority of the empirical method and
the supremacy claimed for direct observation. The poet does not have
to see things to know them" (Peel 117, 222). Benjamin Franklin
Newton, Edward Dickinson's law clerk, taught the poet "a faith in
things unseen" (L282). So when, on the front page of *The Hampshire
and Franklin Express*, in 1855, appeared the aphorism "It is often
said that the effect of a little Science is to make men skeptical; of
much, to make them reverential" (qtd. in Peel 281), one can well
imagine the 24-year-old Dickinson nodding her head in agreement,
and thereby subordinating science to religion. Nevertheless, as Robin
Peel is careful to emphasize, it is probably more accurate to think of
Dickinson's metaphor for the relation between science and religion
as "a tennis match" (107) and of her art as more of a "hybrid of scientific observation and poetic speculation" than as a preoccupation
with religion (80). Emily Dickinson's rich conversation was indeed
primarily scientific in nature, for, as Peel also points out, "nineteenth-
century dialogue-books...consciously created...science for women

and children" (162). For Peel, even Dickinson's key phrase "out opon Circumference" rings scientifically. *Eccentric* he remarks, means not so much psychologically as scientifically "off center, away from the center" (148).

Thus it can be said of Dickinson what Frank M. Meola writes of Emerson, that

[a]t times it seems, Emerson wanted to overwhelm himself with the world's material reality, as if in a determined effort to correct his perpetual tendency to idealize and dream. Harsh truth became his Sancho Panza. On at least one well-known, unsettling occasion, he apparently went to extremes, seeking out the horror of untransfigured reality; the March 29, 1832, entry in his journal contains one matter-of-fact statement: "I visited [late wife] Ellen's tomb & opened the coffin." There is no further description or comment. (119)

Dickinson's version of "the horror of untransfigured reality" was the large body of her lugubrious, voice-from-the-grave poems (Poe comes to mind here, as well), an inescapable implication of which was the nineteenth-century, state-of-the-art-scientific incompatibility between belief in the world as materialistic and faith in a world elsewhere. She would have approved of how Emerson made this same point:

The religion that is afraid of science [Emerson writes] dishonors God & commits suicide. It acknowledges that it is not equal to the whole of truth, that it legislates, tyrannizes over a village of God's empire but is not the immutable universal law. Every influx of atheism, of skepticism is thus made useful as a mercury pill assaulting & removing a diseased religion & making way for truth. (Journal entry for March 4, 1831, qtd. in Meola 116)

Should creation "science" take note?

Why did Emily Dickinson, unlike Helen Hunt Jackson, Frances Osgood, and Lydia Sigourney, survive into the twenty-first century? Such Dickinson-influenced writers as Lucy Brock-Broido, Alice Fulton, Jorey Graham, Robert Hass, Susan Howe, Cristine Hume, Marilynne Robinson, Larissa Szporluk, and Charles Wright provide cases in point (see Fathi; Annie Finch). Perhaps it was because authors living in this young century and in the last were attracted to her "strategies of indirection to represent awe toward the unknown" (Fathi 78). Perhaps it was because such authors gravitated toward her prescient perspective on subjects like death, God, the death of God, despair, and the ineffable (see 81–88). From the vantage point of this book, however, it was finally because she established not only a "philosophical or idea-based presence" in contemporary poetry (78), but also a scientific or hypothesis-based presence there.

Emily Dickinson's Rich Conversation: Poetry, Philosophy, Science, then, has attempted to illustrate how Dickinson's literal and figurative dialogue with a range of Anglo-Americans focuses on the material world. She reimagines Wordsworth's and Emerson's "natural method-ism" as her faith in experience. She carries Locke's sense-based reason to its logical conclusion—that is, she turns the empirical evangelism of Methodism founder John Wesley and of Dickinson friend Charles Wadsworth into her evangelical empiricism. She makes Darwin's evolutionary biology her bone-pick with God. As a palliative to the postexperiential perspective of her pre-Modern pessimism, she writes the late-Romantic version of Keats's "poetry of earth." She thereby earns optimism in, thereby holds out hope for, the here and now.

What difference does Dickinson's allegiance to dialogue make to her art of knowledge, as distinct from her art of belief? The answer is that Locke's epistemology in general and the laboratory procedures of cutting-edge scientists in particular guide her verses on steam technology, geology and astronomy, the healing arts, and natural selection. Despite its respect for, its nostalgia for, faith, this canon-within-her-canon searches out things seen, as opposed to envisioning the unseen. Thus, just as Dickinson's much-penetrating eye can "see," like Wordsworth and Darwin, "into the life of things," so her skepticism can amplify Shelley's "voice...to repeal / Large codes of fraud and woe." And thus, although Dickinson's realism can prove harsh, her wisdom can stay salutary—that is, her empirical voice can turn experience into words. Her poems of physical and life science can even substitute grounded imagination for a diminished thing—namely, attenuated faith. Demythologizing the religious enthusiasm of Wesley and of Wadsworth, Dickinson found, for her part, that "the mere sense of living" was "joy enough," perhaps even for all who would take heart from her watchword: "Experiment escorts us last - ."

In sum, Emily Dickinson's art belongs to a global context. Sometimes consciously and sometimes subconsciously, she engages Anglo-American poetry, on the one hand, and Anglo-American philosophy and science, on the other. She keeps her counsel as she moderates debate and seeks consensus within her select society of partners in discussion. When the influence is direct, it is perhaps less finally anxious than auspiciously mutual, for her language thrives alongside Wordsworth's, Emerson's, Locke's, and Darwin's. When the influence is indirect, critical insight yet flows from comparison/contrast

between the words of these and other such unwitting participants in
Emily Dickinson's rich conversation and her equally epistemological,
just as scientifically methodical letters and poems. This interdisciplinary, historical, and biographical approach to her works has drama-
tized her faith in experience and in experiment alike. However barely,
however surprisingly, the Apollonian imagination can thus edge out
the Dionysiac in the late-Romantic thought and practice of the "lady
whom the people call the *Myth*."

APPENDIX A

EMPIRICISM AND EVANGELICALISM: A COMBINATION OF ROMANTICISM

The twin pioneers of transatlantic revivalism, John Wesley (1703–1791) and Jonathan Edwards (1703–1758), absorbed and spiritualized the sensationalist epistemology of John Locke (1632–1704) and then passed along to the nineteenth century their empirical idiom of evangelical expression. As a direct as well as indirect result of this complex process of cultural osmosis, such British Romantics as William Blake, William Wordsworth, Samuel Taylor Coleridge, Percy Bysshe Shelley, and John Keats could conceive of the physical senses as portals to epiphany and not just as analogies of spiritual insight. As an illustrative Anglo-American trio of late-Romantic writers, Thomas Carlyle, Alfred, Lord Tennyson, and Ralph Waldo Emerson continued to blend what Wordsworth called "the language of the sense" with what Coleridge, anticipating the fin-de-siècle apprehension of art as religion, and vice versa, called "poetic faith."[1] Emily Dickinson (1830–1886), herself as much of a late-Romantic as of a Victorian-American (anti-Romantic) or pre-Modern poet, also gravitated toward the amalgamation of scientific method with the varieties of religious experience.[2] Like her precursors and contemporaries on the high- to late-Romantic arc of literary history, the ark back and forth across the Atlantic, Dickinson grew more apt to expect truth, joy, and grace, like Locke, Wesley, and Edwards, than like Marx, Nietzsche, or Freud to suspect consciousness as false.

Thus, as distinct from Euro-continental Romanticism of either a French rationalist or a German idealist stripe, Anglo-American Romanticism generated language at once empirical and evangelical. For example, this local habitation of the long Romantic Movement from the late eighteenth to the second half of the nineteenth century perceived rather than deduced or intuited "whatsoever things" were true, honest, just, pure, lovely, and "of good report" (compare Phil 4:8). On the one hand, in a skeptical turn, this binational brand of Romanticism proclaimed a twofold imperative—namely, *Trust in Experiment! Test Religion!* On the other hand, with guileless receptivity Romantic Anglo-America could also dwell in the possibility of the spiritual sense, perhaps even reimagining as worth a try in an "age of wonder" (Holmes) the warm heart of faith. At any rate, so radically immanent were both the philosophy and the religion of eighteenth- to nineteenth-century Anglo-America that English-speaking Romanticism stayed grounded, for better or worse, in spiritual as well as in natural experience.

To be sure, if one may read back-in-time Stephen Jay Gould's phrase for the proper relation between science and religion in the twentieth century, the empiricism and the evangelicalism of Romantic Anglo-America could seem to be "non-overlapping magisteria." Moreover, if one may apply to the shortcomings of religion Keats's language for the limits of the creative imagination or of "poetic faith," faith could scarcely move mountains "so well / As she is fam'd to do, deceiving elf" (compare Keats, "Ode to a Nightingale" [1819], lines 73–74). Nevertheless, Anglo-American Romantic writers anticipated that through dust and heat but for better not worse, faith in experience would lead to an experience of faith. Experience and faith emerged from this climate, this transatlantic weather, as "Contraries" that did not so much clash or meld as produce "progression" (witness Blake's dialectical terms in *The Marriage of Heaven and Hell* [1790–1793], Plate Three). Instead of nihilistic unbelief, constructive skepticism informed all that the Anglo-American century from 1770 to 1870 found resonant in "the burthen of the mystery," and in mystery itself (Wordsworth, "Tintern Abbey," line 38).

This appendix, having epitomized the series-to-date, can now signal how this book differs from previous installments in this ongoing project in Anglo-American cultural poetics. Without precluding a future study of Dickinson's spiritual experience per se, the present, sixth volume of this historical, interdisciplinary approach to English-language Romanticism constitutes a strategic drawing back from the emphasis in Volume 5 on Dickinson's experience/faith fusion. Of course, her perennial human yearning for transcendence drew her toward dialectic in the first place.[3] Still, she rarely hesitated to apply Ockham's razor to what was not absolutely required to explain the case at hand. Scarcely ever did her blessed rage for order foreclose her aesthetic choice to stick with physical evidence. She more often tended to migrate from evangelical training to empirical discipline than tried to reconcile the two on any paradoxical, counterintuitive, or oxymoronic ground of providential chance, on the one hand, or of random grace, on the other. The emphasis of the present book lies less on the empirical thesis and the evangelical antithesis of her poetic synthesis (for that case, though, see Chapter 4 of Brantley *Experience and Faith*) than on the more philosophical and scientific than religious flow of her literary conversation. Hers was not so much the destination of system as the journey of method.

Appendix B

Locke and Wesley:
An Essence of Influence

Does the great principle of empiricism—namely, that one must see for oneself and be in the presence of the thing one knows—extend to evangelicalism? Does each of these -isms operate along a continuum joining emotion to intellect? Does one of these methodologies link the external to words through ideas of sensation as though perception were mediation? Does the other link the external to words through ideals of sensation as though grace were perception? If empiricism refers to direct impact from, and includes immediate contact with, objects and subjects in time and place, does evangelicalism entertain the similarly reciprocating notions that religious truth is concerned with experiential presuppositions, and that experience itself need not be nonreligious?

Yes, since John Locke's influence on John Wesley and Wesley's Locke on Wesley's followers can constitute the twofold case in point. This nexus of thought and feeling connected the sense-based reason of British empiricism to the spiritual sense of immediate, if not traditional, revelation. This mode of philosophy and of theology morphed the analogy between sense perception and spiritual sense into experience/faith continuum, and perhaps even into experience-faith identity. Wesley spread this state-of-the-art word of natural to spiritual efficacy throughout his parish, the world. Thus his transatlantic revival became an experiment in life force and took on the forceful life of an experiment. His all-encompassing alignment of the Enlightenment with heart religion laid the groundwork for proexperience heart leaps of Romantic Anglo-America, and shows to this day how different from neoclassical evangelism is its science-averse offshoot in the twenty-first-century reaches of the post-Modern world.

It may be helpful, in this appendix, to summarize those previous arguments of this series that pertain to Wesley's immersion in Locke's *Essay concerning Human Understanding* (1690). Wesley, after all, will figure prominently in this book about how Emily Dickinson's experience/faith dialogue favored experience at the expense of, though with continuing respect for, faith. Locke's rational empiricism galvanized Wesley to express the ineffable occurrence of sense-like grace through the language of sense-based method. It was as though natural and spiritual experience could be one and the same. Besides being scriptural, classical, and colloquial, Wesley's prose was pervasively philosophical. His rich and strange but readable hybrid, his composite thought nameable as philosophical theology, harked back to British empiricism, and leaped forward to evangelical practice in the nineteenth-century Anglo-American world.

Here, preliminary to the analytical as well as chronological concentration on Wesley's decisive decade of the 1740s, is a narrative overview of his empirical study. In 1730, intrigued by an obscure follower of Locke, Peter Browne, bishop of Cork and Ross during the 1720s and 1730s, Wesley abridged Browne's *Procedure, Extent, and Limits of Human Understanding* (1728), a theologizing of empiricism. In 1763, Wesley published his condensation of Browne's work in Wesley's anthology of science, *A Survey of the Wisdom of God in the Creation: or a Compendium of Natural Philosophy*, which formed one of Wesley's many educational enterprises. In 1781, Wesley wrote annotations to Locke's *Essay*, and published them, with extracts from the *Essay*, in Wesley's serial for his followers, *The Arminian Magazine*, during 1782–1784. Thus generations of laity encountered empiricism per se as well as empirical evangelicalism. It is especially significant that Wesley took women seriously as philosophical and theological discussion partners, encouraging their abilities as did few of his contemporaries.

Well before, long after, and as catalyst of his strange warming of the heart at a quarter to nine on the evening of May 24, 1738, in Aldersgate Street, London, Wesley was steeped in Locke's sense-based theory of knowledge. A spiritual watershed of English cultural life, Wesley's conversion had as much to do with the tabula rasa of Wesley's mind, and hence with the times and places of Wesley's sense experience, as with the state of his soul. Thus, besides designating the devotional exercises of his Holy Club at Oxford during the 1730s, and besides referencing the religious discipline of his followers thereafter, Wesley's intellectual as well as emotional, originary brand of Methodism denotes their induction of knowledge from experience.

The decade to conjure with is the 1740s, when Wesley developed his Locke-derived breakthrough in experience/faith conundrums. For example, just as Locke's view that words correspond to things through ideas led him to advocate a simple style (see the discussion of *Essay* 3 in Brantley *Locke* 31–33), so his theory of language informed Wesley's *Character of a Methodist* (1742), and turned this message into an intellectual treatise:

> The most obvious, easy, common words, wherein our meaning can be conveyed [Wesley writes], we prefer before others, both on ordinary occasions, and when we speak of the things of God. We never, therefore, willingly or designedly, deviate from the usual way of speaking, unless when we express scripture truths in scripture words, which, we presume, no Christian will condemn. (Jackson 8:340)

Of course, both Locke and Wesley recognized the fundamentally metaphorical and analogical nature of language, and hence they both acknowledged, as well, the potential for arbitrariness and imprecision in the capacity of words to represent and communicate truths, whether natural or spiritual. Still, if only at the level of diction, both the philosopher and the preacher held that simplicity and clarity of speech could augur purity, stability, reliability, and transparency of understanding.

The combination of message and intellectual treatise in *An Earnest Appeal to Men of Reason and Religion* (1743) kept not only the Bible but also Locke's *Essay* in the direct line of Wesley's central vision:

> You know [Wesley writes emphatically and at length]...that before it is possible for you to form a true judgment of the things of God, it is absolutely necessary that you have a clear apprehension of them, and that your ideas thereof be all fixed, distinct, and determinate. And seeing our ideas are not innate, but must all originally come from our senses, it is certainly necessary that you have senses capable of discerning objects of this kind—not those only which are called "natural senses," which in this respect profit nothing, as being altogether incapable of discerning objects of a spiritual kind, but spiritual senses, exercised to discern spiritual good and evil...
>
> And till you have these internal senses, till the eyes of your understanding are opened, you can have no apprehension of divine things, no idea of them at all. Nor consequently, till then, can you either judge truly or reason justly concerning them, seeing your reason has no ground whereon to stand, no materials to work upon. (Cragg 56–57)

The sense-based word choice—namely, "materials," "ground," "eyes," "internal senses," "natural senses," "objects," and "things"—constitutes perhaps the fullest statement of Wesley's spiritual sense. The philosophical demand for empiricism, which in Locke's is rational as well as sense-based, is also met in Wesley's far from antirational concept of inspiration, which he associates with terms such as "discern," "reason," "understanding," "ideas," "apprehension," and "judgment." As though to maintain Locke's balance between reason and its ground, Wesley indicates a radically metaphorical, far from arbitrary relation between rational apprehension and the spiritual sense. Consistent with his endorsement of tabula rasa as the first principle of theology as well as of philosophy, he signals his dependence on, as well as his affinity for, Locke's method. The operative phrase, the heart of the matter, in Wesley's words "not those only which are called 'natural senses,'" is *natural senses.*

To be sure, in suggesting that sense perception is crucial to religion, Wesley avoids ever claiming that one can often, or even finally, stand on any common ground between experience and faith. Like *An Essay concerning Human Understanding, An Earnest Appeal to Men of Reason and Religion* stresses that natural understanding cannot easily, or ever clearly, apprehend spiritual truth: "What then [Wesley asks] will your reason do here? How will it pass from things natural to spiritual? From the things that are seen to those that are not seen? From the visible to the invisible world? What a gulf is here!" (Cragg 57). Nevertheless, faith is defined by Wesley not simply in accordance with scripture but even according to a balance between the sensing and the reasoning powers per se:

> [Faith] [Wesley observes] is the feeling of the soul, whereby a believer perceives, through the "power of the highest overshadowing him" [see Luke 1:35] both the existence and the presence of him in whom he "lives, moves, and has his being" [see Acts 17:28], and indeed the whole invisible world, the entire system of things eternal. And hereby, in particular, he feels "the love of God shed abroad in the heart" [see Romans 3:5]. (Cragg 47)

By *feeling*, Wesley does not mean "inner trend of belief" so much as "faith in relation to the senses," for *An Earnest Appeal to Men of Reason and Religion* speaks of "faith" in reference to "the eye," "the ear," and even "taste" (see, e.g., Cragg 46). Wesley's definition, finally, both by its diction ("whereby a believer *perceives")* and by its development throughout the treatise, intimates his view that religious feeling, like sense data, comprises matter for the mind to work upon. Thus the *Earnest Appeal* pays homage to Locke explicitly, or at least perspicuously. This important but surprising document of the growth of Wesley's mind during the 1740s draws an analogy between faith and empirical observation: "Faith is with regard to the spiritual world what sense is with regard to the natural" (Cragg 46). The precisely analogical structure of this breakthrough in religious epistemology rests on such far from arbitrary, if not radically metaphorical, association of faith with the natural senses that one hears here the identification of experience with faith that was to mark Methodism as a phenomenal new species of philosophical theology.

From 1745 through 1748, Wesley wrote letters to Mr. John Smith (an alias for Thomas Secker, bishop of Oxford and later bishop of Canterbury) in which appears such an arresting statement as this: "To this day, I have abundantly more temptation... to be... a philosophical sluggard, than an itinerant Preacher" (Telford 2:68). Throughout these letters, Wesley combines evangelistic goals with his love of philosophical theology, and especially pronounced is his Locke-derived method, for even to traditional revelation he applies Locke's as well as Descartes's skepticism. "I am as fully assured to-day [Wesley discloses to Smith], as I am of the rising of the sun, that the scriptures are of God. I cannot possibly deny or doubt of it now; yet I may doubt of it tomorrow; as I have done heretofore a thousand times, and that after the fullest assurance preceding" (Telford 2:92). Thus, the mind remains open even after carefully searching for, and apparently finding, what is not subject to doubt. The letters to Smith, moreover, acknowledge both poles of Locke's method, for the sense-based nature of mind is implicit in Wesley's phraseology "so far as men can judge from their eyes and ears" (Telford 2:44).

Rise and progress, a phrase characteristic of eighteenth-century British book titles, as in *The Rise and Progress of Religion in the Soul* (1742) by Philip Doddridge, assumes the British philosophy of experience. When Wesley writes Smith that "we are speaking, not of the progress, but of the first rise, of faith" (Telford 2:48), he suggests, for one thing, that no more than knowledge does faith exist innately and, for another, that faith, like knowledge, must be datable by exact moments in personal history. "It cannot be, in the nature of things [Wesley tells Smith], that a man should be filled with this peace, and joy, and love, by the inspiration of the Holy Spirit, without perceiving it as clearly as he does the light of the sun" (Telford 2:64). Thus, just as one knows what one experiences naturally, so one has faith in what one encounters spiritually.[1]

In a sermon entitled "The Great Privilege of Those that are Born of God" (1748), Wesley affirms a real correspondence between universally describable experience and experience that, though possible for all, would remain quite ineffable were it not for Locke's linguistic instrument of analogy-cum-metaphor. With regard to the interpenetration of sense perception and the world of here and now, "The Great Privilege" sounds precisely Locke-initiated:

> No sooner is the child born into the world [Wesley teaches], than he... *feels* the air with which he is surrounded, and which pours into him from every side, as fast as he alternately breathes it back, to sustain the flame of life: and hence springs a continual increase of strength, of motion, and of sensation; all the bodily senses being now awakened, and furnished with their proper objects. (*Sermons* 76; Wesley's emphasis)

In this passage, the mind's wakeful involvement with sense data is just as clear as in whole sections of *An Essay concerning Human Understanding* where Locke insists that the mind's response to sense experience is almost at one with what one needs to know about the world. The entire sermon preaches that "the circumstances of the natural birth" provide "the most easy way to understand the spiritual" (*Sermons* 175)—that is, that the invisible world is familiar to twice-born people whose spiritual sense parallels the limited but sufficient operation of the natural faculties. Wesley's description here of "senses, whereby alone we can discern the things of God" bespeaks a vital interaction—namely, what is "continually received" is "continually rendered back" (*Sermons* 176). At the mental level, and with reference to the senses, spiritual experience is depicted throughout "The Great Privilege" as coalescence, as near identification, with the condescension of God. Thus Wesley's alternation, nay oscillation, between reason- and sense-based wording signifies, again and again, that through immediate revelation God and man are en-sphered, or rather that a clear intercourse occurs not just between man as object and God as subject but even between man as subject and God as object.

A *Letter to the Reverend Dr. Conyers Middleton* (1749), finally, expresses a paradoxically Locke-consistent theology of immediate revelation:

> Traditional evidence [Wesley admits, concerning the Bible] is of an extremely complicated nature, necessarily including so many and so various considerations, that only men of a strong and clear understanding can be sensible of its full force. On the contrary, how plain and simple is this; and how level to the lowest capacity! Is not this the sum: "One thing I know; I was blind, but now I see"? [see John 9:25].

An argument so plain, that a peasant, a woman, a child, may feel all its force.

The traditional evidence of Christianity stands, as it were, a great way off; and therefore, although it speaks loud and clear, yet makes a less lively impression. It gives us an account of what was transacted long ago, in far distant times as well as places. Whereas the inward evidence is intimately present to all persons, at all times, and in all places. (Jackson 10:75–76)

The language here does not so much look down on women (see the discussion, in part I of this book, of Wesley's protofeminist streak) as democratically affirm the at once reason-strong and all but sensate capacity of all people to see the spiritual as well as natural object as in itself it really is. Wesley's attitude toward scripture here does not so much anticipate the Higher Criticism of the Bible during the nineteenth century as subordinate Bible reading to near-identity between sense perception of natural knowledge and immediate revelation of the Holy Spirit's ongoing and unfolding truth.[2] Although Wesley is sedulous here to manifest reticence about just how much one can know from spiritual sense and discernment—there is no mere knowingness of self-indulgent enthusiasm in this passage—his fully epistemological tone signals his relative confidence in immediate revelation as avenue to enlightenment.

Is it not so [Wesley asks Middleton]? Let impartial reason speak. Does not every thinking man want a window, not so much in his neighbour's, as in his own, breast? He wants an opening there, of whatever kind, that might let in light from eternity. He is pained to be thus feeling after God so darkly and uncertainly: to know so little of God, and indeed so little of any beside material objects. He is concerned, that he must see even that little not directly, but in the dim, sullied glass of sense; and consequently so imperfectly and obscurely, that it is all a mere enigma still.

Now, these very desiderata faith supplies. It gives a more extensive knowledge of things invisible, showing what eye had not seen, nor ear heard, neither could it enter into our heart to conceive [see I Cor. 2:9]. And all these it shows in the clearest light, with the fullest certainty and evidence. For it does not leave us to receive our notice of them by mere reflection from the dull glass of sense; but resolves a thousand enigmas of the highest concern by giving faculties suited to things invisible. (Jackson 10:74–75)

Couched in the doubly empirical context of a not-so-buried optics metaphor (notice the lens-focusing implication of "*resolves* a thousand enigmas") and experientially philosophical language for and from the Bible, this statement is more than in keeping with *An Essay concerning Human Understanding*. The avowal epitomizes Wesley's at once spiritual and natural mode of knowing and of speaking—that is, his brand of faith as less different from, than enhansive and extensive of, the senses.

Wesley not only drew an analogy between sense perception and revelation but also attempted, in an almost more than merely metaphorical manner, to bridge the gap between natural and spiritual experience. Insofar as he shaped an eighteenth- and nineteenth-century kind of thought and feeling, the empirical and the evangelical understanding of experience came together for the Anglo-American middle class. British authors as late as Thomas Carlyle and Alfred, Lord Tennyson and American authors as late as Ralph Waldo Emerson and Emily Dickinson descended intellectually as well as spiritually from Wesley insofar as all four of these writers of belletristic prose and of poetry accepted as well as theologized empiricism. This quartet grounded transcendentalism in mind and world, balanced religious myths and religious morality with scientific reverence for fact and detail, allied this-worldly assumptions with spiritual discipline, and shared the rational and sense-respecting reliance on experience as the less royal than public road to natural knowledge and divine truth alike.

Appendix C

Wadsworth and Dickinson:
A Marriage of Minds

Second only to Brooklyn Congregational Reverend Henry Ward Beecher in national clerical renown (Applegate; Strickland), Philadelphia Presbyterian Reverend Charles Wadsworth inspired in Emily Dickinson a decades-long series of honorifics. These range from her deferential, near-infantalized "my Shepherd from 'Little Girl'-hood" to her allusive "My Philadelphia" (compare Antony to Cleopatra: "My Egypt") to her heartfelt "my closest earthly friend" and "my dearest earthly friend" to her affective but formal and professionally correct "beloved Clergyman" and "My Clergyman" (L750, L765, L766, L790, and L807). Alfred Habegger's brief for Wadsworth as the addressee of Dickinson's sexually charged "Master Letters" (L187, L233, and L248) is judiciously understated (Habegger 419–23). If Habegger is correct, and he is far from alone in proposing Wadsworth as "Master," then these three letters are the only ones known, at present, from Dickinson to Wadsworth.[1] The (so far) sole surviving communication from Wadsworth to Dickinson (L248a) is undated: it consists of two brief sentences of vague, rather perfunctory pastoral counseling, as though it were a routine response to a parishioner's request for spiritual guidance and comfort. Although the record shows just a pair of face-to-face meetings between Wadsworth and Dickinson, one in 1860 and the other in 1880 (were there other such encounters?), the emotional tinges and the passionate character of their relationship have formed the focus of educated guesses by Habegger, Pollak, Shurr, Strickland, and others. Their collective investigation, based on parallels between Wadsworth's sermons and Dickinson's letters and poems, has proved quite plausible, as well as inherently intriguing.

This appendix, for its part in this necessarily more provisional than definitive scholarly conversation, suggests a cerebral twist to the possibility of a romantic attachment between the preacher and the poet. Yes, their intellectual as well as emotional love for one another, like the friendship between George Bernard Shaw and Ellen Terry, stayed largely an epistolary embodiment. But Wadsworth's letters to Dickinson could well have referenced his sermons, and hers to him probably enclosed her poems. The circumstantial but strong evidence that she read his printed works—namely, a striking set of verbal as well as gist-specific correspondences between his and her works—is gathered cumulatively throughout this book, and to some extent serves this appendix, as well.[2] For instance, the fact that during the early 1880s, Wadsworth's friends the Clark brothers delivered to Dickinson (or sent her) a collection of Wadsworth's sermons will figure prominently here. The most important and surprising aspect of the Wadsworth/ Dickinson connection, if this essay comes near the mark, was their "marriage of true minds."[3] Notwithstanding how clearly this union may appear to have been the sublimation of their powerful (but suppressed) psychosexual energies, this interaction of two rather opposite, yet mutually attracted, mentalities constituted, nonetheless, the subject-to-subject drama of their composite consciousness.

Charles Wadsworth and Emily Dickinson may have met in March 1855, during a visit paid by Dickinson and her sister, Lavinia, to their Philadelphia friends, the Coleman family. The Colemans may have belonged to, and were from time to time undoubtedly among, Wadsworth's congregation at the Arch Street Presbyterian Church.[4] In the Presbyterian language of *The Life and Letters of Emily Dickinson* (1924) by Dickinson's niece, Martha Dickinson Bianchi (daughter of Susan and Austin Dickinson), the "two predestined souls" were "kept apart only by a high sense of duty."[5] Although Bianchi's Dickinson-loves-Wadsworth story is a melodramatic outpouring full of embellishment, if not hyperbole (Bianchi was working from distant memories of events), her account contains more than a grain of truth.[6] This appendix, while erring on the side of caution, will select quotations from Bianchi's narrative and blend these markers of romance with such indications less of romance than of mind-marriage as Dickinson's letters to the Clark brothers, several of her other letters, and certain poems. Certain love-theme dimensions of literary history in general and of Dickinson's cultural milieu in particular will also prove pertinent to this discussion. Thus, in an Anglo-American atmosphere of compatibility and, for that matter, of interdependence between romance and intellect, Dickinson tilted, however slightly, away from heart and soul, and toward mind.

Although Wadsworth traveled to the Dickinson family homestead in Amherst, Massachusetts, in 1860, "the one word he implored," according to Bianchi's account of the journey, "Emily would not say" (Dickinson's recluse-like behavior began at about that time). In 1863, perhaps because his parishioners had disapproved of his pro-Southern leanings (this detail is not in Bianchi, though), Wadsworth "silently withdrew with his wife and an only child" to Calvary Presbyterian Church in San Francisco, "a continent's width remote" (savor Bianchi's flourish). In 1869, he accepted a second Philadelphia pastorate, the Third Reformed Dutch Church, and, in 1880, while serving Immanuel Presbyterian Church, Philadelphia, he visited Dickinson again. In 1882, after a throat ailment had begun to hinder his career, he died at 68, four years before her demise at 55.

If, with however large a grain of salt, one may credit Bianchi's reading of motivation, Dickinson appeared scarcely inclined to cause "the inevitable destruction of another woman's life." Mrs. Jane Wadsworth (this indeed has a ring of truth) "knew nothing of this instantaneous, overwhelming, impossible love." After 1860, "without stopping to look back," Dickinson, if one can countenance more of Bianchi's rather overblown but chronologically convincing prose, "fled to her own home for refuge—as a wild thing running from whatever it may be that pursues." She henceforth, if one may recover the kernel of biographical conceivability from Bianchi's sentimental, and somewhat condescending (even belittling), language,

> went on alone in the old house under the pines...From this time on she clung more intensely to the tender shadows of her father's home. She still saw her friends and neighbors from time to time, but even then her life had begun to go on in hidden ways...Her little form flitted tranquil through the sunny small industries of her day, until night gave her the right to watch with her flowers and liberated fancies.

Only "Sister Sue" (here, there may well be much psychosexual and psychosocial verisimilitude in what Bianchi has to say) knew that "love had been home to [Emily Dickinson] for an instant."

To be sure, Bianchi's story of hopeless love might seem formulaic, might be negligible as mere boilerplate allusion to "One Word More" (1855) by Robert Browning, three lines of which presage, from the man's point of view, Bianchi's implication of a double life for Wadsworth and for Dickinson alike:

> God be thanked [Browning writes], the meanest of his creatures
> Boasts two soul-sides, one to face the world with,
> One to show a woman when he loves her! (17:15–7).

Perhaps Bianchi's narrative is just a pale, failed micro-version of a triple-decker, Victorian-era romance. Nevertheless, lovers of biography will want to keep Bianchi's sepia diptych on an at-hand shelf in the storehouse of resources for interpreting the life and art of Emily Dickinson. Does Dickinson's love poetry, for instance, suggest that she was looking for a father figure? Sixteen years older than she (the same age difference obtains between Mr. Knightley and Emma Woodhouse), Wadsworth held maturity, "a certain age," in common with such other Dickinson-admired men as Benjamin Franklin Newton, Samuel Bowles (he was only four years her senior, though), Thomas Wentworth Higginson, and Otis Lord.[7] One thinks, in this connection, of another December-May romance, a love-match historically, yet not substantively, far removed from Wadsworth and from Dickinson—namely, the Bible story of Boaz and Ruth (was their body-and-soul-mating, for all practical purposes, the first, most complete romantic comedy in the West?).

The words already quoted from Bianchi jibe with the ideas and, for that matter, with the negative and positive diction of Dickinson's poems and letters. The poet, as fleeing "wild thing," comments on the primal fear of her speaker in "I started Early - Took my Dog - ," in which a dreamlike but masculine sea hotly but unsuccessfully pursues the poet's wily self-projection (Fr656; Dickinson elsewhere, though, feels *no* ambivalence about "Wild nights!" of love-making! [Fr269, line 1]). "Her father's home" brings to mind her decision, taken at about age thirty, not "to cross my Father's ground [i.e., the Homestead] to any House or town" (L330). Her "hidden ways" parallel the main idea of her melancholy poem "I tie my Hat - I crease my Shawl - ," in which her (lovelorn?) persona withdraws not only from the world into her (father's?) home but also (shades of Miss Havisham) from her surrounding house into herself (Fr522). Thus the "instantaneous" and "overwhelming" quality of Emily Dickinson's love for Charles Wadsworth, as Bianchi portrays it, turns out to be directly proportional to the "impossibility" of this love, as Bianchi reports on it. The "instantaneous" and "overwhelming," if unfulfilled, quality of the poet's love for the preacher, however, "dwell[s] in Possibility - " indeed (Fr466, line 1)—that is, lingers in her "liberated fancies," her creative imagination, and her accomplished poems (her blooming "flowers"), where, as Tennyson would have it,

'Tis better to have loved and lost
Than never to have loved at all.
                    (*In Memoriam* [1850] 27:15–16)

Bianchi's conclusion—that is, that Dickinson's *"instant*aneous" and "overwhelming" love for Wadsworth "had been home [to her] for an *instant*"—echoes the poet's muted insight, her lyrical implication, that even star-crossed, and hence fleeting, love graciously leaves behind, and beautifully preserves in amber, the "Soul's Superior *instants*" (Fr630, line 1; emphasis added).[8]

If aficionados of Dickinson's poetry appear unlikely to confirm Bianchi's details—Wadsworth had two small children in 1863, not one—then neither need her readers do entirely without Bianchi's version of events. Of course, William Wordsworth's "spots of time" and all the consequent proto-Joycean epiphanies, quasi-mystical unions, and quasi-divine afflatuses of nineteenth-century poetry pertain to the literary-historical inspirations of Emily Dickinson's writings.[9] Still, something was at work in her life, and thence in her imagination, besides purely aesthetic influence, and if it was not her love for Susan Dickinson or for Charles Wadsworth, or for Otis Lord, or for all three or for someone else, then it was her encounters with otherness through others, and with others through otherness. *Something* in the poet's personal history, after all, surely feels of sufficient importance to steady and to center her art, for which Bianchi's witness serves well enough as a flawed but working model. The "romance" aspect of *The Life and Letters of Emily Dickinson* issues Bianchi's call for biographical criticism, however speculative in tendency such biographical criticism must be.[10] Some of the particulars of Bianchi's book appear exaggerated, even preposterous, but, whatever her reliability, Dickinson's niece was as close to the poet as almost anyone else, and the mystique of her account comes across as perennially indicative of what lively insights the biographical critic of Dickinson's art can generate. Bianchi concludes that the Myth of Amherst was "as truly a nun as any avowed celibate, but the altar she served was veiled from every eye save that of God." Perhaps "altar" signifies here the religious otherness of Wadsworth's presence in Dickinson's poetry.

In August 1882, four months after Wadsworth's death, Dickinson declared to his friend James D. Clark, "He was my Shepherd from 'Little Girl'hood, and I cannot conjecture a world without him, so noble was he always—so fathomless—so gentle" (L766).[11] Now this poet never praised anyone or anything lightly. As far as she was concerned, the inconceivability of a world without Wadsworth signaled her love for him, notwithstanding her implication of a father/daughter, or a minister/protégée-parishioner, arrangement between them. Her love for him, she implies, has endured, if not from "'Little Girl'hood," then for well over two decades. Her romantic as well as

mentor/student allegiance to a man of deep mystery—she would be
equally fathomless to him—vies as the main event of her life—and
ranks as perhaps the chief fact behind the metaphors of her love poems
(along with her friendship for Sue, of course).[12]

To be sure, William H. Shurr's twofold belief (a) that Wadsworth
and Dickinson consummated their love and (b) that she had an
abortion has made Shurr's readers definitely wince.[13] Nevertheless,
although Dickinson's "historical reality" and her "imaginative transformations" are two different things, scarcely interrelating literally,
the former underpins the latter, and vice versa.[14] So Bianchi's report
can lead into an interpretive clearing. Bianchi's Presbyterian diction—
recall "two predestined souls…kept apart only by a high sense of
duty"—finds excellent match in Dickinson's Presbyterian idiom. Such
words as "Synods" and such mysteries as "The Presbyterian Birds
can now resume their Meeting" (Fr1400B, line 4; Fr1620, line 3)
can reinforce Habegger's near-location of the Presbyterian minister
in Dickinson's "Master" poems.[15] The creative imagination flowers,
after all, whenever love germinates.[16] Thus, if Dickinson's personal
history in fact forms part of her imagination, then Wadsworth makes
much difference to her poetry. Perhaps he even makes all the difference in it, inspiring her 40 fascicles in particular (roughly 45 percent
of her 1,789 lyrics).[17]

The Wadsworth/Dickinson connection, at any rate, can become
an ascendant means of reading Dickinson's poems biographically, if
only because, until recently, the love between preacher and poet has
suffered scholarly neglect compared with the understandable peak
of interest in Susan Dickinson.[18] To complement romance, one may
analyze the intellectual character of the Wadsworth/Dickinson friendship. This "marriage of true minds" becomes no less dynamic for sub-
limating, trends even more explosive for repressing, Eros. Martha
Nussbaum's phrases "upheavals of *thought*" and "the *intelligence
of emotions*" (emphasis added) prove apropos. Just as Dickinson's
love for Wadsworth stays truer for developing mind, as well as soul
and heart, so her poems plot "abundant recompense" for embodied
presence.[19]

The Wadsworth/Dickinson connection, accordingly, marks the
poet's maturity. "Friendship often ends in love, but love in friendship
never." Schoolgirl Dickinson copied this proverb on the inside back
cover of her edition (1838) of the works of Vergil.[20] The budding
poet shared the conventional view, handed down from Rochefoucauld
to Sterne to Byron, that in the behavior of men toward women, and
perhaps even of women toward men, love and friendship must remain

mutually exclusive.[21] Alongside the adult Dickinson's "reading" of Wadsworth, her reading of Keats and of Emerson, as this appendix can now roundly conclude, probably changed her thinking, undoubtedly mended the view captured by the schoolgirl's jotting.

Through conning Keats, first, Dickinson would have known that friendship and love can turn out nothing if not simultaneously viable. "Love and friendship" together make up, for Keats, the "crown" of "happiness" that "sits high / Upon the forehead of humanity" (compare Keats, *Endymion: A Poetic Romance* [1818] 1:776–77). Keats adds, for good measure, that the "entanglements" of friendship with love—that is, the friction between, and the interpenetration of, these concepts—grow "[r]icher," and "far / More self-destroying," than even that mystical

> moment [when humanity] step[s]
> Into a sort of oneness, and our state
> Is like a floating spirit's.
> (*Endymion* 1:778–802)

As far as Wadsworth's presence in Dickinson's poetry goes, her art, like Keats's canon, demonstrates that friendship/love can comprise an alternative to, as well as a fountain of, mysticism (Wadsworth's faith, after all, if Part I of this book pans out, can feel considerably less retrospectively preternatural than boldly sense-related). Thus, proving neither the same nor regressive from one to the other, friendship and love can emerge from Dickinson's experience, and move into her words, as progressive from one to the other, and as, for that matter, overlapping, imbricated.

For Emerson and his circle, too (ultimately including Dickinson), friendship and love together represent the blessings of life.[22] "We are associated in adolescent and adult life," Emerson writes,

> with some friends, who, like skies and waters, are coextensive with our idea; who, answering each to a certain affection of the soul, satisfy our desire on that side; whom we lack power to put at such focal distance from us, that we can mend or even analyze them. We cannot chuse but love them...[M]uch intercourse with a friend has supplied us with a standard of excellence, and has increased our respect for the resources of God who thus sends a real person to outgo our ideal. ("Nature" [1837] in Murphy, ed., 1:844)

Emerson's phrase "a certain affection of the soul" couches his synthesis of friendship with love in the language of Jonathan Edwards.

John Wesley's abridgment of *Edwards's Treatise concerning Religious Affections* (1746; abridged 1773) imports "a certain affection of the soul" into British sensibility, adding binational resonance to the religious background of Emerson's friendship/love coalescence and of his friendship-love interpenetration.[23] As one places Dickinson's thinking in this Anglo-American context, one thinks, as well, of the friendship-love synthesis in such Romantic-era doctrines of sympathy as those of Blake, Coleridge, and Shelley.[24]

"A man," declares Emerson (one could substitute "Emily Dickinson" and change, as well, the gender of the following personal pronouns), "will see his character emitted in the events that seem to meet, but which exude from and accompany him" ("Fate" [1852] in Whicher, ed., 349). "Some people," Emerson continues, "are made up of rhyme, coincidence, omen, periodicity, and presage: they meet the person they seek; what their companion prepares to say to them, they first say to him; and a hundred signs apprise them of what is about to befall."[25] Dickinson, it is true, might seem little thus to favor whom she meets. The persistent view of her as a lonely heart, as an eccentric loner, after all, can yet mislead her readers. Nonetheless, through her personae, she characterizes the dialogue of love/friendship as the impetus to knowledge, perhaps even more than as the aid to belief (or so this book everywhere signals). Giving rise to her signature theme of wonder, of awe mixed with fear, her friendship/love combination will not let her go (compare Hosea 11:4), and it augurs her more than merely metaphorical connection with worldly reality as the proxy for unworldly faith. Thus, according to the larger perspective of this book, the truth as well as the grace and joy that the poet offers her readers is what she also continually receives from her array of such incarnate to ghostly beloveds as Wadsworth. Just as friendship and love, for Dickinson, cross over from one to the other, so the others and the otherness of her life form the phenomenal to numinous, if primarily the phenomenal, dimension of her aesthetic vision.

The quality of Dickinson's "marriage of true minds" is that it lasts, for, though her combination of friendship with love can waver, it scarcely vanishes. Of course, she refused to marry Judge Lord, to whom she explained, "'No' is the wildest word we consign to Language" (L562). Still, she wrote to Judge Lord regularly, and, during the many years when she received virtually no other visitors, she saw him. Her even greater love for Susan Dickinson and for Charles Wadsworth lasted for decades, despite the inevitable friction in even these relationships. Dickinson was not so much at once, as alternately, in love and friends with all such members of her social circle, but her mind stayed married to theirs in Blake's best tradition of "marriage" not as "reconciliation" but as "the sustained tension, without victory or suppression, of co-present oppositions."[26]

Susan Dickinson gets most of the credit, nowadays, for inspiring some of the best love poetry in the language. Habegger faults this focus, however, for "trying to see [Emily] Dickinson through a single lens."[27] At some risk of using a "single lens" here, yet often acknowledging the power of Susan Dickinson to stimulate biographical assumptions about, and approaches to, Dickinson's art, this appendix, and indeed this book, seek to correct the imbalance to which Habegger often refers. One may take the poet's superlative language "dearest earthly friend" seriously. One may proceed heuristically, as though Charles Wadsworth were "first among equals" in Dickinson's sometimes really imagined and sometimes imaginatively real social circle.

"Finally," Christopher Benfey concludes, "Dickinson suggests that we can relinquish certainty in our relations to others, and yet acknowledge our relatedness to them. She will often call this relation one of 'nearness.'"[28] Thus, without necessarily excluding eroticism, however ungratified; passion, however shackled; or romance, however unfulfilled, from her mix of friendship and love, she nonetheless represents both friendship and love as at all times reflecting not only varying degrees of heartfelt emotion but also heaping measures of mind-filled soul.[29] Things equal to the same thing, one learns in school, are equal to each other. Love is equal to "the marriage of true minds"; so is friendship; therefore, with apologies to Rochefoucauld et al., friendship and love can prove equal to one another, perhaps for men and women in particular. Dickinson, paradoxically, finds this axiom *empirically* true.

In large part because of its unwillingness to "bend with the remover to remove," a poem that Dickinson composed in, or about, 1882, the year of Wadsworth's death, would appear to take the measure of the poet's "marriage" to the preacher, and perhaps even of his to her:

My Wars are laid away in Books -
I have one Battle more -
A Foe whom I have never seen
But oft has scanned me o'er -
And hesitated me between
And others at my side,
But chose the Best - Neglecting me - till
All the rest have died -
How sweet if I am not forgot

> By Chums that passed away -
> Since Playmates at threescore and ten
> Are such a scarcity -
>   (Fr1579)

Habegger reasons that "the Best" (line 7) means Wadsworth, who died on April 1, and that "Books - " (line 1) means the 40 fascicles, the manuscript books or the more than 800 poems that Dickinson might well have addressed to Wadsworth even as Wordsworth—what a fortuitous coincidence of names!—wrote *The Prelude* (1805 version) for Coleridge.[30] Thus "My Wars are laid away in Books - " appears to take for granted the central role among Dickinson's poetic personae, as well as within her social circle, of the man whom she calls "my Clergyman" (L790). Poised between her having written about him and her faint, all but unexpressed hope of seeing him in heaven, she pays tribute in these lines to his importance to her on earth. The poem might well identify Wadsworth as the chief muse of Dickinson's art.

According to Thomas H. Johnson, the editor of the first of the (so far) two complete variorum editions of Emily Dickinson's poems, "The handwriting of 'Those - dying then,' suggests that the lines might have been written after the death of Charles Wadsworth on 1 April 1882" (*Poems* 3:713 n):

> Those - dying then,
> Knew where they went -
> They went to God's Right Hand -
> That Hand is amputated now
> And God cannot be found -
>
> The abdication of Belief
> Makes the Behavior small -
> Better an ignis fatuus
> Than no illume at all -
>   (Fr1581)

These late-career lines nag at Roger Lundin's effort to anatomize Dickinson's belief, haunting both Lundin's study and the previous volume in the present series of arguments concerning the evangelical as well as empirical language of Anglo-American Romanticism.[31] As Charles R. Anderson understands Dickinson's expression of her tough mind here, the poem "sums up her lifelong problem as that of one who was cut off from simple faith by the new currents of thought in her day, mildly envious of the orthodox older generations" (257). The pessimism of the poem contrasts sharply with Dickinson's hard-earned optimism elsewhere.[32] Her lament appears personal, and "hope without belief" (Lambert 15) is about the best face that could be put upon it. Johnson's biographical approach to "Those - dying then" magnifies more intensely than even the history-of-ideas emphasis in Lundin's sweeping study Dickinson's apprehension of the abdication, mutilation, or death of God. If God, by Dickinson's implication, is "changed, changed utterly" for the worse, then the death of Wadsworth confirms a dreadful cosmic mutation from divine plenitude and presence to the most unbearable emptiness and absence conceivable (compare Yeats, "Easter 1916" [1920], line 79). The horror, the horror, of Wadsworth's death epitomizes Dickinson's stake in the larger demise announced in parallel but exclusively philo-sophical terms by her contemporary Nietzsche, and "Those - dying then" can even suggest that Wadsworth and Dickinson included nihilism as an appalling but inescapable topic of their philosophical/ scientific/theological conversation.

To capture the interpersonally conditioned American atmosphere in which Wadsworth and Dickinson breathed, and which she breathed into her words, witness a passage from *A Week on the Concord and Merrimac Rivers* (1849) by Henry David Thoreau. Imagine Dickinson saying the following words to Wadsworth as part of instructions about "how a Friend [or beloved] will address his [or her] Friend [or beloved]" (Thoreau's [expanded] language):

> I never asked thy leave to let me love thee [Thoreau writes],—I have a right. I love thee not as something private and personal, which is your own, but as something universal and worthy of love, which I have found...You are the fact in a fiction,—you are the truth more strange and admirable than fiction. Consent only to be what you are. I alone will never stand in your way. This is what I would like,—to be as inti-mate with you as our spirits are intimate,—respecting you as I respect my ideal. Never to profane one another by word or action, even by a thought. Between us, if necessary, let there be no acquaintance. (Qtd. in Shurr 126–27)

Shurr cites this passage in order to establish "in miniature much of the same emotional galaxy" in which Wadsworth and Dickinson "oper-ated" (127), and "You are the fact in a fiction,—you are the truth more strange and admirable than fiction" speaks volumes about her life/art paradox, and about the sphere of her beloveds, alike. Thoreau's words provide the flavor of the disembodied but real love that Dickinson feels for Wadsworth, and perhaps even vice versa. *Ideal*, for instance, is cho-sen over, and possibly selected to the exclusion of, mere *acquaintance* (this word, if it implies Geoffrey Chaucer's bawdy meaning, does so with abundant intellectual recompense for such signification).[33]

Arlo Bates's identification of Dickinson's chief trait, "emotional *thought*" (emphasis added), most fully describes, though, what she and Wadsworth hold in common.[34] The "emotional galaxy" of their love contains more tension, more psychological and psychosexual urgency, than Thoreau's passage suggests love ever reflects. Their "emotional galaxy," in fact, leads to more intellectual colloquy than Thoreau appears to think either possible or desirable in even the most loving kinds of friendship. Thus, the ever increasing and the increasingly satisfying complexities of their relationship are doubly assured. Dickinson calls Wadsworth "my Clergyman" with proprietary intensity and with propriety—that is, with respect for the mind of her prime partner in discussion.[35]

The pastoral counselor/spiritual aspirant model of Dickinson's emotionally intellectual relationship with Wadsworth is "a more excellent way" for nineteenth-century men and women to have followed than, say, the teacher/pupil condescension suffered by Elizabeth Peabody at the hands of then Harvard president John Kirkland.[36] Kirkland warns Peabody that when a woman "is raised by genius and knowledge above the level of her sex, her neglect of...attentions called femininities, will more than counterbalance all her advantages and reduce her below all other women" (qtd. in Marshall 61). Dickinson accomplishes much and leads an eventful life with a little help from her male friends and mentors. This means not just brother Austin, legal aid Newton, journalists Lyman and Bowles, and lawyer Lord but ministers or ministers-to-be or former ministers Aaron Colton, Daniel Bliss, John Grant, John Gould, J. L. Jenkins, Washington Gladden, Horace Bushnell, Edwards A. Park, Thomas Wentworth Higginson, and Ralph Waldo Emerson.[37] Whether or not Dickinson's friendship with, and love for, Wadsworth is "first" among all these "equals," their intellectual as well as emotional parity with her, their "marriage of [their] true minds" to her mind, indeed entails a give-and-take, rather than a top-down, kind of instruction. The "fellowship of kindred *minds*" (emphasis added) is the philosophical and scientific, as well as theological, "tie that binds" the poet to the preacher with all the cohesion that she would ever know or could ever need to know on this earth.[38]

Walter Pater epitomizes the nineteenth-century kind of affection-with-wisdom that distinguishes the Wadsworth/Dickinson sensibility.

While all melt under our feet [Pater writes], we may well grasp at any exquisite passion, or...the face of one's friend. Not to discriminate every moment some passionate attitude in those about us, and in the very brilliancy of their gifts some tragic dividing of forces on their ways, is, on this short day of frost and sun, to sleep before evening. (Conclusion to *The Renaissance* [1873])

The preacher and the poet together occupied terra that grew firm, if not sacred, because of the hard, gem-like flame of their loving friendship. Their "marriage of true minds / Admit[ted] [few] impediments," if one may redirect here the truths of the Bard (in Sonnet 116 [1609], lines 1–2). The love between Wadsworth and Dickinson neither depended on face-to-face encounter nor, again to apply to their case the words of Dickinson's favorite author, "[bent] with the remover to remove" (Sonnet 116, line 4).

NOTES

INTRODUCTION

1. For Emily Dickinson's lifelong love of William Shakespeare's art as the primal scene of literature, see, e.g., Wolff, 165, 176, 205, 280, 352.
2. See, respectively, Virginia Woolf, *A Room of One's Own* (1929); Shakespeare, Sonnet 30 (1609), line 1; and Wallace Stevens, "The Idea of Order at Key West" (1935), line 56. Quotations of British and American authors, unless otherwise indicated, are from Damrosch et al., eds., and Baym et al., eds. For a comparison of Shakespeare and Dickinson, focusing on plays rather than sonnets and giving meaning to her lyric poems as dramatic monologues, if not dialogues, see Finnerty. For a comparison of Virginia Woolf and Emily Dickinson, based on their shared debt to Shakespeare, see Novy, ed. As Dickinson almost daily recorded her manuscript self-projections, she absorbed words written by others; therefore, juxtaposing her words with those of these fellow-writers can constitute the means of reconstructing her conversation. This method can work, whether these various master figures were all but literally at her side, or more than figuratively on her horizon, or both.
3. For an exposition of Henry Sussman's phrase "between the registers," see Chapter 4 of Sussman. These words epitomize Sussman's goal of collapsing distinctions among poetry, philosophy, and religion. The subtitle of Sussman's *The Task of the Critic* (2005)—namely, *Poetics, Philosophy, Religion*—parallels the subtitle of this book (*Poetry, Philosophy, Science*). Religion, though, forms the subtext of this book, even as science does of Sussman's.
4. Gravil *Romantic Dialogues* 95–96, 99–100, 106, 140, 147, 236. Gravil argues that the American Renaissance builds on, rather than attacks or parodies, British Romanticism. In his view, Cooper, Emerson, Thoreau, Hawthorne, Poe, Melville, Whitman, and Dickinson strive to supplement British Romantic tentativeness, doubt, indirection, failure, and compromise with American Romantic liberation, self-confidence, and perfection. Shira Wolosky, similarly, understands Dickinson in dialogue with American authors: Dickinson's poetic, Wolosky argues, constitutes "a register of the world" (*Poetry and Public Discourse* 30). For a pioneering study of the binational emphasis of this book, see Lease *Anglo-American Encounters*. Gravil recognizes two "equally

viable stances for American literati" (xii), one represented by James
Fenimore Cooper's antagonism toward British literary authority, and
the other by Elizabeth Palmer Peabody's participation in that authority. Nicholas Nardini discerns "a third tack" among British as well
as American writers—namely, a stance "look[ing] past all questions
of nations and language, to some universal grounding in 'nature'"
(160–61).

5. Paul Crumbley's *Winds of Will: Emily Dickinson and the Sovereignty
of Democratic Thought* (2010) does not claim interest, on Dickinson's
part, in women's rights, abolition, or war, but Crumbley's emphasis on
her dialogical method, and on her multiple choices (her choosing not
choosing), carries the American experiment in democratic sovereignty
to its logical, proper conclusion. If one were to write the companion
volume on Dickinson's religious thought, it might be titled *Winds of
Will: Emily Dickinson and the Arminian (Free-Will) Character of Her
Soul-Competence*. Crumbley's two books understand the indeterminacy of Dickinson's dialogic style as the simultaneous existence of her
Gothic, Romantic, sentimental, and evangelical discourses. To these,
in the spirit of this book, one might add her empirical voice at the top
of her less indeterminate than possible triangle of Romantic, empirical, and evangelical perspectives, with Gothic and sentimental off to
one side, and lower down.

6. Quotations of the Bible are from Dickinson's choice among trans-
lations—namely, the King James Version (Capps). The nineteenth
century was the high watermark of this perennial favorite among
English-language renderings (Alter; Gordon Campbell 148–76). The
KJV is holding its own (Bloom *Shadow*). Dickinson's KJV, she writes,
"stills, incites, infatuates—blesses and blames" (L965). Thus, like
Horace Bushnell's and Edwards Amasa Park's mid-nineteenth-century
understanding of biblical metaphor as multilayered in meaning, and
unlike the unitary-criterion doctrinal emphasis of Charles Hodge's
midcentury Princeton Reformed propositional theology, Dickinson's
Bible retains the power to "elude stability" (L693). Thanks go to
Jennifer Leader for sharing her understanding of American theological history. Ann Douglas, for her part, suggests that, along with Parks
and Bushnell, Dickinson admired Charles Wadsworth for "turning
religion into literature" (Ann Douglas 150).

7. This refers to Carl Sandberg's refrain in *The People, Yes* (1936).

8. Ann Rigney's way of branding the major means by which Sir Walter
Scott unwittingly achieved his "afterlives"—i.e., his ongoing and
great, yet almost universally unacknowledged, cultural influence—
is "invisible suffusions" (2). Rigney demonstrates, for instance, the
unrecognized but pervasive pertinence of Edward Waverly's creative
suspension between two loves—Flora and Rose—to the present-day
"strong weakness" of a Briton's pledging allegiance to England and
to Scotland at one and the same time. Even Hardy, notwithstanding

his reputation for pessimism, called his philosophy "meliorism," from the Latin, "to make better."

9. For the philosophical and scientific language of "known unknowns," etc., see Zizek.

10. Compare, respectively, Hardy, "In Tenebris" (1902), line 24; Beckett, *Waiting for Godot* (1952); Conrad, *Heart of Darkness* (1902); Yeats, "The Second Coming" (1919), line 5; and Wordsworth, "Ode: Intimations of Immortality" (1802–1804), line 126.

11. Compare Wordsworth, *The Prelude* (1850) 6:609. For Dickinson's prefiguring of Modernism, see Dickie; Porter. Robert Langbaum's studies of the arc from Romantic to Modern concentrate on intuition, self-expression, and unmediated vision (*Poetry* 35–36), to which this book adds sense perception, pragmatic appeal, and sensory insight. Langbaum's emphasis on Modern-era fragmentation, disjunction, and disequilibrium (*Word* xiii–xiv) will influence (see part II) how this book interprets Modernism in relation to Dickinson.

12. Dickinson channeled works she had not read, but which were central to her concerns, such as John Keats's "Epistle to John Hamilton Reynolds" (1817). Dickinson's living counterparts in this almost more than merely metaphorical/imaginary discussion, would have replied to her, were it not that only 10 of her 1,789 lyrics appeared in print during her lifetime, and these not only against her will but also considerably altered. Such fellow-writers would have selected her for their society of belles lettres, inasmuch as their works often paralleled hers in both form and content.

13. Since Emily Dickinson called her poems flowers, and since *flowers* can mean "extracts from literary works" (Potter 114), it appears more than plausible to think of Dickinson's poems not only as excerpts from but also as part and parcel of that larger poem called literary history.

14. Compare Herman Melville, "Bartleby the Scrivener" (1853). For a pairing of Melville and Dickinson, based on how in their analogous garrets they raised symbolic rather than economic capital, see Kearns. No hint of community, similarly, leavens Emerson's journal entry for April 17, 1827: "I feel a joy in my solitude that the merriment of vulgar society can never communicate" (qtd. in Meola 115).

15. Candidates for Dickinson's "permanent earthly beloved" include her "dearest earthly friend" (L807), the Reverend Charles Wadsworth (Habegger; Longsworth "'Latitude'"; Sewall *Life*; Shurr; Strickland); her sister-in-law Susan Huntington Gilbert Dickinson, wife of Austin (Bennett; Hart; Smith); her confidantes Kate Scott Anthon (Patterson *Riddle*) and Samuel Bowles, editor of *The Springfield Republican* (Farr); and her father Edward's liege companion and fellow-lawyer (later judge) Otis Lord (Walsh). One suspects that, if it was any of these (Lyndall Gordon calls it none of the above, not wanting Dickinson to be thus overidentified with any man), or if it was yet

another (this book will mention others), her beloved was only one in number (though she remained the friend of each candidate). See also Eberwein "Lovers."

16. Compare, respectively, Keats, "This Living Hand" (late 1819?), line 6; Yeats, "The Second Coming" (1920), line 5; and Wordsworth, "Lines Written a Few Miles above Tintern Abbey" (1798), line 49.

17. The unforgettable but potentially misleading name "lady whom the people call the *Myth*" was given to Dickinson by her friend and early editor Mabel Loomis Todd, who was simply epitomizing how the citizens of Amherst, Massachusetts, thought of their admittedly eccentric neighbor. For Dickinson as a not-so-reclusive poet, see Richard B. Sewall's still-magisterial critical biography. If Dickinson did not always deliberately speak with, or talk back to, her written others, her scarcely lonely "Soul," nonetheless, was not simply or entirely home alone. Although she met people face to face more often than one might think, given that "the people" still often regard this "lady" as a recluse, words affected her less often by the hearing of her physical ear than through print. She met her boon companions primarily on the pages of her books in her upstairs room, where she kept to herself incongruously to share their outreach or fellow-feeling.

18. For a path-finding essay on Dickinson's global concerns, see Giles. For a state-of-the-art discussion of Dickinson as a domestic poet, see Mudge. One thinks, in this connection, of Ben Jonson's double-edged view of Shakespeare (a) that he was the "Soul of the age!" and (b) that "He was not of an age, but for all time!" ("To the Memory of My Beloved Master, William Shakespeare, and What He Hath Left Us" [1623], lines 17, 43).

19. Jürgen Habermas's watchword "the unforced force of the better argument" can apply to the open-endedness of poetic quest, as well as of philosophical and scientific inquiry (Habermas 78). For a less admiring view of Habermas, see New and Reedy, eds., *Theology*, xv–xix. The injunction "Stop in the name of the law!" is satirized in Michel Foucault's critique of aesthetically inimical Western power (Foucault 31).

20. For Bloomian interpretation emphasizing Dickinson's *anxiety* of influence, see Diehl *Dickinson*; Homans. Just as in Dickinson's poems and letters one can hear her conversation with her fellow-authors in the long Romantic Movement, so one can take heart from the gender-complementary model generated by Stuart Curran. Curran juxtaposes the style and substance of male and female poet-pairs without favoring one sex. Beth Lau's collection of essays tests the paradigm, and shows how male/female pairings of "fellow-Romantics" "inhabited the same or overlapping...milieus and...expressed many shared aspirations, convictions, anxieties, and conflicts" (2). The same could be said of the pairing of almost any male Romantic author with Dickinson. Annie Finch argues that Dickinson "survived into the twentieth and

twenty-first century" because she was a "hybrid" poet who mixed what Louise Bogan calls the female "line of feeling" with what Bogan calls the male "line of truth" (Bogan qtd. in Finch 28).

21. This detail of the poet's interior decoration justifies inflecting how she said she saw—i.e., "New *Englandly*" (Fr256, line 7; emphasis added). Dickinson saw, in other words, less from her American than from her *Anglo*-American perspective. Three other Britain-derived images on the "text" of her wall were pictures of Windsor Castle, of Elizabeth Barrett Browning, and of George Eliot (Longsworth "'Latitude'" 49). For Dickinson and Barrett Browning, see Swyderski. For Dickinson and George Eliot, see Wolff 534, 555–57.

22. See, respectively, Blake, *All Religions Are One* (c. 1788), and Wordsworth, "Lines Composed a Few Miles above Tintern Abbey" (1798), line 38.

23. For the philosophical transcendentalism of the British Romantics, see Notopoulos; Newman Ivey White. For their religious transcendentalism, see Barth; Brantley *Experience* 165–89; Roe; Ryan; Ulmer. Colin Jager has recently concluded, contra legions of secularizing critics, that the "intentionality" embraced by British Romantics logically committed them to "divine intentionality" (224). Describing an arc from the Enlightenment to Romanticism, Jager's interpretation demonstrates a self-critical "tradition of natural theology," "substantially continuous" from Hume to Blake, in which "practice" is preferred to "argument" (36–37). For Dickinson, as she was influenced by the religious transcendentalism of British Romantic writers and of Emerson (and for that matter of John Wesley and of Jonathan Edwards), see Brantley *Experience* 116–64. For subject/object coalescence and interpenetration as the key to the British Romantics' theme of sense perception and their love of paradox, see Clarke; Wasserman "The English Romantics." For a classic argument that Wordsworth introduced this empirically philosophical emphasis of British Romantic "epistemology," see Davies.

24. For the importance of science to the British Romantic imagination, see Bate *Romantic*; Holmes; Gaull; Grinnell; Macfarlane; McKusick; Milnes; Nichols; Rigby. Jane Donahue Eberwein draws a distinction between Dickinson's "scientifically detached observational skills" and "the counter-influence of Transcendental Romanticism" ("Outgrowing Genesis?" 15). But there is not such a sharp distinction, perhaps, between Dickinson's "observational skills" and the *empirical* streak of *Anglo-American* Romanticism.

25. For the prominence of Scottish Common Sense philosophy in Edward Dickinson's library, see Capps. For signs of the Common Sense School in Emily Dickinson's poetry, see Deppman *Trying to Think*. For the importance of the Common Sense School in eighteenth- to nineteenth-century America, see Manning.

26. This wording is indebted to that of Denis Donoghue in another context: "Even to write against something is to take one's bearings from

it" (*Third Voice* 18). This important and surprising idea will recur throughout this book.

27. Compare Robert Frost, "To Earthward" (1923). Note well the final word of William James's title: *The Varieties of Religious Experience* (1902).

28. For the relation between Charles Darwin's science and literature, and for his science *as* literature, see Beer; Levine; David Locke. George Levine points to the metaphorical and paradoxical character of Darwin's language, and to Darwin's comic rather than tragic tone. For the centrality of the phrase "poetic faith" to Romantic-era thought, see Coleridge, *Biographia Literaria* (1817), Chapter 14.

29. For a recent perspective on the American importation through James Marsh and John Dewey of Coleridge's British Romantic domestication of German idealism, see Harvey "Coleridge's."

30. See the discussion in Patterson *Riddle* Chapter 1. Of "Wild nights - wild nights!" Sharon Leiter writes: "On the physical level, the image of the speaker as a boat mooring in a harbor reverses the roles inherent in male and female anatomy. The observation has led...to a homoerotic interpretation. If the poem is about Dickinson's love for another woman (the most likely candidate would be her sister-in-law, Susan Huntington Gilbert Dickinson), the problem is eliminated" (232).

31. See Gerard Manley Hopkins, "I Wake and Feel the Fell of Dark, Not Day" (1885). Here is the full passage: "I am gall, I am heartburn. God's most deep decree / Bitter would have me taste: my taste was me; / Bones built in me, flesh filled, blood brimmed the curse. // Selfyeast of spirit a dull dough sours. I see / The lost are like this, and the scourge to be / As I am mine, their sweating selves; but worse" (lines 9–14). For the constructed nature of self-fashioning, see Greenblatt *Renaissance*.

32. In 1969, Richard Howard dedicated a volume of dramatic monologues to Robert Browning: "[T]o the great poet of otherness...who said, as I should like to say, 'I'll tell my state as though 'twere none of mine'" (qtd. in Abrams et al., eds., 2:1,229). Does Browning anticipate T. S. Eliot's formula: "The more perfect the artist, the more completely separate in him will be the man who suffers and the mind which creates" (qtd. in Kirchwey 19)?

33. This conflates Walt Whitman's language in "Song of Myself," line 1,314, with Dickinson's in line 3 of "Obtaining but our own extent" (Fr1573). Agnieszka Salska's philosophically perceptive comparison of Whitman with Dickinson argues that, for them, "the self is central" (36); Dickinson's in Salska's view, however, is more circumscribed and isolated (Salska adduces Whitman's as "kosmos" ["Song of Myself" 34:1]). Salska emphasizes such inward-looking poems of Dickinson's as "How happy is the little Stone" (Fr1570). This book, on the other hand, suggests the dialogical and scientific as well as philosophical

senses in which Dickinson's poetic concerns match those of Whitman in "Song of Myself" 4:2–4: "People I meet, the effect upon me of my early life, or the ward and city I live in, or the nation, / The latest dates, discoveries, inventions, societies, authors old and new, / My dinner, dress, associates, looks, compliments, dues." Dickinson's "central consciousness" (Salska's phrase) radiates as far and wide as Whitman's, as in her lines "The Only News I know / Is Bulletins all Day / From Immortality" (Fr820, lines 1–3).

34. E. Derek Taylor 522. See also E. Derek Taylor and Melvyn New, eds. Mary Astell's Christian feminism calls ascetically for Protestant nunneries. See Astell's *Serious Proposal to the Ladies* (1694) and Astell's *Reflections upon Marriage* (1700).

35. Wesley respected Norris's otherworldly, sense-suspicious Christian Platonism, but Wesley's conversations with Mary Pendarves, as with Miss March, Mary Bishop, Hannah Ball, Anne Foard, Damaris Perronnet, and his mother, Susannah, showed that Locke had won the battle. For a study of the Wesley/Pendarves connection— i.e., their common interest in the Locke-derived method of British Enlightenment theology—see Brantley *Locke* 103–105, 111–12, 116, 205, 252. The focus on Mary Pendarves's importance in Brantley *Locke* is now supplemented by Molly Peacock's fascinating, welcome account of Mrs. Delany (formerly Mrs. Pendarves) as a collage or flower-mosaic artist beginning at age 72. Peacock mentions Wesley only in passing, but Peacock's labor of love is a model of research.

36. Beginning with his 11 sisters, whose father referred to his "sixty feet of daughters," Edwards showed respect for the intelligence of women. See Marsden *Jonathan* 18–19, 68, 93–95, 99, 105–109, 128, 172, 241–42, 254, 510. Recent overviews of the role of women in the transatlantic revival (see Andrews; Mack) have emphasized emotion.

37. Debby Applegate offers the fullest account of the affair, which constitutes as much of a late-nineteenth-century paradigm shift in the history of male/female sexual relations as the Austin Dickinson/ Mabel Loomis Todd affair (see Gay; Longsworth *Austin and Mabel*). For a pioneering study of the nineteenth-century intellectual alliance between ministers and their female parishioners, see Douglas.

38. Just as some have drawn convincing theological parallels between Wadsworth's sermons and Dickinson's poems (see Huffer; Lease; Paul M. Miller; Sewall *Life* 2:449–54), so a future installment in this series of arguments will join this conversation. This book, meanwhile, focuses on what has not been thoroughly undertaken—i.e., a philosophical and scientific comparison between their two bodies of work.

39. Religious specifics in Dickinson's poetry are well established. See Eberwein *Dickinson*; Linda Freedman; Keane *Emily;* Lundin; McIntosh; Elisa New; Oberhaus. Elisa New's suggestion that Dickinson rebelled against Emerson's bias against theology supplements the emphasis on Emerson in this book. This book, however, will conclude that

208 NOTES

Dickinson's empirical procedure, her faith in experience, trumps her evangelical yearning or experience of faith. Of course, poems like "'Arcturus' is his other name" (Fr117) are antiscience, and Dickinson credits Benjamin Franklin Newton for teaching her "faith in things unseen" (L282). Still, just as science in Dickinson's experience is "part of an intellectual tennis match in which the other player is always going to be religion" (Peel 107), so science often wins this game of hers.

40. Habegger writes well of Dickinson's "Calvinist evangelicalism" (10–13; see also 4, 7, 101–103, 167–69, 174, 196–205, 282–85, 287, 309–12). This is a more accurate label than the vague, seventeenth-century term *Puritanism*, but the religious motif that this book will continue to include adds *Arminianism* to the mix. Jacobus Arminius's doctrine of free will, as opposed to John Calvin's of predestination, explains the reverence for experience in many of Wadsworth's sermons and in most of Dickinson's poems. The controversy begun by Arminian John Wesley and Calvinist Jonathan Edwards reached dénouement during the Second Great Awakening, resolving itself in favor of Jacobus Arminius in the sermon-poem nexus of Wadsworth (despite Wadsworth's Calvinist/Presbyterian beginnings) and Dickinson. Dickinson perhaps persuaded Wadsworth to come down on her side. In any case, the Arminian view of experience as open-ended characterizes the religious pole of Dickinson's oscillation between experiential philosophy and experiential faith. The erotic motor of seventeenth-century Puritanism will figure in a planned book in this series, about the religious roots of Wadsworth and of Dickinson alike; meanwhile, see Leverenz *Language*. For an exploration of Edwards's central paradox, that "the freedom of a moral agent is compatible with determinism," see Crisp (57). For the experiential emphasis of nineteenth-century Presbyterianism, see Marsden *Evangelical Mind*.

41. Dickinson heard or read other ministers for other reasons. Jane Eberwein points out that she "heard more sermons from [Aaron] Colton than from any other clergyman"; Colton "took a kindly and hopeful approach to Calvinist doctrine" ("Ministerial" 8, 10). Horace Bushnell and Edwards Park were appealing to Dickinson because these progressive Congregationalists learned from Coleridge to emphasize a theology of feeling rather than intellect (Peel 301–302).

42. For a comparison of Wesley's style and that of Edwards, see Brantley *Coordinates* 7–42. This comparison depicts these twin pioneers of transatlantic revivalism in philosophical as well as theological terms; for exclusively religious comparisons of the two, see Hindmarsh. As far as Wadsworth's spoken words were concerned, he was "one of the most renowned orators in America, on a par with Henry Ward Beecher" (Strickland 103). He "impressed believers and unbelievers alike, including Mark Twain, who heard him in San Francisco and liked his humorous glare" (Habegger 330). This humor comes

across, as well, in Wadsworth's written words. Mark Twain's response to Wadsworth suggests that the dialogue between nineteenth-century ministers and their *male* auditors merits attention, too. Witness the connection between Joseph Hopkins Twichell and Mark Twain (Strong). Dickinson's art stands taller than Wadsworth's, perhaps even by homiletic standards: Jane Eberwein often argues for Dickinson's connoisseurship of sermons, and hence for Dickinson's alternately earnest and satirical sermons and antisermons in lyrics (see, for instance, Eberwein "Ministerial"). Wadsworth, though, avoided hackneyed phrases and ideas.

43. Keats's "naturalized imagination" (Stillinger 99–118) prophesied his "poetry of earth" (compare Keats, "The Poetry of Earth Is Never Dead" [1817]).

44. "Human beings" in general, as David Brooks writes concerning cognitive science in particular, "are engaged every second in all sorts of silent conversation—with the living and the dead, the near and the far." For an overview of cognitive science, see Schacter. For cognitive science and Romanticism, see Richardson. For cognitive science and Dickinson, see Freeman "Cognitive." Just as Dickinson knew that she could "re-create a [literary] conversation" with "the dead" because they leave "textual traces of themselves" that "make themselves heard in the voices of the living" (Greenblatt *Shakespearean* 1), so in the spirit of her age, understanding science as dialogue (see Peel 162–63), she conversed with her scientific precursors and contemporaries.

45. Blake's marginalium is in response to a statement by Joshua Reynolds— namely, "Enthusiastic admiration seldom promotes knowledge." See Blake's Marginalia in a copy of Reynolds's *Works* (1798; qtd. in Bentley 52–53).

46. Dickinson's first reviewer, Arlo Bates, admired her "emotional thought," which her thorough biographer Richard B. Sewall, echoing Wordsworth, praised as her "ideas felt on the pulses, in the bloodstream" (see the quotation and discussion of Bates's review in Sewall "Teaching Dickinson" 31). Compare Wordsworth's "Lines Written a Few Miles above Tintern Abbey" (1798), lines 27–30.

47. Dickinson's circle imagery, Shira Wolosky argues, parallels Emerson's "Circles" (1844): "The life of man [Emerson writes] is a self-evolving circle, which, from a ring imperceptibly small, rushes on all sides outwards to new and larger circles, and that without end...The instinct of man presses eagerly outward to the impersonal and illimitable" (qtd. in Wolosky "Dickinson's Emerson" 136). There is thus something metaphysical in the idea of Dickinson as *eccentric*, which, Peel points out, "means off center, away from the center" (148).

48. The word *inane* derives from the paleoscientific language of Lucretius, yet in Shelley's hands widens cyclically and "transcendentally."

49. Cynthia MacKenzie, Marietta Messmer, and Marta Werner, among others, have demonstrated the aesthetic excellence of Dickinson's

letters. The Dickinson Editing Collective will make available the many "books" Dickinson sent to her correspondents. Dickinson's letters make up one side of a substantial as well as passionate conversation.

50. For a classic, still explanatory study of the mimetic, pragmatic, expressive, and objective functions of art, see Abrams *Mirror*. Contrary to the received description of lyric as introspective, and in spite of the pervasiveness of Descartes's isolated self, the expressive function of Dickinson's art modulates into her other-directed appeal or audience orientation. For the lyric genre as preeminently subjective, see Hardy. For a provocative recent view of the Cartesian *cogito* as a deleterious interpolation into the Romantic-era culture of the Western world, see Breuggemann 2–4. Virginia Jackson deplores the "lyricization" of Dickinson's poetry—i.e., the habit of interpreting Dickinson's poetry through the paradigm of the "expressive romantic" lyric (7). Jackson recommends connecting Dickinson's poetry to its manuscript context, and hence to Dickinson's role as an engaged, almost impersonal public writer. Perhaps Jackson's reading of Dickinson's poetry is not as far removed from Romanticism as Jackson implies, though, since Gravil, for one, has emphasized the dialogism, and hence the pragmatic function, of Romantic art.

51. Kershner 17; emphasis added. Dickinson wrote almost wholly in hymn or ballad quatrains—i.e., she usually alternated iambic tetrameter with iambic trimeter. For Dickinson's ironizing of hymns like those of Watts, see England and Sparrow; Gelpi "Emily Dickinson's Word"; Weisbuch. For Charles Wesley's hymns as belles lettres, see Brantley "Charles." Victoria Morgan's full-length study of Dickinson and the hymn tradition depicts the poet's sisterhood of female hymn singers, transcribers, writers, and composers. In Morgan's view, they were all engaged, especially Dickinson, in sometimes conventional and sometimes unconventional exchanges with their hymn singing, transcribing, writing, and composing brothers. For Dickinson and revival testimony, see Brantley *Experience* 116–64. One of Dickinson's favorite stories, Harriet E. Prescott Spofford's "Circumstance" (1860), features "grand and sweet Methodist hymns," as a seventeenth-century Maine frontierswoman's means of parrying a panther attack (qtd. in David Cody 59).

52. The dialogical theory of M. M. Bakhtin whereby "I can mean what I say, but only *indirectly*, at a second remove, in words I take and give back to the community according to the protocols it establishes" is pertinent throughout this book (see, e.g., the conclusion). Bakhtin would add, "My voice can mean, but only with others: at times in chorus, but at the best of times in a dialogue." See Michael Holquist's concise and accurate paraphrase of Bakhtin's position, qtd. in Greenblatt, ed., *Allegory* 165. Bakhtin's dialogical theory set a precedent for interpreting literature against the background of oral culture. He and his followers, however, thought of such culture in

almost exclusive relation to narrators and characters in belletristic fiction. See R. B. Kershner's application of Bakhtin's theory to James Joyce's comic fiction (Kershner 17–22).

53. For folk, popular, and elite culture as background to Dickinson's poetry, see St. Armand.

54. For a recent, comprehensive history of the Royal Society, see Bryson, ed. John Wesley was steeped in Milton (see Herbert), and so would have known of the religious connotations of the word *society*, as in Milton's echo of Revelation 21:1–7 in his elegy "Lycidas" (1635): "There entertain him all the Saints above, / In solemn troops, and sweet Societies / That sing, and singing in their glory move, / And wipe the tears for ever from his eyes" (lines 178–81). Wesley organized his hymn-singing followers into religious "Societies." He also knew, however, the philosophical meaning of the word *society*, as in Locke's social contract (see Dreyer). *Society*, then, is Wesleyan argot for fellowship among Methodist, methodized, disciplined believers, truth-seekers. All these implications of the word, philosophical and scientific as well as religious, apply to Dickinson's concept *society*.

1 PROCLAIMING EMPIRICISM

1. In a letter to William Wordsworth, written perhaps in early January 1815, Charles Lamb regretted that the editor of *The Quarterly*, William Gifford, had omitted from Lamb's review of Wordsworth's *Excursion* (1814) Lamb's argument for Wordsworth's poetry as "natural methodism." Lamb thought that Wordsworth would have liked such an interpretation: "I regret only that I did not keep a copy. I am sure you would have been pleased with it, because I have been feeding my fancy for some months with the notion of pleasing you" (Lamb 2:149). See also Brantley *Wordsworth's* 8, 135, 142, 174.

2. Thus the phrase *natural methodism* serves on the Anglo-American Romantic scene to complement but at the same time to tone down the phrase *Natural Supernaturalism* there. According to the Euro-continental drift of M. H. Abrams's classic argument for the relation between British and Euro-continental Romanticism, Natural Supernaturalism gives a German idealist, Teutonic twist to the late-Romantic imagination of, say, Sage of Chelsea Thomas Carlyle, who makes full use of this uppercase phrase in his *Sartor Resartus* (1831) (see Abrams *Natural*; see also Cazamian). In the early and middle phases of Carlyle's career, where his true genius lay, the Sage, too, can sound like a "Natural Methodist," yet with the stipulation that his temperament stayed rather more transcendental-izing than Emily Dickinson's ever was, as though Carlyle thought of "natural methodism" as Natural Methodism. For Carlyle as this kind of an Anglo-American writer, as distinct from being German Romantic at heart, see Brantley *Coordinates* 43–76.

3. In a mode of analysis harking back to William James and German Romantic theologian Friedrich Schleiermacher, Stanford University psychological anthropologist T. M. Luhrmann examines the religious emotion cultivated by such contemporary evangelicals as the Pentecostals of the Vineyard Christian Fellowship in Chicago and Northern California. Luhrmann's title, *When God Talks Back: Understanding the American Evangelical Relationship with God* (2012), parallels the emphasis in this book on poetic, philosophical, and scientific conversation.

4. For the language of John Locke in John Wesley's Kingswood School rules—the ban on holidays, the injunction against play, and the insistence on simplicity of diet and starkness of accommodation—see Body 56–61. These rules enforce nurture against nature and carry tabula rasa to its logical conclusion.

5. For the leading role of Locke's *Essay* in the curriculum at Wesley's Kingswood School, see Body 33. For the pervasive influence of Locke's *Essay* on Wesley's revival, see Brantley *Locke* 27–102. For the pioneering study of Locke's influence on Wesley, see Hindley. For the impact of Locke's *Two Treatises on Government* on Wesley's idea of community or of social contract, see Dreyer. Dreyer's investigation can give additional Locke- as well as Wesley-drenched meaning to Emily Dickinson's signature utterance: "The Soul selects her own Society - " (Fr409, line 1).

6. For perspective on George Berkeley's "bundling" or "clustering" of sense impressions, see Brantley *Locke* 9, 18–19, 73, 145, 229n.23.

7. For soul-competence on the nineteenth- to twentieth-century American revival scene (especially Baptist), see Bloom *American* 111–43. For postmodern-evangelical sensibility, see, e.g., books by Joel Osteen.

8. Charles Wadsworth's description of the intellectual scholar is the polar opposite of John Wesley's of the ideal clergyman as an unaffected man of God whose well-prepared sermons should avoid "a dull, dry, formal manner" and be delivered earnestly and from memory without any lolling of the elbows. See the discussion in Brantley *Wordsworth's* 25–28. Clergy who sound like Wadsworth's portrait of professors are satirized in William Cowper *The Task* 2:419–26 and in Wordsworth *The Prelude* 7:546–56.

9. For an overview of Dickinson's friendship with Wadsworth, including the probable facilitating-importance of Elizabeth and Josiah Gilbert Holland, see Sewall *Life* 2:444–62, 2:729–41. See also Lease 4, 6.

10. For the friendship between Thomas Wentworth Higginson and Emily Dickinson, see Benfey; Wineapple. Howard N. Meyer's recent edition of selected works by the prolific Higginson can serve as an ongoing basis for grasping how influential a figure Higginson was in general, as well as in Emily Dickinson's lifetime of writing.

11. For the argument that Eliza Coleman brought Dickinson and her sister, Lavinia, to hear Wadsworth preach (philosophically?) at the

NOTES213

Arch Street Presbyterian Church, Philadelphia, in March 1855, see Leyda 1:lxxvi–lxxvii. Besides Wadsworth, as Alfred Habegger points out, two ministerial candidates for intellectual and even philosophical compatibility with Dickinson are Horace Bushnell and Edwards A. Park (311–13).

12. See Sewall *Life* 2:262–68; Leyda 1:29, 1:37, 1:323, 2:33. For the nationwide context of nineteenth-century women's education in science, see Peel 144, 146, 176.

13. For sustained perspective on Wordsworth's theme of exalted humility, see Brantley *Wordsworth's* 37–65.

14. See, respectively, Percy Bysshe Shelley, "Adonais" (1821), line 418; and Shelley, *Prometheus Unbound* (1819), act 3, scene 1, line 204. Shelley thinks of *inane* as "the vacancy that nevertheless holds in itself the potentiality of all that is" (Wasserman *Subtler* 209).

15. Shelley, "Adonais," line 418. Again Frost's "To Earthward" proves apropos. The alternately heady and earthward excursions in Wordsworth's *Excursion* (1814) anticipate Shelley's.

16. Many of Dickinson's personae, for that matter, choose never to strike out for the empyrean in the first place. They may venture out into nature but go no further, stopping well short of "darting their spirit's light" into the universe. Thus they resemble Robert Frost's persona in "To Earthward" (1923).

17. Jerusha Hall McCormack understands Dickinson's style as a form of mid-nineteenth-century "telegraphese" (dashes, ellipses, and capitalized nouns).

18. For Dickinson's somewhat less Wadsworth-related mastery of mathematics, chemistry, botany, ornithology, and entomology, see Brantley *Experience* 35, 55–62, 90–93, 96–102. Peel addresses the first three of these disciplines and also such pseudosciences as mesmerism, animal magnetism, phrenology, and spiritualism (330–60). It is as though Dickinson completed bits and pieces of the epic that at 25 Coleridge planned would reflect mathematics, hydrostatics, optics, astronomy, botany, metallurgy, fossilism, chemistry, geology, anatomy, and medicine (Johnston 507). For Dickinson's ethnocentrism, see Erkkila.

19. Wadsworth would agree with Thomas Chalmers's 1833 reading and Edward Hitchcock's 1851 reading of the biblical six days of creation as metaphorically a long time (for Chalmers's and Hitchcock's views on the subject, see Eberwein "Outgrowing Genesis?").

20. The December 1859 issue of *The Atlantic Monthly,* to which the Dickinson family subscribed, included the lyric "The Northern Lights and the Stars" and an article "The Aurora Borealis" (Peel 197).

21. Sources as otherwise widely divergent as Newton and the Calvinists used astronomy as an argument, respectively, for modesty and for humility. For Newton, see Dyson. For the Calvinists, see Eberwein "'Where'" 13. Contrast the perhaps overweening epistemological confidence of Steven Weinberg's astronomical science.

22. Sources as otherwise widely divergent as author Poe and astronomer Denison Olmsted used star-gazing as an occasion for egotistical sublimity in the former case and for observer participation in the latter. For Poe, see Delbanco 274. For Olmsted's presence in the immediate Dickinson milieu, see Ricca. Compare Peel on how Dickinson's slant truth parallels the image deflection and the angled lenses of telescopes (248–49).

23. Susan Dickinson's library contained O. M. Mitchell's praise of the "extraordinary powers of Leverrier as a mathematical astronomer" and of his research on "the motions of Mercury" (qtd. in Peel 268).

24. For the possibility that Dickinson writes of Caroline and not of William Herschel in her poem "Nature and God - I neither knew" (Fr803), and for the prominence of such other women astronomers as Maria Mitchell, see Peel 344–45.

25. Just as Kant declares that "Two things fill my mind... the starry heavens above me, and the moral law within me," so Dickinson's poem, here, links the ephemerality of stars to that of humankind, and vice versa (qtd. in Peel 280).

26. Whereas astronomy provides the occasion of "wonder" for the "Romantic science" (Holmes) of Keats in his "On First Looking into Chapman's Homer" (1816), Dickinson's late-Romantic-era personae can experience more terror in astronomical meditation than the exaltation of sublimity. Just as astronomy made Emerson lose his faith (Peel 236) and terrified Ishmael (Delbanco 160), so Dickinson's astral contemplation was fraught.

27. To the more than 30 names Darwin places on his list of predecessors in the fourth edition of *Origin* (1866), Rebecca Stott adds many more. These notably include Abraham Trembley, Trembley's nephew Charles de Bonnet, and their teacher, René-Antoine Feuchault da Réaumour. The entomologist Trembley, in particular, used his interest in asexually producing polyps to ask why, if man is so clearly the crown of creation, God did not give him this remarkable means of perpetuating his kind! Stott strongly emphasizes the collaborative, conversational interaction among Darwin's predecessors and credits Darwin with his generous acknowledgment of the scientific community. Charles de Bonnet, incidentally, is well known for first identifying the syndrome with which his name is still linked—namely, the hallucination of multiple images that often replace darkness whenever one is suffering from failing vision.

28. Compare Henry Ward Beecher in 1872: "I do not participate a particle with those that dread the idea of man's having sprung from some lower form of existence; all that I ask is that you show me how I got clear from monkeys, and then I am quite satisfied to have had only one for an ancestor... I want to know where I am going; I don't care where I came from" (qtd. in Kirkby "'[W]e thought'" 10). Kirkby points to a "sprightly manner" and "a lightness about

the response to evolutionary issues, a whimsy and humor which belies the seriousness of what might be regarded as world-shattering new ideas," and then adds, "There is a kind of carnavalization of evolutionary themes" (9).

29. In 1869, *The Springfield Daily Republican* quoted Thomas Henry Huxley's declaration concerning Samuel Wilberforce that he would prefer being "descended from a respectable monkey" than from a "bishop of the English church, who can put his brains to no better use than to ridicule science and misrepresent its cultivation" (qtd. in Kirkby "'[W]e thought'"12).

30. Jane Donahue Eberwein thinks of Darwin's "eye" as "retrospective" and contrasts it with Dickinson's "that looks toward heaven" ("Outgrowing Genesis?" 12). Dickinson's "prospective eye" may have as much to do with the driving force of natural selection, however, as with eschatological concerns.

31. According to Gravil "Locksley," Tennyson's monodrama *Maud* (1855) forms a major influence on Dickinson's 40 fascicles, her manuscript books.

32. Hitchcock began writing to Darwin in 1845, and the third edition (1861) of *The Origin* considers bird origins in the light of Hitchcock's writings on fossilized bird footprints from the Connecticut Valley (see Kirkby "'[W]e thought'" 7–8).

33. These words from *In Memoriam* constitute the chief poetic result of Tennyson's perspective on Robert Chambers's proto-Darwin *Vestiges of the Natural History of Creation* (1844).

34. To reference General Benjamin F. Butler's occupation of New Orleans, Butler played God there egregiously. He earned himself the nickname "Beast"; see the discussion in Sandberg *Abraham* 246–47. In fairness to General Butler, and in contrast to "Mrs Dr Stearns"'s evident view of him, the Massachusetts general "grew ever more steadfast" in defending the one thousand fugitive contraband slaves at Fortress Monroe. Butler argued that they "were not only contraband: they had become free" (Goodheart 338).

35. For a less historical and more theoretical view of the poem, and also for a more theological but no less negative view of it, see Franke's argument that "The missing All - prevented Me" "articulates the principle that the Nothing is the All, the Absolute" (71). "The missing All - prevented Me" counterbalances an article (1872) by Dr. Hedge in *The Springfield Republican*: "[Science] yet refreshes and expands the idea of God by new revelations of the hights [*sic*] and depths and infinite riches of the wondrous All" (qtd. in Kirkby "'[W]e thought'" 11). The optimistic element of Dickinson's poems on evolution can remain if "excitement and exhilaration" (Kirkby "'[W]e thought'" 4) arise from "All things swept sole away," for "This is immensity" (Fr1548, lines 1–2).

36. A January 1873 *Scribner's* essay on "Victorian Poets" laments from the standpoint of late-nineteenth-century women the post-Darwin plight

of poetry: "The truth is that our school-girls and spinsters who wan-
der down the lanes with Darwin, Huxley, and Youmans under their
arms; or, if they carry Tennyson, Longfellow, and Morris, read them
in the light of spectrum analysis, or test them by the economics of
Mill and Bain" (qtd. in Kirkby "'[W]e thought'" 14). As a September
1877 *Scribner's* essay on "The Poetry of the Future" contends, "[i]f
the extinction of a single individual has been so sung as to be cause
for tears, what pathos must there not lie in the extinction of whole
species, genera, and families?" (qtd. in Kirkby "'[W]e thought'" 14).
Thus Darwin's 1831 voyage on *The Beagle* did not so much culminate
"Romantic science" (see Holmes) as instigate the scientific worldview
of late Romanticism and of early Modernism. Darwin writes that we
"behold the face of nature bright with gladness" but "do not see
or we forget, that the birds which are idly singing round us mostly
live on insects or seeds, and are thus constantly destroying life; or
we forget how largely these songsters, or their eggs, or their nest-
lings, are destroyed by birds and beasts of prey" (*Origin* 52 qtd. in
Eberwein "Outgrowing Genesis?" 17). Dickinson's bird that "bit an
Angle Worm in halves / And ate the fellow, raw" (Fr359) and her
"Nature" that "sometimes sears a Sapling - / Sometimes - scalps a
Tree" (Fr457) is poetry, nonetheless, of however new or however
tough-minded a kind (see Eberwein "Outgrowing Genesis?").

37. Kirkby's conclusion is apropos: "Dickinson explored both the wonder and the emotional toll of a darwinized natural world" ("'[W]e
thought'" 27). For philosopher Thomas Nagel, evolution is not random, for Nagel believes in a "cosmic predisposition" to moral value,
meaning, and consciousness (7). Nagel's idea of a natural teleology,
though, remains difficult to square with the overwhelming reality
of species extinction. Darwin's truth entails not purpose (for natural selection finds little point even in the biological power to create)
but "eternal fierce destruction" where "the greater on the less feeds
evermore" (compare Keats, "Epistle to John Hamilton Reynolds"
[1818], lines 95, 97).

38. By contrast, a writer in *Harper's New Monthly* for November 1862 is
"appalled" that "the Man as well as the Fly" must "depend" on the
"immensity of individual *facts*" (emphasis in original) and on "the
incontrovertible laws of Nature" (qtd. in Peel 321–22).

39. Compare, respectively, Matthew Arnold, "The Function of Criticism
at the Present Time" (1864), and Wordsworth, *The Prelude* (1850)
14:76. Alexandra Socarides suggests that Dickinson's sense of playful
paradox grows stronger, and somewhat darker, as her career develops.
Socarides describes a roughly chronological movement of Dickinson's
thought and practice from order (i.e., fascicles, loose sheets) to disorder (i.e., late fragments).

40. Compare, e.g., Coleridge's definition of "poetic faith" as "the willing
suspension of disbelief" in *Biographia Literaria* (1817), Chapter 14.

2 GUIDING EXPERIMENT

1. "The Philosophy of Enthusiasm," by J. Clifford Hindley, links Moravian theology to Wesley's conversion on May 24, 1738, in Aldersgate Street, London. Hindley emphasizes, however, that Wesley's "empiricist conditioning" taught him so much respect for experience as the necessary ground of knowledge that his distinctive quest for "a direct experience of the divine love" was in the first instance, and ultimately, quasi-philosophic (107–108; hence the emphasis added to Hindley's word *philosophy*).

2. These three phrases—namely, "the dogged aggregation of phenomena," "abstract reasoning," and "complicated mathematics"— comprise the chief elements in "the story of science and the Royal Society" (Gleick qtd. in Bryson, ed., 180). According to the perspective of part I, Dickinson's select society of partners in dialogue perpetuated the "innovation" that "marked the [Royal] Society out for success," again to borrow the language of James Gleick (qtd. in Bryson, ed., 181–82). The Royal Society's "way of making knowledge was to talk about it," Gleick concludes (183). The same goes for Dickinson's Royal Society-descended select society.

3. As an example of the subtlety, enchantment, or mystery that might even yet occur as the empirical quintessence of logical positivism, consider what Peter Geach, as reported in Kenny, has called "Ludwig's Self-Trap." Wittgenstein's early *Tractatus Logico-Philosophicus* maintained that "[t]he right method of philosophy [and, for that matter, of poetry?] would be to say nothing except what can be said, that is to say the propositions of natural science." But that sentence, as Wittgenstein later recognized, is no such proposition! The verification principle that "meaningful propositions were either analytic or capable of verification or falsification by experience" was itself neither analytic nor empirical! Such exercise of both/and logic, such relish of ambiguity, is not far from Emily Dickinson's rich conversation about poetry, philosophy, science. For subtle discussion of "Ludwig's Self-Trap," see Kenny.

4. Compare Shelley, "Mont Blanc" (1817), lines 80–81. By "Large codes of fraud," does Shelley mean papal bulls? By "Large codes of...woe," does Shelley mean ironically to contrast the enlightened domestic policy of the "Code Napoleon" with Napoleon's ruinous foreign wars? For the influence of Napoleon on British Romanticism, see Bainbridge.

5. See, respectively, Emerson, "Experience" [1844], qtd. in Murphy 1:944; Wordsworth, "Expostulation and Reply" (1798), line 24; and Emily Dickinson, Fr1433 (1876), line 1.

6. English readers' favorite Frenchman, accordingly, was Montaigne, who rejected "the more doctrinaire projections of the essayist's French readers" in favor of his own easygoing, pragmatic, antitheoretical, tolerant, secular, and joyful "woolliness" (Chester 8).

7. The "logical extreme and consequence of Protestant individualism," according to Albert Gelpi, flowed from the "antinomian element" of Anne Hutchinson's legacy, which "elevated individual gnosis above community consensus" (Gelpi "Long Shadow" 109). "As American Puritanism became tempered and secularized by Unitarianism and then Transcendentalism," Gelpi concludes, "the antinomian saint became the antinomian artist" (109). This insight can apply to "On a Columnar Self - ."

8. For the pre-1975, prefundamentalist-era "soul-competence" of such traditional, mainline Southern Baptists as E. Y. Mullins, who coined the phrase and who inspired old-line Baptists like former president Jimmy Carter, see Bloom *American* 131–44. Here is a promising line of thought: To compare Dickinson's Congregational heritage with Baptist tradition would nuance her theological language.

9. To poems such as "On a Columnar Self - " and "I saw no Way - the Heavens were stitched - " (Fr633), Shira Wolosky demonstrates, on the one hand, the relevance of Emerson's essay "Circles" (1844), declaring that "the instinct of man presses eagerly outward to the impersonal and illimitable" (qtd. in Wolosky "Dickinson's Emerson" 136). On the other hand, Wolosky emphasizes, in Dickinson's case, the more modest halves of her and Emerson's binary oppositions of selfhood (e.g., limitation/expansion, extension/intensity, and constrictive circles/infinite circumference).

10. Kher's emphasis on Dickinson's "multidimensional reality" (2), Greg Johnson's on her poetics of inward quest, Benfey's on her skepticism concerning intersubjectivity, and Kimpel's on her prephilosophical state of bafflement or of perplexity—all emphasize philosophy in general, rather than philosophers in particular. The collection of essays edited by Jed Deppman, Marianne Noble, and Gary Lee Stonum, a work in progress, will draw parallels between Dickinson's poetry and such philosophers of the late nineteenth and early twentieth century as Charles Pierce and Martin Heidegger.

11. For the merits of polytheism over monotheism, see Schwartz.

12. See the discussion and quotation in Leib 40; emphasis added. See also Hannay.

13. It seems worth noting, though, that as prologue to Marx, Locke's *Second Treatise* assumes that laborers prove worthy of their hire (compare Luke 10:7): "The Ploughman's Pains [Locke writes], the Reaper's and Thresher's Toil, and the Baker's Sweat, is to be counted into the Bread we eat: the labor of those who broke the Oxen, who digged and wrought the Iron and Stones, who felled and framed the Timber employed about the Plough, Mill, Oven, or any other Utensils, which are a vast Number, requisite to this Corn, from its being feed to be sown to its being made Bread, must all be charged to the account of Labor" (qtd. in Waldron 174).

14. Jeremy Waldron's argument for John Locke as an "equality-radical" (5) carries implications for Locke's philosophy. "The members of the laboring class," C. B. Macpherson's reading of Locke asserts, "do not and cannot live a fully rational life" (qtd. in Waldron 85), but in Waldron's words, Locke insists on "the fundamental adequacy of even the meanest intellect" (87). Waldron, correspondingly, refutes Macpherson's narrow understanding of Lockean "property" as tangible possessions (126); Locke's concept, in Waldron's highlighting, features life, liberty, and labor (173–75). Locke, as Waldron understands him, "believed it was possible to use human reason—to sift the customs of the world and determine at least for some of them whether or not they were in uniformity with the requirements of natural law" (168). Thus Waldron shows how "Locke's opposition to innateism does not lead him to relativism" (168). Waldron's eye for all that Locke says about equality scrutinizes such vivid but neglected views as Locke's implication of crossovers, even oneness (a principle of *e pluribus unum*), among species ("women have conceived by Drills [mandrills]...[and the *Essay* continues:] I once saw a Creature that was the issue of a Cat and a Rat" (qtd. in Waldron 65). No hierarchical chain of being for Locke!

15. Jeremy Waldron's argument for John Locke as an "equality-radical" (5) carries implications for Locke's political theory in general and his attitude toward women in particular. The *First Treatise* thunders "No!" to slavery as though the peculiar institution were the last abuse on earth ever likely to win the approval of Magna Carta heirs of whatever class: "Slavery [Locke proclaims] is so vile and miserable an Estate of Man, and so distinctly opposite to the generous Temper and Courage of our Nation; that 'tis hardly to be conceived, that an *Englishman*, much less a Gentleman, should plead for 't" (qtd. in Waldron 199). At the outset of his book, and as a persistent motif, Waldron contests Lorenne Clark's verdict that Locke's theory displays "unequivocally sexist assumptions" (qtd. in Waldron 23). As Waldron sums up Locke's view, "If we have sinned, that is true of Eve [and of Adam] only [and not necessarily of all other women and men]. If Eve was subordinated to her husband by her greater transgression, that is true of Eve only [and not necessarily of all other wives]" (27). For more than six pages in the *First Treatise*, Locke elaborates on the inclusion of mothers in the fifth commandment (Waldron 39). Waldron's ear for Locke's "logic of contractarianism" hears Locke acknowledging women's parental authority, their property, and even their marital partnership (123); Waldron makes good use of Melissa Butler's pioneering essay, "Early Liberal Roots of Feminism: John Locke and the Attack on Patriarchy" (1978). As Waldron points out, Locke praised a 1696 sermon by Rebecca Collier, observing that "women had the honor first to publish the resurrection of the Lord of Love" (41–42).

16. Padgett Powell's tour de force, *The Interrogative Mood* (2009), comes to mind as an early-twenty-first-century version of an entirely interrogative theodicy, insofar as Powell's belletristic prose asks why, and nothing else but why, every which way from Sunday. Each question-sentence in the novel, and there is no other kind of sentence in it, amounts to a why addressed to whoever or whatever will or will not answer.

17. "Like Whitman," Nancy Mayer writes, "Dickinson uses plant life as an emblem of all lives, and especially human life, but while Whitman's 'single sprout' is important because of what it has in common with all living things, Dickinson's flower, although it may be 'any happy Flower,' is important because of its irreplaceable singularity" (9).

18. As early as the 1790s, though, in his poems on the Salisbury Plain, Wordsworth's nature could be "not the picturesque landscape associated with him from the Lake District, nor is it Nature with any supportive metaphysical principle or god term behind it. On the contrary, it is more like the grimly competitive nature of Malthus and later of Charles Darwin" (Johnston 484).

19. For a more admiring though still a clear-eyed assessment of *The Excursion* in general and of the Wanderer in particular, see Gravil "Is…?"

20. After the manner of Darwin's final book, on earthworms, Dickinson would rather regard earthworms as "Our little / Kinsmen" (Fr932, line 1) than agree with "Our Pastor [who] says we are a 'Worm'" (L193). Thus "religion," for Dickinson, "could offend human pride more sharply than Darwin" (Eberwein "Outgrowing Genesis?" 17). There is more human dignity in Darwin's science, Dickinson implies, than in Calvinist theology (see also Peel 312).

21. Compare another example of Dickinson's sarcasm: "How many barefoot shiver I trust their Father knows who saw not fit to give them shoes" (L207).

22. Dickinson's emphasis on the humanity of Christ is not the same as in Emerson or in Jones Very, for both of whom the common ground between each man or woman and Jesus is not tragic suffering but egotistical sublimity, a spark of the divine.

23. Darwin's argument that "makes the whole world kin," Asa Gray writes, "discomposes us" (qtd. in Eberwein "Outgrowing Genesis?" 16). "With Gray providing Dickinson's introduction to Darwin," Jane Eberwein observes, "it is no wonder that she recognized explosive potential in the new scientific thinking" (15). Also like Gray, though, and perhaps in part because of him, Dickinson was capable of responding bravely, with pluck. Kirkby "'[W]e thought'" demonstrates (18) that Dickinson's language—"I was thinking, today—as I noticed, that the 'Supernatural,' was only the Natural, disclosed" (L280)—makes prose poetry out of the prose of evolutionary theologian Asa Gray.

24. Opening conversation about Emily Dickinson's theodicy, Barton Levi St. Armand has described the poet's association of cats with the playfully cruel nature of the Calvinist God. Focusing on folk-art images of vengefully fearsome felines, St. Armand is not methodologically concerned, as a means of scientifically intensifying the issue, to bring Darwin's cat-and-mouse metaphor into the picture of nineteenth-century theodicy. In Shira Wolosky's view (*Emily*), the Civil War caused Dickinson's questions concerning providential justice. Dickinson developed not so much a question/response theodicy, after the manner of Milton or of Tennyson, and perhaps even of Job, as a series of challenging questions without ready answers, along the lines of Blake's "The Tyger," yet with less bard-like voice than Genesis J-writer drollery. Her theodicean's dialogue emerges from this big picture as even more tough-minded than Darwin's, but God remains as much her desired addressee as Job's or as Hopkins's. Thus the interrogative mood of her quarrel with God draws on both the nineteenth-century condition of her theodicy-heritage and the historical sweep of this theological tradition. For conversation about these matters, thanks are due to Jane Donahue Eberwein.

25. Darwin's wife, Emma, asked him a poignant question: "[M]ay not the habit in scientific pursuits of believing nothing till it is proved, influence your mind too much in other things which cannot be proved in the same way, & which if true are likely to be above our comprehension?" (qtd. in Kirkby "'[W]e thought" 20–21). In the margin of this letter, Darwin wrote: "When I am dead, know that many times, I have kissed & cried over this." Dickinson out-Darwins Darwin, Kirkby argues, at least in the sense that she took a certain pleasure in "shocking her constituency" (21), as in the straight-out Darwinism of Fr747, Fr101, Fr39, and Fr1668.

26. The suggestion here that Dickinson was even more tough-minded in her understanding of evolutionary biology than Darwin brings to mind the courageous cases of modern-day evangelicals who, having read such neo-atheists as Sam Harris, Daniel Dennett, Richard Dawkins, and Christopher Hitchens, are suffering the consequences of concurring with Darwin. Having often lost their jobs, friends, and spouses, these converts to nonbelief can seem even more courageous than the Myth of Amherst, who lost little on account of speaking out. Such former parishioners, former pastors, and children of pastors as Jerry DeWitt, Nate Phelps, Dan Barker, Darrel Ray, Amanda Schneider, and Teresa MacBain do not still wrestle with God's angel. Instead, they seek natural blessing from one another in such online networks as the Clergy Project, Recovering from Religion, the United Coalition of Reason, the Secular Student Alliance, and the Freedom from Religion Foundation. At "Freethinker" gatherings even in the Bible Belt, most recently at the "Reason Rally" in Washington DC (March 2012), DeWitt-like sentiment abounds: "What makes me

different [DeWitt testifies] is that process didn't stop, and it took me all the way. In the end, I couldn't help feeling that all religion, even the most loving kind, is just a speed bump in the progress of the human race." See the discussion in Worth. Is struggling, if not former, evangelical Dickinson a forerunner of this movement? Perhaps, but her poetry never comes as close to the movement as, say, *Religion and the Human Prospect* (2006), in which Alexander Saxton scrutinizes religion through the lens of evolutionary biology, concluding that creed, perhaps even as this note is being written, is outliving its usefulness as an adaptive tool.

27. Dickinson's doubts, according to Virginia H. Oliver, constituted her "efforts to pile up evidence for belief" (16).

28. Although Blake's "Tyger" is theodicy, his "A Vision of the Last Judgment" might cast theodicy out: "The Last Judgment [will be, Blake warns] when all those are Cast away who trouble Religion with Questions concerning Good & Evil or Eating of the Tree of those Knowledges or Reasonings which hinder the Vision of God turning all into a Consuming fire" (see Blackstock).

29. See, besides Keane *Emerson* and Carafiol, the further-groundbreaking recent essay by Samantha Harvey and her forthcoming book.

30. Jeremy Waldron's argument for John Locke as an "equality-radical" (5) carries implications for religious and literary history alike. "No Man," Locke writes, "is so wholly taken up with the Attendance on the Means of Living, as to have no spare Time at all to think of his Soul, and inform himself in Matters of Religion [one thinks in this regard of Dickinson's 'Soul's' 'Society - ' (Fr409, line 1) and of her spider-artist's ruggedly self-reliant, as well as thoroughly cryptic, self-generation of natural knowledge and spiritual truth ('himself himself inform' appears particularly well Locke-expressed; see Fr1163, line 6)]" (Locke's *Essay* qtd. in Waldron 87). Waldron demonstrates that Locke gives "serious consideration" to the possibility that "basic equality *must* be grounded in a religious connection" (14; Waldron's emphasis). The "equality-radical" of Locke's "Christian Foundations" (Waldron 5), as opposed to the exclusionary strain of Christianity, means for the early twenty-first century that the phrase *liberal Christianity* need prove no mere oxymoron. If Locke's "equality-radical" Christianity strengthened the late-Enlightenment to early-Romantic fight against the slave trade led by liberal-evangelical William Wilberforce, Locke's concern for the rights of the poor resurfaces, too, among such now-prominent, moderate-to-liberal evangelicals as Barry Hankins, Ron Sider, Rich Cizik, Darren Cushman Wood, and Jim Wallis. These, and even to a considerably lesser extent such conservative evangelicals as Pat Robertson, James Dobson, Ralph Reed, and Richard Land (notice the strange absence of women from such lists), are moving away from preoccupation with sexual sin and toward concern for practical charity, environmentalism ("creation care"), terrorism, the Gaza Strip,

HIV/AIDS, the IMF, and the World Bank. The Locke-orientation of John Wesley's thought leads not only to Wesley's quasi-epistemological doctrine of the spiritual sense but also to the egalitarian basis of his respect for the poor and of his practice of charity. His encouragement of women preachers harks back to Locke's praise for the sermon art of Rebecca Collier. Ultimately the Christian as well as empirical Locke and the empirical as well as Christian Wesley inspired the natural to spiritual autobiography that as this series of arguments has maintained for 40 years forms a genre of Anglo-American Romanticism.

31. For a sampling of Dickinson's nonrational witness, see "'Hope' is the thing with feathers - " (Fr314), "The Soul's superior instants" (Fr630), "A Tooth opon our Peace" (Fr694), "The Spirit is the Conscious Ear - " (Fr718), "The Admirations - and Contempts - of time - " (Fr830), "The Soul's distinct connection" (Fr901), "Love - is ante-rior to Life - " (Fr980), "The Infinite a sudden Guest - " (Fr1344), and "Whoever disenchants" (Fr1475). For Locke's Christianity, see Locke, *The Reasonableness of Christianity* (1695).

32. See, respectively, Locke *Essay* 2.7.10 (Nidditch 131) and Blake, *There Is No Natural Religion: Second Series* (1788), Plate IV.

33. See, respectively, Wordsworth, "Elegiac Stanzas" (1807), line 15; and "Tintern Abbey," line 149. For Dickinson's allusions to the lines from "Elegiac Stanzas," see L315 and L394.

34. For this theme in Wordsworth, see Brantley *Wordsworth's* Chapter 1.

35. By contrast, Richard Holmes places Romanticism and Robin Peel places Dickinson in the immediate context of science alone.

3 GAINING LOSS

1. See William Blake, *The Marriage of Heaven and Hell* (1792), Plate 14. For a pioneering comparison of Blake and Dickinson, see the recent essay by Alan Blackstock.

2. Compare Hardy, "The Darkling Thrush" (1900), line 24. See also premier Australian poet Les Murray's perhaps too-dismissive diagnosis of Modernists, who, Murray concludes, wrote out of a "pathological state [of] depression" (qtd. in Coetzee 6). Murray has a point, though; see A. N. Wilson 1–18. For a discussion of the paradigmatic Modern *aboulie* or lack of will, see Louis Menand's recent review-essay on T. S. Eliot ("Practical Cat"). The state of near-depression in which Eliot wrote "The Waste Land" (1922) can sound like Dickinson's most pessimistic poems of aftermath: "I have gone through some ter-rible agony myself," Eliot writes, "which I do not understand yet, and which has left me utterly bewildered and dazed"; or this: "I have been boiled in a hell-broth" (qtd. in Menand ["Cats" 45]; Menand puts this depression down to Eliot's disastrous marriage to Vivienne Haigh-Wood and also to Eliot's concern about the state of Europe and America after World War I). Yeats thought of himself as "among

the last Romantics," but even as such—as well as in his up-to-date Modern toughness—he writes a definitive three lines on aftermath of which Dickinson or of which Wordsworth, for that matter, would be proud:

Now that my ladder's gone,
I must lie down where all the ladders start,
In the foul rag and bone shop of the heart.

("The Circus Animals' Desertion" [1939], lines 38–40)
Perhaps the most optimistically Romantic-sounding of the Moderns can be Joyce; his ultimately affirming Molly Bloom ("Yes," she declares) illustrates near-comic to comic genius. For a discussion of Dickinson's poems of aftermath as a harbinger of Modern-era pessimism, see Porter 9–24.

3. Joanne Feit Diehl's study of the Romantics' influence on Dickinson downplays Romantic-era toughness and highlights the poet's rebellion against their tenderness.

4. Compare Wordsworth, *The Prelude* (1850) 6:606. For the theme of joy in literary history, see Potkay.

5. For overviews of continuity from Romanticism to Modernism, see Bornstein; Carlos Baker *The Echoing Green.*

6. Dickinson, Prose Fragment 71, Johnson, ed., *Complete Poems* 3:923. Kenneth R. Johnston similarly finds in such poems by Wordsworth as "There Was a Boy" (1798) a pattern characteristic of high Romanticism in general and of Wordsworth's in particular—namely, "infinite gain from finite loss" (Johnston 639).

7. See Byron's journal entry for November 27, 1813. Byron may be quoting Joseph Miller (1684–1738), who joined the Drury Lane Company in 1709.

8. Dickinson, Prose Fragment 49, Johnson, ed., *Complete Poems* 3:919. Compare Dickinson's letter to Thomas Wentworth Higginson, after the death of his wife: "Dear friend, I think of you so wholly that I cannot resist to write again, to ask if you are safe? Danger is not at first, for then we are unconscious, but in the after—slower—Days…Love is it's own rescue, for we—at our supremest, are but it's trembling Emblems" (L522).

9. For a recent survey of Friedrich Nietzsche's standard ideas, see Solomon 3–18.

10. Compare Eliot, "The Hollow Men" (1925). See also Wordsworth, "The Happy Warrior" (1807) and "Prospectus" to *The Recluse* (1814), line 87.

11. Shelley, "When the Lamp Is Shattered" (1824), lines 7–8, 29–32. Compare George Meredith's cycle of seizains, *Modern Love* (1862). Meredith increases the pessimism of Shelley's view.

12. For a discussion of "soul-competency," see Bloom *American Religion* 111–43. The term comes from turn-of-the-twentieth-century Southern Baptist leader E. Y. Mullins. The term can serve as a good label for

the religion-leaning, yet grounded, individualism of Romantic Anglo-America (see Brantley *Coordinates* and *Anglo-American*). See also Wallace Stevens, "Sunday Morning" (1915), line 120.

13. Compare Byron, "Maid of Athens, Ere We Part" (1812), line 17. See Chapter 2 ("Susan Gilbert"), Chapter 3 ("Master"), Chapter 5 ("Sisterhood"), and Chapter 6 ("The Wife - Without the Sign"), in Pollak 59–104, 133–89. See also Lundin; Menand *Metaphysical*.

14. For Dickinson's eye-trouble, see Guthrie. For Dickinson as a "daughter of prophecy" (the phrase comes from the Book of Joel), see Doriani.

15. Wordsworth, "Tintern Abbey," lines 73–74, 87–88; Wordsworth, "Ode: Intimations of Immortality," line 188.

16. Wolosky *Emily* 155–57.

17. See Perry Miller; Edmund Morgan.

18. Regarding Dickinson's expression of "the psychological pain of loss," Robin Peel argues, persuasively, that Dickinson "cannot convince herself, or the listener, that pain is really doing her any good" (340). Dickinson, Peel concludes, offers a clinical and chilling "reversal of the Pygmalion story" (342). Dickinson's "Breathing Woman Yesterday" has become a statue (see Peel's discussion, 340–42, of Fr1088, lines 7–8).

19. For Dickinson and Frost, see Keller *Kangaroo*. For Dickinson and Stevens, see Dickie.

20. See, respectively, Eliot, "The Love Song of J. Alfred Prufrock" (1910–11), line 122; and Wordsworth, "Elegiac Stanzas" (1807), line 58.

21. See, respectively, Mossberg 171–72; Barker 169–70; L807; L776.

22. Dickinson's "so-called abstract images," Margaret H. Freeman concludes, "are grounded in her physical and intellectual experience of...the universe around her" (267). "My Life had stood - a Loaded Gun - ," in Freeman's view, is the signature lyric of Dickinson's "cognitive poetics." This means that Dickinson's brain puts the world together, for her metaphors are products of the embodied mind.

23. "Where I have lost, I softer tread - ," written in 1860, laments the loss of Charles Wadsworth, perhaps even more than that of Susan Dickinson, not through death but through spatial separation or psychological estrangement. Emily Dickinson's word "dusk" (Fr158, line 10) recalls her pet name for Wadsworth, "Dusk Gem" (L776). Given William H. Shurr's argument for Wadsworth as the inspiration of Dickinson's love poems, it is surprising that nowhere does he mention "Where I have lost, I softer tread - ." This exception proves the rule of Shurr's thoroughness, if not of his relentlessness, in pursuing the idea of Wadsworth as "Master."

24. William Harmon and Hugh C. Holman define *aporia*, a presiding idea of Deconstruction, as "a point of undecidability, which locates the site at which the text most obviously undermines its own rhetorical structure, dismantles, or deconstructs itself" (36).

25. Wordsworth, "Expostulation and Reply" (1798), line 7. For defense mechanisms in Dickinson's poetry, see John Cody.

26. Keats to George and Thomas Keats, December 21, 27 [?], 1817.

27. This discussion is indebted to conversations with the late Susan Manning about Dickinson's "White - unto the White Creator - " and Melvyn New about Voltaire's *Candide* (1759) and Johnson's *Dictionary* (1755). The *Dictionary* calls on John Dryden to illustrate the meaning of *candid* (white):
    The box receives all black: but, pour'd from thence,
    The stones come candid forth, the hue of innocence.

28. T. S. Eliot's comment on Donne comes to mind: "A thought to Donne was an experience; it modified his sensibility" (qtd. in Menand "Practical Cat" 46).

29. In Dickinson's imagery of whiteness, there may be, as Robin Peel points out, a suggestion of science in the service of Puritanism, and vice versa. "For it is important to reemphasize the enthusiasm of Protestants for science," Peel writes, "as part of their campaign to discredit the perceived flaws in the reasoning of the Catholic Church. The Catholic Descartes had argued that the prism changes pure white light into colors, which are the impure forms. Newton (1642–1727) is best known in the history of astronomy for his theories of motion and description of gravity, but his pioneering work on optics allowed him to demonstrate that white light is impure. He demonstrated that, although a prism separates white light into colors, a second prism does not change red, for example, into any other color. Red, therefore, is one of the pure colors...[Jonathan] Edwards's early essay on color, in 'Notes on Natural Science,' suggests that he was familiar with Newton's *Opticks*" (253). If whiteness, in philosophical terms, denotes tabula rasa for Dickinson, then it may also denote, scientifically speaking, the sense in which the white heat of her poetic vocation was not so much purity, as a primary truth; not so much an other-worldly, as a worldly kind of reality.

30. See, respectively, Wordsworth, Preface to *Lyrical Ballads* (1798); and Dickinson, Fr320, lines 7–8.

31. See, respectively, Wasserman *Subtler* 236; Eric G. Wilson *Coleridge's Melancholia*; and *The Spiritual History of Ice* 151–57.

32. See, respectively, Dickinson Fr466, line 1; and Shelley, "Adonais" (1821), line 463.

33. In 2003, Harold Bloom remarked, "I suspect my central essay on Romanticism is 'The Internalization of Quest Romance' in *Romanticism and Consciousness* [1970]." Bloom had argued, therein, that the Romantics psychologize the love, desire, and enchantment found in medieval Christian romance. See the discussion of Bloom in Judith Page 188–94, esp. 192. For parallels between Dickinson as a paradoxically engaged recluse and her father Edward's canny withdrawal/nonwithdrawal from politics, see Hutchison.

4 DESPAIRING HOPE

1. With the first quotation, here, compare Robin Peel's discussion of Emily Dickinson's perspective on "the mysterious hollowness of life" in "Finding is the first act" (Fr910) (Peel 373). With the second quotation, here, compare Dickinson's letter to Maria Whitney, written during the summer of 1883: "You speak of 'disillusion.' That is one of the few subjects on which I am an infidel. Life is so strong a vision, not one of it shall fail. Not what the stars have done, but what they are to do, is what detains the sky... To have been made alive is so chief a thing, all else inevitably adds. Were it not riddled by partings, it were too divine" (L860).

2. If scholars hit the mark in exploring how Dickinson's point of view stays stable, even this interpretation need not imply either that any given lyric of hers or that her canon as a whole is static. For a list of studies concluding that her oeuvre is constant in outlook, see the discussion in Barnstone. For her part, Aliki Barnstone emphasizes not a set of discrete stages in, nor an obvious timeline for, Dickinson's development but, instead, recurrent shifts in focus between differing stances. Barnstone's argument highlights Dickinson's fluid but persistent "self-conversion" from Calvinism to Transcendentalism and back (9ff.). Similar to such shifts in focus is the notion of oscillation in this book, except that here, each extreme of the alternating process includes enough of the other for dialogue to occur at any given time.

3. Compare Wordsworth, "Resolution and Independence" (1807), line 49, and Coleridge, "Dejection: An Ode" (1802).

4. See, respectively, Pollak 202; John Cody; Porter; Fr314, line 1; Fr1424, line 1; Fr1493, line 1. Dickinson's persistent but secularized hope, as expressed in such poems as these, may be contrasted with Melville's doubt (registered in his *Clarel* [1876]) whether any sort of hope can coexist, in the end, with science: "Shall Science then / Which solely dealeth with this thing / Named Nature, shall she ever bring / One solitary hope to men?" (qtd. in Delbanco 280–82).

5. This view parallels Robin Peel's: Darwin and Dickinson alike "recognized that, in the struggle for life, there is a need to *adapt* to ensure survival. Dickinson's poems are strategies in adaptation. The poetry teaches a psychological, rather than a biological, process of adaptation, but the poems are part of a conscious survival strategy nonetheless. Dickinson's work contains a rhetoric quite in accord with the scientific recognition that forces operate in human life in a way that often overrides careful human planning" (293; Peel's emphasis).

6. Compare Ephesians 5:6; Colossians 4:5; Romans 5:3.

7. Compare Shelley's simultaneously personal and cultural injunction "to hope, till Hope creates / From its own wreck the thing it contemplates" (*Prometheus Unbound* [1820], act 4, lines 573–74).

8. This observation is indebted to Sewall "Teaching."

9. Compare Blake, *The Marriage of Heaven and Hell*, Plates 7–10.
10. See, respectively, Shelley, "Mont Blanc" (1817), lines 80–1; and Dylan Thomas, "In My Craft, or Sullen Art" (1946), line 1.
11. For the all but permanent afterlife of Byron's "Prisoner," its influence on literature as late as the works of William Ernest Henley, see Buckley.
12. In a recent book for the informed general reader, Sam Harris builds on the scientific work of Daniel Wegner and Benjamin Libet to argue that "[f]ree will is an illusion. Our wills are simply not of our own making. Thoughts and intuitions emerge from background causes of which we are unaware and over which we exert no conscious control" (8). There is consciousness, though, which allows us what even Wegner calls "perceived control" (qtd. in Menaker 20). Consciousness, concludes Daniel Menaker concerning all these issues, "may not tell us what to do, but it does tell us what we do means—oh, and what beauty is" (20). Thus consciousness, if not free will—and indeed consciousness as the practical equivalent of free will—remains useful in areas where belief in free will has always held sway—namely, religion, law, and morality. Dickinson would have included philosophy and science among those very areas.
13. See the quotation and discussion of Thomas Carlyle's *Past and Present* (1843) in Ikeler 6–7.
14. John Wesley's central doctrine of responsible grace, according to Randy L. Maddox, reconciles divining grace (Eastern Christianity), free grace (Lutheran tradition), sovereign grace (Reformed tradition), co-operant grace (Arminian tradition), sanctifying grace (radical Reformed tradition), and mediated grace (Catholic tradition).
15. The empirical/evangelical dialectic of Romantic Anglo-America consistently describes the Calvinist/Arminian controversy and the Arminian ascendancy as glosses on eighteenth- to nineteenth-century literary development (Brantley *Coordinates; Anglo-American*). For Dickinson's Calvinist strain, see Eberwein "'Where - Omnipresence - fly?.'" The life of Henry Ward Beecher, whose "gospel of love" resists father Lyman's doctrine of depravity, illustrates the triumph, for better or worse, of Arminianism (Applegate). For political implications of the Arminian ascendancy during the increasingly democratic nineteenth century, see Hatch.
16. Meanwhile, see Brantley *Experience* 15, 90–93, 139, 198, 237 n.25.
17. See, respectively, Wordsworth, Preface to *Lyrical Ballads* (1802) and Keats, "Ode on Melancholy" (1819), lines 23, 28.
18. Compare Wordsworth, "A Slumber Did My Spirit Seal" (1798), line 7; Shelley, *Prometheus Unbound* (1819), act 3, scene 1, line 204; and Shelley, "Adonais" (1821), line 463. "Science will not trust us with another world," Dickinson writes (L395). No Thomas Henry Huxley could have had a stronger sense of the transience, change, variation, and adaptation specified by Darwinian thought than the

manifest set of perceptions on offer in an 1856 letter from Dickinson
to her cousin John Graves: "Much that is gay—have I to show, if
you were with me, John, upon this April grass—then there are *sadder* features—here and there, *wings* half gone to dust, that fluttered
so, last year—a mouldering plume, an empty house, in which a bird
resided. Where last year's flies, their errand ran, and last year's *crickets
fell!* We, too, are flying—fading, John—and the song 'here lies,' soon
upon lips that love us now—will have hummed and ended...It is a
jolly thought to think that we can be Eternal—when air and earth
are *full* of lives that are gone—and done—and a conceited thing
indeed, this promised Resurrection!" (L184; Dickinson's emphasis).
Thus empirically based doubts about the Christian afterlife, evident
in her thinking as early as her twenty-sixth year, led to Dickinson's
quasi-Arminian idea of willing, of choosing, heaven in the here and
now—"Paradise is of the Option," she writes (Fr1125, line 1; see the
discussion in Gilliland; McCullough). Dickinson's concept of naturalized immortality can mean, as well, a mind not so much still living
after the death of the body as, while yet part of it, uncircumscribed
by time and space (see Fr373, Fr630, Fr653, Fr725, Fr817, Fr1166,
Fr1486, and Fr1662).

19. Cynthia MacKenzie's concordance to the letters is an invaluable
    resource, which, together with Jack L. Capps's demonstration of
    Dickinson's wide range of reading, points well beyond the necessar-
    ily limited range of evidence in this, or in any other, book on her
    poetry.

20. That more tender singing is emphasized in Brantley *Experience.*

CONCLUSION

1. Compare, respectively, Stevens, "Of Modern Poetry" (1940), line 2,
   and Blake, *The Marriage of Heaven and Hell* (1790–1793), Plate 10,
   line 7.

2. See Keats's letter to Benjamin Bailey, November 22, 1817. Bailey was
   an Anglican minister. For Keats's relation to Dissent, see Roe.

3. For Darwin's sympathy for religion, despite the nonreligious direction of his thought, see Frank Burch Brown; Janet Browne.

4. Such examples of nineteenth-century Higher Criticism as David
   Friedrich Strauss's *Das Leben Jesu* (1835–1836) and Ernest Renan's *Vie
   de Jésus* (1863) employed scientific standards of evidence and brought
   methods of linguistics, anthropology, and literary criticism to bear on
   biblical analysis. "Its practitioners set biblical stories in perspective as
   records compiled by unidentified and sometimes contradictory authors
   over vast time-spans, responding to different historical conditions, and
   inflected by myths of neighboring peoples" (Eberwein "Outgrowing
   Genesis?" 20). In this regard, Jane Eberwein's most recent synthesis—
   the subtitle of "Outgrowing Genesis?" is "Dickinson, Darwin, and the

Higher Criticism"—examines such poems as "It always felt to me - a wrong" (Fr521) and "Better than Music!" (Fr378). The former flatly states, "No Moses there can be" (line 6). The latter limns "Eden" as "a legend - dimly told - " (line 15).

5. For the view that evolutionary biology and Judaeo-Christian faith are "non-overlapping magisteria," see Gould. The ability to compartmentalize experience and faith is close to the literary temperament, as in F. Scott Fitzgerald's declaration that "[t]he test of a first-rate intelligence is the ability to hold two opposed ideas in the mind at the same time, and still retain the ability to function" (69). The fact that Emily Dickinson possessed this ability did not prevent her from favoring the philosophical and the scientific.

6. For cognitive science as a cooperative undertaking, see Schacter. For cognitive science as an approach to reading the Romantics as a scientific group, see Richardson.

7. See, respectively, Richard Wilbur, "Love Calls Us to the Things of This World" (1955), and Abrams, ed., 2:60. M. H. Abrams has reference here to what he thinks Blake means by "the marriage of heaven and hell."

8. The word *pathetic* is not necessarily pejorative. It relates to pathos. But *fallacy* is pejorative. See the discussion in Harmon and Holman, under *pathetic fallacy*. See also John Ruskin, "Of the Pathetic Fallacy" (1856), volume 3, part 4, chapter 12. Ruskin's example is from Coleridge's "Christabel" (1800): "The one red leaf, the last of the clan, / That dances as often as dance it can." From pejorative implication Ruskin exempts personification. Compare Dickinson's Experiment.

9. Elizabeth Barrett Browning, "How Do I Love Thee?" (1850), lines 11–12, and T. S. Eliot, "The Waste Land" (1922), line 430, apply to Dickinson's case.

10. Pinch 531–33. See also Eric G. Wilson *Coleridge's* and Potkay.

11. Compare, respectively, Wordsworth, "Tintern Abbey," line 48, and Hopkins, "No Worst, There Is None" (1918), line 6.

12. Compare, respectively, Fr1404, line 7, and Keats, "Ode on Melancholy" (1819), line 15.

13. Menand, for historical reasons of philosophy and science, emphasizes late-nineteenth- and early-twentieth-century pessimism, and Carlos Baker *Echoing Green*, Bornstein, Favret, Fussell, and Howells do, too, but these five also acknowledge, in Modernism, a hopeful remnant of philosophy, science, religion, and Romanticism.

14. Beethoven, song cycle, opus 98. The lyrics are by Aloys Jeitteles. In 1849, Franz Liszt transcribed "*An Die Ferne Geliebte*" for piano, and Estela Kersenbaum Olevsky, musical advisor for the television documentary "Angles of a Landscape: The Poet in Her Bedroom," produced for the Emily Dickinson Museum, played the piece as an accompaniment. Dickinson played some of Beethoven's works

for piano (Cooley). For musical settings of Dickinson's verse, see Lowenberg.

15. George Steiner's views can appear to be commensurate with the arguments of Bryan Boyd, Denis Dutton, Eric R. Kandel, and Mark Pagel for a Darwinian aesthetic. All of these, Steiner included (though Steiner only alludes to Darwin), attempt a Darwinian vindication of art by emphasizing the utilitarian power of art to enhance human fitness of various kinds. Thus all of these thinkers might inflect Kant's definition of art as follows: "*purposiveness* without purpose," not "purposiveness *without purpose.*" But Steiner's views are more art-appropriate, more nonutilitarian, than those of Boyd, Dutton, Kandel, and Pagel. Thanks go to Professor Emeritus Michael Cass for his rich conversation about the works of George Steiner.

16. Compare Kershner's phrasing, in his study of Joyce (15–21).

17. Compare Michael Holquist's paraphrase of the almost exclusively fiction-oriented "dialogism" of M. M. Bakhtin: "I can mean what I say, but only *indirectly*, at a second remove, in words I take and give back to the community according to the protocols it establishes. My voice can mean, but only with others: at times in chorus, but at the best of times in a dialogue" (qtd. in Greenblatt, ed., *Allegory* 165).

18. See Martin Buber qtd. in Breuggemann 2.

19. For a discussion of Locke's "double conformity" thesis that things may conform to ideas and that ideas may conform to words (*Essay*, Book 3), see Aarsleff. For a lucid historical survey of such issues of linguistic theory as the perennial question of, the ongoing status of, aesthetic representation, see Beale.

20. One can easily imagine the negative reaction of the poet of "Experiment escorts us last - " to the various post-Modern US foreign policy departures from the Anglo-American birthright of empiricism. "In the summer of 2002," Ron Suskind writes, "a senior advisor to [president George W.] Bush…told me something" that "I now believe gets to the very heart of the Bush presidency": "The aide [Suskind continues] said that guys like me were 'in what we call the reality-based community,' which he defined as people who 'believe that solutions emerge from your judicious study of discernible reality.' I nodded and murmured something about enlightenment principles and empiricism. He cut me off. 'That's not the way the world really works anymore,' he continued. 'We're an empire now, and when we act, we create our own reality. And while you're studying that reality—judiciously, as you will—we'll act again, creating other new realities, which you can study too, and that's how things will sort out. We're history's actors, and you, all of you, will be left to just study what we do" (21).

21. Dickinson's loved ones and friends basked in, inspired, her 1,049 extant letters (she wrote myriads more) and also benefited from, also affected, the lyric mastery of her 1,789 poems (she incorporated many lyrics in the texts of her letters and enclosed many more in the

envelopes). Dickinson's leading role in her wide correspondence "fills spaces" for "controlled acts of self-representation" and appropriates "a multiplicity of discursively constructed voices in an inter-generic dialogic exchange" (Messmer 77). The Dickinson Editing Collective is in the process of publishing the many "books" Dickinson wrote to all these various correspondents. "Sister Sue," Wadsworth, and Higginson proved especially prominent among her fellow-aficionados of reading and writing and of literature and criticism. Hitchcock and Wadsworth ranked equally high among those beloveds of hers who, in the select society of her imagination and of her mind, are arrayed among her philosophical and scientific (as well as religious) partners in discussion.

22. At the August 2010 Emily Dickinson International Society Conference held in Oxford, England, 29 sessions celebrated her works. The following poem serves as Dickinson's signature lyric of encouragement to all who would understand her challenging but parsable canon:

> Good to hide, and hear 'em hunt!
> Better, to be found,
> If one care to, that is,
> The Fox fits the Hound -
>
> Good to know, and not tell -
> Best, to know and tell.
> Can one find the rare Ear
> Not too dull -
>
> (Fr945)

In these lines is summed up the pragmatic/democratic outreach of Emily Dickinson's art of knowledge.

APPENDIX A   EMPIRICISM AND EVANGELICALISM

1. See, respectively, Wordsworth, "Lines Written a Few Miles above Tintern Abbey" (1798), line 108, and Coleridge, *Biographia Literaria* (1817), Chapter 14.

2. The empirical/evangelical dialectic of Romantic Anglo-America can appear to foresee, though scarcely to preempt, the psychologically anthropological findings of T. M. Luhrmann. In her study of John Wimber's Vineyard Movement of evangelical churches, Luhrmann cultivates an almost more than William James-like sympathy for how these congregations school their members "to experience the supernatural with their senses," and hence to encounter or, in the vile vernacular, "friend" God personally (Luhrmann 36).

3. Perhaps no better way exists to describe how Emily Dickinson's yearning for transcendence is a universal human trait than in the language of Oliver Sacks: "To live on a day-to-day basis is insufficient

for human beings; we need to transcend, transport, escape; we need meaning, understanding, and explanation; we need to see over-all patterns in our lives. We need hope, the sense of a future. And we need freedom (or, at least, the illusion of freedom) to get beyond ourselves, whether with telescopes and microscopes and our ever-burgeoning technology, or in states of mind that allow us to travel to other worlds, to rise above our immediate surroundings" (40). The first of Sacks's three additional sentences in this vein proves equally applicable to Dickinson: "Many of us find Worthsworthian 'intimations of immortality' in nature, art, creative thinking, or religion; some people can reach transcendent states through meditation or similar trance-inducing techniques, or through prayer and spiritual exercises. But drugs offer a shortcut; they promise transcendence on demand. These shortcuts are possible because certain chemicals can directly stimulate many complex brain functions" (40).

APPENDIX B   LOCKE AND WESLEY

1. One thinks here of Mark Noll's discussion of "power evangelism," "a phrase originating with Lonnie Frisbee and the title of one of [John] Wimber's best-known books, which stresses tangible signs from the Holy Spirit as the key to Christian conversion" (Noll 25).
2. For a portrait of the Friday Masowe Apostolic Church of Zimbabwe, which has discarded the Bible in favor of direct experience of the Holy Spirit, see Engelke.

APPENDIX C   WADSWORTH AND
DICKINSON

1. As Georgiana Strickland kindly points out in correspondence, biographers favoring Wadsworth include Whicher (1928), Thomas H. Johnson (1965), Gelpi (1965), Sewall (1974), Shurr (1983), Lease (1990), Habegger (2001), and Longsworth (2001). Other candidates and their sponsors, as Strickland also observes in correspondence, are: Edward Hunt, first husband of Helen Hunt Jackson (Pollitt, 1930); George Gould (Taggard, 1930); Kate Scott Anthon (Patterson, 1951 *Riddle*); Bowles (Ward, 1961; Farr, 1992; Lambert, 1996; and Arnold, 1998); Susan Dickinson (Hart and Smith, 1998); Richard Dickinson, a cousin, said to be a minister in Philadelphia at the same time as Wadsworth (Waugh, 1990); and William Smith Clark (Ruth Owen Jones, 2002). Wolff and Keller, Strickland emphasizes, say the whole love affair is imaginary on Dickinson's part, perhaps a conscious fiction. Franklin, ed., *The Master Letters*, "rejects the fictional aspect but takes no stand on who the recipient was or whether copies of the letters were actually mailed" (Strickland in correspondence).

"So if popularity is evidence," she reasons, "Wadsworth wins over Bowles and all the rest." "This is of course a ridiculous way to look at this question," Strickland concludes, "but it says something about Dickinson scholarship—that despite frequent statements that it doesn't really matter, many scholars have strong feelings about this question. The story certainly feeds a strong public desire for a romance."

2. The evidence that Wadsworth sent his sermons to Dickinson as part of his dialogue with her is here based on text/poem comparison. For an overview of the Wadsworth/Dickinson friendship, including the facilitating importance of Dickinson's friends Elizabeth and Josiah Gilbert Holland (who appear to have mediated the correspondence by receiving and transmitting letters), see Sewall *Life* 2:444–46, 2:729–41. See also Reynolds 31 and Lease 4, 6.

3. To describe the relationship between Wadsworth and Dickinson, the word *connection* might seem inappropriate, harsh, blunt, and even salacious. In eighteenth-century Britain, however, as in Selina, the Countess of Huntington's *Connection*, the term carried the connotation of intellectual-salon-like circles of male/female evangelical conversation (see Brantley *Locke* 103–28).

4. As Georgiana Strickland carefully argues in print, "The church's early membership records have apparently been lost; neither the present minister of the Arch Street (formerly West Arch Street) Church, the Reverend George Clayton Ames (visit of June 28, 2003) nor Kenneth Ross at the Presbyterian Historical Society (phone conversation of March 9, 2004) has knowledge of their location. Longsworth... notes that Mrs. Coleman's letter of transfer from the Amherst College Church, dated 1856, is now at South Church in Middletown, Connecticut, suggesting that she did not establish church membership in either Princeton or Philadelphia" (Strickland endnote 22).

5. For all quotations from Bianchi's biography, see Bianchi *Life* 46–49.

6. What Bianchi calls "the inward drama" of Dickinson's "romance" with Wadsworth gives "befitting dignity" to "the true inspiration of the love poems." Bianchi's memoir adds that her mother, father, Lavinia, and Mattie Gilbert "told me specifically" that the romance "left a permanent effect upon my aunt's life and vision." In support of Wadsworth as Master, Bianchi quotes letters to her from "the wife of a first cousin of Aunt Emily" and from a great-granddaughter of Samuel Fowler Dickinson. She cites an early reviewer: "There are poems here printed in respect to love that never could have been written without experience." She sums up with Louis Untermeyer: "Emily tells the whole story of her love, her first rebellious desire, her inner negation, her resignation, her waiting for reunion in Eternity. There is nothing more to add except irrelevant names and unimportant street numbers." See Bianchi *Face to Face* 51–53. Strickland closes: "Whatever the reason for Bianchi's choice of Wadsworth as the lover, and whatever its truth or fictionality, it has remained a fixture—and a lightning

rod—in Dickinson biography and criticism ever since" (Strickland endnote 29).

7. Compare Jane Austen, *Emma* (1816). For Dickinson and Newton—he worked in Edward Dickinson's law office and introduced Dickinson to Emerson's poetry—see Sewall *Life* 2:400–04. For Dickinson and Bowles, see Farr. For Dickinson and Higginson, see Wineapple. For Dickinson and Lord, see Guthrie; Walsh.

8. One may borrow a phrase from what one should hereby acknowledge as a primarily religious poem.

9. See Wordsworth, *The Prelude* (1850) 12:216. For discussion of the nineteenth-century commonplaces enumerated earlier, see Langbaum *Word*; Losey.

10. Lundin makes good use of Martha Dickinson Bianchi's biography.

11. See the account of Dickinson's correspondence with James Dickson Clark and Charles H. Clark, concerning their mutual friend, Charles Wadsworth, in Habegger 416–21.

12. For an example of how Dickinson uses the word *fathomed* in its sexual sense, see Fr1742, line 7.

13. Discussing a series of poems that William H. Shurr calls "The Pregnancy Sequence," Shurr concludes:

> The solution [to Dickinson's pregnancy by Charles Wadsworth, namely abortion] seems unthinkable ... until we recall that 1861 and 1862 were the years of her greatest emotional and mental crisis, that Dickinson was sick and bedridden for a whole summer at this time, that there was something profoundly shattering in her experience of "marriage," that she nevertheless had compelling reasons to assert repeatedly that she was married, that the family doctors and the family medical histories for all the Dickinsons are recorded except for these years, and that Dickinson's sister-in-law next door, Susan, was routinely procuring abortions from the year of her marriage in 1856 until the birth of her first child in 1861. Nor should we exclude from this sequence the fact that in 1862 Wadsworth abruptly and unaccountably (considering his professional success in Philadelphia) put a whole continent between himself and Dickinson—surely a prudent move for a professional man, to remove himself from possible scandal. (149, 170–88, esp. 179–80)

For serious scholarly reservations about Shurr's approach, see Tanter; Habegger 715. Farr and Shoobridge deeply reconsider the "master letters," yet they make no mention of Shurr's work, which has been not only snubbed but ridiculed when it was not ignored. Perhaps enough time has passed and enough biographers have found Wadsworth the likely "Master" so that students of Dickinson's poetry may reconsider the possibility of a Wadsworth/Dickinson attachment. They would be well advised to do so warily, however, for feelings in the Dickinson world run high.

14. In an understatement, Alfred Habegger comments, "Shurr gives the fullest and most attentive treatment [of a series of poems he calls 'The Pregnancy Sequence'] but tends to override historical reality and take Emily Dickinson's imaginative transformations literally" (715).

15. Judith Farr identifies 132 "Poems for Master," as distinct from 94 "Poems for Sue."

16. With regard to Thomas Mann and his social circle, Anthony Heilbut develops Mann criticism from Heilbut's hypothesis that whenever love germinates the creative imagination flowers, though erotic love for Mann's characters often ends in death. Shurr draws an analogy between his argument for Wadsworth as Dickinson's muse and that of James E. Miller for Vivienne Eliot, T. S. Eliot's wife, as a constant presence in Eliot's supposedly "impersonal" poetry (see *Marriage* 71).

17. The case for Wadsworth as Dickinson's muse boasts more evidence than, say, Kenneth R. Johnston's theory of Wordsworth as a spy against the French. Yet Johnston's reviewers rightly praise his biographical approach to Wordsworth's art. Speculation can be directly proportional to good critical results as in the cases of the biblical J-writer, Homer, many medieval authors, and Shakespeare. See James Butler; Bloom *The Book of J*; Hartog; Wood.

18. A foretaste of Polly Longsworth's argument for Wadsworth as "Master" appears in Longsworth's "'Latitude.'" Habegger announces: "There are enough clues pointing to the minister [as the choice for Master] that he is the one we will consider as occasion offers" (421). For overviews of the case for Sue, see Dobson; Hart; Hart and Smith; Smith. Both/and logic is in order as where Pollak gives equal attention to Wadsworth and Susan in *Anxiety* 59–104.

19. Wordsworth, "Tintern Abbey," line 42.

20. Tynan "Scholars." Thanks to W. B. Gerard for his information about this source. Young woman Dickinson understandably misidentified the aphorism of clergyman, sportsman, gambler, suicide, and author of the collection of aphorisms *Lacon* (1820–2; 2 volumes)—Charles Caleb Colton—as belonging to Robert Browning.

21. Rochefoucauld: "True love, however rare, is still more common than true friendship." Sterne: "Love is *nothing* without sentiment, / And sentiment is still *less* without love" (Sterne's emphasis). Byron: "A mistress never is nor can be a friend. While you agree, you are lovers; and when it is over, anything but friends." See the quotation and discussion of François de la Rochefoucauld, *Maxims* (1665), in *The World Book Encyclopedia* (1975), s. v. "La Rochefoucauld, Duc de." See also Laurence Sterne, *A Sentimental Journey*, Melvyn New, ed., 63, where he uses the French: "l'amour n'est *rien* sans sentiment, / Et le sentiment est encore *moins* sans amour." See, finally, George Gordon, Lord Byron, *Letters and Journals*, journal entry for November 24, 1813.

22. Carlos Baker's group biography, *Emerson among the Eccentrics* (1996), emphasizes the compatibility between friendship and love. See also Sharp; Crain; Leverenz *Manhood*; Robert K. Martin *Hero*.
23. For the centrality of *A Treatise concerning Religious Affections* to Jonathan Edwards's works and in the history of ideas, see Marsden *Edwards* 284–90. John Wesley's abridgment provides shorthand perspective on the emotional, intellectual, and spiritual background to Anglo-American belles lettres of the nineteenth century: see Brantley *Coordinates* 7–42.
24. See, e.g., Judith Page's recent study of Romantic-era sympathy (esp. 1–20).
25. Emerson, "Fate" (1852), in Whicher, ed., 349. The social grace of such a passage contrasts with the egotistical sublime in the "Transparent Eye-ball" section of Emerson's "Nature" (1836) and throughout his "Self-Reliance" (1841); even these essays, however, can well appear more other-directed than they have often seemed to be (see Brantley *Anglo-American* 177–92).
26. Abrams, ed., *The Norton Anthology of English Literature: Fifth Edition* 2:60. M. H. Abrams interprets what Blake must have meant by his phrase "the marriage of heaven and hell."
27. Habegger xv, 268, 368, 372, 418, 598, 715, esp. xv.
28. Benfey 64. Christopher Benfey's reading of Dickinson's "Split the Lark - and you'll find the Music - " is particularly persuasive (93).
29. Mark 12:33. Compare body, emotion, reason, and imagination in Blake's cosmology (Ault). Wesley's quadrilateral—scripture, reason, tradition, and experience (Maddox 36–40)—parallels Blake's and foreshadows, like his, Dickinson's discovery of mind, soul, and heart in friendship and in love alike.
30. Habegger 471. "My Wars are laid away in Books - " (Fr1579) provides Habegger with the title of his critical biography and serves him, in effect, as Emily Dickinson's signature poem.
31. See Lundin 4, 34, 78, 134, 149. See also Brantley *Experience* 144, 154, 155.
32. The pessimism of "Those - dying then" (Fr1581) also contrasts somewhat with Melville's imagery of ignis fatuus. Dickinson's second stanza is not as tough-minded as Melville even as early as his first story, "Fragments of a Writing Desk" (1839), in which the narrator, perhaps repeating Melville's chagrin over his father's futile dreamquests, curses the "absurd conceits" that "inflated his brain," "the ignis fatuus, that danced so provokingly before me" (see the quotation and discussion in Delbanco 27). In the first stanza, however, Dickinson outdoes Melville himself in truth-acknowledgment of an unflinching kind. Dickinson's near-blasphemous imagery of God's amputated hand epitomizes the literary boldness that her refusal to publish freed her to develop. Compare Melville's imagination of Ahab

"with a crucifixion in his face": a pious editor changed this to: "an apparently eternal anguish in his face" (qtd. in Delbanco 178).

33. See D. W. Robertson, Jr.,'s discussion of "The Miller's Tale" (1400) by Geoffrey Chaucer (Robertson 382–86, 468–69).

34. See the quotation and discussion in Sewall "Teaching" 31, of the first review of Emily Dickinson's poetry, by Arlo Bates.

35. The Wadsworth/Dickinson romance approaches the philosophical concept of friendship to be found in the discourse of Gilles Deleuze and Félix Guattieri: "The friend who appears in philosophy no longer stands for an extrinsic persona, an example or empirical circumstance, but rather for a presence that is intrinsic to thought, a condition of possibility of thought itself" (Deleuze and Guattieri 2–3). Dickinson's concept of friendship is as conversational, philosophical, and scientific as that of Emerson in his essay on "Friendship" (1841), which, as Frank M. Meola paraphrases it, means that "[i]n a nation of individuals,...ideas would be tested and reworked in perpetual dialogues, and as proper citizens we would all be on lifelong journeys of self-reinvention, encountering the other in ourselves, ourselves in others" (123).

36. Compare I Corinthians 12:31. Galatians 3:28 is also apropos.

37. Eberwein; Guthrie; Habegger 311–3; Sewall *Life*.

38. Inspired by his decision not to accept a larger pastorate in London, the Reverend Dr. John Fawcett (1740–1817) stayed at his small church in Wainsgate and wrote

> Blest be the Tie that Binds
> Our hearts in Christian love;
> The fellowship of kindred minds
> Is like to that above.

See Fawcett (1772). As a farewell or, rather, antifarewell hymn, "Blest be the Tie that Binds" parallels Emily Dickinson's lifelong interest in the theme of parting as an existential, as well as spiritual, problem. Recall her lines:

> Parting is all we know of heaven,
> And all we need of hell.
>   (Fr1773, lines 7–8)

WORKS CITED

Aarsleff, Hans. *From Locke to Saussure: Essays on the Study of Language and Intellectual History.* Minneapolis: U of Minnesota P, 1982.

Abrams, M. H. *The Mirror and the Lamp: Romantic Theory and the Critical Tradition.* New York: Oxford UP, 1954.

———. *Natural Supernaturalism: Tradition and Revolution in Romantic Literature.* New York: W. W. Norton, 1971.

——— et al., eds. *The Norton Anthology of English Literature,* 6th ed. 2 Vols. New York: W. W. Norton, 1998.

Alter, Robert. *Pen of Iron: American Prose and the King James Bible.* Princeton, NJ: Princeton UP, 2010.

Anderson, Charles R. *Stairway of Surprise: Emily Dickinson's Poetry.* New York: Holt, Rinehart and Winston, 1960.

Anderson, Douglas. "Presence and Place in Emily Dickinson's Poetry." *New England Quarterly* 57 (June 1984): 205–24.

Andrews, Dee E. *The Methodists and Revolutionary America, 1760–1800: The Shaping of an Evangelical Culture.* Princeton, NJ: Princeton UP, 2000.

Applegate, Debby. *The Most Famous Man in America: The Biography of Henry Ward Beecher.* New York: Doubleday, 2006.

Astell, Mary. *A Serious Proposal to the Ladies.* London: Printed for Richard Wilkin, 1694.

———. *Some Reflections upon Marriage.* London: John Nutt, Stationers-Hall, 1700.

Ault, Donald. *Narrative Unbound: Re-Visioning Blake's* The Four Zoas. Barrytown, FL: Station Hill P, 1987.

Bainbridge, Simon. *Napoleon and English Romanticism.* Cambridge: Cambridge UP, 1995.

Baker, Carlos. *The Echoing Green: Romanticism, Modernism, and the Phenomena of Transference in Poetry.* Princeton, NJ: Princeton UP, 1984.

———. *Emerson among the Eccentrics: A Group Portrait.* New York: Viking, 1996.

Baker, Nicholson. *U and I: A True Story.* New York: Random House, 1991.

Barber, Frank Louis. *The Philosophy of John Wesley.* Toronto: Ryerson Press, 1923.

Barker, Wendy. *Lunacy of Light: Emily Dickinson and the Experience of Metaphor.* Carbondale and Edwardsville: Southern Illinois UP, 1987.

Barnstone, Aliki. *Changing Rapture: Emily Dickinson's Poetic Development.* Hanover, NH: UP of New England, 2007.

Barrett, Paul H. et al., eds. *The Collected Papers of Charles Darwin*. 2 Vols. Ithaca, NY: Cornell UP, 1987.

Barth, J. Robert. *Romanticism and Transcendence: Wordsworth, Coleridge, and the Religious Imagination*. Columbia: U of Missouri P, 2003.

Bate, Jonathan. *English Literature: A Very Short Introduction*. New York: Oxford UP, 2012.

———. *Romantic Ecology: Wordsworth and the Environmental Tradition*. London: Routledge, 1991.

Baym, Nina et al., eds. *The Norton Anthology of American Literature*, 5th ed. New York: W. W. Norton, 1998.

Beale, Walter H. *Learning from Language: Symmetry, Asymmetry, and Literary Humanism*. Pittsburgh: U of Pittsburgh P, 2009.

Beer, Gillian. "Darwinism and Romanticism." Penrith, England: Humanities-Ebooks, 2010.

Benfey, Christopher. *Emily Dickinson and the Problem of Others*. Amherst: U of Massachusetts P, 1984.

Bennett, Paula. *Emily Dickinson: Woman Poet*. Iowa City: U of Iowa P, 1991.

Bentley, G. E., Jr. *The Stranger from Paradise: A Biography of William Blake*. New Haven and London: Yale UP, 2001.

Bianchi, Martha Dickinson. *Emily Dickinson Face to Face*. New York: Houghton Mifflin, 1932.

———. *The Life and Letters of Emily Dickinson*. Boston: Houghton Mifflin, 1924.

Blackstock, Alan. "Dickinson, Blake, and the Hymnbooks of Hell." *The Emily Dickinson Journal* 20.2 (November 2011): 33–60.

Bloom, Harold. *The American Religion: The Emergence of the Post-Christian Nation*. New York: Simon and Schuster, 1992.

———. *The Anatomy of Influence: Literature as a Way of Life*. New Haven, CT: Yale UP, 2011.

———. *The Book of J*. Translated from the Hebrew by David Rosenberg; interpreted by Harold Bloom. New York: Grove Weidenfeld, 1990.

———. *How to Read and Why*. New York: Scribners, 2000.

———. *The Shadow of a Great Rock: A Literary Appreciation of the King James Bible*. New Haven, CT: Yale UP, 2011.

———. *Shakespeare: The Invention of the Human*. New York: Riverhead Books, 1998.

———. *The Western Canon: The Books and School of the Ages*. New York, San Diego, and London: Harcourt, Brace and Company, 1994.

———, ed. *Modern Critical Views: Alfred Lord Tennyson*. New York: Chelsea House, 1985.

Body, Alfred H. *John Wesley and Education*. London: Epworth Press, 1936.

Bornstein, George. *Transformations of Romanticism in Yeats, Eliot, and Stevens*. Chicago: U of Chicago P, 1976.

Boyd, Brian. *Why Lyrics Last: Evolution, Cognition, and Shakespeare's Sonnets*. Cambridge, MA: Harvard UP, 2012.

WORKS CITED 241

Brantley, Richard E. *Anglo-American Antiphony: The Late Romanticism of Tennyson and Emerson*. Gainesville: UP of Florida, 1994.

———. "Charles Wesley's Experiential Art." *Eighteenth-Century Life* 11 (May 1987): 1–11.

———. *Coordinates of Anglo-American Romanticism: Wesley, Edwards, Carlyle, and Emerson*. Gainesville: UP of Florida, 1993.

———. *Experience and Faith: The Late-Romantic Imagination of Emily Dickinson*. 2004. Reprint. New York: Palgrave Macmillan, 2008.

———. *Locke, Wesley, and the Method of English Romanticism*. Gainesville: UP of Florida, 1984.

———. *Wordsworth's "Natural Methodism."* New Haven, CT: Yale UP, 1975.

Breuggemann, Walter. *Disruptive Grace: Reflections on God, Scripture, and the Church*. Ed. Carolyn J. Sharp. Minneapolis: Fortress, 2011.

Brooks, David. "Tools for Thinking." *The New York Times*, March 29, 2011: A31.

Brown, Frank Burch. *The Evolution of Darwin's Religious Views*. Macon, GA: Mercer UP, 1986.

Browne, Janet. *Darwin's Origin of Species: A Biography*. London: Atlantic Books, 2006.

Browne, Peter. *The Procedure, Extent, and Limits of Human Understanding*, 2nd ed. London: W. Innys, 1729.

Bryson, Bill, ed. *Seeing Further: The Story of Science, Discovery, and the Genius of the Royal Society*. New York: William Morrow, 2010.

Buckley, Jerome H. *William Ernest Henley: A Study in the "Counter-Decadence" of the Nineties*. Princeton, NJ: Princeton UP, 1945.

Budick, Emily Miller. *Emily Dickinson and the Life of Language: A Study in Symbolic Poetics*. Baton Rouge: Louisiana State UP, 1986.

Bunyan, John. *The Pilgrim's Progress*. 1678. Ed. W. R. Owens. Oxford: Clarendon, 2003.

Bushell, Sally. *Text as Process: Creative Composition in Wordsworth, Tennyson, and Dickinson*. Charlottesville and London: U of Virginia P, 2009.

Butler, James. Rev. of *The Hidden Wordsworth*, by Kenneth R. Johnston. *The Wordsworth Circle* 30 (Autumn 1999): 173–75.

Butler, Jon. *Awash in a Sea of Faith: Christianizing the American People*. Cambridge, MA: Harvard UP, 1992.

Butler, Melissa. "Early Liberal Roots of Feminism: John Locke and the Attack on Patriarchy." *American Political Science Review* 72 (1978): 135–50.

Bynum, W. F. *The History of Medicine*. New York: Oxford UP, 2008.

Byron, George Gordon, Lord. *Byron's Letters and Journals*. Ed. Leslie A. Marchand. Volume 3: 1813–14. Cambridge, MA: Harvard UP, 1974.

Cameron, Sharon. *Choosing Not Choosing: Dickinson's Fascicles*. Chicago: U of Chicago P, 1992.

———. "'A Loaded Gun': Dickinson and the Dialectic of Rage." *PMLA* 93 (May 1978): 423–37.

Campbell, Gordon. *Bible: The Story of the King James Version, 1611–2011*. New York: Oxford UP, 2010.

Campbell, Ted. "The Origins and Early Growth of Methodism, 1730–1791." *The Ashgate Research Companion on World Methodism*. Ed. William Gibson. Aldershot, England, and Burlington, VT: Ashgate, 2012.

Capps, Jack L. *Emily Dickinson's Reading: 1836–1886*. Cambridge, MA: Harvard UP, 1966.

Carafiol, Peter. *Transcendent Reason: James Marsh and the Forms of Romantic Thought*. Gainesville: U of Florida P, 1982.

Cazamian, Louis. *Carlyle*. Translated by E. K. Brown. 1912. Reprint. Hamden, CT: Archon Books, 1966.

Chambers, Robert. *Vestiges of the Natural History of Creation*. 1844. Rockville, MD: IndyPublish, 2004.

Chester, Timothy. "Man for Our Time?" *TLS*, May 7, 2010: 5–8.

Clarke, Colin C. *Romantic Paradox: An Essay on the Poetry of Wordsworth*. London: Routledge & Kegan Paul, 1966.

Cody, David. "'When one's soul's at a white heat': Dickinson and the 'Azarian School.'" *The Emily Dickinson Journal* 19.1 (2010): 30–59.

Cody, John. *After Great Pain: The Inner Life of Emily Dickinson*. Cambridge, MA: Harvard UP, 1971.

Coetzee, J. M. "The Angry Genius of Les Murray." *The New York Review of Books*, September 29, 2011: 17–21.

Coghill, Sheila, and Thom Tammaro, eds. *Visiting Emily: Poems Inspired by the Life and Work of Emily Dickinson*. Iowa City: U of Iowa P, 2000.

Collier, Frank Wilbur. *Back to Wesley*. New York: Methodist Book Concern, 1924.

"Colton, Charles Caleb." *Chambers's Biographical Dictionary*. Edinburgh: W. R. Chambers, 1898.

Cooley, Carolyn Lindley. *The Music of Emily Dickinson's Poems and Letters: A Study of Imagery and Form*. Jefferson, NC: Mcfarland and Company, Inc., 2003.

Cragg, Gerald R., ed. *The Appeals to Men of Reason and Religion and Certain Related Open Letters*. Vol. 11 of *The Works of John Wesley*. Ed. Frank Baker. Oxford: Clarendon P, 1975.

Crain, Caleb. *American Sympathy: Men, Friendship, and Literature in the New Nation*. New Haven: Yale UP, 2001.

Crews, Harry. *All We Need of Hell: A Novel*. New York: HarperCollins, 1988.

Crisp, Oliver D. *Jonathan Edwards on God and Creation*. New York: Oxford UP, 2012.

Crumbley, Paul. "Dickinson's Dialogic Voice." *The Emily Dickinson Handbook*. Ed. Gudrun Grabher, Roland Hagenbüchle, and Cristanne Miller. Amherst: U of Massachusetts P, 1998. 93–112.

———. *Inflections of the Pen: Dash and Voice in Emily Dickinson*. Lexington: U of Kentucky P, 1996.

———. *Winds of Will: Emily Dickinson and the Sovereignty of Democratic Thought*. Tuscaloosa: U of Alabama P, 2010.

Culler, Jonathan. *Structuralist Poetics: Structuralism, Linguistics, and the Study of Literature.* Ithaca, NY: Cornell UP, 1975.

Curnock, Nehemiah, ed. *The Journal of the Rev. John Wesley, A. M.* 8 Vols. London: Robert Culley, 1909.

Curran, Stuart. "The I Altered." *Romanticism and Feminism.* Ed. Anne Mellor. Bloomington: Indiana UP, 1988. 17–26.

Damrosch, David et al., eds. *The Longman Anthology of British Literature: First Edition.* 2 Vols. New York: Longman, 1999.

Darwin, Charles. *On the Origin of Species.* 1859. Darwin: A Norton Critical Edition. 3rd ed. Ed. Philip Appleman. New York: Norton, 2001.

Davies, Hugh Sykes. "Wordsworth and the Empirical Philosophers." *The English Mind: Studies in the English Moralists Presented to Basil Willey.* Ed. Hugh Sykes Davies and George Watson. Cambridge: Cambridge UP, 1964.

Delbanco, Andrew. *Melville: His World and Work.* New York: Alfred A. Knopf, 2005.

Deleuze, Gilles, and Félix Guattieri. *What Is Philosophy?* London: Verso, 1994.

Deppman, Jed. "'I Could Not Have Defined the Change': Rereading Dickinson's Definition Poetry." *The Emily Dickinson Journal* 11.1 (2002): 49–80.

———. *Trying to Think with Emily Dickinson.* Amherst: U of Massachusetts P, 2008.

Dickie, Margaret. *Lyric Contingencies: Emily Dickinson and Wallace Stevens.* Philadelphia: U of Pennsylvania P, 1991.

Dickinson, Emily. *Emily Dickinson's Herbarium: A Facsimile Edition.* Ed. Leslie A. Morris. Cambridge, MA: Harvard UP, 2006.

Diehl, Joanne Feit. *Dickinson and the Romantic Imagination.* Princeton, NJ: Princeton UP, 1981.

———. "'Ransom in a Voice': Language as Defense in Dickinson's Poetry." *Feminist Critics Read Emily Dickinson.* Ed. Suzanne Juhasz. Bloomington: Indiana UP, 1983.

Dobson, Joanne. *Dickinson and the Strategies of Reticence: The Woman Writer in Nineteenth-Century America.* Bloomington: Indiana UP, 1989.

Doddridge, Philip. *The Rise and Progress of Religion in the Soul.* 1742. Charleston, SC: Nabu P, 2010.

Dolan, Elizabeth A. *Seeing Suffering in Women's Literature of the Romantic Era.* Aldershot, England, and Burlington, VT: Ashgate, 2008.

Donoghue, Denis. "The Discreet Charms of the Bourgeoisie." *New England Review* 32.3 (2011): 87–95.

———. *The Third Voice: Modern British and American Verse Drama.* Princeton, NJ: Princeton UP, 1959.

Doriani, Beth Maclay. *Emily Dickinson: Daughter of Prophecy.* Amherst: U of Massachusetts P, 1996.

Douglas, Ann. *The Feminization of American Culture.* New York: Knopf, 1977.

Downey, Charlotte. "Emily Dickinson's Appeal for a Child Audience," *Dickinson Studies* 55 (Spring 1985): 21–31.

Dreyer, Frederick. "Faith and Experience in the Thought of John Wesley." *The American Historical Review* 88 (February 1983): 12–30.

Dutton, Denis. *The Art Instinct: Beauty, Pleasure, and Human Evolution.* New York: Bloomsbury P, 2009.

Dyson, Freeman. "What Price Glory?" *The New York Review of Books,* June 10, 2010: 8–12.

Eberwein, Jane Donahue. "'Dangerous Fruit of the Tree of Knowledge': Mary Anne Evans, Emily Dickinson, and Strauss's *Das Leben Jesu.*" *The Emily Dickinson Journal* 21.2 (2012): 1–19.

———. "Dickinson and Calvin's God." *Emily Dickinson International Society Bulletin* 13 (November/December 2001): 29–30.

———. *Dickinson: Strategies of Limitation.* Amherst: U of Massachusetts P, 1985.

———. "Lovers, Speculation About." *An Emily Dickinson Encyclopedia.* Ed. Jane Donahue Eberwein. Westport, CT: Greenwood, 1998.

———. "Ministerial Interviews and Fathers in Faith." *The Emily Dickinson Journal* 9.2 (2000): 6–15.

———. "Outgrowing Genesis? Dickinson, Darwin, and the Higher Criticism." *Dickinson and Philosophy.* Ed. Marianne Noble, Jed Deppmann, and Gary Lee Stonum. Cambridge: Cambridge UP, 2013. 1–35.

———. Rev. of *Experience and Faith,* by Richard E. Brantley. *The Emily Dickinson Journal* 15.1 (2006): 96–100.

———. "'Where - Omnipresence - Fly?' Calvinism as Impetus to Spiritual Amplitude." *The Emily Dickinson Journal* 14.2 (2005): 12–23.

Edwards, Jonathan. *An Extract from a Treatise concerning Religious Affections.* Ed. John Wesley. In Vol. 23 of *The Works of the Rev. John Wesley.* 32 Vols. Bristol: J. Paramore, 1771–74.

Engelke, Matthew. *A Problem of Presence: Beyond Scripture in an African Church.* Berkeley: U of California P, 2007.

England, Martha, and John Sparrow. *Hymns Unbidden: Donne, Herbert, Blake, Emily Dickinson, and the Hymnographers.* New York: New York Public Library, 1966.

Erkkila, Betsy. "Emily Dickinson and Class." *American Literary History* 4 (Spring 1992): 1–27.

Farr, Judith. *The Passion of Emily Dickinson.* Cambridge, MA: Harvard UP, 1992.

Fathi, Fanoosh. "'Tell all the Truth but tell it slant - ': Dickinson's Poetics of Indirection in Contemporary Poetry." *The Emily Dickinson Journal* 17.2 (2008): 77–99.

Favret, Mary A. *War at a Distance: Romanticism and the Making of Modern Wartime.* Princeton NJ: Princeton, UP, 2009.

Fawcett, John. "Blest be the Tie that Binds." 1772. *Hymns Adapted to the Circumstances of Public Worship and Private Devotion.* Leeds: G. Wright and Son, 1782.

Felstiner, John, ed., trans. *Selected Poems and Prose of Paul Celan*. New York: W. W. Norton, 2001.

Finch, Annie. "My Father Dickinson: On Poetic Influence." *The Emily Dickinson Journal* 17.2 (2008): 24–38.

Finch, A. R. C. "Dickinson and Patriarchal Meter: A Theory of Metrical Codes." *PMLA* 102.2 (March 1987): 166–76.

Finnerty, Páraic. *Emily Dickinson's Shakespeare*. Amherst and Boston: U of Massachusetts P, 2006.

Fish, Stanley. "One University Under God?" *The Chronicle of Higher Education*, January 7, 2005: 13.

Fitzgerald, F. Scott. *The Crack-Up*. Ed. Edmund Wilson. New York: Charles Scribner's Sons, 1931.

Foucault, Michel. *The Order of Things: An Archaeology of the Human Science*. New York: Vintage, 1994.

Franke, William. "'The Missing All': Emily Dickinson's Apophatic Poetics." *Christianity & Literature* 58.1 (Autumn 2008): 61–80.

Franklin, Ralph W., ed. *The Manuscript Books of Emily Dickinson*. 2 Vols. Cambridge, MA: Belknap P of Harvard UP, 1981.

Freedman, Linda. *Emily Dickinson and the Religious Imagination*. Cambridge: Cambridge UP, 2011.

Freedman, William. "Dickinson's 'I Like to See It Lap the Miles.'" *The Explicator* 41 (Spring 1982): 30–32.

Freeman, Margaret H. "A Cognitive Approach to Dickinson's Metaphors." *The Emily Dickinson Handbook*. Ed. Gudrun Grabher, Roland Hagenbüchle, and Cristanne Miller. Amherst: U of Massachusetts P, 1998. 258–72.

———. "George Eliot and Emily Dickinson: Poets of Play and Possibility." *The Emily Dickinson Journal* 21.2 (2012): 37–58.

Frost, Robert. *The Selected Prose of Robert Frost*. Ed. Hyde Cox and Edward Connery Lathem. New York: Random House, 1979.

Fulton, Alice. "'Her Moment of Brocade': The Reconstruction of Emily Dickinson." *Parnassus: Poetry in Review* 15.1 (1989): 9–44.

Fussell, Paul. *The Great War and Modern Memory*. 1975. New York: Oxford UP, 2000.

Garbowsky, Maryanne M. *The House without the Door: A Study of Emily Dickinson and the Illness of Agoraphobia*. Madison, NJ: Fairleigh Dickinson UP, 1989.

Gardner, Thomas. *A Door Ajar: Contemporary Writers and Emily Dickinson*. New York: Oxford UP, 2006.

Gaull, Marilyn. "'Conjecturing a Climate': The Discovery of Transatlantic Weather." *Symbiosis: A Journal of Anglo-American Literary Relations* 15.1 (April 2011): 17–28.

Gay, Peter. *The Bourgeois Experience*. 2 Vols. New York: Oxford UP, 1984–1986.

Gelpi, Albert. "Emily Dickinson's Long Shadow: Susan Howe and Fanny Howe." *The Emily Dickinson Journal* 17.2 (2008): 100–12.

———. "Emily Dickinson's Word: Presence as Absence, Absence as Presence." *American Poetry* 4 (Winter 1987): 41–50.

Gilbert, Sandra, and Susan Gubar. *The Madwoman in the Attic: The Woman Writer and the Nineteenth-Century Literary Imagination*. 1979. 2nd ed. New Haven, CT: Yale UP, 2000.

Giles, Paul. "'The Earth Reversed Her Hemispheres': Dickinson's Global Antipodality." *The Emily Dickinson Journal* 20.1 (2011): 1–21.

Gilliland, Don. "Textual Scruples and Dickinson's 'Uncertain Certainty.'" *The Emily Dickinson Journal* 18.2 (2009): 38–62.

Godwin, William. *The Enquirer*. London: J. Johnson, 1797.

———. *An Enquiry Concerning Political Justice, and Its Influence on Morals and Happiness*. 1793. Reprint. Toronto: U of Toronto P, 1946.

Goodheart, Adam. *1861: The Civil War Awakening*. New York: Knopf, 2011.

Gordon, Lyndall. *Lives Like Loaded Guns: Emily Dickinson and Her Family's Feuds*. New York: Penguin Group, 2010.

Gould, Stephen Jay. *Time's Arrow, Time's Cycle: Myth and Metaphor in the Discovery of Geological Time*. Cambridge, MA: Harvard UP, 1987.

Gravil, Richard. "Emily Dickinson (and Walt Whitman): The Escape from 'Locksley Hall.'" *Symbiosis: A Journal of Anglo-American Literary Relations* 7.1 (April 2003): 56–75.

———. "Is The Excursion a Metrical Novel?" *The Wordsworth Circle* 42.2 (Spring 2011): 31–36.

———. *Romantic Dialogues: Anglo-American Continuities, 1776–1862*. New York: St. Martin's Press, 2000.

Gray, John. "The Return of an Illusion." *The New Republic*, June 23, 2011: 29.

Greenblatt, Stephen J. *Renaissance Self-Fashioning: From More to Shakespeare*. Chicago: The U of Chicago P, 1980.

———. *Shakespearean Negotiations*. Berkeley: U of California P, 1988.

———. *The Swerve: How the World Became Modern*. New York: W. W. Norton, 2012.

———, ed. *Allegory and Representation*. Baltimore, MD: Johns Hopkins UP, 1981.

Grinnell, George. *The Age of Hypochondria: Interpreting Romantic Health and Illness*. New York: Palgrave Macmillan, 2010.

Guthrie, James R. *Emily Dickinson's Vision: Illness and Identity in Her Poetry*. Gainesville: UP of Florida, 1998.

Habegger, Alfred. *My Wars Are Laid Away in Books*. New York: Random House, 2001.

Habermas, Jürgen. *The Philosophic Discourse of Modernity: Twelve Lectures*. Boston, MA: MIT P, 1990.

Hankins, Barry. *The Second Great Awakening and the Transcendentalists*. Westport, CT: Greenwood Publishing Group, 2004.

Hannay, Alastair. *Kierkegaard: A Biography*. New York: Cambridge UP, 2001.

Hardy, Barbara Nathan. *The Advantage of Lyric: Essays on Feeling in Poetry*. Bloomington: Indiana UP, 1977.

Harmon, William, and C. Hugh Holman. *A Handbook to Literature*. 7th ed. Upper Saddle River, NJ: Prentice Hall, 1996.

Harris, Sam. *Free Will*. New York: Free Press, 2012.

Harrison, Kathryn. "I am, Therefore I Want." *The New York Review of Books*, November 6, 2005: 22.

Hart, Ellen Louise. "The Encoding of Homoerotic Desire: Emily Dickinson's Letters and Poems to Susan Dickinson, 1850–1886." *Tulsa Studies in Women's Literature* 9 (1990): 251–72.

Hart, Ellen Louise, and Martha Nell Smith, eds. *Open Me Carefully: Emily Dickinson's Intimate Letters to Susan Huntington Dickinson*. Ashfield, MA: Paris P, 1998.

Hartog, François. *Memories of Odysseus: Frontier Tales from Ancient Greece*. Trans. Janet Lloyd. Chicago: U of Chicago P, 2001.

Harvey, Samantha. "Coleridge's American Revival: James Marsh, John Dewey, and the Legacy of Vermont Transcendentalism." *Symbiosis: A Journal of Anglo-American Literary Relations* 15.1 (2011): 77–103.

———. *Transatlantic Transcendentalism: Coleridge, Emerson, and the Romantic Triad*. Edinburgh, Scotland: U of Edinburgh P, 2013.

Hatch, Nathan O. *The Democritization of American Christianity*. New Haven, CT: Yale UP, 1989.

Heilbut, Anthony. *Thomas Mann: Eros and Literature*. Berkeley: U of California P, 1997.

Herbert, T. Walter. *John Wesley as Editor and Author*. Princeton, NJ: Princeton UP, 1940.

Herbert, T. Walter, Jr. *Moby Dick and Calvinism: A World Dismantled*. New Brunswick, NJ: Rutgers UP, 1977.

Hindley, J. Clifford. "The Philosophy of Enthusiasm." *The London Quarterly and Holborn Review* 182 (1957): 99–109, 199–210.

Hindmarsh, D. Bruce. "The Reception of Jonathan Edwards by Early Evangelicals in England." *Jonathan Edwards at Home and Abroad: Historical Memories, Cultural Movements, Global Horizons*. Ed. David W. Kling and Douglas A. Sweeney. Columbia: U of South Carolina P, 2003. 207–10.

Hirsch, E. D., Jr. *The Aims of Interpretation*. Chicago: U of Chicago P, 1975.

Holmes, Richard. *The Age of Wonder: How the Romantic Generation Discovered the Beauty and Terror of Science*. New York: Pantheon, 2009.

Holquist, Michael. "The Politics of Representation." *Allegory and Representation*. Ed. Stephen J. Greenblatt. Baltimore: Johns Hopkins UP, 1981. 163–83.

Homans, Margaret. *Women Writers and Poetic Identity: Dorothy Wordsworth, Emily Brontë, and Emily Dickinson*. Princeton, NJ: Princeton UP, 1980.

Howells, Richard. "Resinking the Titanic: Hubris, Nemesis, and the Modern World." *Symbiosis: A Journal of Anglo-American Literary Relations* 1 (October 1997): 151–58.

Huffer, Mary Lee Stephenson. *Emily Dickinson's Experiential Poetics and Rev. Dr. Charles Wadsworth's Rhetoric of Sensation: The Intellectual Friendship between the Poet and a Pastor*. Lewiston, NY: Edwin Mellen P, 2007.

Hulme, T. E. "Romanticism and Classicism." *Speculations: Essays on Humanism and the Philosophy of Art*. Ed. Herbert Read. New York: Harcourt, Brace and Company, 1936. 113–40.

Hurst, J. F. *John Wesley , the Methodist*. 1904. Reprint. Whitefish, MT: Kessinger Publications, 1999.

Hutchison, Coleman. "'Eastern Exiles': Dickinson, Whiggery and War." *The Emily Dickinson Journal* 13.2 (2004): 1–26.

Ikeler, A. Abbott. *Puritan Temper and Transcendental Faith: Carlyle's Literary Vision*. Columbus: Ohio State UP, 1972.

Jackson, Thomas, ed. *The Works of the Rev. John Wesley, A. M.* 14 Vols. 1829–31. Reprint. Grand Rapids, MI: Zondervan P, 1958.

Jackson, Virginia. *Dickinson's Misery: A Theory of Lyric Reading*. Princeton, NJ: Princeton UP, 2005.

Jager, Colin. *The Book of God: Secularization and Design in the Romantic Era*. Philadelphia: U of Pennsylvania P, 2007.

James, William. *The Varieties of Religious Experience*. 1902. New York: Touchstone, 1997.

Jeffrey, Francis. "Wordsworth's Excursion." *The Edinburgh Review, or Critical Journal* 24 (November 1814): 14.

Johnson, Greg. *Emily Dickinson: Perception and the Poet's Quest*. Tuscaloosa: U of Alabama P, 1985.

Johnson, Samuel. *Samuel Johnson's Dictionary: Selections from the 1755 Work that Defined the English Language*. Ed. Jack Lynch. New York: Walker, 2003.

Johnson, Thomas H., ed. *The Complete Poems of Emily Dickinson*. 3 Vols. Cambridge, MA: Harvard UP, 1955.

Johnston, Kenneth R. *The Hidden Wordsworth: Poet, Lover, Rebel, Spy*. New York: Norton, 2001.

Jones, Rowena Revis. "'A Royal Seal': Emily Dickinson's Rite of Baptism." *Religion and Literature* 18 (Fall 1986): 29–51.

Jones, Ruth Owen. "'Neighbor - and friend - and Bridegroom -': William Smith Clark as Emily Dickinson's Master Figure." *The Emily Dickinson Journal* 11.2 (Fall 2002): 48–85.

Juhasz, Suzanne. "Reading Dickinson Doubly." *Women's Studies* 16 (1989): 217–21.

———. "Tea and Revolution: Emily Dickinson Populates the Mind." *Essays in Literature* 12 (Spring 1985): 145–50.

———. *The Undiscovered Continent: Emily Dickinson and the Space Within*. Bloomington: Indiana UP, 1983.

———. "'To Make a Prairie': Language and Form in Emily Dickinson's Poems about Mental Experience." *Ball State University Forum* 21 (Spring 1980): 12–25.

Kandel, Eric R. *The Age of Insight: The Quest to Understand the Unconscious in Art, Mind, and Brain, from Vienna 1900 to the Present*. New York: Random House, 2012.

Keane, Patrick J. *Emerson, Romanticism, and Intuitive Reason: The Transatlantic "Light of All Our Day."* Columbia: U of Missouri P, 2005.

———. *Emily Dickinson's Approving God: Divine Design and the Problem of Suffering*. Columbia: U of Missouri P, 2008.

Kearns, Michael. *Writing for the Street, Writing in the Garret: Melville, Dickinson, and Private Publication*. Columbus: Ohio State UP, 2010.

Keller, Karl. "Alephs, Zahirs, and the Triumph of Ambiguity: Typology in Nineteenth-Century American Literature." *Literary Uses of Typology from the Late Middle Ages to the Present*. Ed. Earl Miner. Princeton, NJ: Princeton UP, 1977.

———. *The Only Kangaroo among the Beauty: Emily Dickinson and America*. Johns Hopkins UP, 1979.

Kenny, Anthony. "True Believers." *TLS*, June 22, 2012: 24.

Kershner, R. B. *Joyce, Bakhtin, and Popular Literature: Chronicles of Disorder*. Chapel Hill: U of North Carolina P, 1989.

Kher, Indra Nath. *The Landscape of Absence: Emily Dickinson's Poetry*. New Haven, CT: Yale UP, 1974.

Kimpel, Ben. *Emily Dickinson as Philosopher*. Lewiston, NY: Edwin Mellen P, 1981.

Kincaid, James. *Tennyson's Major Poems: The Comic and Ironic Patterns*. New Haven, CT: Yale UP, 1975.

Kirchwey, Karl. "Man of Many Voices." *The New York Times Book Review*, April 25, 2010: 19.

Kirkby, Joan. "'A Crescent Still Abides': Emily Dickinson and the Work of Mourning." *Wider than the Sky: Essays and Meditations on the Healing Power of Emily Dickinson*. Ed. Cindy MacKenzie and Barbara Dana. Kent, OH: Kent State UP, 2007. 129–40.

———. "'[W]e thought Darwin had thrown "the Redeemer" Away': Darwinizing with Emily Dickinson." *The Emily Dickinson Journal* 19.1 (2010): 1–29.

Lamb, Charles. *The Letters of Charles Lamb to which are added those of his sister Mary Lamb*. Ed. E. V. Lucas. 8 Vols. London: J. M. Dent & Sons and Methuen & Company, 1935.

Lambert, Robert Graham. *The Prose of a Poet: A Critical Study of Emily Dickinson's Letters*. Lewiston, NY: Edwin Mellen P, 1996.

Langbaum, Robert. *The Poetry of Experience: The Dramatic Monologue in Modern Literary Tradition*. London: Chatto and Windus, 1957.

———. *The Word from Below: Essays in Modern Literature and Culture*. Madison: U of Wisconsin P, 1987.

Lau, Beth, ed. *Fellow Romantics: Male and Female British Writers, 1790–1835*. Aldershot, England, and Burlington, VT: Ashgate, 2009.

Lease, Benjamin. *Anglo-American Encounters: England and the Rise of Anglo-American Literature*. Cambridge: Cambridge UP, 1981.

———. *Emily Dickinson's Reading of Men and Books: Sacred Soundings*. Basingstoke, England: Macmillan, 1990.

Leder, Sharon, with Andrea Abbott. *The Language of Exclusion: The Poetry of Emily Dickinson and Christina Rossetti*. New York: Greenwood Press, 1987.

Leib, Erin. "Both/And." *The New Republic*, February 11, 2002: 38–41.

Leiter, Sharon. *Critical Companion to Emily Dickinson: A Literary Reference to Her Life and Work*. New York: Facts on File, 2006.

Leonard, Douglas Novich. "Certain Slants of Light: Exploring the Art of Dickinson's Fascicle 13." *Approaches to Teaching Dickinson' Poetry*. Ed. Robin Riley Fast and Christine Mack Gordon. New York: Modern Language Association of America, 1989. 124–33.

———. "Emily Dickinson's Religion: 'An Ablative Estate.'" *Christian Scholar's Review* 13.4 (1984): 333–48.

Lethem, Jonathan. "The Ecstasy of Influence." *Harper's*, February 2007: 18–23.

Leverenz, David. *Language of Puritan Feeling: An Exploration in Literature, Psychology, and Social History*. New Brunswick, NJ: Rutgers UP, 1980.

———. *Manhood and the American Renaissance: The Rhetoric of Narrative in Fiction and Film*. Ithaca, NY: Cornell UP, 1990.

Levine, George. *Darwin the Writer*. New York: Oxford UP, 2011.

Leyda, Jay, ed. *The Years and Hours of Emily Dickinson*. 2 Vols. New Haven, CT: Yale UP, 1960.

Locke, David. *Science as Writing*. New Haven, CT: Yale UP, 1992.

Locke, John. *Some Thoughts Concerning Education*. London: A. and J. Churchill, 1693.

Longsworth, Polly. *Austin and Mabel*. Amherst: U of Massachusetts P, 1984.

———. "'Latitude of Home': Life in the Homestead and the Evergreens." *The Dickinsons of Amherst*. Ed. Christopher Benfey et al. Hanover, NH: UP of New England, 2001.

Losey, Jay. "'Demonic Epiphany': The Denial of Death in Larkin and Heaney." *Moments of Moment: Aspects of the Literary Epiphany*. Ed. William Tigges. Atlanta: Rodopi, 1999.

Lowenberg, Carlton. *Musicians Wrestle Everywhere: Emily Dickinson and Music*. Berkeley, CA: Fallen Leaf P, 1992.

Luhrmann, T. M. *When God Talks Back: Understanding the American Evangelical Relationship with God*. New York: Knopf, 2012.

Lundin, Roger. *Emily Dickinson and the Art of Belief*. Grand Rapids, MI: William B. Eerdmans, 1998.

Macfarlane, Robert. *Mountains of the Mind: Adventures in Reaching the Summit*. New York: Random House, 2009.

Mack, Phyllis. *Heart Religion in the British Enlightenment: Gender and Emotion in Early Methodism*. Cambridge: Cambridge UP, 2008.

MacKenzie, Cynthia, ed. *Concordance to the Letters of Emily Dickinson*. Boulder: UP of Colorado, 2000.

MacLean, Kenneth. *John Locke and English Literature of the Eighteenth Century*. 1936. Reprint. New York: Russell & Russell, 1962.

Maddox, Randy L. *Responsible Grace: John Wesley's Practical Theology*. Nashville, TN: Kingswood Books, 1994.

Manning, Susan. *Fragments of Union: Making Connections in Scottish and American Writing*. London: Palgrave Macmillan, 2002.

2

Marsden, George M. *The Evangelical Mind and the New School Presbyterian Experience: A Case Study of Thought and Theology in Nineteenth-Century America*. New Haven, CT: Yale UP, 1970.

———. *Jonathan Edwards: A Life*. New Haven, CT: Yale UP, 2004.

Marshall, Megan. *The Peabody Sisters: Three Women Who Ignited American Romanticism*. New York: Houghton Mifflin Harcourt, 2006.

Marston, Jane. "Metaphorical Language and Terminal Illness: Reflections upon Images of Death." *Literature and Medicine* 5 (1986): 109–21.

Martin, Robert Bernard. *Tennyson: The Unquiet Heart*. New York: Oxford UP, 1980.

Martin, Robert K. *Hero , Captain, Stranger: Male Friendship, Social Critique, and Literary Form in the Sea Novels of Herman Melville*. Chapel Hill: U of North Carolina P, 1986.

Martin, Wendy. *An American Triptych: Anne Bradstreet, Emily Dickinson, Adrienne Rich*. Chapel Hill: U of North Carolina P, 1984.

Mayer, Nancy. "The Back Story: The Christian Narrative and Modernism in Dickinson's Poetry." *The Emily Dickinson Journal* 17.2 (2008): 1–23.

McClave, Heather. "Emily Dickinson: The Missing All." *Southern Humanities Review* 14 (Winter 1989): 1–12.

McCormack, Jerusha Hall. "Domesticating Delphi: Emily Dickinson and the Electromagnetic Telegraph." *American Quarterly* 55.4 (2003): 569–601.

McCullough, Gerald. "The Influence of Arminius on American Theology." *Man's Faith and Freedom: The Theological Influence of Jacobus Arminius*. Ed. Gerald McCullough. Nashville, TN: Abingdon P, 1962.

McGilchrist, Iain. *The Master and His Emissary: The Divided Brain and the Making of the Western World*. New Haven, CT: Yale UP, 2010.

McIntosh, James. *Nimble Believing: Dickinson and the Unknown*. Ann Arbor: U of Michigan P, 2000.

McKusick, James C. *Green Writing: Romanticism and Ecology*. New York: Palgrave Macmillan, 2000.

Menaker, Daniel. "Have It Your Way." *The New York Times Book Review*, July 15, 2012: 20.

Menand, Louis. *The Metaphysical Club*. New York: Farrar, Straus, and Giroux, 2001.

———. "Practical Cat: How Eliot Became Eliot." *The New Yorker*, September 19, 2011: 44–47.

Meola, Frank M. "Emerson between Faith and Doubt." *New England Review* 52.3 (2011): 111–23.

Messmer, Marietta. *A Vice for Voices: Reading Emily Dickinson's Correspondence*. Amherst: U of Massachusetts P, 2001.

Meyer, Howard N., ed. *The Magnificent Activist: The Writings of Thomas Wentworth Higginson, 1823–1911*. New York: Da Capo Press, 2000.

Miller, Cristanne. "How 'Low Feet' Stagger: Descriptions of Language in Dickinson's Poetry." *Feminist Critics Read Emily Dickinson*. Ed. Suzanne Juhasz. Bloomington: Indiana UP, 1983.

Miller, Paul M. "The Relevance of the Rev. Charles Wadsworth to the Poet Emily Dickinson." *Higginson Journal* 6 (Spring 1991): 1–69.

Miller, Perry. *Errand into the Wilderness.* Cambridge, MA: Harvard UP, 1956.

Milnes, Tim. *The Truth about Romanticism: Pragmatism and Idealism in Keats, Shelley, Coleridge.* Cambridge: Cambridge UP, 2010.

Milosz, Czeslaw. *The Land of Ulro.* New York: Farrar, Straus, Giroux, 1984.

Morey, Frederick L. "Dickinson-Kant: The First Critique." *Dickinson Studies* 60 (Autumn 1986): 1–70.

———. "Dickinson-Kant, Part II (covering the second critique, that of Practical Reason)." *Dickinson Studies* 64 (Autumn 1987): 3–30.

———. "Dickinson-Kant, Part III: The Beautiful and the Sublime." *Dickinson Studies* 67 (Autumn 1988): 3–60.

Morgan, Edmund S. *Visible Saints: The History of a Puritan Idea.* Ithaca, NY: Cornell UP, 1965.

Morgan, Robert. *Lions of the West.* Chapel Hill, NC: Shannon Ravenel, 2011.

Morgan, Victoria N. *Emily Dickinson and Hymn Culture: Tradition and Experience.* Aldershot, England, and Burlington, VT: Ashgate, 2010.

Mossberg, Barbara. *When a Writer Is a Daughter.* Bloomington: Indiana UP, 1983.

Motion, Andrew. *Keats.* New York: Farrar, Straus, and Giroux, 1997.

Mudge, Jean McClure. *Emily Dickinson and the Image of Home.* Amherst: U of Massachusetts P, 1975.

Murphy, Francis, ed. *The Norton Anthology of American Literature*, 2nd ed. 2 Vols. New York: W. W. Norton, 1985.

Nagel, Thomas. *Mind and Cosmos: Why the Materialist Neo-Darwinian Conception of Nature Is Almost Certainly False.* New York: Oxford UP, 2012.

Nardini, Nicholas. "Henry Reed's American Wordsworth: Romantic Universality across the Atlantic." *Symbiosis* 15.2 (October 2011): 155–72.

New, Elisa. "Difficult Writing, Difficult God: Emily Dickinson's Poems Beyond Circumference." *Religion & Literature* 18.3 (1986): 1–27.

New, Melvyn. "Laurence Sterne." *The Cambridge Companion to English Novelists.* Ed. Adrian Poole. Cambridge: Cambridge UP, 2009. 63–79.

———, ed. *The Florida Edition of the Works of Laurence Sterne.* Gainesville: UP of Florida, 1978–.

New, Melvyn, and Gerard Reedy, SJ, eds. *Theology and Literature in the Age of Johnson: Resisting Secularism.* Dover: U of Delaware P, 2012.

Nichols, Ashton. *Beyond Romantic Ecocriticism: Toward Urbanatural Roosting.* New York: Palgrave Macmillan, 2011.

Nidditch, Peter, ed. *An Essay Concerning Human Understanding.* 1690. By John Locke. Oxford: Clarendon Press, 1975.

Noll, Mark. "Among the Believers." *The New Republic*, September 13, 2012: 23–28.

Notopoulos, James A. *The Platonism of Shelley: A Study of Platonism and the Poetic Mind.* Durham, NC: Duke UP, 1949.

Novy, Marianne, ed. *Women's Re-Visions of Shakespeare: On the Responses of Dickinson, Woolf, Rich, H. D., George Eliot, and Others.* Champaign-Urbana: U of Illinois P, 1990.

Nussbaum, Martha C. *Upheavals of Thought: The Intelligence of Emotions.* Cambridge: Cambridge UP, 2001.

Oberhaus, Dorothy Huff. *Emily Dickinson's Fascicles: Method and Meaning.* University Park: Pennsylvania State UP, 1995.

O'Hara, Daniel T. "'The Designated Light': Irony in Emily Dickinson." *Boundary 2: An International Journal of Literature and Culture* 7.3 (1979): 175–98.

Oliver, Virginia H. *Apocalypse of Green: A Study of Emily Dickinson's Eschatology.* New York: Peter Lang, 1989.

O'Neill, Michael. *The Human Mind's Imaginings: Conflict and Achievement in Shelley's Poetry.* Oxford: Clarendon Press, 1989.

Osteen, Joel. *Every Day a Friday: How to Be Happier 7 Days a Week.* Nashville, TN: FaithWords, 2012.

———. *Your Best Life Now: 7 Steps to Living at Your Full Potential.* Brentwood, TN: Warner Faith, 2004.

Packer, Barbara L. *Emerson's Fall: A New Interpretation of the Major Essays.* New York: Continuum, 1982.

Page, Judith. *Imperfect Sympathies: Jews and Judaism in British Romantic Literature.* New York: Palgrave, 2004.

Pagel, Mark. *Wired for Culture: Origins of the Human Social Mind.* New York: W. W. Norton, 2012.

Patterson, Rebecca. *Emily Dickinson's Imagery.* Amherst: U of Massachusetts P, 1979.

———. *The Riddle of Emily Dickinson.* Boston: Houghton Mifflin, 1951.

Peacock, Molly. *The Paper Garden: Mrs. Delany Begins Her Life's Work at 72.* Toronto: McClellan & Stewart, 2010.

Peel, Robin. *Emily Dickinson and the Hill of Science.* Teaneck, NJ: Fairleigh Dickinson UP, 2010.

Peltason, Timothy. *Reading* In Memoriam. Princeton, NJ: Princeton UP, 1985.

Peterfreund, Stuart. *Turning Points in Natural Theology from Bacon to Darwin: The Way of the Argument from Design.* New York: Palgrave Macmillan, 2012.

Peters, Sally. *Bernard Shaw: The Ascent of the Superman.* New Haven, CT: Yale UP, 1996.

Pfau, Thomas. *Romantic Moods: Paranoia, Trauma, and Melancholy, 1790–1840.* Baltimore: Johns Hopkins UP, 2005.

Philip, Jim. "Valley News: Emily Dickinson at Home and Beyond." *Nineteenth-Century American Poetry.* Ed. A. Robert Lee. Totowa, NJ: Barnes and Noble, 1985.

Pickering, Samuel F. *John Locke and Children's Books in Eighteenth-Century England*. Knoxville: U of Tennessee P, 1981.

Pinch, Adela. Rev. of *Against Happiness*, by Eric G. Wilson, and *The Story of Joy*, by Adam Potkay. *European Romantic Review* 21.4 (August 2010): 531–36.

Pollak, Vivian R. *Dickinson: The Anxiety of Gender*. Ithaca, NY: Cornell UP, 1984.

Porter, David. *Emily Dickinson: The Modern Idiom*. Cambridge, MA: Harvard UP, 1981.

Potkay, Adam. *The Story of Joy: From the Bible to Late Romanticism*. Cambridge: Cambridge UP, 2007.

Potter, Lois. *The Life of William Shakespeare: A Critical Biography*. Oxford: Wiley-Blackwell, 2012.

Powell, Padgett. *The Interrogative Mood: A Novel?* New York: Ecco, 2009.

Pulos, C. E. *The Deep Truth: A Study of Shelley's Skepticism*. Lincoln: U of Nebraska P, 1954.

Putnam, Hilary. *Realism with a Human Face*. Cambridge, MA: Harvard UP, 1990.

Reynolds, David S. *Beneath the American Renaissance: The Subversive Imagination in the Age of Emerson and Melville*. Cambridge, MA: Harvard UP, 1989.

Ricca, Brad. "Emily Dickinson: Learn'd Astronomer." *The Emily Dickinson Journal* 9.2 (2000): 96–108.

Richardson, Alan. *British Romanticism and the Science of the Mind*. Cambridge: Cambridge UP, 2001.

Ricks, Christopher. *Tennyson*. New York: Palgrave Macmillan, 1989.

Ricoeur, Paul. *Freud and Philosophy*. Translated by Denis Savage. Cambridge: Cambridge UP, 1970.

Rigby, Catherine E. *Topographies of the Sacred: The Poetics of Place in European Romanticism*. Charlottesville: U of Virginia P, 2004.

Rigney, Ann. *The Afterlives of Walter Scott: Memory on the Move*. New York: Oxford UP, 2012.

Rilke, Rainer Maria. *The Selected Poetry of Rainer Maria Rilke*. Ed. Stephen Mitchell. New York: Vintage Books, 1989.

Robertson, D. W., Jr. *A Preface to Chaucer: Studies in Medieval Perspectives*. Princeton, NJ: Princeton UP, 1962.

Robinson, John. *Emily Dickinson: Looking to Canaan*. London: Faber, 1986.

"Rochefoucauld, Duc de la." *The World Book Encyclopedia*. Chicago: Encyclopedia Center, 1975.

Roe, Nicholas. *John Keats and the Culture of Dissent*. Oxford: Clarendon P, 1998.

Roszak, Theodore. "In Search of the Miraculous." *Harper's* January 1981: 54–62.

Rousseau, G. S. "John Wesley's *Primitive Physick* (1747)." *Harvard Library Bulletin* 16 (July 1968): 242–56.

Ruef, Martin. "Strong Ties, Weak Ties and Islands: Structural and Cultural Predictors of Organizational Innovation." *Industrial and Corporate Change* 11 (2002): 427–49.

Ruskin, John. "Of the Pathetic Fallacy." *Modern Painters.* 1856. London: George Allen, 1906. Part 4, chapter 12.

Ryan, Robert M. *The Romantic Reformation: Religious Politics in English Literature, 1789–1824.* Cambridge: Cambridge UP, 1997.

Sacks, Oliver. "Altered States: Self-experiments in Chemistry." *The New Yorker,* August 27, 2012: 40–47.

Salska, Agnieszka. *Walt Whitman and Emily Dickinson: Poetry of the Central Consciousness.* Philadelphia: U of Philadelphia P, 1985.

Sandberg, Carl. *Abraham Lincoln: The Prairie Years and the War Years.* 1954. New York: Harcourt, 1982.

———. *The People, Yes.* New York: Harcourt, Brace, 1936.

Saxton, Alexander. *Religion and the Human Prospect.* New York: Monthly Review P, 2006.

Schacter, Daniel L. *The Seven Sins of Memory: How the Mind Forgets and Remembers.* New York: Mariner Books, 2002.

Scherrer, Grace B. "A Study of Unusual Verb Constructions in the Poems of Emily Dickinson." *American Literature* 7.1 (1935): 37–46.

Scholnick, Robert. "'The Password Primeval': Whitman's Use of Science in 'Song of Myself.'" *Studies in the American Renaissance* (1986): 385–425.

Schulz, Kathryn. *Being Wrong: Adventures in the Margin of Error.* New York: Ecco Press, 2011.

Schwartz, Regina M. *The Curse of Cain: The Violent Legacy of Monotheism.* Chicago: U of Chicago P, 1997.

Sewall, Richard B. *The Life of Emily Dickinson.* 2 Vols. 1974. Reprint. New York: Farrar, Straus, and Giroux, 1980.

———. "Teaching Dickinson: Testimony of a Veteran." *Approaches to Teaching Dickinson's Poetry.* Ed. Robin Riley Fast and Christine Mack Gordon. New York: Modern Language Association of America, 1989. 30–38.

Sharp, Ronald A. *Friendship and Literature: Spirit and Form.* Durham, NC: Duke UP, 1986.

Shelston, Alan, ed. *Thomas Carlyle: Selected Writings.* 1971. Reprint. Harmondsworth, England: Penguin, 1986.

Shoobridge, Helen. "'Reverence for each Other Being the Sweet Aim': Dickinson Face to Face with the Masculine." *The Emily Dickinson Journal* 9.1 (2000): 87–111.

Showalter, Elaine. *Inventing Herself: Claiming a Feminist Intellectual Heritage.* New York: Simon & Schuster, 2001.

Shurr, William H. *The Marriage of Emily Dickinson: A Study of the Fascicles.* Lexington: UP of Kentucky, 1983.

Simpson, Jeffrey E. "The Dependent Self: Emily Dickinson and Friendship." *Dickinson Studies* 45 (June 1983): 35–42.

Slater, Joseph, ed. *The Correspondence of Emerson and Carlyle.* New York: Columbia UP, 1964.

Smith, Martha Nell. *Rowing in Eden: Rereading Emily Dickinson.* Austin: U of Texas P, 1992.

Socarides, Alexandra. *Dickinson Unbound: Paper, Process, Poetics.* New York: Oxford UP, 2012.

Solomon, Robert C. *Living with Nietzsche: What the Great "Immoralist" Has to Teach Us.* New York: Oxford UP, 2003.

Spellman, W. M. *John Locke and the Problem of Depravity.* Oxford: Clarendon, 1988.

St. Armand, Barton Levi. *Emily Dickinson and Her Culture: The Soul's Society.* Cambridge: Cambridge UP, 1984.

Steiner, George. *Errata: An Examined Life.* New Haven, CT: Yale UP, 1999.

———. *The Poetry of Thought: From Hellenism to Celan.* New York: New Directions, 2012.

Stillinger, Jack. "Imagination and Reality in the Odes of Keats." *The Hoodwinking of Madeline, and Other Essays on Keats's Poems.* Urbana: U of Illinois P, 1971.

Stocks, Kenneth. *Emily Dickinson and the Modern Consciousness: A Poet of Our Time.* New York: St. Martin's, 1988.

Stott, Rebecca. *Darwin's Ghosts: The Secret History of Evolution.* New York: Spiegel & Grau, 2012.

Strickland, Georgiana. "Emily Dickinson's Philadelphia." *The Emily Dickinson Journal* 13.2 (2004): 79–115.

Strong, Leah A. *Joseph Hopkins Twichell, Mark Twain's Friend and Pastor.* Athens: U of Georgia P, 1966.

Suskind, Ron. "Faith, Certainty and the Presidency of George W. Bush." *The New York Times Magazine* (October 4, 2004): 14–28.

Sussman, Henry. *The Task of the Critic: Poetics, Philosophy, Religion.* New York: Fordham UP, 2005.

Swingle, L. J. *The Obstinate Questionings of English Romanticism.* Baton Rouge: Louisiana State UP, 1987.

Swyderski, Ann. "Dickinson and 'that Foreign Lady - .'" *Symbiosis: A Journal of Anglo-American Literary Relations* 4.1 (April 2000): 51–65.

Tallis, Raymond. "The Truth about Lies: Foucault, Nietzsche, and the Cretan Paradox." *TLS* 5151 (December 2, 2001): 3–4.

Tanter, Marci. Obituary notice of William H. Shurr. *Emily Dickinson International Society Bulletin* 14 (May/June 2002): 14.

Taylor, Charles. *A Secular Age.* Cambridge, MA: Harvard UP, 2007.

Taylor, E. Derek. "Mary Astell's Ironic Assault on John Locke's Theory of Thinking Matter." *Journal of the History of Ideas* 64 (2001): 505–22.

Taylor, E. Derek, and Melvyn New, eds. *Letters Concerning the Love of God, by Mary Astell and John Norris.* Aldershot, England, and Burlington, VT: Ashgate, 2005.

Taylor, Linda J. "Shakespeare and Circumference: Dickinson's Hummingbird and The Tempest." *ESQ: A Journal of the American Renaissance* 2.3 (1977): 252–61.

Telford, John, ed. *The Letters of John Wesley, A. M., Sometime Fellow of Lincoln College, Oxford.* 8 Vols. Ed. John Telford. London: Epworth P, 1933.

Thirlwell, Adam. "Visionary Naturalism." *The New Republic*, June 9, 2011: 27–32.

Thompson, Lawrance. *Melville's Quarrel with God*. Princeton, NJ: Princeton UP, 1952.

Todd, John Emerson. *Emily Dickinson's Use of the Persona*. The Hague and Paris: Mouton, 1973.

Tynan, Trudy. "Scholars Find Emily Dickinson's Schoolgirl Notes." *Associated Press*, June 9, 2000. http://www.salon.com/books/wire/2000/06/09/dickinson/print.html.

Ulmer, William A. *The Christian Wordsworth: 1798–1805*. Albany: State U of New York P, 1971.

Uno, Hiroko. "'Chemical Conviction': Dickinson, Hitchcock, and the Poetry of Science." *The Emily Dickinson Journal* 7.2 (1998): 95–111.

Updike, John. "Novel Thoughts about Fiction Writers with Metaphysics on their Minds." *The New Yorker*, August 21 and 28, 1995: 105–14.

Van Leer, David. *Emerson's Epistemology: The Argument of the Essays*. Cambridge: Cambridge UP, 1986.

Vendler, Helen. *Dickinson*. Cambridge, MA: Harvard UP, 2011.

Wadsworth, Charles. *Sermons*. Brooklyn: Eagle Bookland Job Printing Co., 1905.

———. *Sermons*. New York and San Francisco: A. Ronan & Company, 1869.

———. *Sermons*. Philadelphia: Presbyterian Publishing Co., 1884.

Waldron, Jeremy. *God, Locke, and Equality: Christian Foundations in Locke's Political Thought*. Cambridge: Cambridge UP, 2002.

Walker, Julia M. "Emily Dickinson's Poetic of Private Liberation." *Dickinson Studies* 45 (June 1983): 17–22.

Walsh, John Evangelist. *Emily Dickinson in Love: The Case for Otis Lord*. New Brunswick, NJ: Rutgers UP, 2012.

Wasserman, Earl. "The English Romantics: The Ground of Knowledge." *Studies in Romanticism* 4 (1964): 17–34.

———. *The Subtler Language: Critical Readings of Neoclassic and Romantic Poems*. Baltimore: Johns Hopkins UP, 1959.

Weinberg, Steven. *Dreams of a Final Theory*. New York: Pantheon, 1993.

Weisbuch, Robert. *Emily Dickinson's Poetry*. Chicago: U of Chicago P, 1981.

Werner, Marta L. "'A Woe of Ecstasy': On the Electronic Editing of Emily Dickinson's Late Fragments." *The Emily Dickinson Journal* 16.2 (2007): 26–52.

Wesley, John. *Primitive Physick: or, an Easy and Natural Method of Curing Most Diseases*, 9th ed. London: W. Strahan, 1761.

———. *Sermons on Several Occasions*. London: Epworth P, 1944.

———, ed. Vol. 23 of *The Works of the Rev. John Wesley*. 32 Vols. Bristol: J. Paramore, 1771–74.

Whicher, Stephen E., ed. *Selections from Ralph Waldo Emerson: An Organic Anthology*. Boston: Houghton Mifflin, 1957.

White, Newman Ivey. *Shelley*. New York: Knopf, 1945.

White, Ronald C., Jr. *A. Lincoln: A Biography*. New York: Random House, 2009.

Wilson, A. N. *God's Funeral: The Decline of Faith in Western Civilization*. New York: W. W. Norton, 1999.

Wilson, Eric G. *Against Happiness: In Praise of Melancholy*. New York: Farrar, Straus and Giroux, 2008.

———. *Coleridge's Melancholia: An Anatomy of Limbo*. Gainesville: UP of Florida, 2004.

———. *The Spiritual History of Ice: Romanticism, Science, and the Imagination*. New York: Palgrave Macmillan, 2003.

Wineapple, Brenda. *White Heat: The Friendship of Emily Dickinson and Thomas Wentworth Higginson*. New York: Knopf, 2008.

Wolff, Cynthia Griffin. *Emily Dickinson*. Radcliffe Biography Series. Reading, PA: Addison-Wesley, 1988.

Wolosky, Shira. "Dickinson's Emerson: A Critique of American Identity." *The Emily Dickinson Journal* 9.2 (2000): 134–41.

———. *Emily Dickinson: A Voice of War*. New Haven, CT: Yale UP, 1984.

———. *Poetry and Public Discourse in Nineteenth-Century America*. New York: Palgrave Macmillan, 2010.

Wood, Michael. *Shakespeare*. New York: Basic Books, 2004.

Woolf, Virginia. *A Room of One's Own*. 1929. Ed. Susan Gubar. Boston: Harcourt, 2005.

Worth, Robert F. "God Who?" *The New York Times Magazine*, August 26, 2012: 40–43, 50–51.

Zizek, Slavoj. *The Sublime Object of Ideology*. 1989. New York: Verso, 1997.

Index of Poems Cited

A bird came down the walk, 216n36
A doubt if it be us, 115–16
A prison gets to be a friend, 137
A Science - so the Savans say, 62–64
A tooth upon our peace, 223n21
A wounded deer leaps highest, 103, 104
After great pain a formal feeling comes, 103–13, 128, 147
All things swept sole away, 215n35
Apparently with no surprise, 73, 84–87, 221n25
'Arcturus' is his other name, 170
As by the dead we love to sit, 79
At leisure is the soul, 137–38

Banish air from air, 47
Before I got my eye put out, 141–42
Better than music! for I who heard it, 230n4
By a departing light, 135

Civilization spurns the leopard, 117

Dare you see a would at the 'white heat,' 122

Experience is the angled road, 9, 13
Experiment escorts us last, 25, 34, 73–79, 154, 156, 172, 231n20

"Faith" is a fine invention, 77–79
Finding is the first act, 227n1
From blank to blank, 133
Further in summer than the birds, 145

Good to hide and hear 'em hunt, 232n22
Great streets of silence led away, 229n18

He is alive this morning, 65
"Heavenly Father" - take to thee, 87–92
Hope is a strange invention, 166, 227n4
Hope is a subtle glutton, 227n4
Hope is the thing with feathers, 223n31
How happy is the little stone, 206n33
How the old mountains drip with sunset, 168

I breathed enough to take the trick, 130–31
I can wade grief, 104, 134, 139
I died for beauty but was scarce, 18
I dwell in possibility, 45–46, 122, 190
I felt a funeral in my brain, 147
I had some things that I called mine, 221n25
I held a jewel in my fingers, 118–19
I like a look of agony, 146
I like to see it lap the miles, 47–49
I never lost as much but twice, 221n25
I never saw a moor, 170
I reason earth is short, 92
I saw no way, the heavens were stitched, 25, 45, 78
I started early, 190

I tie my hat - I crease my shawl,
    114, 116–17, 190
If I could tell how glad I was, 79
In many and reportless places,
    127–28
In winter in my room, 235n12
It always felt to me a wrong, 230n4
It would never be common more I
    said, 109–13, 116
It's easy to invent a life, 221n25
I've dropped my brain, my soul is
    numb, 225n18

Like some old fashioned miracle, 134
Lo at my problem bending, 79
Love is anterior to life, 79, 223n31

Many cross the Rhine, 18
My life closed twice before its close,
    119, 238n38
My life had stood a loaded gun,
    119–20, 225n22
My wars are laid away in books,
    195–96

Nature and God, I neither knew,
    214n24
Nature sometimes sears a sapling,
    216n36
No crowd that has occurred, 229n18
None can experience stint, 135

Of all the sounds despatched abroad,
    27, 72
Of bronze and blaze, 52–54, 156
On a columnar self, 73, 79–83, 129,
    154, 218n7–8
One crucifixion is recorded only, 79

Paradise is of the option, 229n18
Perception of an object costs, 10, 13
Publication is the auction, 122, 139

Severer service of myself, 144, 146
She went as quiet as the dew, 55–57
Soto! Explore thyself, 170

Split the lark and you'll find the
    music, 237n28
Superiority to fate, 140

Tell all the truth but tell it slant, 27,
    74–75
The admirations and contempts of
    time, 223n31
The bobolink is gone, 192
The brain is wider than the sky, 40
The day that I was crowned,
    50–51, 65
The difference between despair,
    108–9
The fact that earth is heaven, 3, 94
The going from a world we know,
    229n18
The infinite a sudden guest, 223n31
The lilac is an ancient shrub, 23, 69
The missing all prevented me, 13,
    64–66, 215n35
The only news I know, 207n33
The rat is the concisest tenant, 66
The robin's my criterion for tune,
    61, 71, 76
The soul has bandaged moments,
    135–36
The soul selects her own society,
    5–6, 149–50, 167–68, 212n5,
    217n2
The soul's distinct connections,
    223n31
The soul's superior instants, 149,
    223n31, 229n18
The spirit is the conscious ear,
    223n31
The whole of it came not at once, 89
The worthlessness of earthly things,
    192
Their height in heaven comforts
    not, 26, 229n18
There is a languor of the life, 114
There is a pain so utter, 114–15
There's a certain slant of light, 86,
    122, 168, 226n30
They say that "time assuages," 132

This consciousness that is aware, 229n18

This is my letter to the world, 6, 99

This was in the white of the year, 100, 105, 146–48, 156, 159

This world is not conclusion, 26, 94, 229n18

Those cattle smaller than a bee, 67

Those dying then, 91, 196

Those not live yet, 229n18

Tis so appalling it exhilarates, 91

To whom the mornings stand for night, 109

Too happy time dissolves itself, 131–32

We learn it in retreating, 134

What mystery pervades a well, 78

When we stand on the tops of things, 67

Where I have lost, I softer tread, 118–20, 225n23

White - unto the white creator, 122, 226n27

Whoever disenchants, 223n31

Wild nights - wild nights!, 18, 190, 206n30

Wonder is not precisely knowing, 18

Zeros taught us phosphorus, 141

INDEX

Aarsleff, Hans, 231n19
Abbott, Andrea, 80
Abrams, M.H., 211
Anatomy of Influence, The
    (Bloom), 8
Anatomy of the World, An
    (Donne), 23
Anderson, Charles R., 196
Anderson, Douglas, 142
Applegate, Debby, 187, 207n37,
    228n15
Arminian evangelicalism, 21, 53, 55,
    65, 70, 87, 95, 140, 208n40,
    228n15, 229n18
Arminius, Jacobus, 208n40
Arnold, Matthew, 27, 94, 129, 138,
    151, 169
Asolando (Browning), 72
Astell, Mary, 20
astronomy, 26, 28, 38, 46, 52–57,
    72, 96–97, 147, 169, 172
atheism, 13, 89, 91, 136, 171,
    221n26
Ault, Donald, 237n29

Bachelard, Gaston, 148
Baker, Carlos, 230n13, 237n22
Baker, Nicholson, 129
Bakhtin, M.M., 210n52, 231n17
Barnstone, Aliki, 113, 227n2
Barrett, Paul, 92
Barrett Browning, Elizabeth, 34
Barthes, Roland, 157, 165
Bate, Jonathan, 168
Bates, Arlo, 198, 209n46
Beale, Walter H., 231n19

Beckett, Samuel, 4, 169
Beer, Gillian, 92, 206n28
Bennett, Paula, 42
Bentham, Jeremy, 79
Berkeley, George, 42
Bianchi, Martha Dickinson, 145,
    188–92, 234n6
biology, 14, 37, 46, 61–66, 70, 72,
    83, 89–91, 94, 97, 153, 162,
    164, 172, 216n37, 221n26,
    227n5, 230n5
Bishop, Elizabeth, 161
Blake, William
    Dickinson's style and, 5, 8, 85,
        153, 162
    "Enthusiastic Admiration" and, 23
    lack of mentions in Dickinson's
        letters, 150
    love and, 194–95
    *Marriage of Heaven and Hell,
        The*, 127, 176
    perception and, 104–5, 175
    "Poetic Genius" and, 9
    "Proverbs of Hell" and, 132
    science and, 153, 155, 175
    Tennyson and, 84
    theodicy and, 83–84, 91, 222n28
    There Is No Natural Religion, 105
    transcendentalism and, 10
    "Tyger, The," 83, 221n24, 222n28
Bloom, Harold, 8, 17, 45, 91, 138,
    156, 192
Body, Alfred H., 212n4
Bowles, Camilla Parker, 107
Bowles, Samuel, 59, 190, 198, 234n1
Boyd, Bryan, 231

Breuggemann, Walter, 210n50
Brooks, David, 209n44
Brown, Frank Burch, 63
Browne, Peter, 180
Browne, Thomas, 113
Browning, Robert, 19, 72, 189, 206n32
Budick, Emily Miller, 111, 136
Bunyan, John, 74
Bushell, Sally, 165
Butler, Benjamin F., 64–65, 215n34
Butler, Jon, 16
Butler, Melissa, 219n15
Bynum, W.F., 57
Byron, George Gordon, Lord, 65, 105, 125–27, 137, 150, 192

Calvinism, 21, 53, 55, 65, 67, 70, 84, 86–88, 95, 140
Cameron, Sharon, 9, 64, 75, 116
Capps, Jack, 202n6, 205n25, 229n19
Carlyle, Thomas
   Dickinson's style and, 8, 77–79, 121, 155, 162
   doing and, 138
   Emerson and, 77–78
   empiricism and, 77–78, 93, 162, 175
   lack of mentions in Dickinson's letters, 150
   postexperience and, 121–22
   science and, 77–79
   transcendentalism and, 68
   Wesley and, 186
Cazamian, Louis, 78
Celan, Paul, 169–70
Chalmers, Thomas, 213n19
Chambers, Robert, 215n33
Chester, Timothy, 217n6
Civil War, 72, 108, 164, 221
Clark, James D., 191
Cody, David, 210n51
Cody, John, 27, 114, 139
Coghill, Sheila, 169
Coleman, Eliza, 39, 43, 188, 212n11, 234n4

Coleridge, Samuel Taylor
   "Aeolian Harp, The," 97
   "Conversation Poems," 2
   Dickinson's style and, 8, 125, 155, 162
   lack of mentions in Dickinson's letters, 150
   love and, 194
   melancholy and, 158
   reason and, 79, 81, 93
   science and, 79, 175
   theodicy and, 91
   transcendentalism and, 68
   Wordsworth and, 93, 196
   "Work without Hope," 86
Collier, Frank Wilbur, 61
Collier, Rebecca, 219n15, 223n30
Cooper, James Fenimore, 201, 202
Cragg, Gerald R., 181–83
Crashaw, Richard, 23
Crews, Harry, 119
Crisp, Oliver, 208n40
Crumbley, Paul, 2, 202n5
Culler, Jonathan, 79
Curnock, Nehemiah, 57
Curran, Stuart, 204n20

Darwin, Charles
   Dickinson's style and, 14–17, 20, 22–23, 28, 72, 81, 99, 129, 153, 156, 161–62, 164, 172
   empiricism and, 16–17, 37
   mentions in Dickinson's letters, 150
   religion and, 61–68, 89–92, 172
   science and, 4, 46, 61–68, 74, 96–99, 108
   theodicy and, 83–86
   Wadsworth and, 15
   see also natural selection
Davies, Hugh Sykes, 205n23
Dawkins, Richard, 221n26
Delbanco, Andrew, 65, 214n26, 237n32
Deleuze, Gilles, 238n35
Deppman, Jed, 145–46, 218n10

Descartes, Rene, 40, 69, 78, 183,
   210n50, 226n29
Dewey, John, 93, 206n29
Dickie, Margaret, 117
Dickinson, Austin, 1, 3, 39, 59, 64,
   188, 198
Dickinson, Edward, 11, 13, 22,
   26, 48, 97, 170, 203n15,
   207n36
Dickinson, Susan Huntington
   Gilbert
   daughter, 188
   fantasies about, 18
   hopelessness and, 126
   letters to, 106–7
   loss and, 109
   love and, 126, 191–92, 194–95
   physical absence and, 144, 159
Diehl, Joanne Feit, 60, 85, 110,
   204n20, 224n3
Doddridge, Philip, 183
Dolan, Elizabeth, 71
Donne, John, 23
Donoghue, Denis, 103, 148, 163,
   205n26
Doriani, Beth Maclay, 16
Douglas, Ann, 202n6, 207n37
Downey, Charlotte, 49
Dreyer, Frederick, 211n54, 212n5
Drummond, William, 72
Dutton, Denis, 231n15

Eberwein, Jane Donahue, 15, 21,
   137, 140, 205n24, 208n41,
   209n42, 215n30, 220n23
Edwards, Jonathan, 175, 193–94,
   205n23, 208n40, 226n29
Edwards, Sarah Pierpont, 21
Eliot, T.S., 105, 112, 121, 161
Emerson, Ralph Waldo
   Carlyle and, 77–78
   conversation and, 22
   Dickinson's style and, 8, 10,
     16–17, 22, 28, 45–46, 76,
     106, 121, 153, 155, 161–62,
     168, 198

empiricism and, 48, 53–55, 63,
   68, 164
experience and, 138–40, 145,
   166, 172
Keane on, 93
love and, 193–94
mentions in Dickinson's letters,
   150
Meola on, 171
"Nature," 48, 55
postexperience and, 106–7,
   121–22
reality and, 81–82, 85–86
science and, 72, 76
self-reliance and, 140
son's death and, 85, 112–13
theodicy and, 85–86
transcendentalism and, 10, 21,
   153, 186
Wesley and, 186
Wordsworth and, 175
empiricism
   Carlyle and, 77–78, 93, 162, 175
   Darwin and, 16–17, 37
   Emerson and, 48, 53–55, 63, 68,
     164
   Keats and, 34–35, 46, 53, 57, 60,
     175–76
   Locke and, 11–12, 37–46, 51, 54,
     57–58, 60, 67–70, 175
   Shelley and, 72, 76, 175
   Tennyson and, 59, 63, 66, 175
   transcendentalism and, 78
   Wadsworth and, 37–39, 42–51,
     55–63, 67, 69–70, 78, 172
   Wesley and, 33, 37–46, 49,
     52–54, 57–61, 63, 65–67,
     69–70, 163–64, 166, 172
   Wordsworth and, 3–4, 33–38, 45,
     48, 53, 56–57, 69–70, 175–76
experience
   Emerson and, 138–40, 145, 166,
     172
   Locke and, 122, 129
   Tennyson and, 83–84, 93
   Wadsworth and, 95–96, 166

experience—*Continued*
  Wesley and, 72, 77, 82–83, 90,
    95–96, 98–99
  Wordsworth and, 72, 93–94,
    96–98, 172
  see also postexperience

Farr, Judith, 126, 235n13, 236n15
Fathi, Fanoosh, 171
Fawcett, John, 238n38
Felstiner, John, 169–70
feminism, 21, 42, 83, 149, 185
Finch, Annie, 171, 204 n20
Finch, A.R.C., 112
Fish, Stanley, 36
Fitzgerald, Edward, 113–14
Fitzgerald, F. Scott, 230n5
Foucault, Michel, 204
Franke, William, 215n35
Franklin, Benjamin, 158
Franklin, Ralph, 54, 74
Freedman, William, 49
Freeman, Margaret H., 119–20,
    225n22
Frost, Robert, 2, 45, 69, 112, 129,
    143, 157, 161
  "Birches," 45
Fuller, Margaret, 21
Fulton, Alice, 110, 171

Garbowsky, Maryanne, 110, 112,
    115, 117, 131
Gardner, Thomas, 169
Gaull, Marilyn, 70
Gay, Peter, 207n37
Geertz, Clifford, 71–72
Gelpi, Albert, 118, 218n7
geology, 38, 46, 49–51, 57, 63, 72,
    83, 96, 172
Gilbert, Sandra, 142
Giles, Paul, 204n18
Gilliland, Don, 229n18
Godwin, William, 71, 120
Goodheart, Adam, 215n34
Gordon, Lyndall, 203n15
Gould, Stephen Jay, 66, 176, 230n5

Gravil, Richard, 2, 84–85, 201n4,
    210n50
Gray, Asa, 89, 220n23
Gray, John, 74
Great Awakenings, 12, 68, 70, 98,
    208n40
Greenblatt, Stephen J., 14, 209n44
Gubar, Susan, 142
Guthrie, James, 61, 63, 225n14

Habegger, Alfred, 21, 187, 192,
    195–96, 208n40, 213n11,
    236n14
Habermas, Jurgen, 204n19
Hankins, Barry, 21, 222n30
Hardy, Thomas, 4, 85, 104, 151,
    157, 161, 202n8
Harmon, William, 225n24, 230n8
Harris, Sam, 221n26, 228n12
Harrison, Frederick, 79
Harrison, Kathryn, 127
Hatch, Nathan O., 228n15
Heilbut, Anthony, 236n16
Herbert, George, 23
Herbert, T. Walter, 211n54
Herbert, T. Walter, Jr., 90
Higginson, Thomas Wentworth, 13,
    18, 43, 80, 190, 198, 212n10,
    232n21
Hindley, J. Clifford, 217n1
Hindmarsh, D. Bruce, 208n42
Hirsch, E.D., 1–2, 161
Hitchcock, Edward, 44, 49, 63,
    213n19, 232n21
Holland, Elizabeth and Josiah
    Gilbert, 42, 60, 234n2
Holland, Theodore, 42
Holman, Hugh C., 225n24, 230n8
Holmes, Richard, 176, 214n26,
    216n36, 223n35
Hopkins, Gerard Manley, 19, 22, 91,
    115, 132, 138, 158, 206n31,
    221n34
Howard, Richard, 206n32
Howe, Susan, 171
Howells, Richard, 47, 230n13

Huffer, Mary Lee Stephenson, 207n38
Hulme, T.E., 23
Hurst, J.F., 41, 65
Hutchinson, Anne, 218n7

idealism, 17, 40, 45–46, 54, 69, 73–82, 93, 96, 156, 162, 175
Ikeler, A., 228n13
Industrial Revolution, 48–49, 96

Jackson, Helen Hunt, 40, 49, 52, 57, 67, 77, 171, 181, 185
Jackson, Virginia, 210n50
Jager, Colin, 205n23
James, Henry, 54
James, William, 12, 212n3, 232n2
Jefferson, Thomas, 78, 87, 103–4
Jeffrey, Francis, 37
Johnson, Greg, 142, 218n10
Johnson, Thomas H., 196–97
Jones, Rowena Revis, 51
Jones, Ruth Owen, 143
Joyce, James, 191, 224n2
Juhasz, Suzanne, 46, 81, 108, 139

Kandel, Eric R., 231n15
Kant, Immanuel, 80–81
Keane, Patrick J., 15, 84–90, 93
Kearns, Michael, 203n14
Keats, John
    despair and, 138, 143
    Dickinson's style and, 6, 8, 34–35, 59, 69, 138, 154–55, 159
    empiricism and, 34–35, 46, 53, 57, 60, 175–76
    Endymion: A Poetic Romance, 193
    "Epistle to John Hamilton Reynolds," 203n12, 216n37
    "Eve of Saint Agnes, The," 10
    "How Many Bards," 10
    Hyperion: A Fragment, 97
    Lamia, 19
    letters, 113, 229n2
    "naturalized imagination" and, 162, 209n43

"Ode on a Grecian Urn," 53, 66, 95
"Ode to a Nightingale," 35, 57, 107, 176
"On First Looking into Chapman's Homer," 46, 214n26
"On Sitting Down to Read King Lear Again," 66
"Poetry of Earth Is Never Dead, The," 12, 34, 162, 172
    postexperience and, 104, 120, 122
    Stillinger and, 162
"This Living Hand," 60, 204n16
Keller, Karl, 51, 63
Kenny, Anthony, 217n3
Kershner, R.B., 210n51, 211n52, 231n16
Kher, Indra Nath, 218n10
Kierkegaard, Soren, 81–82
Kimpel, Ben, 110, 218n10
Kincaid, James, 114
Kipling, Rudyard, 156
Kirchwey, Karl, 206n32
Kirkby, Joan, 15, 91, 168, 198
Kirkland, John, 198

Lamb, Charles, 33, 35–37, 68–70, 83, 153, 197, 211n1
Lambert, Robert Graham, 197
Langbaum, Robert, 104, 148, 203n11
"Lapis Lazuli" (Yeats), 90
Lease, Benjamin, 17, 201n4
Leder, Sharon, 80
Leib, Erin, 82, 90
Leiter, Sharon, 5, 206n30
Leonard, Douglas Novich, 133–34, 140, 168–69
Lethem, Jonathan, 168
Leverenz, David, 208n40
Levine, George, 206n28
Leyda, Jay, 6, 125
Lincoln, Abraham, 48, 69

Locke, John
  Astell and, 20
  Dickinson's style and, 12–17,
    20–23, 28, 51, 153, 156,
    161, 163–65, 172
  empiricism and, 11–12, 37–46,
    51, 54, 57–58, 60, 67–70, 175
  experience and, 122, 129
  language and, 167
  religion and, 20–21
  science and, 14–17, 72, 76, 78,
    81, 83, 93, 95–99
  society and, 150
  transcendentalism and, 40
  Wadsworth and, 12–13, 42
  Wesley and, 11–12, 163, 179–86
Longsworth, Polly, 205n21, 207n37,
  234n4, 236n18
Lord, Otis P., 63, 143, 191, 194,
  198
Lowenberg, Carlton, 231n14
Luhrmann, T.M., 212n3, 232n2
Lundin, Roger, 5, 36, 72, 196–97
Lyman, Joseph, 24, 198, 228n15

Mack, Phyllis, 207n36
MacKenzie, Cynthia, 209n49,
  229n19
MacLean, Kenneth, 76
Maddox, Randy, 228n14, 237n39
Manning, Susan, 205n25, 226n27
Marsden, George, 21
Marsh, James, 93, 206n29
Marshall, Megan, 198
Marston, Jane, 111
Martin, Robert Bernard, 59
Martin, Wendy, 49, 136, 138
Marx, Karl, 82, 175, 218n13
materialism, 20, 34, 79, 82, 91, 171
mathematics, 55, 73–75, 78–79, 160,
  213n18, 214n23, 217n2
Mayer, Nancy, 220n17
McClave, Heather, 64
McCormack, Jerusha Hall, 213n17
McGann, Jerome, 165
meliorism, 4, 203n8

Melville, Herman, 5, 65, 90,
  203n14, 227n4, 237n32
Menaker, Daniel, 228n12
Menand, Louis, 223n2, 230n13
Meola, Frank M., 171, 203n14,
  238n35
Messmer, Marietta, 232n21
Methodism, 33, 36–37, 40, 61,
  70, 77, 92, 96, 99, 210n51,
  211n2
Meyer, Howard N., 212n10
Miller, Cristanne, 110
Miller, Joseph, 224n7
Milosz, Czeslaw, 86
Milton, John, 27, 84, 90–92, 108,
  143, 149, 211n54, 221n24
Montaigne, Michel de, 217n6
Morey, Frederick L., 80, 162
Morgan, Victoria, 210n51
Mossberg, Barbara, 115
Motion, Andrew, 59
Mudge, Jean McClure, 128
Murphy, Francis, 22, 48, 54–55, 78,
  82, 93, 106–7, 112, 121, 139,
  145, 193

Nagel, Thomas, 216n37
Nardini, Nicholas, 202n4
natural methodism, 33–37, 68–70,
  96, 98, 153, 156, 164, 172,
  211n1–2
natural selection, 14–15, 23, 38,
  61–63, 66, 83–84, 90, 155,
  172, 215n30, 216n37
  see also Darwin, Charles
Natural Supernaturalism, 68–69,
  211n2
  see also supernatural
naturalized imagination, 22, 26, 98,
  145, 162, 209n43
negative capability, 120, 154, 166
New, Elisa, 207n39
New, Melvyn, 207n34, 226n27,
  236n21
Newton, Benjamin Franklin, 170,
  190, 198, 208n39

Newton, Isaac, 9, 52–53, 213n21, 226n29
Nidditch, Peter, 40, 42
Nietzsche, Friedrich, 71, 88, 105, 139, 175, 197
Noll, Mark, 233n1
Norcross, Frances and Louise, 147
Norris, John, 20, 207n35
Notopoulos, James A., 26, 205n23
Novy, Marianne, 201n2
Nussbaum, Martha, 90, 192

O'Hara, Daniel T., 142
Olmsted, Denison, 214n22
O'Neill, Michael, 9
Osgood, Frances, 171
"Outgrowing Genesis?" (Eberwein), 15, 205n24, 213n19, 215n30, 216n36, 220n20, 229n4

Packer, Barbara, 112–13
Pagel, Mark, 231n15
Paradise Lost (Milton), 27, 84, 90
Pater, Walter, 122, 161, 198–99
Patterson, Rebecca, 117, 142, 206n30
Peabody, Elizabeth, 198, 202n4
Peacock, Molly, 207n35
Peacock, Thomas Love, 39
Peel, Robin, 15, 38, 170–71, 208n39, 209n47, 213n18, 214n22, 223n35, 225n18, 226n29, 227n1
Peltason, Timothy, 131, 143
Pendarves, Mary Granville, 21, 207n45
pessimism
  aftermath and, 106, 108, 112–14, 116, 223n2, 224n2
  Dickinson and, 4, 9, 72, 108–9, 111–14, 125, 147, 230n13, 237n32
  Eliot and, 223n2
  Hardy and, 203n8
  hope and, 137, 147, 159–60
  Keats and, 172

Meredith and, 224n11
Modernism and, 157, 224n2
"poetic faith" and, 90
post-Modernism and, 104
postexperience and, 104, 106–9, 118, 128, 133, 137, 164
Romanticism and, 112, 120–21, 159, 172
Tennyson and, 121
Wadsworth and, 196
Yeats and, 90
  see also meliorism
Peters, Sally, 144
Pfau, Thomas, 157
Philip, Jim, 49
Pickering, Samuel, 41
Poe, Edgar Allan, 46, 171, 214n22
"poetry of earth," 12, 34, 69, 162, 172, 209n43
  see also Keats, John
Pollak, Vivian, 103, 112, 115, 117, 126, 144–45, 187
Porter, David, 224n2
postexperience
  Carlyle and, 121–22
  Emerson and, 106–7, 121–22
  pessimism and, 104, 106–9, 118, 128, 133, 137, 164
  Tennyson and, 121–22
  see also experience
Potter, Lois, 203n13
Powell, Padgett, 220n16
Prescott, Harriet E., 210
Prince Charles, 107
Pulos, C. E., 9, 26, 72
Putnam, Hilary, 71

rationalism, 17, 40, 45–46, 69, 71, 74–75, 78–79, 99, 156, 175
Reynolds, Joshua, 209n45
Ricca, Brad, 214n22
Rich, Adrienne, 161
Richardson, Alan, 209n44, 230n6
Ricks, Christopher, 113
Ricoeur, Paul, 95
Rigney, Ann, 202n8

Rilke, Rainer Maria, 155
Robinson, John, 46, 112, 117, 140, 142, 171
Rochefoucauld, Francois de la, 192, 195
Root, Abiah, 39, 41
Roszak, Theodore, 166
Rousseau, G.S., 57
Ruef, Martin, 6

Sacks, Oliver, 232–33n3
Salska, Agnieszka, 206–7n33
Sartor Resartus (Carlyle), 8, 77–79, 211n2
Scott, Walter, 58, 202
Scottish Common Sense School, 11, 97, 205
Secker, Thomas, 183
Sewall, Richard B., 24, 49, 51, 62, 74, 79, 81, 161, 204n17, 207n38, 209n46
Shakespeare, William
  Dickinson and, 1, 5, 28, 66, 84, 201n2, 204n18
  language and, 19
Shelley, Mary, 71
Shelley, Percy Bysshe
  "Adonais," 26
  despair and, 130, 132, 147
  Dickinson's style and, 8–9, 130, 132, 155, 162, 194
  Emerson and, 106
  empiricism and, 72, 76, 175
  "Hymn to Intellectual Beauty," 157
  "intense inane," 78
  lack of mention in Dickinson's letters, 150
  Locke and, 44–45
  love and, 106
  Lyman and, 24
  "Mont Blanc," 9, 25, 81, 122
  Prometheus Unbound, 26
  realism and, 162, 172
  theodicy and, 87
  transcendentalism and, 26

"World's Great Age Begins Anew, The," 111
Shoobridge, Helen, 235n13
Showalter, Elaine, 83
Shurr, William H., 19, 187, 192, 197, 225n23, 235n13, 236n14
Sigourney, Lydia, 171
Steiner, George, 14, 160–61, 231n15
Stevens, Wallace, 5, 85, 112, 153, 161
Stillinger, Jack, 98, 104, 162
Stocks, Kenneth, 133
Strickland, Georgiana, 187, 208n42, 233n1, 234n4
Subtler Language, The (Wasserman), 98
supernatural, 69, 153, 220n23, 232n2
  see also Natural Supernaturalism
Sussman, Henry, 201n3
Swingle, L.J., 39, 72, 106

Tallis, Raymond, 72
Tanter, Marci, 235n13
Taylor, Charles, 87
Taylor, E. Derek, 207n34
Taylor, Linda J., 112
technology, 38, 46, 57, 72, 164, 166, 172
Tennyson, Alfred Lord
  afterlife and, 159
  Blake and, 84
  Bushell and, 165
  Dickinson's style and, 8, 162
  empiricism and, 59, 63, 66, 175
  experience and, 83–84, 93
  "Flower in the Crannied Wall," 145–46
  In Memoriam, 107, 113–14, 121, 131, 138, 143–44, 190
  love and, 143–45
  mentions in Dickinson's letters, 150
  postexperience, 121–22
  Romanticism and, 138

science and, 89
  theodicy and, 83–84, 91, 155
  Wesley and, 186
theodicy
  Blake and, 83–84, 91, 222n28
  Bloom and, 91
  Coleridge and, 91
  Darwin and, 83–86
  Dickinson and, 73, 83–92,
    221n24
  Emerson and, 85–86
  natural selection and, 155
  Powell and, 220n16
  Shelley and, 87
  St. Paul and, 87
  Tennyson and, 83–84, 91, 155
  Wordsworth and, 85–86
Thomas, Dylan, 64, 132, 156
Thoreau, Henry David, 197–98
Tilton, Elizabeth, 21
Todd, John Emerson, 23
Todd, Mabel Loomis, 6, 204n17,
    207n37
Transcendentalism
  Blake and, 10
  Carlyle and, 68, 186
  Coleridge and, 68
  Dickinson and, 10–11, 25–26,
    68, 70, 111, 162–63, 166,
    186
  Emerson and, 10, 21, 153,
    162–63, 186
  empiricism and, 78
  experiment and, 25, 34
  Locke and, 40
  natural methodism and, 3, 164
  religion and, 21
  Shelley and, 26
  Tennyson and, 186
  Wadsworth and, 20–21
  Wordsworth and, 70
Tynan, Trudy, 236n20

Uno, Hiroko, 117
Untermeyer, Louis, 234n6
Updike, John, 129, 149

Van Leer, David, 68
Vendler, Helen, 5

Wadsworth, Charles
  astronomy and, 55–57
  correspondence with Dickinson,
    187–99
  Darwin and, 15–17, 61–63
  Dickinson's style and, 11–17,
    28, 72, 82, 126–27, 140, 144,
    147–48, 153, 156, 159, 161
  empiricism and, 37–39, 42–51,
    55–63, 67, 69–70, 78, 172
  experience and, 95–96, 166
  friendship with Dickinson, 108,
    118, 120, 137, 163–64, 167
  geology and, 49–51
  Locke and, 12–13, 42
  medicine and, 57–60
  Romanticism and, 42, 98–99
  scholarship and, 42–43
  transcendentalism and, 20–21
  views on technological
    development, 45–47
  Wesley and, 11–15, 20–23, 153,
    163–64
Waldron, Jeremy, 58, 218n13,
    219n14–15, 222n30
Walker, Julia, 46
Walsh, John Evangelist, 143,
    203n15
Wasserman, Earl, 98
Waverly, Edward, 202n8
Weinberg, Steven, 213n21
Werner, Marta, 19, 209n49
Wesley, John
  despair and, 129, 139, 150
  Dickinson's style and, 14–16, 20,
    28, 153, 156, 161
  Edwards and, 194
  empiricism and, 33, 37–46, 49,
    52–54, 57–61, 63, 65–67,
    69–70, 163–64, 166, 172
  evangelicalism, 166, 172, 175
  experience and, 72, 77, 82–83,
    90, 95–96, 98–99

Wesley, John—*Continued*
  Locke and, 11, 179–86
  medicine and, 57–60
  Methodism and, 11
  natural methodism and, 35
  Romanticism and, 15–16
  Wadsworth and, 11–15, 20–23, 153, 163–64
Whicher, Stephen, 63, 194
White, Ronald C., 69
Whitman, Walt, 20, 23, 38, 201n4, 206n33, 220n17
Wilbur, Richard, 161
Wilson, A.N., 151
Wilson, Eric G., 158
Wittgenstein, Ludwig, 217n3
Wolff, Cynthia Griffin, 63, 110, 112, 129, 133, 139
Wolosky, Shira, 110, 133–35, 201n4, 209n47, 218n9, 221n24
Woolf, Virginia, 113, 161
Wordsworth, William
  Bushell and, 165
  "Characteristics of a Child Three Years Old," 167
  despair and, 125, 127, 132, 135, 137, 143–50, 158
  Dickinson's style and, 3–4, 6, 8–9, 16–17, 22–23, 28, 125, 155–56, 161–62, 164–67
  "Elegiac Stanzas," 85
  empiricism and, 3–4, 33–38, 45, 48, 53, 56–57, 69–70, 175–76

  Excursion, 86
  experience and, 72, 93–94, 96–98, 172
  experiment and, 25
  "Happy Warrior," 105
  "language of the sense," 98
  "Lines Written a Few Miles above Tintern Abbey," 98, 155–56, 158, 176
  Locke and, 78
  love and, 191, 196
  "master light," 93
  "My Heart Leaps Up," 22, 143
  natural methodism and, 153, 156, 172
  "Ode: Intimations of Immortality," 83, 93, 107–8, 132, 145, 148, 150
  postexperience, 104–5, 107–8, 113, 120, 122
  Recluse, The, 25, 69
  "Resolution and Independence," 127
  Romanticism and, 3
  science and, 4
  Steiner and, 160
  theodicy and, 85–86
  transcendentalism and, 25
Worth, Robert, 222n26

Yeats, William Butler, 4, 6, 90, 112, 139, 161, 197, 223n2

Lighting Source UK Ltd.
Milton Keynes UK
UKOW03n1201200214

2268336UK00004B/38/P